Lewis Campbell, Benjamin Jowett

The Epistles of St. Paul to the Thessalonians, Galatians and Romans

Lewis Campbell, Benjamin Jowett

The Epistles of St. Paul to the Thessalonians, Galatians and Romans

ISBN/EAN: 9783744774475

Printed in Europe, USA, Canada, Australia, Japan

Cover: Foto ©Lupo / pixelio.de

More available books at **www.hansebooks.com**

THE
EPISTLES OF ST. PAUL
TO THE
THESSALONIANS, GALATIANS AND ROMANS

ESSAYS AND DISSERTATIONS

BY THE LATE
BENJAMIN JOWETT, M.A.
MASTER OF BALLIOL COLLEGE
REGIUS PROFESSOR OF GREEK IN THE UNIVERSITY OF OXFORD
DOCTOR IN THEOLOGY IN THE UNIVERSITY OF LEYDEN

EDITED BY
LEWIS CAMPBELL, M.A., LL.D.
EMERITUS PROFESSOR OF GREEK IN THE UNIVERSITY OF ST. ANDREWS

LONDON
JOHN MURRAY, ALBEMARLE STREET
1894

CONTENTS

	PAGE
ESSAY ON THE INTERPRETATION OF SCRIPTURE	1–101
Differences of interpretation partly traditional partly the result of growth in thought	1–3
Mystical and logical tendencies	3, 4
Rhetorical tendencies	4, 5
Illustration from classical literature	6–8
Difficulty of recovering the original meaning	8, 9
A history of interpretation	9–14
Inspiration	14–22
The apologetic temper	22–24
Anachronisms	24, 25
The ideal and actual	26–39
Relation between Old and New Testaments	39, 40
Preliminary questions	40–42
Necessity of inquiry	42–46
Interpret Scripture like any other book	47–51
Interpret Scripture from itself	52–54
Continuity of Scripture	54–58
Language of Scripture	58–65
Special features of New Testament language	65–68
Rhetorical or logical element	68–70
Modes of thought	70–72
Interpretation distinguished from application	73–80
Unity of Scripture	80–82
The words of Christ	82–85
Lessons of the Old Testament	85, 86
Apprehension of original meaning inconsistent with typical and conventional interpretations	87, 88
Transitional conceptions of Christianity	88–90
Effect on Theology and on Life	90–92
Sectarian differences	92–94
Christian Missions	94, 95
Scripture in education	95–97
Sermons	97, 98
Bearing of the subject on the position of the clergy	98–101

CONTENTS

ESSAY ON CONVERSION AND CHANGES OF CHARACTER 102–132
    Spiritual conflict described in Romans VII . . 102
    Christianity in the modern world . . . 102, 103
    The suddenness and permanence of early conversions 103–106
    Conversion of whole multitudes at once . . 107–110
    Re-action in spiritual life 110–112
    Reality of conversion in modern times . . 112–117
    Critical moments in life 117–121
    Changes of feeling 121–123
    Impressions 123
    Reasonable convictions 123, 124
    Influence of circumstances 124
    Struggle between good and evil . . . 125, 126
    The power of God 126, 127
    The love of Christ 127–129
    Prayer 129, 130
    Reality of religious influences 130–132

ESSAY ON CONTRASTS OF PROPHECY 133–151
    Conflicting statements of the Old Testament as quoted by St. Paul 133, 134
    Old Testament chronology 134, 135
    Misuse of prophecy 135
    Aspects of prophecy 135, 136
    Human element in prophecy 136–138
    Real connexion of Old and New Testaments . 139, 140
    The day of the Lord 140–143
    Rejection and restoration of Israel . . . 143–146
    Transition from the nation to the individual . 146–149
    Mercy and not sacrifice 149–151

ESSAY ON CASUISTRY 152–176
    Morality and circumstances 152
    Question of meats and drinks 152, 153
    Meats offered to idols 153, 154
    Things and persons common or unclean . . 154, 155
    The rule of Christian prudence . . . 155–157
    The law of Christian courtesy 157, 158
    The law of individual conscience . . . 158, 159
    The law of Christian freedom 159, 160
    A scrupulous conscience 161–164
    Practical consistency 164, 165
    The truth shall make you free 166
    Modern casuistry 166, 167

	PAGE
The counter-reformation	167, 168
Intricacy of human action	168, 169
Casuistry become a science	169–171
The evils of casuistry	171–176

ESSAY ON NATURAL RELIGION . . 177–246
    St. Paul's point of view 177–179
    Philosophical aspect of the same question . 179–181
    Ignorance and responsibility 181–183
    Christianity and Heathenism 183–185
    Religions of the world 185–195
    Missionary enterprise 195–198
    God in nature 198–205
    Natural and revealed religion . . . 205–208
    Primitive man 208–211
    Growth of early religions 211–214
    Relation to morality 215–218
    Stages of natural religion . . . 218, 219
    Greek religion 219–221
    Greek philosophy 221, 222
    Roman religion 222, 223
    Stoic and Epicurean 223, 224
    Unconscious influence of religion on men in general 225
    Arguments for the being of a God . . . 226, 227
    Final Causes 227–231
    The great First Cause 231–234
    Idea of Law 234–239
    The Church and the world . . . 239–246

ESSAY ON RIGHTEOUSNESS BY FAITH . . 247–272
    Revival of the doctrine at the Reformation . 247–250
    Statement of the question 250, 251
    Luther and St. Paul 252, 253
    Real significance 253, 255
    Jewish conception of righteousness . . 255, 256
    The opposition of the Law and the Spirit . 256, 257
    Grace and Faith in St. Paul . . . 257, 258
    Corresponding facts 258, 259
    St. Paul and Christ 259, 260
    Liberty and assurance . . . 260, 261
    Modern aspect of the doctrine . . 262–265
    Justification as an act on God's part . 265, 266
    Faith the mainspring of religious life . 266, 267
    Personal character of salvation . 267, 268
    Belief in the kingdom of Christ . . 268

	PAGE
Is unbelief sinful?	269
Human imagery	269, 270
Religious confidence	270, 271
Faith and Love	271, 272
ESSAY ON THE LAW AS THE STRENGTH OF SIN	273–303
The Law at once the cause of sin and the preparation for the Gospel	273, 274
The paradox in St. Paul	274–276
The Bible the easiest and hardest of books	276–279
St. Paul's conception of the Law	279, 280
Old Testament notions and Alexandrian ideas	280, 281
Conception of sin	281–283
'Conscientia peccati'	283, 284
Personal experience of St. Paul	284–286
'Original sin'	286, 287
Illustration from morality	287, 288
Opposition of positive and moral	288–290
Analogies in the modern world	291, 292
Society	292–296
The weak conscience	296, 297
Speculative difficulties	297–300
Science and Faith	300–303
ESSAY ON THE OLD TESTAMENT	304–307
The first believers had no New Testament	304, 305
How they read the Old Testament	305, 306
Consequent interlacing of Old and New	306, 307
The Old Testament cannot be dispensed with	307
ESSAY ON THE IMPUTATION OF THE SIN OF ADAM	308–316
Slender foundation in the New Testament	308–310
St. Paul's meaning in the passages quoted	310–312
Traces of the doctrine in the Apocrypha and Rabbinical writings	312, 313
The doctrine can have no meaning now	313–315
St. Paul intends to teach a nobler lesson	315, 316
ESSAY ON ATONEMENT AND SATISFACTION	317–369
'Substitution' immoral and unscriptural	317, 318
The argument from Scripture	318–325
The prophetic view of sacrifice	325, 326
The teaching of Christ	326–329
The mysteriousness of the death of Christ	329, 330
The language of the Epistles	330–336
The Epistle to the Hebrews	336–339

	PAGE
The history of Theology	340-342
Patristic period	343-347
Scholastic Theology from Anselm to Abelard	347-350
Doctrine of the reformers, Luther to Grotius	350-352
Logical and metaphysical theories	352-359
Logical discussion in England	353, 354
German Theology, Kant, Schelling, Hegel	354-359
Not a new theory, but a new method	359, 360
A sacrifice—but what sacrifice?	360, 361
The Divine Ransom	361, 362
Christ died for us	362
Less figurative views	362, 363
Union with Christ	363, 364
The greatest moral act in the world	364-366
Personal religion	366, 367
Eternal truths, and passing controversies	367-369

ESSAY ON PREDESTINATION AND FREE WILL . . 370-409

A question of religion and philosophy	370, 371
Dominant ideas	371-375
Historical considerations	375-378
Predestination national or individual	379
Individuality and freedom	379, 380
The elect of God	380, 381
Calvinism and Romans IX.	381, 382
Election transferred from the nation to the Christian Church	382-385
Evidence of religious feeling	385, 386
Philosophical fatalism	386-388
Infinity	388, 389
Omnipotence	389, 390
Omniscience and foreknowledge	390-392
Consciousness of dependence on God	392, 393
Return to fact and nature	394, 395
Cause and effect	395-399
Illusions of language	399, 400
Mind and body	400
Development	400, 401
'Anima Mundi'	401, 402
Degrees of necessity	402-404
Uniformity of human actions :—statistics	404-406
Consciousness of freedom	406, 407
Freedom and obligation	407, 408
Importance of circumstances	408, 409

DISSERTATIONS

ON

THEOLOGICAL SUBJECTS CONNECTED WITH THE STUDY OF

ST. PAUL'S EPISTLES

INCLUDING AN ESSAY ON

THE INTERPRETATION OF SCRIPTURE

ESSAY

ON THE

INTERPRETATION OF SCRIPTURE

It is a strange, though familiar fact, that great differences of opinion exist respecting the Interpretation of Scripture. All Christians receive the Old and New Testament as sacred writings, but they are not agreed about the meaning which they attribute to them. The book itself remains as at the first; the commentators seem rather to reflect the changing atmosphere of the world or of the Church. Different individuals or bodies of Christians have a different point of view, to which their interpretation is narrowed or made to conform. It is assumed, as natural and necessary, that the same words will present one idea to the mind of the Protestant, another to the Roman Catholic; one meaning to the German, another to the English interpreter. The Ultramontane or Anglican divine is not supposed to be impartial in his treatment of passages which afford an apparent foundation for the doctrine of purgatory or the primacy of St. Peter on the one hand, or the three orders of clergy and the divine origin of episcopacy on the other. It is a received view with many, that the meaning of the Bible is to be defined by that of the Prayer-book; while there are others who interpret 'the Bible and the Bible only' with a silent reference to the traditions of the Reformation. Philosophical differences are in the background, into which the differences about Scripture also resolve themselves. They seem to run up at last into a difference of opinion respecting Revelation itself—whether given beside the human faculties or through them, whether an interruption of the laws of nature or their perfection and fulfilment.

This effort to pull the authority of Scripture in different directions is not peculiar to our own day; the same phenomenon appears in the past history of the Church. At the Reformation, in the Nicene or Pelagian times, the New Testament was the ground over which men fought; it might also be compared to the armoury which furnished them with weapons. Opposite aspects of the truth which it contains were appropriated by different sides. 'Justified by faith without works' and 'justified by faith as well as works' are equally Scriptural expressions; the one has become the formula of Protestants, the other of Roman Catholics. The fifth and ninth chapters of the Romans, single verses such as 1 Cor. iii. 15; John iii. 3, still bear traces of many a life-long strife in the pages of commentators. The difference of interpretation which prevails among ourselves is partly traditional, that is to say, inherited from the controversies of former ages. The use made of Scripture by Fathers of the Church, as well as by Luther and Calvin, affects our idea of its meaning at the present hour.

Another cause of the multitude of interpretations is the growth or progress of the human mind itself. Modes of interpreting vary as time goes on; they partake of the general state of literature or knowledge. It has not been easily or at once that mankind have learned to realize the character of sacred writings—they seem almost necessarily to veil themselves from human eyes as circumstances change; it is the old age of the world only that has at length understood its childhood. (Or rather perhaps is beginning to understand it, and learning to make allowance for its own deficiency of knowledge ; for the infancy of the human race, as of the individual, affords but few indications of the workings of the mind within.) More often than we suppose, the great sayings and doings upon the earth, 'thoughts that breathe and words that burn,' are lost in a sort of chaos to the apprehension of those that come after. Much of past history is dimly seen and receives only a conventional interpretation, even when the memorials of it remain. There is a time at which the freshness of early literature is lost ; mankind have turned rhetoricians, and no longer write or feel in the spirit which created it. In this unimaginative period in which sacred or ancient writings are partially unintelligible, many methods have been taken at different times to adapt the ideas of the past to the wants of the present. One age has wandered into the flowery paths of allegory,

'In pious meditation fancy fed.'

Another has straitened the liberty of the Gospel by a rigid application of logic, the former being a method which was at first more naturally applied to the Old Testament, the latter to the New. Both methods of interpretation, the mystical and logical, as they may be termed, have been practised on the Vedas and the Koran, as well as on the Jewish and Christian Scriptures, the true glory and note of divinity in these latter being not that they have hidden mysterious or double meanings, but a simple and universal one, which is beyond them and will survive them. Since the revival of literature, interpreters have not unfrequently fallen into error of another kind from a pedantic and misplaced use of classical learning ; the minute examination of words often withdrawing the mind from more important matters. A tendency may be observed within the last century to clothe systems of philosophy in the phraseology of Scripture. But 'new wine cannot thus be put into old bottles.' Though roughly distinguishable by different ages, these modes or tendencies also exist together; the remains of all of them may be remarked in some of the popular commentaries of our own day.

More common than any of these methods, and not peculiar to any age, is that which may be called by way of distinction the rhetorical one. The tendency to exaggerate or amplify the meaning of simple words for the sake of edification may indeed have a practical use in sermons, the object of which is to awaken not so much the intellect as the heart and conscience. Spiritual food, like natural, may require to be of a certain bulk to nourish the human mind. But this 'tendency to edification' has had an unfortunate influence on the interpretation of Scripture. For the preacher almost necessarily oversteps the limits of actual knowledge, his feelings overflow with the subject; even if he have the power, he has seldom the time for accurate thought or inquiry. And in the course of years spent in writing, perhaps, without study, he is apt to persuade himself, if not others, of the truth of his own repetitions. The trivial consideration of making a discourse of sufficient length is often a reason why he overlays the words of Christ and his Apostles with commonplaces. The meaning of the text is not always the object which he has in view, but some moral or religious lesson which he has found it necessary to append to it; some cause which he is pleading, some error of the day which he has to combat. And while in some passages he hardly dares to trust himself with the full force of Scripture (Matt. v. 34; ix. 13; xix. 21: Acts v. 29), in others he extracts more from words than they really imply (Matt. xxii. 21; xxviii. 20: Rom. xiii. 1; &c.), being more eager to guard against the abuse of some precept than to enforce it, attenuating or adapting the utterance of prophecy to the requirements or to the measure of modern times. Any one who has ever written sermons is aware how hard it is to apply Scripture to the wants of his hearers and at the same time to preserve its meaning.

The phenomenon which has been described in the preceding pages is so familiar, and yet so extraordinary, that it requires an effort of thought to appreciate its true nature. We do not at once see the absurdity of the same words having many senses, or free our minds from the illusion that the Apostle or Evangelist must have written with a reference to the creeds or controversies or circumstances of other times. Let it be considered, then, that this extreme variety of interpretation is found to exist in the case of no other book, but of the Scriptures only. Other writings are preserved to us in dead languages—Greek, Latin, Oriental, some of them in fragments, all of them originally in manuscript. It is true that difficulties arise in the explanation of these writings, especially in the most ancient, from our imperfect acquaintance with the meaning of words, or the defectiveness of copies, or the want of some historical or geographical information which is required to present an event or character in its true bearing. In comparison with the wealth and light of modern literature, our knowledge of Greek classical authors, for example, may be called imperfect and shadowy. Some of them have another sort of difficulty arising from subtlety or abruptness in the use of language; in lyric poetry especially, and some of the earlier prose, the greatness of the thought struggles with the stammering lips. It may be observed that all these difficulties occur also in Scripture; they are found equally in sacred and profane literature. But the meaning of classical authors is known with comparative certainty; and the interpretation of them seems to rest on a scientific basis. It is not, therefore, to philological or historical difficulties that the greater part of the uncertainty in the interpretation of Scripture is to be attributed. No ignorance of Hebrew or Greek is sufficient to account for it. Even the Vedas and the Zendavesta, though beset by obscurities of language probably greater than are found in any portion of the Bible, are interpreted, at least by European scholars, according to fixed rules, and beginning to be clearly understood.

To bring the parallel home, let us imagine the remains of some well-known Greek author, as Plato or Sophocles, receiving the same treatment at the hands of the world which the Scriptures have experienced. The text of such an author, when first printed by Aldus or Stephens, would be gathered from the imperfect or miswritten copies which fell in the way of the editors; after awhile older and better manuscripts come to light, and the power of using and estimating the value of manuscripts is greatly improved. We may suppose, further, that the readings of these older copies do not always conform to some received canons of criticism. Up to the year 1550, or 1624, alterations, often proceeding on no principle, have been introduced into the text; but now a stand is made—an edition which appeared at the latter of the two dates just mentioned is invested with authority; this authorized text is a *pièce de résistance* against innovation. Many reasons are given why it is better to have bad readings to which the world is accustomed than good ones which are novel and strange—why the later manuscripts of Plato or Sophocles are often to be preferred to earlier ones—why it is useless to remove imperfections where perfect accuracy is not to be attained. A fear of disturbing the critical canons which have come down from former ages is, however, suspected to be one reason for the opposition. And custom and prejudice, and the nicety of the subject, and all the arguments which are intelligible to the many against the truth, which is intelligible only to the few, are thrown into the scale to preserve the works of Plato or Sophocles as nearly as possible in the received text.

Leaving the text, we proceed to interpret and translate. The meaning of Greek words is known with tolerable certainty; and the grammar of the Greek language has been minutely analyzed both in ancient and modern times. Yet the interpretation of Sophocles is tentative and uncertain; it seems to vary from age to age : to some the great tragedian has appeared to embody in his choruses certain theological or moral ideas of his own age or country; there are others who find there an allegory of the Christian religion or of the history of modern Europe. Several schools of critics have commented on his works; to the Englishman he has presented one meaning, to the Frenchman another, to the German a third; the interpretations have also differed with the philosophical systems which the interpreters espoused. To one the same words have appeared to bear a moral, to another a symbolical meaning; a third is determined wholly by the authority of old commentators; while there is a disposition to condemn the scholar who seeks to interpret Sophocles from himself only, and with reference to the ideas and beliefs of the age in which he lived. And the error of such an one is attributed not only to some intellectual but even to a moral obliquity which prevents his seeing the true meaning.

It would be tedious to follow into details the absurdity which has been supposed. By such methods it would be truly said that Sophocles or Plato may be made to mean anything. It would seem as if some *Novum Organum* were needed to lay down rules of interpretation for ancient literature. Still one other supposition has to be introduced which will appear, perhaps, more extravagant than any which have preceded. Conceive then that these modes of interpreting Sophocles had existed for ages; that great institutions and interests had become interwoven with them, and in some degree even the honour of nations and churches—is it too much to say that in such a case they would be changed with difficulty, and that they would continue to be maintained long after critics and philosophers had seen that they were indefensible?

No one who has a Christian feeling would place classical

on a level with sacred literature; and there are other particulars in which the preceding comparison fails, as, for example, the style and subject. But, however different the subject, although the interpretation of Scripture requires 'a vision and faculty divine,' or at least a moral and religious interest which is not needed in the study of a Greek poet or philosopher, yet in what may be termed the externals of interpretation, that is to say, the meaning of words, the connexion of sentences, the settlement of the text, the evidence of facts, the same rules apply to the Old and New Testaments as to other books. And the figure is no exaggeration of the erring fancy of men in the use of Scripture, or of the tenacity with which they cling to the interpretations of other times, or of the arguments by which they maintain them. All the resources of knowledge may be turned into a means not of discovering the true rendering, but of upholding a received one. Grammar appears to start from an independent point of view, yet inquiries into the use of the article or the preposition have been observed to wind round into a defence of some doctrine. Rhetoric often magnifies its own want of taste into the design of inspiration. Logic (that other mode of rhetoric) is apt to lend itself to the illusion, by stating erroneous explanations with a clearness which is mistaken for truth. 'Metaphysical aid' carries away the common understanding into a region where it must blindly follow. Learning obscures as well as illustrates; it heaps up chaff when there is no more wheat. These are some of the ways in which the sense of Scripture has become confused, by the help of tradition, in the course of ages, under a load of commentators.

The book itself remains as at the first, unchanged amid the changing interpretations of it. The office of the interpreter is not to add another, but to recover the original one; the meaning, that is, of the words as they struck on the ears or flashed before the eyes of those who first heard and read them. He has to transfer himself to another age; to imagine that he is a disciple of Christ or Paul; to disengage himself from all that follows. The history of Christendom is nothing to him; but only the scene at Galilee or Jerusalem, the handful of believers who gathered themselves together at Ephesus, or Corinth, or Rome. His eye is fixed on the form of one like the Son of man, or of the Prophet who was girded with a garment of camel's hair, or of the Apostle who had a thorn in the flesh. The greatness of the Roman Empire is nothing to him; it is an inner not an outer world that he is striving to restore. All the after-thoughts of theology are nothing to him; they are not the true lights which light him in difficult places. His concern is with a book in which, as in other ancient writings, are some things of which we are ignorant; which defect of our knowledge cannot, however, be supplied by the conjectures of fathers or divines. The simple words of that book he tries to preserve absolutely pure from the refinements or distinctions of later times. He acknowledges that they are fragmentary, and would suspect himself, if out of fragments he were able to create a well-rounded system or a continuous history. The greater part of his learning is a knowledge of the text itself; he has no delight in the voluminous literature which has overgrown it. He has no theory of interpretation; a few rules guarding against common errors are enough for him. His object is to read Scripture like any other book, with a real interest and not merely a conventional one. He wants to be able to open his eyes and see or imagine things as they truly are.

Nothing would be more likely to restore a natural feeling on this subject than a history of the Interpretation of Scripture. It would take us back to the beginning; it would present in one view the causes which have darkened the meaning of words in the course of ages; it would clear away the remains of dogmas, systems, controversies, which are encrusted upon them. It would show us the 'erring fancy' of interpreters assuming sometimes to have the

Spirit of God Himself, yet unable to pass beyond the limits
of their own age, and with a judgement often biassed by
party. Great names there have been among them, names
of men who may be reckoned also among the benefactors of
the human race, yet comparatively few who have understood
the thoughts of other times, or who have bent their minds
to 'interrogate' the meaning of words. Such a work would
enable us to separate the elements of doctrine and tradition
with which the meaning of Scripture is encumbered in our
own day. It would mark the different epochs of interpretation from the time when the living word was in process of
becoming a book to Origen and Tertullian, from Origen to
Jerome and Augustine, from Jerome and Augustine to
Abelard and Aquinas; again, making a new beginning with
the revival of literature, from Erasmus, the father of Biblical
criticism in more recent times, with Calvin and Beza for his
immediate successors, through Grotius and Hammond, down
to De Wette and Meyer, our own contemporaries. We should
see how the mystical interpretation of Scripture originated
in the Alexandrian age; how it blended with the logical
and rhetorical; how both received weight and currency
from their use in support of the claims and teaching of the
Church. We should notice how the 'new learning' of the
fifteenth and sixteenth centuries gradually awakened the
critical faculty in the study of the sacred writings; how
Biblical criticism has slowly but surely followed in the
track of philological and historical (not without a remoter
influence exercised upon it also by natural science); how,
too, the form of the scholastic literature, and even of notes
on the classics, insensibly communicated itself to commentaries on Scripture. We should see how the word
inspiration, from being used in a general way to express
what may be called the prophetic spirit of Scripture, has
passed, within the last two centuries, into a sort of technical
term; how, in other instances, the practice or feeling of
earlier ages has been hollowed out into the theory or system

of later ones. We should observe how the popular explanations of prophecy as in heathen (Thucyd. ii. 54), so also in Christian times, had adapted themselves to the circumstances of mankind. We might remark that in our own country, and in the present generation especially, the interpretation of Scripture had assumed an apologetic character, as though making an effort to defend itself against some supposed inroad of science and criticism; while among German commentators there is, for the first time in the history of the world, an approach to agreement and certainty. For example, the diversity among German writers on prophecy is far less than among English ones. That is a new phenomenon which has to be acknowledged. More than any other subject of human knowledge, Biblical criticism has hung to the past; it has been hitherto found truer to the traditions of the Church than to the words of Christ. It has made, however, two great steps onward—at the time of the Reformation and in our day. The diffusion of a critical spirit in history and literature is affecting the criticism of the Bible in our own day in a manner not unlike the burst of intellectual life in the fifteenth or sixteenth centuries. Educated persons are beginning to ask, not what Scripture may be made to mean, but what it does. And it is no exaggeration to say that he who in the present state of knowledge will confine himself to the plain meaning of words and the study of their context may know more of the original spirit and intention of the authors of the New Testament than all the controversial writers of former ages put together.

Such a history would be of great value to philosophy as well as to theology. It would be the history of the human mind in one of its most remarkable manifestations. For ages which are not original show their character in the interpretation of ancient writings. Creating nothing, and incapable of that effort of imagination which is required in a true criticism of the past, they read and explain the thoughts of former times by the conventional modes of their own. Such a history would form a kind of preface or prolegomena to the study of Scripture. Like the history of science, it would save many a useless toil; it would indicate the uncertainties on which it is not worth while to speculate further; the by-paths or labyrinths in which men lose themselves; the mines that are already worked out. He who reflects on the multitude of explanations which already exist of the 'number of the beast,' 'the two witnesses,' 'the little horn,' 'the man of sin,' who observes the manner in which these explanations have varied with the political movements of our own time, will be unwilling to devote himself to a method of inquiry in which there is so little appearance of certainty or progress. These interpretations would destroy one another if they were all placed side by side in a tabular analysis. It is an instructive fact, which may be mentioned in passing, that Joseph Mede, the greatest authority on this subject, twice fixed the end of the world in the last century and once during his own lifetime. In like manner, he who notices the circumstance that the explanations of the first chapter of Genesis have slowly changed, and, as it were, retreated before the advance of geology, will be unwilling to add another to the spurious reconcilements of science and revelation. Or, to take an example of another kind, the Protestant divine who perceives that the types and figures of the Old Testament are employed by Roman Catholics in support of the tenets of their church, will be careful not to use weapons which it is impossible to guide, and which may with equal force be turned against himself. Those who have handled them on the Protestant side have before now fallen victims to them, not observing as they fell that it was by their own hand.

Much of the uncertainty which prevails in the interpretation of Scripture arises out of party efforts to wrest its meaning to different sides. There are, however, deeper reasons which have hindered the natural meaning of the text from immediately and universally prevailing. One of these is the unsettled state of many questions which have an important but indirect bearing on this subject. Some of these questions veil themselves in ambiguous terms; and no one likes to draw them out of their hiding-place into the light of day. In natural science it is felt to be useless to build on assumptions; in history we look with suspicion on *a priori* ideas of what ought to have been; in mathematics, when a step is wrong, we pull the house down until we reach the point at which the error is discovered. But in theology it is otherwise; there the tendency has been to conceal the unsoundness of the foundation under the fairness and loftiness of the superstructure. It has been thought safer to allow arguments to stand which, although fallacious, have been on the right side, than to point out their defect. And thus many principles have imperceptibly grown up which have overridden facts. No one would interpret Scripture, as many do, but for certain previous suppositions with which we come to the perusal of it. 'There can be no error in the Word of God,' therefore the discrepancies in the books of Kings and Chronicles are only apparent, or may be attributed to differences in the copies:—'It is a thousand times more likely that the interpreter should err than the inspired writer.' For a like reason the failure of a prophecy is never admitted, in spite of Scripture and of history (Jer. xxxvi. 30: Isa. xxiii: Amos vii. 10–17); the mention of a name later than the supposed age of the prophet is not allowed, as in other writings, to be taken in evidence of the date (Isa. xlv. 1). The accuracy of the Old Testament is measured not by the standard of primaeval history, but of a modern critical one, which, contrary to all probability, is supposed to be attained; this arbitrary standard once assumed, it becomes a point of honour or of faith to defend every name, date, place, which occurs. Or to take another class of questions, it is said that 'the various theories of the origin of the three first Gospels are all equally unknown to the Holy Catholic Church,' or as another writer of a different school expresses himself, 'they tend to sap the inspiration of the New Testament.' Again, the language in which our Saviour speaks of His own union with the Father is interpreted by the language of the creeds. Those who remonstrate against double senses, allegorical interpretations, forced reconcilements, find themselves met by a sort of presupposition that 'God speaks not as man speaks.' The limitation of the human faculties is confusedly appealed to as a reason for abstaining from investigations which are quite within their limits. The suspicion of Deism, or perhaps of Atheism, awaits inquiry. By such fears a good man refuses to be influenced; a philosophical mind is apt to cast them aside with too much bitterness. It is better to close the book than to read it under conditions of thought which are imposed from without. Whether those conditions of thought are the traditions of the Church, or the opinions of the religious world—Catholic or Protestant—makes no difference. They are inconsistent with the freedom of the truth and the moral character of the Gospel. It becomes necessary, therefore, to examine briefly some of these prior questions which lie in the way of a reasonable criticism.

§ 2.

Among these previous questions, that which first presents itself is the one already alluded to—the question of inspiration. Almost all Christians agree in the word, which use and tradition have consecrated to express the reverence which they truly feel for the Old and New Testaments. But here the agreement of opinion ends; the meaning of inspiration has been variously explained, or more often passed over in silence from a fear of stirring the difficulties that would arise about it. It is one of those theological terms which may be regarded as 'great peacemakers,' but which are also sources of distrust and misunderstanding.

For while we are ready to shake hands with any one who uses the same language as ourselves, a doubt is apt to insinuate itself whether he takes language in the same senses—whether a particular term conveys all the associations to another which it does to ourselves—whether it is not possible that one who disagrees about the word may not be more nearly agreed about the thing. The advice has, indeed, been given to the theologian that he 'should take care of words and leave things to themselves ;' the authority, however, who gives the advice is not good—it is placed by Goethe in the mouth of Mephistopheles. Pascal seriously charges the Jesuits with acting on a similar maxim—excommunicating those who meant the same thing and said another, holding communion with those who said the same thing and meant another. But this is not the way to heal the wounds of the Church of Christ ; we cannot thus 'skin and film' the weak places of theology. Errors about words, and the attribution to words themselves of an excessive importance, lie at the root of theological as of other confusions. In theology they are more dangerous than in other sciences, because they cannot so readily be brought to the test of facts.

The word inspiration has received more numerous gradations and distinctions of meaning than perhaps any other in the whole of theology. There is an inspiration of superintendence and an inspiration of suggestion; an inspiration which would have been consistent with the Apostle or Evangelist falling into error, and an inspiration which would have prevented him from erring; verbal organic inspiration by which the inspired person is the passive utterer of a Divine Word, and an inspiration which acts through the character of the sacred writer; there is an inspiration which absolutely communicates the fact to be revealed or statement to be made, and an inspiration which does not supersede the ordinary knowledge of human events ; there is an inspiration which demands infallibility in matters of doctrine, but allows for mistakes in fact. Lastly, there is a view of inspiration which recognizes only its supernatural and prophetic character, and a view of inspiration which regards the Apostles and Evangelists as equally inspired in their writings and in their lives, and in both receiving the guidance of the Spirit of truth in a manner not different in kind but only in degree from ordinary Christians. Many of these explanations lose sight of the original meaning and derivation of the word; some of them are framed with the view of meeting difficulties; all perhaps err in attempting to define what, though real, is incapable of being defined in an exact manner. Nor for any of the higher or supernatural views of inspiration is there any foundation in the Gospels or Epistles. There is no appearance in their writings that the Evangelists or Apostles had any inward gift, or were subject to any power external to them different from that of preaching or teaching which they daily exercised; nor do they anywhere lead us to suppose that they were free from error or infirmity. St. Paul writes like a Christian teacher, exhibiting all the emotions and vicissitudes of human feeling, speaking, indeed, with authority, but hesitating in difficult cases and more than once correcting himself, corrected, too, by the course of events in his expectation of the coming of Christ. The Evangelist 'who saw it, bare record, and his record is true: and he knoweth that he saith true' (John xix. 35). Another Evangelist does not profess to be an original narrator, but only 'to set forth in order a declaration of what eye-witnesses had delivered,' like many others whose writings have not been preserved to us (Luke i. 1, 2). And the result is in accordance with the simple profession and style in which they describe themselves; there is no appearance, that is to say, of insincerity or want of faith; but neither is there perfect accuracy or agreement. One supposes the original dwelling-place of our Lord's parents to have been Bethlehem (Matt. ii. 1, 22), another Nazareth (Luke ii. 4); they trace his genealogy in different ways; one mentions the thieves blaspheming, another has preserved to after-ages the record of the penitent thief; they appear to differ about the day and hour of the Crucifixion; the narrative of the woman who anointed our Lord's feet with ointment is told in all four, each narrative having more or less considerable variations. These are a few instances of the differences which arose in the traditions of the earliest ages respecting the history of our Lord. But he who wishes to investigate the character of the sacred writings should not be afraid to make a catalogue of them all with the view of estimating their cumulative weight. (For it is obvious that the answer which would be admitted in the case of a single discrepancy, will not be the true answer when there are many.) He should further consider that the narratives in which these discrepancies occur are short and partly identical—a cycle of tradition beyond which the knowledge of the early fathers never travels, though if all the things that Jesus said and did had been written down, 'the world itself could not have contained the books that would have been written' (John xx. 30; xxi. 25). For the proportion which these narratives bear to the whole subject, as well as their relation to one another, is an important element in the estimation of differences. In the same way, he who would understand the nature of prophecy in the Old Testament, should have the courage to examine how far its details were minutely fulfilled. The absence of such a fulfilment may further lead him to discover that he took the letter for the spirit in expecting it.

The subject will clear of itself if we bear in mind two considerations:—First, that the nature of inspiration can only be known from the examination of Scripture. There is no other source to which we can turn for information; and we have no right to assume some imaginary doctrine of inspiration like the infallibility of the Roman Catholic Church. To the question, 'What is inspiration?' the first answer therefore is, 'That idea of Scripture which we gather from the knowledge of it.' It is no mere *a priori* notion, but one to which the book is itself a witness. It is a fact which we infer from the study of Scripture—not of one portion only, but of the whole. Obviously then it embraces writings of very different kinds – the book of Esther, for example, or the Song of Solomon, as well as the Gospel of St. John. It is reconcileable with the mixed good and evil of the characters of the Old Testament, which nevertheless does not exclude them from the favour of God, with the attribution to the Divine Being of actions at variance with that higher revelation, which He has given of himself in the Gospel; it is not inconsistent with imperfect or opposite aspects of the truth as in the Book of Job or Ecclesiastes, with variations of fact in the Gospels or the books of Kings and Chronicles, with inaccuracies of language in the Epistles of St. Paul. For these are all found in Scripture; neither is there any reason why they should not be, except a general impression that Scripture ought to have been written in a way different from what it has. A principle of progressive revelation admits them all; and this is already contained in the words of our Saviour, 'Moses because of the hardness of your hearts;' or even in the Old Testament, 'Henceforth there shall be no more this proverb in the house of Israel.' For what is progressive is necessarily imperfect in its earlier stages, and even erring to those who come after, whether it be the maxims of a half-civilized world which are compared with those of a civilized one, or the Law with the Gospel. Scripture itself points the way to answer the moral objections to Scripture. Lesser difficulties remain, but only such as would be found commonly in writings of the same age or country. There is no more reason why imperfect narratives should be excluded from Scripture than imperfect grammar; no more ground for expecting that the New Testament would be logical or Aristotelian in form, than that it would be written in Attic Greek.

The other consideration is one which has been neglected by writers on this subject. It is this—that any true doctrine of inspiration must conform to all well-ascertained facts of history or of science. The same fact cannot be true and untrue, any more than the same words can have two opposite meanings. The same fact cannot be true in religion when seen by the light of faith, and untrue in science when looked at through the medium of evidence or experiment. It is ridiculous to suppose that the sun goes round the earth in the same sense in which the earth goes round the sun; or that the world appears to have existed, but has not existed during the vast epochs of which geology speaks to us. But if so, there is no need of elaborate reconcilements of revelation and science; they reconcile themselves the moment any scientific truth is distinctly ascertained. As the idea of nature enlarges, the idea of revelation also enlarges; it was a temporary misunderstanding which severed them. And as the knowledge of nature which is possessed by the few is communicated in its leading features at least to the many, they will receive with it a higher conception of the ways of God to man. It may hereafter appear as natural to the majority of mankind to see the providence of God in the order of the world, as it once was to appeal to interruptions of it.

It is true that there is a class of scientific facts with which popular opinions on theology often conflict and which do not seem to conform in all respects to the severer conditions of inductive science: such especially are the facts relating to the formation of the earth and the beginnings of the human race. But it is not worth while to fight on this debateable ground a losing battle in the hope that a generation will pass away before we sound a last retreat. Almost all intelligent persons are agreed that the earth has existed for myriads of ages; the best informed are of opinion that the history of nations extends back some thousand years before the Mosaic chronology; recent discoveries in geology may perhaps open a further vista of existence for the human species, while it is possible, and may one day be known, that mankind spread not from one but from many centres over the globe; or as others say, that the supply of links which are at present wanting in the chain of animal life may lead to new conclusions respecting the origin of man. Now let it be granted that these facts, being with the past, cannot be shown in the same palpable and evident manner as the facts of chemistry or physiology; and that the proof of some of them, especially of those last mentioned, is wanting; still it is a false policy to set up inspiration or revelation in opposition to them, a principle which can have no influence on them and should be rather kept out of their way. The sciences of geology and comparative philology are steadily gaining ground; many of the guesses of twenty years ago have become certainties, and the guesses of to-day may hereafter become so. Shall we peril religion on the possibility of their untruth? on such a cast to stake the life of man implies not only a recklessness of facts, but a misunderstanding of the nature of the Gospel. If it is fortunate for science, it is perhaps more fortunate for Christian truth, that the admission of Galileo's discovery has for ever settled the principle of the relations between them.

A similar train of thought may be extended to the results of historical inquiries. These results cannot be barred by the dates or narrative of Scripture; neither should they be made to wind round into agreement with them. Again, the idea of inspiration must expand and take them in. Their importance in a religious point of view is not that they impugn or confirm the Jewish history, but that they show more clearly the purposes of God towards the whole human race. The recent chronological discoveries from Egyptian monuments do not tend to overthrow revelation, nor the Ninevite inscriptions to support it. The use of them on either side may indeed arouse a popular interest in them; it is apt to turn a scientific inquiry into a semi-religious controversy. And to religion either use is almost equally injurious, because seeming to rest truths important to human life on the mere accident of an archaeological discovery. Is it to be thought that Christianity gains anything from the deciphering of the names of some Assyrian and Babylonian kings, contemporaries chiefly with the later Jewish history? As little as it ought to lose from the appearance of a contradictory narrative of the Exodus in the chamber of an Egyptian temple of the year B. C. 1500. This latter supposition may not be very probable. But it is worth while to ask ourselves the question, whether we can be right in maintaining any view of religion which can be affected by such a probability.

It will be a further assistance in the consideration of this subject, to observe that the interpretation of Scripture has nothing to do with any opinion respecting its origin. The meaning of Scripture is one thing; the inspiration of Scripture is another. It is conceivable that those who hold the most different views about the one, may be able to agree about the other. Rigid upholders of the verbal inspiration of Scripture, and those who deny inspiration altogether, may nevertheless meet on the common ground of the meaning of words. If the term inspiration were to fall into disuse, no fact of nature, or history, or language, no event in the life of man, or dealings of God with him, would be in any degree altered. The word itself is but of yesterday, not found in the earlier confessions of the reformed faith; the difficulties that have arisen about it are only two or three centuries old. Therefore the question of inspiration, though in one sense important, is to the interpreter as though it were not important; he is in no way called upon to determine a matter with which he has nothing to do, and which was not determined by fathers of the Church. And he had better go on his way and leave the more precise definition of the word to the progress of knowledge and the results of the study of Scripture, instead of entangling himself with a theory about it.

It is one evil of conditions or previous suppositions in the study of Scripture, that the assumption of them has led to an apologetic temper in the interpreters of Scripture. The tone of apology is always a tone of weakness, and does injury to a good cause. It is the reverse of 'ye shall know the truth, and the truth shall make you free.' It is hampered with the necessity of making a defence, and also with previous defences of the same side; it accepts, with an excess of reserve and caution, the truth itself, when it comes from an opposite quarter. Commentators are often more occupied with the proof of miracles than with the declaration of life and immortality; with the fulfilment of the details of prophecy than with its life and power; with the reconcilement of the discrepancies in the narrative of the infancy, pointed out by Schleiermacher, than with the importance of the great event of the appearance of the Saviour—'*To this end was I born and for this cause came I into the world that I should bear witness unto the truth.*' The same tendency is observable also in reference to the Acts of the Apostles and the Epistles, which are not only brought into harmony with each other, but interpreted with a reference to the traditions of existing communions. The natural meaning of particular expressions, as for example: 'Why are they then baptized for the dead?' (1 Cor. xv. 29), or the words 'because of the angels' (1 Cor. xi. 10); or, 'this generation shall not pass away until all these things be fulfilled' (Matt. xxiv. 34); or, 'upon this rock will I build my Church' (Matt. xvi. 18), is set aside in favour of others, which, however improbable, are more in accordance with preconceived opinions, or seem to be more worthy of the sacred writers. The language, and also the text, are treated on the same defensive and conservative principles. The received translations of Phil. ii. 6 ('Who, being in the form of God, thought it not robbery to be equal with God'), or of

Rom. iii. 25 ('Whom God hath set forth to be a propitiation through faith in his blood '), or Rom. xv. 6 ('God, even the Father of our Lord Jesus Christ'), though erroneous, are not given up without a struggle ; the 1 Tim. iii. 16, and 1 John v. 7 (the three witnesses), though the first ('God manifest in the flesh,' ΘΣ for ΟΣ) is not found in the best manuscripts, and the second in no Greek manuscript worth speaking of, have not yet disappeared from the editions of the Greek Testament commonly in use in England, and still less from the English translation. An English commentator who, with Lachmann and Tischendorf, supported also by the authority of Erasmus, ventures to alter the punctuation of the doxology in Rom. ix. 5 ('Who is over all God blessed for ever ') hardly escapes the charge of heresy. That in most of these cases the words referred to have a direct bearing on important controversies is a reason not for retaining, but for correcting them.

The temper of accommodation shows itself especially in two ways: first, in the attempt to adapt the truths of Scripture to the doctrines of the creeds ; secondly, in the adaptation of the precepts and maxims of Scripture to the language or practice of our own age. Now the creeds are acknowledged to be a part of Christianity ; they stand in a close relation to the words of Christ and his Apostles ; nor can it be said that any heterodox formula makes a nearer approach to a simple and scriptural rule of faith. Neither is anything gained by contrasting them with Scripture, in which the germs of the expressions used in them are sufficiently apparent. Yet it does not follow that they should be pressed into the service of the interpreter. The growth of ideas in the interval which separated the first century from the fourth or sixth makes it impossible to apply the language of the one to the explanation of the other. Between Scripture and the Nicene or Athanasian Creed, a world of the understanding comes in—that world of abstractions and second notions ; and mankind are no longer at the same point as when the whole of Christianity was contained in the words, 'Believe on the Lord Jesus Christ and thou mayest be saved,' when the Gospel centred in the attachment to a living or recently departed friend and Lord. The language of the New Testament is the first utterance and consciousness of the mind of Christ; or the immediate vision of the Word of life (1 John i. 1) as it presented itself before the eyes of His first followers, or as the sense of His truth and power grew upon them (Rom. i. 3, 4); the other is the result of three or four centuries of reflection and controversy. And although this last had a truth suited to its age, and its technical expressions have sunk deep into the heart of the human race, it is not the less unfitted to be the medium by the help of which Scripture is to be explained. If the occurrence of the phraseology of the Nicene age in a verse of the Epistles would detect the spuriousness of the verse in which it was found, how can the Nicene or Athanasian Creed be a suitable instrument for the interpretation of Scripture? That advantage which the New Testament has over the teaching of the Church, as representing what may be termed the childhood of the Gospel, would be lost if its language were required to conform to that of the Creeds.

To attribute to St. Paul or the Twelve the abstract notion of Christian truth, which afterwards sprang up in the Catholic Church, is the same sort of anachronism as to attribute to them a system of philosophy. It is the same error as to attribute to Homer the ideas of Thales or Heraclitus, or to Thales the more developed principles of Aristotle and Plato. Many persons who have no difficulty in tracing the growth of institutions, yet seem to fail in recognizing the more subtle progress of an idea. It is hard to imagine the absence of conceptions with which we are familiar; to go back to the germ of what we know only in maturity; to give up what has grown to us, and become a part of our minds. In the present case, however, the development is not difficult to prove. The statements of Scripture are unaccountable if we deny it; the silence of Scripture is equally unaccountable. Absorbed as St. Paul was in the person of Christ with an intensity of faith and love of which in modern days and at this distance of time we can scarcely form a conception—high as he raised the dignity of his Lord above all things in heaven and earth—looking to Him as the Creator of all things, and the head of quick and dead, he does not speak of Him as 'equal to the Father,' or 'of one substance with the Father.' Much of the language of the Epistles (passages for example such as Rom. i. 2 : Phil. ii. 6) would lose their meaning if distributed in alternate clauses between our Lord's humanity and divinity. Still greater difficulties would be introduced into the Gospels by the attempt to identify them with the Creeds. We should have to suppose that He was and was not tempted; that when He prayed to His Father He prayed also to Himself; that He knew and did not know 'of that hour' of which He as well as the angels were ignorant. How could He have said, 'My God, my God, why hast thou forsaken me'? or, 'Father, if it be possible, let this cup pass from me'? How could He have doubted whether 'when the Son cometh he shall find faith upon the earth'? These simple and touching words have to be taken out of their natural meaning and connexion to be made the theme of apologetic discourses if we insist on reconciling them with the distinctions of later ages.

Neither, as has been already remarked, would the substitution of any other precise or definite rule of faith, as for example the Unitarian, be more favourable to the interpretation of Scripture. How could the Evangelist St. John have said 'the Word was God,' or 'God was the Word' (according to either mode of translating), or how would our Lord Himself have said, 'I and the Father are one,' if either had meant that Christ was a mere man, 'a prophet or as one of the prophets'? No one who takes words in their natural sense can suppose that 'in the beginning' (John i. 1) means, 'at the commencement of the ministry of Christ,' or that 'the Word was with God,' only relates 'to the withdrawal of Christ to commune with God,' or that 'the Word is said to be God,' in the ironical sense of John x. 35. But while venturing to turn one eye on these (perhaps obsolete) perversions of the meanings of words in old opponents, we must not forget also to keep the other open to our own. The object of the preceding remark is not to enter into controversy with them, or to balance the statements of one side with those of the other, but only to point out the error of introducing into the interpretation of Scripture the notions of a later age which is common alike to us and them.

The other kind of accommodation which was alluded to above arises out of the difference between the social and ecclesiastical state of the world, as it exists in actual fact, and the ideal which the Gospel presents to us. An ideal is, by its very nature, far removed from actual life. It is enshrined not in the material things of the external world, but in the heart and conscience. Mankind are dissatisfied at this separation; they fancy that they can make the inward kingdom an outward one also. But this is not possible. The frame of civilization, that is to say, institutions and laws, the usages of business, the customs of society, these are for the most part mechanical, capable only in a certain degree of a higher and spiritual life. Christian motives have never existed in such strength, as to make it safe or possible to entrust them with the preservation of social order. Other interests are therefore provided and other principles, often independent of the teaching of the Gospel, or even apparently at variance with it. 'If a man smite thee on the right cheek turn to him the other also,' is not a regulation of police but an ideal rule of conduct, not to be explained away, but rarely if ever to be literally acted upon in a civilized country; or rather to be acted upon always in spirit, yet not without a reference to the interests of the community. If a missionary were to endanger the public peace and come like the Apostles saying, 'I ought to obey God rather than man,' it is obvious that the most Christian of magistrates could not allow him (say in India or New Zealand) to shield himself under the authority of these words. For in religion as in philosophy there are two opposite poles; of truth and action, of doctrine and practice, of idea and fact. The image of God in Christ is over against the necessities of human nature and the state of man on earth. Our Lord Himself recognizes this distinction, when He says, 'Of whom do the kings of the earth gather tribute?' and 'then are the children free' (Matt. xvii. 26). And again, 'Notwithstanding lest we should offend them,' &c. Here are contrasted what may be termed the two poles of idea and fact.

All men appeal to Scripture, and desire to draw the authority of Scripture to their side; its voice may be heard in the turmoil of political strife; a merely verbal similarity, the echo of a word, has weight in the determination of a controversy. Such appeals are not to be met always by counter-appeals; they rather lead to the consideration of deeper questions as to the manner in which Scripture is to be applied. In what relation does it stand to actual life? Is it a law, or only a spirit? for nations, or for individuals? to be enforced generally, or in details also? Are its maxims to be modified by experience, or acted upon in defiance of experience? Are the accidental circumstances of the first believers to become a rule for us? Is everything, in short, done or said by our Saviour and His Apostles, to be regarded as a precept or example which is to be followed on all occasions and to last for all time? That can hardly be, consistently with the changes of human things. It would be a rigid skeleton of Christianity (not the image of Christ), to which society and politics, as well as the lives of individuals, would be conformed. It would be the oldness of the letter, on which the world would be stretched; not 'the law of the spirit of life' which St. Paul teaches. The attempt to force politics and law into the framework of religion is apt to drive us up into a corner, in which the great principles of truth and justice have no longer room to make themselves felt. It is better, as well as safer, to take the liberty with which Christ has made us free. For our Lord Himself has left behind Him words, which contain a principle large enough to admit all the forms of society or of life; 'My kingdom is not of this world' (John xviii. 36). It does not come into collision with politics or knowledge; it has nothing to do with the Roman government or the Jewish priesthood, or with corresponding institutions in the present day; it is a counsel of perfection, and has its dwelling-place in the heart of man. That is the real solution of questions of Church and State; all else is relative to the history or circumstances of particular nations. That is the answer to a doubt which is also raised respecting the obligation of the letter of the Gospel on individual Christians. But this inwardness of the words of Christ is what few are able to receive; it is easier to apply them superficially to things without, than to be a partaker of them from within. And false and miserable applications of them are often made, and the kingdom of God becomes the tool of the kingdoms of the world.

The neglect of this necessary contrast between the ideal and the actual has had a twofold effect on the Interpretation of Scripture. It has led to an unfair appropriation of some portions of Scripture and an undue neglect of others. The letter is in many cases really or apparently in harmony with existing practices, or opinions, or institutions. In other cases it is far removed from them; it often seems as if the world would come to an end before the words of Scripture could be realized. The twofold effect just now mentioned, corresponds to these two classes. Some texts of Scripture have been eagerly appealed to and made (in one sense) too much of; they have been taken by force into the service of received opinions and beliefs; texts of the other class have been either unnoticed or explained away. Consider, for example, the extraordinary and unreasonable importance attached to single words, sometimes of doubtful meaning, in reference to any of the following subjects:—(1) Divorce; (2) Marriage with a Wife's Sister; (3) Inspiration; (4) the Personality of the Holy Spirit; (5) Infant Baptism; (6) Episcopacy; (7) Divine Right of Kings; (8) Original Sin. There is, indeed, a kind of mystery in the way in which the chance words of a simple narrative, the occurrence of some accidental event, the use even of a figure of speech, or a mistranslation of a word in Latin or English, have affected the thoughts of future ages and distant countries. Nothing so slight that it has not been caught at; nothing so plain that it may not be explained away. What men have brought to the text they have also found there; what has received no interpretation or witness, either in the customs of the Church or in 'the thoughts of many hearts,' is still 'an unknown tongue' to them. It is with Scripture as with oratory, its effect partly depends on the preparation in the mind or in circumstances for the reception of it. There is no use of Scripture, no quotation or even misquotation of a word which is not a power in the world, when it embodies the spirit of a great movement or is echoed by the voice of a large party.

(1) On the first of the subjects referred to above, it is argued from Scripture that adulterers should not be allowed to marry again; and the point of the argument turns on the question whether the words ($\dot{\epsilon}\kappa\tau\dot{o}s$ $\lambda\dot{o}\gamma ov$ $\pi o\rho\nu\epsilon\dot{\iota}as$) 'saving for the cause of fornication,' which occur in the first clause of an important text on marriage, were designedly or accidentally omitted in the second (Matt. v. 32: 'Whosoever shall put away his wife, saving for the cause of fornication, causeth her to commit adultery, and whosoever shall marry her that is divorced committeth adultery;'

compare also Mark x. 11, 12). (2) The Scripture argument in the second instance is almost invisible, being drawn from a passage the meaning of which is irrelevant (Lev. xviii. 18: 'Neither shalt thou take a wife to her sister to vex her, to uncover her nakedness beside the other in her lifetime'): and transferred from the Polygamy which prevailed in Eastern countries 3000 years ago to the Monogamy of the nineteenth century and the Christian Church, in spite of the custom and tradition of the Jews and the analogy of the brother's widow. (3) In the third case the word ($\theta\epsilon\acute{o}\pi\nu\epsilon\nu\sigma\tau\sigma s$) 'given by inspiration of God' is spoken of the Old Testament, and is assumed to apply to the New, including that Epistle in which the expression occurs (2 Tim. iii. 16). (4) In the fourth example the words used are mysterious (John xiv. 26; xvi. 15), and seem to come out of the depths of a divine consciousness; they have sometimes, however, received a more exact meaning than they could truly bear; what is spoken in a figure is construed with the severity of a logical statement, while passages of an opposite tenour are overlooked or set aside. (5) In the fifth instance, the mere mention of a family of a jailer at Philippi who was baptized ('he and all his,' Acts xvi. 33), has led to the inference that in this family there were probably young children, and hence that infant baptism is, first, permissive, secondly, obligatory. (6) In the sixth case the chief stress of the argument from Scripture turns on the occurrence of the word ($\dot{\epsilon}\pi\acute{\iota}\sigma\kappa\sigma\pi\sigma s$) bishop, in the Epistles to Timothy and Titus, which is assisted by a supposed analogy between the position of the Apostles and of their successors; although the term bishop is clearly used in the passages referred to as well as in other parts of the New Testament indistinguishably from Presbyter, and the magisterial authority of bishops in after ages is unlike rather than like the personal authority of the Apostles in the beginning of the Gospel. The further development of Episcopacy into Apostolical succession has often been rested on the promise, 'Lo, I am with you alway, even to the end of the world.' (7) In the seventh case the precepts of order which are addressed in the Epistle to the 'fifth monarchy men of those days,' are transferred to a duty of obedience to hereditary princes; the fact of the house of David, 'the Lord's anointed,' sitting on the throne of Israel is converted into a principle for all times and countries. And the higher lesson which our Saviour teaches: 'Render unto Cæsar the things which are Cæsar's,' that is to say, 'Render unto all their due, and to God above all,' is spoiled by being made into a precept of political subjection. (8) Lastly, the justice of God 'who rewardeth every man according to his works,' and the Christian scheme of redemption, have been staked on two figurative expressions of St. Paul to which there is no parallel in any other part of Scripture (1 Cor. xv. 22: 'For as in Adam all die, even so in Christ shall all be made alive,' and the corresponding passage in Rom. v. 12); notwithstanding the declaration of the Old Testament as also of the New, 'Every soul shall bear its own iniquity,' and 'neither this man sinned nor his parents.' It is not necessary for our purpose to engage further in the matters of dispute which have arisen by the way in attempting to illustrate the general argument. Yet to avoid misconception it may be remarked, that many of the principles, rules, or truths mentioned, as for example, Infant Baptism, or the Episcopal Form of Church Government, have sufficient grounds; the weakness is the attempt to derive them from Scripture.

With this minute and rigid enforcement of the words of Scripture in passages where the ideas expressed in them either really or apparently agree with received opinions or institutions, there remains to be contrasted the neglect, or in some instances the misinterpretation of other words which are not equally in harmony with the spirit of the age. In many of our Lord's discourses He speaks of the 'blessedness of poverty:' of the hardness which they that have riches will experience 'in attaining eternal life.' 'It is easier for a camel to go through a needle's eye,' and 'Son, thou in thy lifetime receivedst thy good things,' and again 'One thing thou lackest, go sell all that thou hast.' Precepts like these do not appeal to our own experience of life; they are unlike anything that we see around us at the present day, even among good men; to some among us they will recall the remarkable saying of Lessing,—'that the Christian religion had been tried for eighteen centuries; the religion of Christ remained to be tried.' To take them literally would be injurious to ourselves and to society (at least, so we think). Religious sects or orders who have seized this aspect of Christianity have come to no good, and have often ended in extravagance. It will not do to go into the world saying, 'Woe unto you, ye rich men,' or on entering a noble mansion to repeat the denunciations of the prophet about 'cedar and vermilion,' or on being shown the prospect of a magnificent estate to cry out, 'Woe unto them that lay field to field that they may be placed alone in the midst of the earth.' Times have altered, we say, since these denunciations were uttered; what appeared to the Prophet or Apostle a violation of the appointment of Providence has now become a part of it. It will not do to make a great supper, and mingle at the same board the two ends of society, as modern phraseology calls them, fetching in 'the poor, the maimed, the lame, the blind,' to fill the vacant places of noble guests. That would be eccentric in modern times, and even hurtful. Neither is it suitable for us to wash one another's feet, or to perform any other menial office, because our Lord set us the example. The customs of society do not admit it; no good would be done by it, and singularity is of itself an evil. Well, then, are the precepts of Christ not to be obeyed? Perhaps in their fullest sense they cannot be obeyed. But at any rate they are not to be explained away; the standard of Christ is not to be lowered to ordinary Christian life, because ordinary Christian life cannot rise, even in good men, to the standard of Christ. And there may be 'standing among us' some one in ten thousand 'whom we know not,' in whom there is such a divine union of charity and prudence that he is most blest in the entire fulfilment of the precept—'Go sell all that thou hast,'—which to obey literally in other cases would be evil, and not good. Many there have been, doubtless (not one or two only), who have given all that they had on earth to their family or friends—the poor servant 'casting her two mites into the treasury,' denying herself the ordinary comforts of life for the sake of an erring parent or brother; that is not probably an uncommon case, and as near an approach as in this life we make to heaven. And there may be some one or two rare natures in the world in whom there is such a divine courtesy, such a gentleness and dignity of soul, that differences of rank seem to vanish before them, and they look upon the face of others, even of their own servants and dependents, only as they are in the sight of God and will be in His kingdom. And there may be some tender and delicate woman among us, who feels that she has a divine vocation to fulfil the most repulsive offices towards the dying inmates of a hospital, or the soldier perishing in a foreign land. Whether such examples of self-sacrifice are good or evil, must depend, not altogether on social or economical principles, but on the spirit of those who offer them, and the power which they have in themselves of 'making all things kin.' And even if the ideal itself were not carried out by us in practice, it has nevertheless what may be termed a truth of feeling. 'Let them that have riches be as though they had them not.' 'Let the rich man wear the load lightly; he will one day fold them up as a vesture.' Let not the refinement of society make us forget that it is not the refined only who are received into the kingdom of God; nor the daintiness of life hide from us the bodily evils of which the rich man and Lazarus are alike heirs. Thoughts such as these have the power to reunite us to our fellow-creatures from whom the accidents of birth, position, wealth have separated us; they soften our hearts towards them, when divided not only by vice and ignorance, but what is even a greater barrier, difference of manners and associations. For if there be anything in our own fortune superior to that of others, instead of idolizing or cherishing it in the blood, the Gospel would have us cast it from us; and if there be anything mean or despised in those with whom we have to do, the Gospel would have us regard such as friends and brethren, yea, even as having the person of Christ.

Another instance of apparent, if not real neglect of the precepts of Scripture, is furnished by the commandment against swearing. No precept about divorce is so plain, so universal, so exclusive as this; 'Swear not at all.' Yet we all know how the custom of Christian countries has modified this 'counsel of perfection' which was uttered by the Saviour. This is the more remarkable because in this case the precept is not, as in the former, practically impossible of fulfilment or even difficult. And yet in this instance again, the body who have endeavoured to follow more nearly the letter of our Lord's commandment, seem to have gone against the common sense of the Christian world. Or to add one more example: Who, that hears of the Sabbatarianism, as it is called, of some Protestant countries, would imagine that the Author of our religion had cautioned His disciples, not against the violation of the Sabbath, but only against its formal and Pharisaical observance; or that the chiefest of the Apostles had warned the Colossians to 'Let no man judge them in respect of the new moon, or of the sabbath-days' (ii. 16).

The neglect of another class of passages is even more surprising, the precepts contained in them being quite practicable and in harmony with the existing state of the world. In this instance it seems as if religious teachers had failed to gather those principles of which they stood most in need. 'Think ye that those eighteen upon whom the tower of Siloam fell?' is the characteristic lesson of the Gospel on the occasion of any sudden visitation. Yet it is another reading of such calamities which is commonly insisted upon. The observation is seldom made respecting the parable of the good Samaritan, that the true neighbour is also a person of a different religion. The words, 'Forbid him not: for there is no man which shall do a miracle in my name, that can lightly speak evil of me,' are often said to have no application to sectarian differences in the present day, when the Church is established and miracles have ceased. The conduct of our Lord to the woman taken in adultery, though not intended for our imitation always, yet affords a painful contrast to the excessive severity with which even a Christian society punishes the errors of women. The boldness with which St. Paul applies the principle of individual judgement, 'Let every man be fully persuaded in his own mind,' as exhibited also in the words quoted above, 'Let no man judge you in respect of the new moon, or of the sabbath-days,' is far greater than would be allowed in the present age. Lastly, that the tenet of the damnation of the heathen should ever have prevailed in the Christian world, or that the damnation of Catholics should have been a received opinion among Protestants, implies a strange forgetfulness of such passages as Rom. ii. 1–16. 'Who rewardeth every man according to his work,' and 'When the Gentiles, which know not the law, do by nature the things contained in the law,' &c. What a difference between the simple statement which the Apostle makes of the justice of God and the 'uncovenanted mercies' or 'invincible ignorance' of theologians half reluctant to give up, yet afraid to maintain the advantage of denying salvation to those who are '*extra palum Ecclesiae!*'

The same habit of silence or misinterpretation extends to words or statements of Scripture in which doctrines are thought to be interested. When maintaining the Athanasian doctrine of the Trinity, we do not readily recall the verse, 'of that hour knoweth no man, no not the Angels of God, *neither the Son*, but the Father' (Mark xiii. 32). The temper or feeling which led St. Ambrose to doubt the genuineness of the words marked in italics, leads Christians in our own day to pass them over. We are scarcely just to the Millenarians or to those who maintain the continuance of miracles or spiritual gifts in the Christian Church, in not admitting the degree of support which is afforded to their views by many passages of Scripture. The same remark applies to the Predestinarian controversy; the Calvinist is often hardly dealt with, in being deprived of his real standing ground in the third and ninth chapters of the Epistle to the Romans. And the Protestant who thinks himself bound to prove from Scripture the very details of doctrine or discipline which are maintained in his Church, is often obliged to have recourse to harsh methods, and sometimes to deny appearances which seem to favour some particular tenet of Roman Catholicism (Matt. xvi. 18, 19; xviii. 18: 1 Cor. iii. 15). The Roman Catholic, on the other hand, scarcely observes that nearly all the distinctive articles of his creed are wanting in the New Testament; the Calvinist in fact ignores almost the whole of the sacred volume for the sake of a few verses. The truth is, that in seeking to prove our own opinions out of Scripture, we are constantly falling into the common fallacy of opening our eyes to one class of facts and closing them to another. The favourite verses shine like stars, while the rest of the page is thrown into the shade.

Nor indeed is it easy to say what is the meaning of 'proving a doctrine from Scripture.' For when we demand logical equivalents and similarity of circumstances, when we balance adverse statements, St. James and St. Paul, the

New Testament with the Old, it will be hard to demonstrate from Scripture any complex system either of doctrine or practice. The Bible is not a book of statutes in which words have been chosen to cover the multitude of cases, but in the greater portion of it, especially the Gospels and Epistles, 'like a man talking to his friend.' Nay, more, it is a book written in the East, which is in some degree liable to be misunderstood, because it speaks the language and has the feeling of Eastern lands. Nor can we readily determine in explaining the words of our Lord or of St. Paul, how much (even of some of the passages just quoted) is to be attributed to Oriental modes of speech. Expressions which would be regarded as rhetorical exaggerations in the Western world are the natural vehicles of thought to an Eastern people. How great then must be the confusion where an attempt is made to draw out these Oriental modes with the severity of a philosophical or legal argument! Is it not such a use of the words of Christ which He Himself rebukes when He says? 'It is the spirit that quickeneth, the flesh profiteth nothing' (John vi. 52, 63).

There is a further way in which the language of creeds and liturgies as well as the ordinary theological use of terms exercises a disturbing influence on the interpretation of Scripture. Words which occur in Scripture are singled out and incorporated in systems, like stones taken out of an old building and put into a new one. They acquire a technical meaning more or less divergent from the original one. It is obvious that their use in Scripture, and not their later and technical sense, must furnish the rule of interpretation. We should not have recourse to the meaning of a word in Polybius, for the explanation of its use in Plato, or to the turn of a sentence in Lycophron, to illustrate a construction of Aeschylus. It is the same kind of anachronism which would interpret Scripture by the scholastic or theological use of the language of Scripture. It is remarkable that this use is indeed partial, that is to say it affects one class of words and not another. Love and truth, for example, have never been theological terms; grace and faith, on the other hand, always retain an association with the Pelagian or Lutheran controversies. Justification and inspiration are derived from verbs which occur in Scripture, and the later substantive has clearly affected the meaning of the original verb or verbal in the places where they occur. The remark might be further illustrated by the use of Scriptural language respecting the Sacraments, which has also had a reflex influence on its interpretation in many passages of Scripture, especially in the Gospel of St. John (John iii. 5 ; vi. 56, &c). Minds which are familiar with the mystical doctrine of the Sacraments seem to see a reference to them in almost every place in the Old Testament as well as in the New, in which the words 'water,' or 'bread and wine' may happen to occur.

Other questions meet us on the threshold, of a different kind, which also affect the interpretation of Scripture, and therefore demand an answer. Is it admitted that the Scripture has one and only one true meaning? Or are we to follow the fathers into mystical and allegorical explanations? or with the majority of modern interpreters to confine ourselves to the double senses of prophecy, and the symbolism of the Gospel in the law? In either case, we assume what can never be proved, and an instrument is introduced of such subtlety and pliability as to make the Scriptures mean anything—'*Gallus in campanili*,' as the Waldenses described it; 'the weathercock on the church tower,' which is turned hither and thither by every wind of doctrine. That the present age has grown out of the mystical methods of the early fathers is a part of its intellectual state. No one will now seek to find hidden meanings in the scarlet thread of Rahab, or the number of Abraham's followers, or in the little circumstance mentioned after the resurrection of the Saviour that St. Peter was the first to enter the sepulchre. To most educated persons in the nineteenth century, these applications of Scripture appear foolish. Yet it is rather the excess of the method which provokes a smile than the method itself. For many remains of the mystical interpretation exist among ourselves; it is not the early fathers only who have read the Bible crosswise, or deciphered it as a book of symbols. And the uncertainty is the same in any part of Scripture if there is a departure from the plain and obvious meaning. If, for example, we alternate the verses in which our Lord speaks of the last things between the day of judgement and the destruction of Jerusalem; or, in the elder prophecies, which are the counterparts of these, make a corresponding division between the temporal and the spiritual Israel; or again if we attribute to the details of the Mosaical ritual a reference to the New Testament; or, once more, supposing the passage of the Red Sea to be regarded not merely as a figure of baptism, but as a pre-ordained type, the principle is conceded; there is no good reason why the scarlet thread of Rahab should not receive the explanation given to it by Clement. A little more or a little less of the method does not make the difference between certainty and uncertainty in the interpretation of Scripture. In whatever degree it is practised it is equally incapable of being reduced to any rule; it is the interpreter's fancy, and is likely to be not less but more dangerous and extravagant when it adds the charm of authority from its use in past ages.

The question which has been suggested runs up into a more general one, 'the relation between the Old and New Testaments.' For the Old Testament will receive a different meaning accordingly as it is explained from itself or from the New. In the first case a careful and conscientious study of each one for itself is all that is required; in the second case the types and ceremonies of the law, perhaps the very facts and persons of the history, will be assumed to be predestined or made after a pattern corresponding to the things that were to be in the latter days. And this question of itself stirs another question respecting the interpretation of the Old Testament in the New. Is such interpretation to be regarded as the meaning of the original text, or an accommodation of it to the thoughts of other times?

Our object is not to attempt here the determination of these questions, but to point out that they must be determined before any real progress can be made or any agreement arrived at in the interpretation of Scripture. With one more example of another kind we may close this part of the subject. The origin of the three first Gospels is an inquiry which has not been much considered by English theologians since the days of Bishop Marsh. The difficulty of the question has been sometimes misunderstood; the point being how there can be so much agreement in words, and so much disagreement both in words and facts; the double phenomenon is the real perplexity—how in short there can be all degrees of similarity and dissimilarity, the kind and degree of similarity being such as to make it necessary to suppose that large portions are copied from each other or from common documents; the dissimilarities being of a kind which seem to render impossible any knowledge in the authors of one another's writings. The most probable solution of this difficulty is, that the tradition on which the three first Gospels are based was at first preserved orally, and slowly put together and written in the three forms which it assumed at a very early period, those forms being in some places, perhaps, modified by translation. It is not necessary to develop this hypothesis farther. The point to be noticed is, that whether this or some other theory be the true account (and some such account is demonstrably necessary), the assumption of such a theory, or rather the observation of the facts on which it rests, cannot but exercise an influence on interpretation. We can no longer speak of three independent witnesses of the Gospel narrative. Hence there follow some other consequences. (1) There is no longer the same necessity as heretofore to reconcile inconsistent narratives; the harmony of the Gospels only means the parallelism of similar words. (2) There is no longer any need to enforce everywhere the connexion of successive verses, for the same words will be found to occur in different connexions in the different Gospels. (3) Nor can the designs attributed to their authors be regarded as the free handling of the same subject on different plans; the difference consisting chiefly in the occurrence or absence of local or verbal explanations, or the addition or omission of certain passages. Lastly, it is evident that no weight can be given to traditional statements of facts about the authorship, as, for example, that respecting St. Mark being the interpreter of St. Peter, because the Fathers who have handed down these statements were ignorant or unobservant of the great fact, which is proved by internal evidence, that they are for the most part of common origin.

Until these and the like questions are determined by interpreters, it is not possible that there should be agreement in the interpretation of Scripture. The Protestant and Catholic, the Unitarian and Trinitarian will continue to fight their battle on the ground of the New Testament. The Preterists and Futurists, those who maintain that the roll of prophecies is completed in past history, or in the apostolical age; those who look forward to a long series of events which are yet to come [ἐς ἀφανὲς τὸν μῦθον ἀνενείκας οὐκ ἔχει ἔλεγχον], may alike claim the authority of the Book of Daniel, or the Revelation. Apparent coincidences will always be discovered by those who want to find them. Where there is no critical interpretation of Scripture, there will be a mystical or rhetorical one. If words have more than one meaning, they may have any meaning. Instead of being a rule of life or faith, Scripture becomes the expression of the ever-changing aspect of religious opinions.

The unchangeable word of God, in the name of which we repose, is changed by each age and each generation in accordance with its passing fancy. The book in which we believe all religious truth to be contained, is the most uncertain of all books, because interpreted by arbitrary and uncertain methods.

§ 3.

It is probable that some of the preceding statements may be censured as a wanton exposure of the difficulties of Scripture. It will be said that such inquiries are for the few, while the printed page lies open to the many, and that the obtrusion of them may offend some weaker brother, some half-educated or prejudiced soul, 'for whom,' nevertheless, in the touching language of St. Paul, 'Christ died.' A confusion of the heart and head may lead sensitive minds into a desertion of the principles of the Christian life, which are their own witness, because they are in doubt about facts which are really external to them. Great evil to character may sometimes ensue from such causes. 'No man can serve two' opinions without a sensible harm to his nature. The consciousness of this responsibility should be always present to writers on theology. But the responsibility is really twofold; for there is a duty to speak the truth as well as a duty to withhold it. The voice of a majority of the clergy throughout the world, the half sceptical, half conservative instincts of many laymen, perhaps, also, individual interest, are in favour of the latter course; while a higher expediency pleads that 'honesty is the best policy,' and that truth alone 'makes free.' To this it may be replied, that truth is not truth to those who are unable to use it; no reasonable man would attempt to lay before the illiterate such a question as that concerning the origin of the Gospels. And yet it may be rejoined once more, the healthy tone of religion among the poor depends upon freedom of thought and inquiry among the educated. In this conflict of reasons, individual judgement must at last decide. That there has been no rude, or improper unveiling of the difficulties of Scripture in the preceding pages, is thought to be shown by the following considerations:

First, that the difficulties referred to are very well known; they force themselves on the attention, not only of the student, but of every intelligent reader of the New Testament, whether in Greek or English. The treatment of such difficulties in theological works is no measure of public opinion respecting them. Thoughtful persons, whose minds have turned towards theology, are continually discovering that the critical observations which they make themselves have been made also by others apparently without concert. The truth is that they have been led to them by the same causes, and these again lie deep in the tendencies of education and literature in the present age. But no one is willing to break through the reticence which is observed on these subjects; hence a sort of smouldering scepticism. It is probable that the distrust is greatest at the time when the greatest efforts are made to conceal it. Doubt comes in at the window, when Inquiry is denied at the door. The thoughts of able and highly educated young men almost always stray towards the first principles of things; it is a great injury to them, and tends to raise in their minds a sort of incurable suspicion, to find that there is one book of the fruit of the knowledge of which they are forbidden freely to taste, that is, the Bible. The same spirit renders the Christian Minister almost powerless in the hands of his opponents. He can give no true answer to the mechanic or artisan who has either discovered by his mother-wit or who retails at second-hand the objections of critics; for he is unable to look at things as they truly are.

Secondly, as the time has come when it is no longer possible to ignore the results of criticism, it is of importance that Christianity should be seen to be in harmony with them. That objections to some received views should be valid, and yet that they should be always held up as the objections of infidels, is a mischief to the Christian cause. It is a mischief that critical observations which any intelligent man can make for himself, should be ascribed to atheism or unbelief. It would be a strange and almost incredible thing that the Gospel, which at first made war only on the vices of mankind, should now be opposed to one of the highest and rarest of human virtues—the love of truth. And that in the present day the great object of Christianity should be, not to change the lives of men, but to prevent them from changing their opinions; that would be a singular inversion of the purposes for which Christ came into the world. The Christian religion is in a false position when all the tendencies of knowledge are opposed to it. Such a position cannot be long maintained, or can only end in the withdrawal of the educated classes from the influences of religion. It is a grave consideration whether we ourselves may not be in an earlier stage of the same religious dissolution, which seems to have gone further in Italy and France. The reason for thinking so is not to be sought in the external circumstances of our own or any other religious communion, but in the progress of ideas with which Christian teachers seem to be ill at ease. Time was when the Gospel was before the age; when it breathed a new life into a decaying world—when the difficulties of Christianity were difficulties of the heart only, and the highest minds found in its truths not only the rule of their lives, but a well-spring of intellectual delight. Is it to be held a thing impossible that the Christian religion, instead of shrinking into itself, may again embrace the thoughts of men upon the earth? Or is it true that since the Reformation 'all intellect has gone the other way'? and that in Protestant countries reconciliation is as hopeless as Protestants commonly believe to be the case in Catholic?

Those who hold the possibility of such a reconcilement or restoration of belief, are anxious to disengage Christianity from all suspicion of disguise or unfairness. They wish to preserve the historical use of Scripture as the continuous witness in all ages of the higher things in the heart of man, as the inspired source of truth and the way to the better life. They are willing to take away some of the external supports, because they are not needed and do harm; also, because they interfere with the meaning. They have a faith, not that after a period of transition all things will remain just as they were before, but that they will all come round again to the use of man and to the glory of God. When interpreted like any other book, by the same rules of evidence and the same canons of criticism, the Bible will still remain unlike any other book; its beauty will be freshly seen, as of a picture which is restored after many ages to its original state; it will create a new interest and make for itself a new kind of authority by the life which is in it. It will be a spirit and not a letter; as it was in the beginning, having an influence like that of the spoken word, or the book newly found. The purer the light in the human heart, the more it will have an expression of itself in the mind of Christ; the greater the knowledge of the development of man, the truer will be the insight gained into the 'increasing purpose' of revelation. In which also the individual soul has a practical part, finding a sympathy with its own imperfect feelings, in the broken utterance of the Psalmist or the Prophet as well as in the fullness of Christ. The harmony between Scripture and the life of man, in all its stages, may be far greater than appears at present. No one can form any notion from what we see around us, of the power which Christianity might have if it were at one with the conscience of man, and not at variance with his intellectual convictions. There, a world weary of the heat and dust of controversy—of speculations about God and man—weary too of the rapidity of its own motion, would return home and find rest.

But for the faith that the Gospel might win again the minds of intellectual men, it would be better to leave religion to itself, instead of attempting to draw them together. Other walks in literature have peace and pleasure and profit; the path of the critical Interpreter of Scripture is almost always a thorny one in England. It is not worth while for any one to enter upon it who is not supported by a sense that he has a Christian and moral object. For although an Interpreter of Scripture in modern times will hardly say with the emphasis of the Apostle, 'Woe is me, if I speak not the truth without regard to consequences,' yet he too may feel it a matter of duty not to conceal the things which he knows. He does not hide the discrepancies of Scripture, because the acknowledgement of them is the first step towards agreement among interpreters. He would restore the original meaning because 'seven other' meanings take the place of it; the book is made the sport of opinion and the instrument of perversion of life. He would take the excuses of the head out of the way of the heart; there is hope too that by drawing Christians together on the ground of Scripture, he may also draw them nearer to one another. He is not afraid that inquiries, which have for their object the truth, can ever be displeasing to the God of truth; or that the Word of God is in any such sense a word as to be hurt by investigations into its human origin and conception.

It may be thought another ungracious aspect of the preceding remarks, that they cast a slight upon the interpreters of Scripture in former ages. The early Fathers, the Roman Catholic mystical writers, the Swiss and German Reformers, the Nonconformist divines, have qualities for which we look in vain among ourselves; they throw an intensity of light upon the page of Scripture which we nowhere find in modern commentaries. But it is not the light of interpretation. They have a faith which seems indeed to have grown dim nowadays, but that faith is not drawn from the study of Scripture; it is the element in which their own mind moves which overflows on the meaning of the text. The words of Scripture suggest to them their own thoughts or feelings. They are preachers, or in the New Testament sense of the word, prophets rather than interpreters. There is nothing in such a view derogatory to the saints and doctors of former ages. That Aquinas or Bernard did not shake themselves free from the mystical method of the Patristic times or the Scholastic one which was more peculiarly their own; that Luther and Calvin read the Scriptures in connexion with the ideas which were kindling in the mind of their age, and the events which were passing before their eyes, these and similar remarks are not to be construed as depreciatory of the genius or learning of famous men of old; they relate only to their interpretation of Scripture, in which it is no slight upon them, to maintain that they were not before their day.

What remains may be comprised in a few precepts, or rather is the expansion of a single one. *Interpret the Scripture like any other book.* There are many respects in which Scripture is unlike any other book; these will appear in the results of such an interpretation. The first step is to know the meaning, and this can only be done in the same careful and impartial way that we ascertain the meaning of Sophocles or of Plato. The subordinate principles which flow out of this general one will also be gathered from the observation of Scripture. No other science of Hermeneutics is possible but an inductive one, that is to say, one based on the language and thoughts and narrations of the sacred writers. And it would be well to carry the theory of interpretation no further than in the case of other works. Excessive system tends to create an impression that the meaning of Scripture is out of our reach, or is to be attained in some other way than by the exercise of manly sense and industry. Who would write a bulky treatise about the method to be pursued in interpreting Plato or Sophocles? Let us not set out on our journey so heavily equipped that there is little chance of our arriving at the end of it. The method creates itself as we go on, beginning only with a few reflections directed against plain errors. Such reflections are the rules of common sense, which we acknowledge with respect to other works written in dead languages; without pretending to novelty they may help us to 'return to nature' in the study of the sacred writings.

First, it may be laid down, that Scripture has one meaning—the meaning which it had to the mind of the Prophet or Evangelist who first uttered or wrote, to the hearers or readers who first received it. Another view may be easier or more familiar to us, seeming to receive a light and interest from the circumstances of our own age. But such accommodation of the text must be laid aside by the interpreter, whose business is, to place himself as nearly as possible in the position of the sacred writer. That is no easy task—to call up the inner and outer life of the contemporaries of our Saviour; to follow the abrupt and involved utterance of St. Paul or of one of the old Prophets; to trace the meaning of words when language first became Christian. He will often have to choose the more difficult interpretation (Gal. ii. 20; Rom. iii. 15, &c.), and to refuse one more in agreement with received opinions, because the latter is less true to the style and time of the author. He may incur the charge of singularity, or confusion of ideas, or ignorance of Greek, from a misunderstanding of the peculiarity of the subject in the person who makes the charge. For if it be said that the translation of some Greek words is contrary to the usages of grammar (Gal. iv. 13), that is not in every instance to be denied; the point is, whether the usages of grammar are always observed. Or if it be objected to some interpretation of Scripture that it is difficult and perplexing, the answer is—'that may very well be—it is the fact,' arising out of differences in the modes of thought of other times, or irregularities in the use of language which no art of the interpreter can evade. One consideration should be borne in mind, that the Bible is the only book in the world written in different styles and at many different times, which is in the hands of persons of all degrees of knowledge and education. The benefit of this outweighs the evil, yet the evil should be admitted—namely, that it leads to a hasty and partial interpretation of Scripture, which often obscures the true one. A sort of conflict arises between scientific criticism and popular opinion. The indiscriminate use of Scripture has a further tendency to maintain erroneous readings or translations; some which are allowed to be such by scholars have been stereotyped in the mind of the English reader; and it becomes almost a political question how far we can venture to disturb them.

There are difficulties of another kind in many parts of Scripture, the depth and inwardness of which require a measure of the same qualities in the interpreter himself. There are notes struck in places, which like some discoveries of science have sounded before their time; and only after many days have been caught up and found a response on the earth. There are germs of truth which after thousands of years have never yet taken root in the world. There are lessons in the Prophets which, however simple, mankind have not yet learned even in theory; and which the complexity of society rather tends to hide; aspects of human life in Job and Ecclesiastes which have a truth of desolation about them which we faintly realize in ordinary circumstances. It is, perhaps, the greatest difficulty of all to enter into the meaning of the words of Christ—so gentle, so human, so divine, neither adding to them nor marring their simplicity. The attempt to illustrate or draw them out in detail, even to guard against their abuse, is apt to disturb the balance of truth. The interpreter needs nothing short of 'fashioning' in himself the image of the mind of Christ. He has to be born again into a new spiritual or intellectual world, from which the thoughts of this world are shut out. It is one of the highest tasks on which the labour of a life can be spent, to bring the words of Christ a little nearer the heart of man.

But while acknowledging this inexhaustible or infinite character of the sacred writings, it does not, therefore, follow that we are willing to admit of hidden or mysterious meanings in them: in the same way we recognize the wonders and complexity of the laws of nature to be far beyond what eye has seen or knowledge reached, yet it is not therefore to be supposed that we acknowledge the existence of some other laws, different in kind from those we know, which are incapable of philosophical analysis. In like manner we have no reason to attribute to the Prophet or Evangelist any second or hidden sense different from that which appears on the surface. All that the Prophet meant may not have been consciously present to his mind; there were depths which to himself also were but half revealed. He beheld the fortunes of Israel passing into the heavens; the temporal kingdom was fading into an eternal one. It is not to be supposed that what he saw at a distance only was clearly defined to him; or that the universal truth which was appearing and reappearing in the history of the surrounding world took a purely spiritual or abstract form in his mind. There is a sense in which we may still say with Lord Bacon, that the words of prophecy are to be interpreted as the words of one 'with whom a thousand years are as one day, and one day as a thousand years.' But that is no reason for turning days into years, or for interpreting the things 'that must shortly come to pass' in the book of Revelation, as the events of modern history, or for separating the day of judgement from the destruction of Jerusalem in the Gospels. The double meaning which is given to our Saviour's discourse respecting the last things is not that 'form of eternity' of which Lord Bacon speaks; it resembles rather the doubling of an object when seen through glasses placed at different angles. It is true also that there are types in Scripture which were regarded as such by the Jews themselves, as for example, the scapegoat, or the paschal lamb. But that is no proof of all outward ceremonies being types when Scripture is silent; —if we assume the New Testament as a tradition running parallel with the Old, may not the Roman Catholic assume with equal reason tradition running parallel with the New? Prophetic symbols, again, have often the same meaning in different places (e.g. the four beasts or living creatures, the colours white or red); the reason is that this meaning is derived from some natural association (as of fruitfulness, purity, or the like); or again, they are borrowed in some of the later prophecies from earlier ones; we are not, therefore, justified in supposing any hidden connexion in the prophecies where they occur. Neither is there any ground for assuming design of any other kind in Scripture any more than in Plato or Homer. Wherever there is beauty and order, there is design; but there is no proof of any artificial design, such as is often traced by the Fathers, in the relation of the several parts of a book, or of the several books to each other. That is one of those mischievous notions which enables us, under the disguise of reverence, to make Scripture mean what we please. Nothing that can be said of the greatness or sublimity, or truth, or depth, or tenderness, of many passages, is too much. But that greatness is of a simple kind; it is not increased by double senses, or systems of types, or elaborate structure, or design. If every sentence was a mystery, every word a riddle, every letter a symbol, that would not make the Scriptures more worthy of a Divine author; it is a heathenish or Rabbinical fancy which reads them in this way. Such complexity would not place them above but below human compositions in general; for it would deprive them of the ordinary intelligibleness of human language. It is not for a Christian theologian to say that words were given to mankind to conceal their thoughts, neither was revelation given them to conceal the Divine.

The second rule is an application of the general principle; 'interpret Scripture from itself,' as in other respects like any other book written in an age and country of which little or no other literature survives, and about which we know almost nothing except what is derived from its pages. Not that all the parts of Scripture are to be regarded as an indistinguishable mass. The Old Testament is not to be identified with the New, nor the Law with the Prophets, nor the Gospels with the Epistles, nor the Epistles of St. Paul to be violently harmonized with the Epistle of St. James. Each writer, each successive age, has characteristics of its own, as strongly marked, or more strongly than those which are found in the authors or periods of classical literature. These differences are not to be lost in the idea of a Spirit from whom they proceed or by which they were overruled. And therefore, illustration of one part of Scripture by another should be confined to writings of the same age and the same authors, except where the writings of different ages or persons offer obvious similarities. It may be said further that illustration should be chiefly derived, not only from the same author, but from the same writing, or from one of the same period of his life. For example, the comparison of St. John and the 'synoptic' Gospels, or of the Gospel of St. John with the Revelation of St. John, will tend rather to confuse than to elucidate the meaning of either; while, on the other hand, the comparison of the Prophets with one another, and with the Psalms, offers many valuable helps and lights to the interpreter. Again, the connexion between the Epistles written by the Apostle St. Paul about the same time (e. g. Romans, 1 and 2 Corinthians, Galatians—Colossians, Philippians, Ephesians—compared with Romans, Colossians—Ephesians, Galatians, &c.) is far closer than of Epistles which are separated by an interval of only a few years.

But supposing all this to be understood, and that by the interpretation of Scripture from itself is meant a real interpretation of like by like, it may be asked, what is it that we gain from a minute comparison of a particular author or writing? The indiscriminate use of parallel passages taken from one end of Scripture and applied to the other (except so far as earlier compositions may have afforded the material or the form of later ones) is useless and uncritical. The uneducated or imperfectly educated person who looks out the marginal references of the English Bible, imagining himself in this way to gain a clearer insight into the Divine meaning, is really following the religious associations of his own mind. Even the critical use of parallel passages is not without danger. For are we to conclude that an author meant in one place what he says in another? Shall we venture to mend a corrupt phrase on the model of some other phrase, which memory, prevailing over judgement, calls up and thrusts into the text? It is this fallacy which has filled the pages of classical writers with useless and unfounded emendations.

The meaning of the Canon '*Non nisi ex Scripturâ Scripturam potes interpretari,*' is only this, 'That we cannot understand Scripture without becoming familiar with it.' Scripture is a world by itself, from which we must exclude foreign influences, whether theological or classical. To get inside that world is an effort of thought and imagination, requiring the sense of a poet as well as a critic—demanding, much more than learning, a degree of original power and intensity of mind. Any one who, instead of burying himself in the pages of the commentators, would learn the sacred writings by heart, and paraphrase them in English, will probably make a nearer approach to their true meaning than he would gather from any commentary. The intelligent mind will ask its own questions, and find for the most part its own answers. The true use of interpretation is to get rid of interpretation, and leave us alone in company with the author. When the meaning of Greek words is once known, the young student has almost all the real materials which are possessed by the greatest Biblical scholar, in the book itself. For almost our whole knowledge of the history of the Jews is derived from the Old Testament and the Apocryphal books, and almost our whole knowledge of the life of Christ and of the Apostolical age is derived from the New; whatever is added to them is either conjecture, or very slight topographical or chronological illustration. For this reason the rule given above, which is applicable to all books, is applicable to the New Testament more than any other.

Yet in this consideration of the separate books of Scripture it is not to be forgotten that they have also a sort of continuity. We make a separate study of the subject, of the mode of thought, in some degree also of the language of each book. And at length the idea arises in our minds of a common literature, a pervading life, an overruling law. It may be compared to the effect of some natural scene in which we suddenly perceive a harmony or picture, or to the imperfect appearance of design which suggests itself in looking at the surface of the globe. That is to say, there is nothing miraculous or artificial in the arrangement of the books of Scripture; it is the result, not the design, which appears in them when bound in the same volume. Or if we like so to say, there *is* design, but a natural design which is revealed to after ages. Such continuity or design is best expressed under some notion of progress or growth, not regular, however, but with broken and imperfect stages, which the want of knowledge prevents our minutely defining. The great truth of the unity of God was there from the first; slowly as the morning broke in the heavens, like some central light, it filled and afterwards dispersed the mists of human passion in which it was itself enveloped. A change passes over the Jewish religion from fear to love, from power to wisdom, from the justice of God to the mercy of God, from the nation to the individual, from this world to another; from the visitation of the sins of the fathers upon the children, to 'every soul shall bear its own iniquity;' from the fire, the earthquake, and the storm, to the still small voice. There never was a time after the deliverance from Egypt, in which the Jewish people did not bear a kind of witness against the cruelty and licentiousness of the surrounding tribes. In the decline of the monarchy, as the kingdom itself was sinking under foreign conquerors, whether springing from contact with the outer world, or from some reaction within, the undergrowth of morality gathers strength; first, in the anticipation of prophecy, secondly, like a green plant in the hollow rind of Pharisaism—and individuals pray and commune with God each one for himself. At length the tree of life blossoms; the faith in immortality which had hitherto slumbered in the heart of man, intimated only in doubtful words (2 Sam. xii. 23; Psalm xvii. 15), or beaming for an instant in dark places (Job xix. 25), has become the prevailing belief.

There is an interval in the Jewish annals which we often exclude from our thoughts, because it has no record in the canonical writings—extending over about four hundred years, from the last of the prophets of the Old Testament to the forerunner of Christ in the New. This interval, about which we know so little, which is regarded by many as a portion of secular rather than of sacred history, was nevertheless as fruitful in religious changes as any similar period which preceded. The establishment of the Jewish sects, and the wars of the Maccabees, probably exercised as great an influence on Judaism as the captivity itself. A third influence was that of the Alexandrian literature, which was attracting the Jewish intellect, at the same time that the Galilean zealot was tearing the nation in pieces with the doctrine that it was lawful to call 'no man master but God.' In contrast with that wild fanaticism as well as with the proud Pharisee, came One most unlike all that had been before, as the kings or rulers of mankind. In an age which was the victim of its own passions, the creature of its own circumstances, the slave of its own degenerate religion, our Saviour taught a lesson absolutely free from all the influences of a surrounding world. He made the last perfect revelation of God to man; a revelation not indeed immediately applicable to the state of society or the world, but in its truth and purity inexhaustible by the after generations of men. And of the first application of the truth which He taught as a counsel of perfection to the actual circumstances of mankind, we have the example in the Epistles.

Such a general conception of growth or development in Scripture, beginning with the truth of the Unity of God in the earliest books and ending with the perfection of Christ, naturally springs up in our minds in the perusal of the sacred writings. It is a notion of value to the interpreter, for it enables him at the same time to grasp the whole and distinguish the parts. It saves him from the necessity of maintaining that the Old Testament is one and the same everywhere; that the books of Moses contain truths or precepts, such as the duty of prayer or the faith in immortality, or the spiritual interpretation of sacrifice, which no one has ever seen there. It leaves him room enough to admit all the facts of the case. No longer is he required to defend, or to explain away, David's imprecations against his enemies, or his injunctions to Solomon, any more than his sin in the matter of Uriah. Nor is he hampered with a theory of accommodation. Still, the sense of 'the increasing purpose which through the ages ran' is present to him, nowhere else continuously discernible or ending in a divine perfection. Nowhere else is there found the same interpenetration of the political and religious element—a whole nation, 'though never good for much at any time,' possessed with the conviction that it was living in the face of God—in whom the Sun of righteousness shone upon the corruption of an Eastern nature—the 'fewest of all people,' yet bearing the greatest part in the education of the world. Nowhere else among the teachers and benefactors of mankind is there any form like His, in whom the desire of the nation is fulfilled, and 'not of that nation only,' but of all mankind, whom He restores to His Father and their Father, to His God and their God.

Such a growth or development may be regarded as a kind of progress from childhood to manhood. In the child there is an anticipation of truth ; his reason is latent in the form of feeling; many words are used by him which he imperfectly understands; he is led by temporal promises, believing that to be good is to be happy always ; he is pleased by marvels and has vague terrors. He is confined to a spot of earth, and lives in a sort of prison of sense, yet is bursting also with a fulness of childish life: he imagines God to be like a human father, only greater and more awful; he is easily impressed with solemn thoughts, but soon 'rises up to play' with other children. It is observable that his ideas of right and wrong are very simple, hardly extending to another life ; they consist chiefly in obedience to his parents, whose word is his law. As he grows older he mixes more and more with others ; first with one or two who have a great influence in the direction of his mind. At length the world opens upon him ; another work of education begins ; and he learns to discern more truly the meaning of things and his relation to men in general. You may complete the image, by supposing that there was a time in his early days when he was a helpless outcast 'in the land of Egypt and the house of bondage.' And as he arrives at manhood he reflects on his former years, the progress of his education, the hardships of his infancy, the home of his youth (the thought of which is ineffaceable in after life), and he now understands that all this was but a preparation for another state of being, in which he is to play a part for himself. And once more in age you may imagine him like the patriarch looking back on the entire past, which he reads anew, perceiving that the events of life had a purpose or result which was not seen at the time; they seem to him bound 'each to each by natural piety.'

'Which things are an allegory,' the particulars of which any one may interpret for himself. For the child born after the flesh is the symbol of the child born after the Spirit. 'The law was a schoolmaster to bring men to Christ,' and now 'we are under a schoolmaster' no longer. The anticipation of truth which came from without to the childhood or youth of the human race is witnessed to within; the revelation of God is not lost but renewed in the heart and understanding of the man. Experience has taught us the application of the lesson in a wider sphere. And many influences have combined to form the 'after life' of the world. When at the close (shall we say) of a great period in the history of man, we cast our eyes back on the course of events, from the 'angel of his presence in the wilderness' to the multitude of peoples, nations, languages, who are being drawn together by His Providence—from the simplicity of the pastoral state in the dawn of the world's day, to all the elements of civilization and knowledge which are beginning to meet and mingle in a common life, we also understand that we are no longer in our early home, to which, nevertheless, we fondly look; and that the end is yet unseen, and the purposes of God towards the human race only half revealed. And to turn once more to the Interpreter of Scripture, he too feels that the continuous growth of revelation which he traces in the Old and New Testament, is a part of a larger whole extending over the earth and reaching to another world.

§ 4.

Scripture has an inner life or soul; it has also an outward body or form. That form is language, which imperfectly expresses our common notions, much more those higher truths which religion teaches. At the time when our Saviour came into the world the Greek language was itself in a state of degeneracy and decay. It had lost its poetic force, and was ceasing to have the sway over the mind which classical Greek once held. That is a more important revolution in the mental history of mankind, than we easily conceive in modern times, when all languages sit loosely on thought, and the peculiarities and idiosyncrasies of one are corrected by our knowledge of another. It may be numbered among the causes which favoured the growth of Christianity. That degeneracy was a preparation for the Gospel—the decaying soil in which the new elements of life were to come forth— the beginning of another state of man, in which language and mythology and philosophy were no longer to exert the same constraining power as in the ancient world. The civilized portion of mankind were becoming of one speech, the diffusion of which along the shores of the Mediterranean sea made a way for the entrance of Christianity into the human understanding, just as the Roman empire prepared the framework of its outward history. The first of all languages, 'for glory and for beauty,' had become the 'common dialect' of the Macedonian kingdoms; it had been moulded in the schools of Alexandria to the ideas of the East and the religious wants of Jews. Neither was it any violence to its nature to be made the vehicle of the new truths which were springing up in the heart of man. The definiteness and absence of reflectiveness in the earlier forms of human speech, would have imposed a sort of limit on the freedom and spirituality of the Gospel; even the Greek of Plato would have 'coldly furnished forth' the words of 'eternal life.' A religion which was to be universal required the divisions of languages, as of nations, to be in some degree broken down. ['*Poena linguarum dispersit homines, donum linguarum in unum collegit.*'] But this community or freedom of language was accompanied by corresponding defects; it had lost its logical precision;

it was less coherent, and more under the influence of association. It might be compared to a garment which allowed and yet impeded the exercise of the mind by being too large and loose for it.

From the inner life of Scripture it is time to pass on to the consideration of this outward form, including that other framework of modes of thought and figures of speech which is between the two. A knowledge of the original language is a necessary qualification of the Interpreter of Scripture. It takes away at least one chance of error in the explanation of a passage; it removes one of the films which have gathered over the page; it brings the meaning home in a more intimate and subtle way than a translation could do. To this, however, another qualification should be added, which is, the logical power to perceive the meaning of words in reference to their context. And there is a worse fault than ignorance of Greek in the interpretation of the New Testament, that is, ignorance of any language. The Greek fathers, for example, are far from being the best verbal commentators, because their knowledge of Greek often leads them away from the drift of the passage. The minuteness of the study in our own day has also a tendency to introduce into the text associations which are not really found there. There is a danger of making words mean too much; refinements of signification are drawn out of them, perhaps contained in their etymology, which are lost in common use and parlance. There is the error of interpreting every particle, as though it were a link in the argument, instead of being, as is often the case, an excrescence of style. The verbal critic magnifies his art, which is really great in Aeschylus or Pindar, but not of equal importance in the interpretation of the simpler language of the New Testament. His love of scholarship will sometimes lead him to impress a false system on words and constructions. A great critic[1] who has commented on

---

[1] [G.] Hermann.

the three first chapters of the Epistle to the Galatians, has certainly afforded a proof that it is possible to read the New Testament under a distorting influence from classical Greek. The tendency gains support from the undefined feeling that Scripture does not come behind in excellence of language any more than of thought. And if not, as in former days, the classic purity of the Greek of the New Testament, yet its certainty and accuracy, the assumption of which, as any other assumption, is only the parent of inaccuracy, is still maintained.

The study of the language of the New Testament has suffered in another way by following too much in the track of classical scholarship. All dead languages which have passed into the hands of grammarians, have given rise to questions which have either no result or in which the importance of the result, or the certainty, if certain, is out of proportion to the labour spent in attaining it. The field is exhausted by great critics, and then subdivided among lesser ones. The subject, unlike that of physical science, has a limit, and unless new ground is broken up, as for example in mythology, or comparative philology, is apt to grow barren. Though it is not true to say that 'we know as much about the Greeks and Romans as we ever shall,' it is certain that we run a danger from the deficiency of material, of wasting time in questions which do not add anything to real knowledge, or in conjectures which must always remain uncertain, and may in turn give way to other conjectures in the next generation. Little points may be of great importance when rightly determined, because the observation of them tends to quicken the instinct of language; but conjectures about little things or rules respecting them which were not in the mind of Greek authors themselves, are not of equal value. There is the scholasticism of philology, not only in the Alexandrian, but in our own times; as in the middle ages, there was the scholasticism of philosophy. Questions of mere orthography, about which there cannot be said to have been a right or wrong, have been pursued almost with a Rabbinical minuteness. The story of the scholar who regretted 'that he had not concentrated his life on the dative case,' is hardly a caricature of the spirit of such inquiries. The form of notes to the classics often seems to arise out of a necessity for observing a certain proportion between the commentary and the text. And the same tendency is noticeable in many of the critical and philological observations which are made on the New Testament. The field of Biblical criticism is narrower, and its materials more fragmentary; so too the minuteness and uncertainty of the questions raised has been greater. For example, the discussions respecting the chronology of St. Paul's life and his second imprisonment: or about the identity of James, the brother of the Lord, or in another department, respecting the use of the Greek article, have gone far beyond the line of utility.

There seem to be reasons for doubting whether any considerable light can be thrown on the New Testament from inquiry into the language. Such inquiries are popular, because they are safe; but their popularity is not the measure of their use. It has not been sufficiently considered that the difficulties of the New Testament are for the most part common to the Greek and the English. The noblest translation in the world has a few great errors, more than half of them in the text; but 'we do it violence' to haggle over the words. Minute corrections of tenses or particles are no good; they spoil the English without being nearer the Greek. Apparent mistranslations are often due to a better knowledge of English rather than a worse knowledge of Greek. It is true that the signification of a few uncommon expressions, e.g. $\dot{\epsilon}\xi o \nu \sigma \acute{\iota} a$, $\dot{\epsilon} \pi \iota \beta a \lambda \acute{\omega} \nu$, $\sigma \nu \nu a \pi a \gamma \acute{o} \mu \epsilon \nu o$, κ.τ.λ., is yet uncertain. But no result of consequence would follow from the attainment of absolute certainty respecting the meaning of any of these. A more promising field opens to the interpreter in the examination of theological terms, such as faith (πίστις), grace (χάρις), righteousness (δικαιοσύνη), sanctification (ἁγιασμός), the law (νόμος), the spirit (πνεῦμα), the comforter (παράκλητος), &c., provided always that the use of such terms in the New Testament is clearly separated (1) from their derivation or previous use in Classical or Alexandrian Greek, (2) from their after use in the Fathers and in systems of theology. To which may be added another select class of words descriptive of the offices or customs of the Apostolic Church, such as Apostle (ἀπόστολος), Bishop (ἐπίσκοπος), Elder (πρεσβύτερος), Deacon and Deaconess (ὁ καὶ ἡ διάκονος). love-feast (ἀγάπαι), the Lord's day (ἡ κυριακὴ ἡμέρα), &c. It is a lexilogus of these and similar terms, rather than a lexicon of the entire Greek Testament that is required. Interesting subjects of real inquiry are also the comparison of the Greek of the New Testament with modern Greek on the one hand, and the Greek of the LXX on the other. It is not likely, however, that they will afford much more help than they have already done in the elucidation of the Greek of the New Testament.

It is for others to investigate the language of the Old Testament, to which the preceding remarks are only in part applicable. And it may be observed in passing of this, as of any other old language, that not the later form of the language, but the cognate dialects, must ever be the chief source of its illustration. For in every ancient language, antecedent or contemporary forms, not the subsequent ones, afford the real insight into its nature and structure. It must also be admitted, that very great and real obscurities exist in the English translation of the Old Testament, which even a superficial acquaintance with the original has a tendency to remove. Leaving, however, to others the consideration of the Semitic languages, which raise questions of a different kind from the Hellenistic Greek, we will offer a few remarks on the latter. Much has been said of the increasing accuracy of our knowledge of the language of the New Testament; the old Hebraistic method of explaining difficulties of language or construction has retired within very narrow limits; it might probably with advantage be confined to still narrower ones—[if it have any place at all except in the Apocalypse or the Gospel of St. Matthew]. There is, perhaps, some confusion between accuracy of our knowledge of language, and the accuracy of language itself; which is also strongly maintained. It is observed that the usages of barbarous as well as civilized nations conform perfectly to grammatical rules; that the uneducated in all countries have certain laws of speech as much as Shakespeare or Bacon; the usages of Lucian, it may be said, are as regular as those of Plato, even when they are different. The decay of language seems rather to witness to the permanence than to the changeableness of its structure; it is the flesh, not the bones, that begins to drop off. But such general remarks, although just, afford but little help in determining the character of the Greek of the New Testament, which has of course a certain system, failing in which it would cease to be a language. Some further illustration is needed of the change which has passed upon it. All languages do not decay in the same manner; and the influence of decay in the same language may be different in different countries; when used in writing and in speaking—when applied to the matters of ordinary life and to the higher truths of philosophy or religion. And the degeneracy of language itself is not a mere principle of dissolution, but creative also; while dead and rigid in some of its uses, it is elastic and expansive in others. The decay of an ancient language is the beginning of the construction of a modern one. The loss of some usages gives a greater precision or freedom to others. The logical element, as for example in the Medieval Latin, will probably be strongest when the poetical has vanished. A great movement, like the Reformation in Germany, passing over a nation, may give a new birth also to its language.

These remarks may be applied to the Greek of the New Testament, which although classed vaguely under the 'common dialect,' has, nevertheless, many features which are altogether peculiar to itself, and such as are found in no other remains of ancient literature. (1) It is more unequal in style even in the same books, that is to say, more original and plastic in one part, more rigid and unpliable in another. There is a want of the continuous power to frame a paragraph or to arrange clauses in subordination to each other, even to the extent in which it was possessed by a Greek scholiast or rhetorician. On the other hand there is a fullness of life, 'a new birth,' in the use of abstract terms, which is not found elsewhere after the golden age of Greek philosophy. Almost the only passage in the New Testament which reads like a Greek period of the time, is the first paragraph of the Gospel according to St. Luke, and the corresponding words of the Acts. But the power and meaning of the characteristic words of the New Testament is in remarkable contrast with the vapid and general use of the same words in Philo about the same time. There is also a sort of lyrical passion in some passages (1 Cor. xiii.; 2 Cor. vi. 6-10; xi. 21-33) which is a new thing in the literature of the world; to which, at any rate, no Greek author of a later age furnishes any parallel. (2) Though written, the Greek of the New Testament partakes of the character of a spoken language; it is more lively and simple, and less structural than ordinary writing—a peculiarity of style which further agrees with the circumstance that the Epistles of St. Paul were not written with his own hand, but probably dictated to an amanuensis, and that the Gospels also probably originate in an oral narrative. (3) The ground colours of the language may be said to be two; first, the LXX.; which is modified, secondly, by the spoken Greek of eastern countries, and by the differences which might be expected to arise between a translation and an original; many Hebraisms would occur in the Greek of a translator, which would never have come to his pen but for the influence of the work which he was translating. (4) To which may be added a few Latin and Chaldee words, and a few Rabbinical formulae. The influence of Hebrew or Chaldee in the New Testament is for the most part at a distance, in the background, acting not directly, but mediately, through the LXX. It has much to do with the clausular structure and general form, but hardly anything with the grammatical usage. Philo, too, did not know Hebrew, or at least the Hebrew Scriptures, yet there is also a 'mediate' influence of Hebrew traceable in his writings. (5) There is an element of constraint in the style of the New Testament, arising from the circumstance of its authors writing in a language which was not their own. This constraint shows itself in the repetition of words and phrases; in the verbal oppositions and anacolutha of St. Paul; in the short sentences of St. John. This is further increased by the fact that the writers of the New Testament were 'unlearned men,' who had not the same power of writing as of speech. Moreover, as has been often remarked, the difficulty of composition increases in proportion to the greatness of the subject; e.g., the narrative of Thucydides is easy and intelligible, while his reflections and speeches are full of confusion; the effort to concentrate seems to interfere with the consecutiveness and fluency of ideas. Something of this kind is discernible in those passages of the Epistles in which the Apostle St. Paul is seeking to set forth the opposite sides of God's dealing with man, e.g., Rom. iii. 1-9; ix., x.; or in which the sequence of the thought is interrupted by the conflict of emotions, 1 Cor. ix. 20; Gal. iv. 11-20. (6) The power of the Gospel over language must be recognized, showing itself, first of all, in the original and consequently variable signification of words ($\pi\iota\sigma\tau\iota\varsigma$, $\chi\acute{\alpha}\rho\iota\varsigma$, $\sigma\omega\tau\eta\rho\acute{\iota}\alpha$), which is also more comprehensive and human than the heretical usage of many of the same terms, e.g., γνῶσις (knowledge), σοφία (wisdom), κτίσις (creature, creation); secondly, in a peculiar use of some constructions, such as δικαιοσύνη Θεοῦ (righteousness of God), πίστις Ἰησοῦ Χριστοῦ (faith of Jesus Christ), ἐν Χριστῷ (in Christ), ἐν Θεῷ (in God), ὑπὲρ ἡμῶν (for us), in which the meaning of the genitive case or of the preposition almost escapes our notice, from familiarity with the sound of it. Lastly, the degeneracy of the Greek language is traceable in the failure of syntactical power; in the insertion of prepositions to denote relations of thought, which classical Greek would have expressed by the case only; in the omission of them when classical Greek would have required them; in the incipient use of ἵνα with the subjunctive for the infinitive; in the confusion of ideas of cause and effect; in the absence of the article in the case of an increasing number of words which are passing into proper names; in the loss of the finer shades of difference in the negative particles; in the occasional confusion of the aorist and perfect; in excessive fondness for particles of reasoning or inference; in various forms of apposition, especially that of the word to the sentence; in the use, sometimes emphatic, sometimes only pleonastic, of the personal and demonstrative pronouns. These are some of the signs that the language is breaking up and losing its structure.

Our knowledge of the New Testament is derived almost exclusively from itself. Of the language, as well as of the subject, it may be truly said, that what other writers contribute is nothing in comparison of that which is gained from observation of the text. Some inferences which may be gathered from this general fact are the following:—
First, that less weight should be given to lexicons, that is, to the authority of other Greek writers, and more to the context. The use of a word in a new sense, the attribution of a neuter meaning to a verb elsewhere passive (Rom. iii. 9 προεχόμεθα), the resolution of the compound

into two simple notions (Gal. iii. 1 προεγράφη), these, when the context requires it, are not to be set aside by the scholar because sanctioned by no known examples. The same remark applies to grammars as well as lexicons. We cannot be certain that διά with the accusative never has the same meaning as διά with the genitive (Gal. iv. 13; Phil. i. 15), or that the article always retains its defining power (2 Cor. i. 17; Acts xvii. 1), or that the perfect is never used in place of the aorist (1 Cor. xv. 4; Rev. v. 7, &c.); still less can we affirm that the latter end of a sentence never forgets the beginning (Rom. ii. 17-21; v. 12-18; ix. 22; xvi. 25-27; &c. &c.). Foreign influences tend to derange the strong natural perception or remembrance of the analogy of our own language. That is very likely to have occurred in the case of some of the writers of the New Testament; that there is such a derangement is a fact. There is no probability in favour of St. Paul writing in broken sentences, but there is no improbability which should lead us to assume, in such sentences, continuous grammar and thought, as appears to have been the feeling of the copyists who have corrected the anacolutha. The occurrence of them further justifies the interpreter in using some freedom with other passages in which the syntax does not absolutely break down. When 'confusion of two constructions,' 'meaning to say one thing and finishing with another,' 'saying two things in one instead of disposing them in their logical sequence,' are attributed to the Apostle; the use of these and similar expressions is defended by the fact that more numerous anacolutha occur in St. Paul's writings than in any equal portion of the New Testament, and far more than in the writings of any other Greek author of equal length.

Passing from the grammatical structure, we may briefly consider the logical character of the language of the New Testament. Two things should be here distinguished, the logical form and the logical sequence of thought. Some ages have been remarkable for the former of these two characteristics; they have dealt in opposition, contradiction, climax, pleonasm, reason within reason, and the like; mere statements taking the form of arguments—each sentence seeming to be a link in a chain. In such periods of literature, the appearance of logic is rhetorical, and is to be set down to the style. That is the case with many passages in the New Testament which are studded with logical or rhetorical formulae, especially in the Epistles of St. Paul. Nothing can be more simple or natural than the object of the writer. Yet 'forms of the schools' appear (whether learnt at the feet of Gamaliel, that reputed master of Greek learning, or not) which imply a degree of logical or rhetorical training.

The observation of this rhetorical or logical element has a bearing on the Interpretation of Scripture. For it leads us to distinguish between the superficial connexion of words and the real connexion of thoughts. Otherwise injustice is done to the argument of the sacred writer, who may be supposed to violate logical rules, of which he is unconscious. For example, the argument of Rom. iii. 19 may be classed by the logicians under some head of fallacy ('Ex aliquo non sequitur omnis'); the series of inferences which follow one another in Rom. i. 16–18 are for the most part different aspects or statements of the same truth. So in Rom. i. 32 the climax rather appears to be an anticlimax. But to dwell on these things interferes with the true perception of the Apostle's meaning, which is not contained in the repetitions of γάρ by which it is hooked together; nor are we accurately to weigh the proportions expressed by his οὐ μόνον—ἀλλὰ καί or πολλῷ μᾶλλον: neither need we suppose that where μέν is found alone, there was a reason for the omission of δέ (Rom. i. 8; iii. 2); or that the opposition of words and sentences is always the opposition of ideas (Rom. v. 7; x. 10). It is true that these and similar forms or distinctions of language admit of translation into

English; and in every case the interpreter may find some point of view in which the simplest truth of feeling may be drawn out in an antithetical or argumentative form. But whether these points of view were in the Apostle's mind at the time of writing may be doubted; the real meaning, or kernel, seems to lie deeper and to be more within. When we pass from the study of each verse to survey the whole at a greater distance, the form of thought is again seen to be unimportant in comparison of the truth which is contained in it. The same remark may be extended to the opposition, not only of words, but of ideas, which is found in the Scriptures generally, and almost seems to be inherent in human language itself. The law is opposed to faith, good to evil, the spirit to the flesh, light to darkness, the world to the believer; the sheep are set 'on his right hand, but the goats on the left.' The influence of this logical opposition has been great and not always without abuse in practice. For the opposition is one of ideas only which is not realized in fact. Experience shows us not that there are two classes of men animated by two opposing principles, but an infinite number of classes or individuals from the lowest depth of misery and sin to the highest perfection of which human nature is capable, the best not wholly good, the worst not entirely evil. But the figure or mode of representation changes these differences of degree into differences of kind. And we often think and speak and act in reference both to ourselves and others, as though the figure were altogether a reality.

Other questions arise out of the analysis of the modes of thought of Scripture. Unless we are willing to use words without inquiring into their meaning, it is necessary for us to arrange them in some relation to our own minds. The modes of thought of the Old Testament are not the same with those of the New, and those of the New are only partially the same with those in use among ourselves at the present day. The education of the human mind may be traced as clearly from the Book of Genesis to the Epistles of St. Paul, as from Homer to Plato and Aristotle. When we hear St. Paul speaking of 'body and soul and spirit,' we know that such language as this would not occur in the Books of Moses or in the Prophet Isaiah. It has the colour of a later age, in which abstract terms have taken the place of expressions derived from material objects. When we proceed further to compare these or other words or expressions of St. Paul with 'the body and mind,' or 'mind' and 'matter,' which is a distinction, not only of philosophy, but of common language among ourselves, it is not easy at once to determine the relation between them. Familiar as is the sound of both expressions, many questions arise when we begin to compare them.

This is the metaphysical difficulty in the Interpretation of Scripture, which it is better not to ignore, because the consideration of it is necessary to the understanding of many passages, and also because it may return upon us in the form of materialism or scepticism. To some who are not aware how little words affect the nature of things it may seem to raise speculations of a very serious kind. Their doubts would, perhaps, find expression in some such exclamations as the following:—'How is religion possible when modes of thought are shifting? and words changing their meaning, and statements of doctrine, though "starched" with philosophy, are in perpetual danger of dissolution from metaphysical analysis?'

The answer seems to be, that Christian truth is not dependent on the fixedness of modes of thought. The metaphysician may analyze the ideas of the mind just as the physiologist may analyze the powers or parts of the bodily frame, yet morality and social life still go on, as in the body digestion is uninterrupted. That is not an illustration only; it represents the fact. Though we had no words for mind, matter, soul, body, and the like, Christianity would remain the same. This is obvious, whether we think of the case of the poor, who understand such distinctions very imperfectly, or of those nations of the earth, who have no precisely corresponding division of ideas. It is not of that subtle or evanescent character which is liable to be lost in shifting the use of terms. Indeed, it is an advantage at times to discard these terms with the view of getting rid of the oppositions to which they give rise. No metaphysical analysis can prevent 'our taking up the cross and following Christ,' or receiving the kingdom of heaven as little children. To analyze the 'trichotomy' of St. Paul is interesting as a chapter in the history of the human mind and necessary as a part of Biblical exegesis, but it has nothing to do with the religion of Christ. Christian duties may be enforced, and the life of Christ may be the centre of our thoughts, whether we speak of reason and faith, of soul and body, or of mind and matter, or adopt a mode of speech which dispenses with any of these divisions.

Connected with the modes of thought or representation in Scripture are the figures of speech of Scripture, about which the same question may be asked: 'What division can we make between the figure and the reality?' And the answer seems to be of the same kind, that 'We cannot precisely draw the line between them.' Language, and especially the language of Scripture, does not admit of any sharp distinction. The simple expressions of one age become the allegories or figures of another; many of those in the New Testament are taken from the Old. But neither is there anything really essential in the form of these figures; nay, the literal application of many of them has been a great stumblingblock to the reception of Christianity. A recent commentator on Scripture appears willing to peril religion on the literal truth of such an expression as 'We shall be caught up to meet the Lord in the air.' Would he be equally ready to stake Christianity on the literal meaning of the words, 'Where their worm dieth not, and the fire is not quenched'?

Of what has been said this is the sum :—'That Scripture, like other books, has one meaning, which is to be gathered from itself without reference to the adaptations of Fathers or Divines; and without regard to *a priori* notions about its nature and origin. It is to be interpreted like other books, with attention to the character of its authors, and the prevailing state of civilization and knowledge, with allowance for peculiarities of style and language, and modes of thought and figures of speech. Yet not without a sense that as we read there grows upon us the witness of God in the world, anticipating in a rude and primitive age the truth that was to be, shining more and more unto the perfect day in the life of Christ, which again is reflected from different points of view in the teaching of His Apostles.'

§ 4.

It has been a principal aim of the preceding pages to distinguish the interpretation from the application of Scripture. Many of the errors alluded to arise out of a confusion of the two. The present is nearer to us than the past; the circumstances which surround us pre-occupy our thoughts; it is only by an effort that we reproduce the ideas, or events, or persons of other ages. And thus, quite naturally, almost by a law of the human mind, the application of Scripture takes the place of its original meaning. And the question is, not how to get rid of this natural tendency, but how we may have the true use of it. For it cannot be got rid of, or rather is one of the chief instruments of religious usefulness in the world: 'Ideas must be given through something;' those of religion find their natural expression in the words of Scripture, in the adaptation of which to another state of life it is hardly possible that the first intention of the writers should be always preserved. Interpretation is the province of few; it requires a finer perception of language, and a higher degree of cultivation than is attained by the majority of mankind. But applications are made by all, from the philosopher reading 'God in History,' to the poor woman who finds in them a response to her prayers, and the solace of her daily life. In the hour of death we do not want critical explanations; in most cases, those to whom they would be offered are incapable of understanding them. A few words, breathing the sense of the whole Christian world, such as 'I know that my Redeemer liveth' (though the exact meaning of them may be doubtful to the Hebrew scholar); 'I shall go to him, but he shall not return to me;' touch a chord which would never be reached by the most skilful exposition of the argument of one of St. Paul's Epistles.

There is also a use of Scripture in education and literature. This literary use, though secondary to the religious one, is not unimportant. It supplies a common language to the educated and uneducated, in which the best and highest thoughts of both are expressed; it is a medium between the abstract notions of the one and the simple feelings of the other. To the poor especially, it conveys in the form which they are most capable of receiving, the lesson of history and life. The beauty and power of speech and writing would be greatly impaired, if the Scriptures ceased to be known or used among us. The orator seems to catch from them a sort of inspiration; in the simple words of Scripture which he stamps anew, the philosopher often finds his most pregnant expressions. If modern times have been richer in the wealth of abstract thought, the contribution of earlier ages to the mind of the world has not been less, but, perhaps greater, in supplying the poetry of language. There is no such treasury of instruments and materials as Scripture. The loss of Homer, or the loss of Shakespeare, would have affected the whole series of Greek or English authors who follow. But the disappearance of the Bible from the books which the world contains, would produce results far greater; we can scarcely conceive the degree in which it would alter literature and language—the ideas of the educated and philosophical, as well as the feelings and habits of mind of the poor. If it has been said, with an allowable hyperbole, that 'Homer is Greece,' with much more truth may it be said, that 'the Bible is Christendom.'

Many by whom considerations of this sort will be little understood, may, nevertheless, recognize the use made of the Old Testament in the New. The religion of Christ was first taught by an application of the words of the Psalms and the Prophets. Our Lord Himself sanctions this application. 'Can there be a better use of Scripture than that which is made by Scripture?' 'Or any more likely method of teaching the truths of Christianity than that by which they were first taught?' For it may be argued that the critical interpretation of Scripture is a device almost of yesterday; it is the vocation of the scholar or philosopher, not of the Apostle or Prophet. The new truth which was introduced into the Old Testament, rather than the old truth which was found there, was the salvation and the conversion of the world. There are many quotations from the Psalms and the Prophets in the Epistles, in which the meaning is quickened or spiritualized, but hardly any, probably none, which is based on the original sense or context. That is not so singular a phenomenon as may at first sight be imagined. It may appear strange to us that Scripture should be interpreted in Scripture, in a manner not altogether in agreement with modern criticism; but would it not be more strange that it should be interpreted otherwise than in agreement with the ideas of the age or country in which it was written? The observation that there is such an agreement, leads to two conclusions which have a bearing on our present subject. First, it is a reason for not insisting on the applications which the New Testament makes of passages in the Old, as their original meaning. Secondly, it gives authority and precedent for the use of similar applications in our own day.

But, on the other hand, though interwoven with literature, though common to all ages of the Church, though sanctioned by our Lord and His Apostles, it is easy to see that such an employment of Scripture is liable to error and perversion. For it may not only receive a new meaning; it may be applied in a spirit alien to itself. It may become the symbol of fanaticism, the cloke of malice, the disguise of policy. Cromwell at Drogheda, quoting Scripture to his soldiers; the well-known attack on the Puritans in the State Service for the Restoration, 'Not every one that saith unto me, Lord, Lord;' the reply of the Venetian Ambassador to the suggestion of Wolsey, that Venice should take a lead in Italy, '*which was only* the Earth is the Lord's and the fulness thereof,' are examples of such uses. In former times, it was a real and not an imaginary fear, that the wars of the Lord in the Old Testament might arouse a fire in the bosom of Franks and Huns. In our own day such dangers have passed away; it is only a figure of speech when the preacher says, 'Gird on thy sword, O thou most mighty.' The warlike passions of men are not roused by quotations from Scripture, nor can states of life such as slavery or polygamy, which belong to a past age, be defended, at least in England, by the example of the Old Testament. The danger or error is of another kind; more subtle, but hardly less real. For if we are permitted to apply Scripture under the pretence of interpreting it, the language of Scripture becomes only a mode of expressing the public feeling or opinion of our own day. Any passing phase of politics or art, or spurious philanthropy, may have a kind of Scriptural authority. The words that are used are the words of the Prophet or Evangelist, but we stand behind and adapt them to our purpose. Hence it is necessary to consider the limits and manner of a just adaptation; how much may be allowed for the sake of ornament; how far the Scripture, in all its details, may be regarded as an allegory of human life—where the true analogy begins—how far the interpretation of Scripture will serve as a corrective to its practical abuse.

Truth seems to require that we should separate mere adaptations from the original meaning of Scripture. It is not honest or reasonable to confound illustration with argument, in theology, any more than in other subjects. For example, if a preacher chooses to represent the condition of a church or of an individual in the present day, under the figure of Elijah left alone among the idolatrous tribes of Israel, such an allusion is natural enough; but if he goes on to argue that individuals are therefore justified in remaining in what they believe to be an erroneous communion—that is a mere appearance of argument which ought not to have the slightest weight with a man of sense. Such a course may indeed be perfectly justifiable, but not on the ground that a prophet of the Lord once did so, two thousand five hundred years ago. Not in this sense were the lives of the Prophets written for our instruction. There are many important morals conveyed by them, but only so far as they themselves represent universal principles of justice and love. These universal principles they clothe with flesh and blood: they show them to us written on the hearts of men of like passions with ourselves. The prophecies, again, admit of many applications to the Christian Church or to the Christian life. There is no harm in speaking of the Church as the Spiritual Israel, or in using the imagery of Isaiah respecting Messiah's kingdom, as the type of good things to come. But when it is gravely urged, that from such passages as 'Kings shall be thy nursing fathers,' we are to collect the relations of Church and State, or from the pictorial description of Isaiah, that it is to be inferred there will be a reign of Christ on earth—that is a mere assumption of the forms of reasoning by the imagination. Nor is it a healthful or manly tone of feeling which depicts the political opposition to the Church in our own day, under imagery which is borrowed from the desolate Sion of the captivity. Scripture is apt to come too readily to the lips, when we are pouring out our own weaknesses, or enlarging on some favourite theme—perhaps idealizing in the language of prophecy the feebleness of preaching or missions in the present day, or from the want of something else to say. In many discussions on these and similar subjects, the position of the Jewish King, Church, Priest, has led to a confusion, partly caused by the use of similar words in modern senses among ourselves. The King or Queen of England may be called the Anointed of the Lord, but we should not therefore imply that the attributes of sovereignty are the same as those which belonged to King David. All these are figures of speech, the employment of which is too common, and has been injurious to religion, because it prevents our looking at the facts of history or life as they truly are.

This is the first step towards a more truthful use of Scripture in practice—the separation of adaptation from interpretation. No one who is engaged in preaching or in religious instruction can be required to give up Scripture language; it is the common element in which his thoughts and those of his hearers move. But he may be asked to distinguish the words of Scripture from the truths of Scripture—the means from the end. The least expression of Scripture is weighty; it affects the minds of the hearers in a way that no other language can. Whatever responsibility attaches to idle words, attaches in still greater degree to the idle or fallacious use of Scripture terms. And there is surely a want of proper reverence for Scripture, when we confound the weakest and feeblest applications of its words with their true meaning—when we avail ourselves of their natural power to point them against some enemy—when we divert the eternal words of charity and truth into a defence of some passing opinion. For not only in the days of the Pharisees, but in our own, the letter has been taking the place of the spirit; the least matters, of the greatest, and the primary meaning has been lost in the secondary use.

Other simple cautions may also be added. The applications of Scripture should be harmonized and, as it were, interpenetrated with the spirit of the Gospel, the whole of which should be in every part; though the words may receive a new sense, the new sense ought to be in agreement with the general truth. They should be used to bring home practical precepts, not to send the imagination on a voyage of discovery; they are not the real foundation of our faith in another world, nor can they, by pleasant pictures, add to our knowledge of it. They should not confound the accidents with the essence of religion—the restrictions and burdens of the Jewish law with the freedom of the Gospel—the things which Moses allowed for the hardness of the heart, with the perfection of the teaching of Christ. They should avoid the form of arguments, or they will insensibly be used, or understood to mean more than they really do. They should be subjected to an overruling principle, which is the heart and conscience of the Christian teacher, who indeed 'stands behind them,' not to make them the vehicles of his own opinions, but as the expressions of justice, and truth, and love.

And here the critical interpretation of Scripture comes in and exercises a corrective influence on its popular use. We have already admitted that criticism is not for the multitude; it is not that which the Scripture terms the Gospel preached to the poor. Yet, indirectly passing from the few to the many, it has borne a great part in the Reformation of religion. It has cleared the eye of the mind to understand the original meaning. It was a sort of criticism which supported the struggle of the sixteenth century against the Roman Catholic Church; it is criticism that is leading Protestants to doubt whether the doctrine that the Pope is Antichrist, which has descended from the same period, is really discoverable in Scripture. Even the isolated thinker, against whom the religious world is taking up arms, has an influence on his opponents. The force of observations, which are based on reason and fact, remains when the tide of religious or party feeling is gone down. Criticism has also a healing influence in clearing away what may be termed the Sectarianism of knowledge. Without criticism it would be impossible to reconcile History and Science with Revealed Religion; they must remain for ever in a hostile and defiant attitude. Instead of being like other records, subject to the conditions of knowledge which existed in an early stage of the world, Scripture would be regarded on the one side as the work of organic Inspiration, and as a lying imposition on the other.

The real unity of Scripture, as of man, has also a relation to our present subject. Amid all the differences of modes of thought and speech which have existed in different ages, of which much is said in our own day, there is a common element in human nature which bursts through these differences and remains unchanged, because akin to the first instincts of our being. The simple feeling of truth and right is the same to the Greek or Hindoo as to ourselves. However great may be the diversities of human character, there is a point at which these diversities end, and unity begins to appear. Now this admits of an application to the books of Scripture, as well as to the world generally. Written at many different times, in more than one language, some of them in fragments, they, too, have a common element of which the preacher may avail himself. This element is twofold, partly divine and partly human; the revelation of the truth and righteousness of God, and the cry of the human heart towards Him. Every part of Scripture tends to raise us above ourselves—to give us a deeper sense of the feebleness of man, and of the wisdom and power of God. It has a sort of kindred, as Plato would say, with religious truth everywhere in the world. It agrees also with the imperfect stages of knowledge and faith in human nature, and answers to its inarticulate cries. The universal truth easily breaks through the accidents of time and place in which it is involved. Although we cannot apply Jewish institutions to the Christian world, or venture in reliance on some text to resist the tide of civilization on which we are borne, yet it remains, nevertheless, to us, as well as to the Jews and first Christians, that 'Righteousness exalteth a nation,' and that 'love is the fulfilling not of the Jewish law only, but of all law.'

In some cases, we have only to enlarge the meaning of Scripture to apply it even to the novelties and peculiarities of our own times. The world changes, but the human heart remains the same: events and details are different, but the principle by which they are governed, or the rule by which we are to act, is not different. When, for example, our Saviour says, 'Ye shall know the truth, and the truth shall make you free,' it is not likely that these words would have conveyed to the minds of the Jews who heard Him any notion of the perplexities of doubt or inquiry. Yet we cannot suppose that our Saviour, were He to come again upon earth, would refuse thus to extend them. The Apostle St. Paul, when describing the Gospel, which is to the Greek foolishness, speaks also of a higher wisdom which is known to those who are perfect. Neither is it unfair for us to apply this passage to that reconcilement of faith and knowledge, which may be termed Christian philosophy, as the nearest equivalent to its language in our own day. Such words, again, as 'Why seek ye the living among the dead?' admit of a great variety of adaptations to the circumstances of our own time. Many of these adaptations have a real germ in the meaning of the words. The precept, 'Render unto Cæsar the things that are Cæsar's, and to God the things that are God's,' may be taken generally as expressing the necessity of distinguishing the divine and human—the things that belong to faith and the things that belong to experience. It is worth remarking in the application made of these words by Lord Bacon, 'Da fidei quae fidei sunt;' that, although the terms are altered, yet the circumstance that the form of the sentence is borrowed from Scripture gives them point and weight.

The portion of Scripture which more than any other is immediately and universally applicable to our own times is, doubtless, that which is contained in the words of Christ Himself. The reason is that they are words of the most universal import. They do not relate to the circumstances of the time, but to the common life of all mankind. You cannot extract from them a political creed; only, 'Render unto Cæsar the things that are Cæsar's,' and 'The Scribes and Pharisees sit in Moses' seat; whatsoever, therefore, they say unto you do, but after their works do not.' They present to us a standard of truth and duty, such as no one can at once and immediately practise—such as, in its perfection, no one has fulfilled in this world. But this idealism does not interfere with their influence as a religious lesson. Ideals, even though unrealized, have effect on our daily life. The preacher of the Gospel is, or ought to be, aware that his calls to repentance, his standard of obligations, his lamentations over his own shortcomings or those of others, do not at once convert hundreds or thousands, as on the day of Pentecost. Yet it does not follow that they are thrown away, or that it would be well to substitute for them mere prudential or economical lessons, lectures on health or sanitary improvement. For they tend to raise men above themselves, providing them with Sabbaths as well as working days, giving them a taste of 'the good word of God' and of 'the powers of the world to come.' Human nature needs to be idealized; it seems as if it took a dislike to itself when presented always in its ordinary attire; it lives on in the hope of becoming better. And the image or hope of a better life—the vision of Christ crucified—which is held up to it, doubtless has an influence; not like the rushing mighty wind of the day of Pentecost; it may rather be compared to the leaven 'which a woman took and hid in three measures of meal, till the whole was leavened.'

The Parables of our Lord are a portion of the New Testament, which we may apply in the most easy and literal manner. The persons in them are the persons among whom we live and move; there are times and occasions at which the truths symbolized by them come home to the hearts of all who have ever been impressed by religion. We have been prodigal sons returning to our Father; servants to whom talents have been entrusted; labourers in the vineyard inclined to murmur at our lot, when compared with that of others, yet receiving every man his due; well-satisfied Pharisees; repentant Publicans:—we have received the seed, and the cares of the world have choked it—we hope also at times that we have found the pearl of great price after sweeping the house—we are ready like the Good Samaritan to show kindness to all mankind. Of these circumstances of life or phases of mind, which are typified by the parables, most Christians have experience. We may go on to apply many of them further to the condition of nations and churches. Such a treasury has Christ provided us of things new and old, which refer to all time and all mankind—may we not say in His own words—'because He is the Son of Man?'

There is no language of Scripture which penetrates the individual soul, and embraces all the world in the arms of its love, in the same manner as that of Christ Himself. Yet the Epistles contain lessons which are not found in the Gospels, or, at least, not expressed with the same degree of clearness. For the Epistles are nearer to actual life—they relate to the circumstances of the first believers, to their struggles with the world without, to their temptations and divisions from within—their subject is not only the doctrine of the Christian religion, but the business of the early Church. And although their circumstances are not our circumstances—we are not afflicted or persecuted, or driven out of the world, but in possession of the blessings, and security, and property of an established religion—yet there is a Christian spirit which infuses itself into all circumstances, of which they are a pure and living source. It is impossible to gather from a few fragmentary and apparently not always consistent expressions, how the Communion was celebrated, or the Church ordered, what was the relative position of Presbyters and Deacons, or the nature of the gift of tongues, as a rule for the Church in after ages;—such inquiries have no certain answer, and, at the best, are only the subject of honest curiosity. But the words, 'Charity never faileth,' and 'Though I speak with the tongues of men and of angels, and have not charity, I am nothing,'—these have a voice which reaches to the end of time. There are no questions of meats and drinks nowadays, yet the noble words of the Apostle remain: 'If meat make my brother to offend, I will eat no flesh while the world standeth, lest I make my brother to offend.' Moderation in controversy, toleration towards opponents or erring members, is a virtue which has been thought by many to belong to the development and not to the origin of Christianity, and which is rarely found in the commencement of a religion. But lessons of toleration may be gathered from the Apostle, which have not yet been learned either by theologians or by mankind in general. The persecutions and troubles which awaited the Apostle no longer await us; we cannot, therefore, without unreality, except, perhaps, in a very few cases, appropriate his words, 'I have fought the good fight, I have finished my course, I have kept the faith.' But that other text still sounds gently in our ears: 'My strength is perfected in weakness,' and 'when I am weak, then am I strong.' We cannot apply to ourselves the language of authority in which the Apostle speaks of himself as an ambassador for Christ, without something like bad taste. But it is not altogether an imaginary hope that those of us who are ministers of Christ, may attain to a real imitation of his great diligence, of his sympathy with others, and consideration for them—of his willingness to spend and be spent in his Master's service.

Such are a few instances of the manner in which the analogy of faith enables us to apply the words of Christ and His Apostles, with a strict regard to their original meaning. But the Old Testament has also its peculiar lessons which are not conveyed with equal point or force in the New. The beginnings of human history are themselves a lesson, having a freshness as of the early dawn. There are forms of evil against which the Prophets and the prophetical spirit of the Law carry on a warfare, in terms almost too bold for the way of life of modern times. There, more plainly than in any other portion of Scripture, is expressed the antagonism of outward and inward, of ceremonial and moral, of mercy and sacrifice. There all the masks of hypocrisy are rudely torn asunder, in which an unthinking world allows itself to be disguised. There the relations of rich and poor in the sight of God, and their duties towards one another, are most clearly enunciated. There the religion of suffering first appears—'adversity, the blessing' of the Old Testament, as well as of the New. There the sorrows and aspirations of the soul find their deepest expression, and also their consolation. The feeble person has an image of himself in the 'bruised reed;' the suffering servant of God passes into the 'beloved one, in whom my soul delighteth.' Even the latest and most desolate phases of the human mind are reflected in Job and Ecclesiastes; yet not without the solemn assertion that 'to fear God and keep his commandments' is the beginning and end of all things.

It is true that there are examples in the Old Testament which were not written for our instruction, and that, in some instances, precepts or commands are attributed to God Himself, which must be regarded as relative to the state of knowledge which then existed of the Divine nature, or given 'for the hardness of men's hearts.' It cannot be denied that such passages of Scripture are liable to misunderstanding; the spirit of the Old Covenanters, although no longer appealing to the action of Samuel, 'hewing Agag in pieces before the Lord in Gilgal,' is not altogether extinguished. And a community of recent origin in America found their doctrine of polygamy on the Old Testament. But the poor generally read the Bible unconsciously; they take the good, and catch the prevailing spirit, without stopping to reason whether this or that practice is sanctioned by the custom or example of Scripture. The child is only struck by the impiety of the children who mocked the prophet; he does not think of the severity of the punishment which is inflicted upon them. And the poor, in this respect, are much like children; their reflection on the morality or immorality of characters or events is suppressed by reverence for Scripture. The Christian teacher has a sort of tact by which he guides them to perceive only the spirit of the Gospel everywhere; they read in the Psalms of David's sin and repentance; of the never-failing goodness of God to Him, and his never-failing trust in Him, not of his imprecations against his enemies. Such difficulties are greater in theory and on paper, than in the management of a school or parish. They are found to affect the half-educated, rather than either the poor, or those who are educated in a higher sense. To be above such difficulties is the happiest condition of human life and knowledge, or to be below them; to see, or think we see, how they may be reconciled with Divine power and wisdom, or not to see how they are apparently at variance with them.

§ 5.

Some application of the preceding subject may be further made to theology and life.

Let us introduce this concluding inquiry with two remarks.

First, it may be observed, that a change in some of the prevailing modes of interpretation is not so much a matter of expediency as of necessity. The original meaning of Scripture is beginning to be clearly understood. But the apprehension of the original meaning is inconsistent with the reception of a typical or conventional one. The time will come when educated men will be no more able to believe that the words, 'Out of Egypt have I called my son' (Matt. ii. 15; Hos. xi. 1), were *intended* by the prophet to refer to the return of Joseph and Mary from Egypt, than they are now able to believe the Roman Catholic explanation of Gen. iii. 15, 'Ipsa conteret caput tuum.' They will no more think that the first chapters of Genesis relate the same tale which Geology and Ethnology unfold than they now think the meaning of Joshua x. 12, 13, to be in accordance with Galileo's discovery.

From the circumstance that in former ages there has been a fourfold or a sevenfold interpretation of Scripture, we cannot argue to the possibility of upholding any other than the original one in our own. The mystical explanations of Origen or Philo were not seen to be mystical; the reasonings of Aquinas and Calvin were not supposed to go beyond the letter of the text. They have now become the subject of apology; it is justly said that we should not judge the greatness of the Fathers or Reformers by their suitableness to our own day. But this defence of them shows that their explanations of Scripture are no longer tenable; they belong to a way of thinking and speaking which was once diffused over the world, but has now passed away. And what we give up as a general principle we shall find it impossible to maintain partially, e. g., in the types of the Mosaic Law and the double meanings of prophecy, at least, in any sense in which it is not equally applicable to all deep and suggestive writings.

The same observation may be applied to the historical criticism of Scripture. From the fact that Paley or Butler were regarded in their generation as supplying a triumphant answer to the enemies of Scripture, we cannot argue that their answer will be satisfactory to those who inquire into such subjects in our own. Criticism has far more power than it formerly had; it has spread itself over ancient, and even modern, history; it extends to the thoughts and ideas of men as well as to words and facts; it has also a great place in education. Whether the habit of mind which has been formed in classical studies will not go on to Scripture; whether Scripture can be made an exception to other ancient writings, now that the nature of both is more understood; whether in the fuller light of history and science the views of the last century will hold out — these are questions respecting which the course of religious opinion in the past does not afford the means of truly judging.

Secondly, it has to be considered whether the intellectual forms under which Christianity has been described may not also be in a state of transition and resolution, in this respect contrasting with the never-changing truth of the Christian life (1 Cor. xiii. 8). Looking backwards at past ages, we experience a kind of amazement at the minuteness of theological distinctions, and also at their permanence. They seem to have borne a part in the education of the Christian world, in an age when language itself had also a greater influence than nowadays. It is admitted that these distinctions are not observed in the New Testament, and are for the most part of a later growth. But little is gained by setting up theology against Scripture, or Scripture against theology; the Bible against the Church, or the Church against the Bible. At different periods either has been a bulwark against some form of error: either has tended to correct the abuse of the other. A true inspiration guarded the writers of the New Testament from Gnostic or Manichean tenets; at a later stage, a sound instinct prevented the Church from dividing the humanity and Divinity of Christ. It may be said that the spirit of Christ forbids us to determine beyond what is written; and the decision of the council of Nicaea has been described by an eminent English prelate[1] as 'the greatest misfortune that ever befel the Christian world.' That is, perhaps, true; yet a different decision would have been a greater misfortune. Nor does there seem any reason to suppose that the human mind could have been arrested in its theological course. It is a mistake to imagine that the dividing and splitting of words is owing to the depravity of the human heart; was it not rather an intellectual movement (the only phenomenon of progress then going on among men) which led, by a sort of necessity, some to go forward to the completion of the system, while it left others to stand aside? A veil was on the human understanding in the great controversies which absorbed the Church in earlier ages; the cloud which the combatants themselves raised intercepted the view. They did not see—they could not have imagined—that there was a world which lay beyond the range of the controversy.

And now, as the Interpretation of Scripture is receiving another character, it seems that distinctions of theology, which were in great measure based on old interpretations, are beginning to fade away. A change is observable in the manner in which doctrines are stated and defended; it is no longer held sufficient to rest them on texts of Scripture, one, two, or more, which contain, or appear to contain, similar words or ideas. They are connected more closely with our moral nature; extreme consequences are shunned; large allowances are made for the ignorance of mankind. It is held that there is truth on both sides; about many questions there is a kind of union of opposites; others are admitted to have been verbal only; all are regarded in the light which is thrown upon them by church history and religious experience. A theory has lately been put forward, apparently as a defence of the Christian faith, which denies the objective character of any of them. And there are other signs that

[1] [Kaye, Bishop of Lincoln, d. 1853.]

times are changing, and we are changing too. It would be scarcely possible at present to revive the interest which was felt less than twenty years ago [1] in the doctrine of Baptismal Regeneration; nor would the arguments by which it was supported or impugned have the meaning which they once had. The communion of the Lord's Supper is also ceasing, at least in the Church of England, to be a focus or centre of disunion—

'Our greatest love turned to our greatest hate.'

A silence is observable on some other points of doctrine around which controversies swarmed a generation ago. Persons begin to ask what was the real difference which divided the two parties. They are no longer within the magic circle, but are taking up a position external to it. They have arrived at an age of reflection, and begin to speculate on the action and reaction, the irritation and counter-irritation, of religious forces; it is a common observation that 'revivals are not permanent;' the movement is criticized even by those who are subject to its influence. In the present state of the human mind, any consideration of these subjects, whether from the highest or lowest or most moderate point of view, is unfavourable to the stability of dogmatical systems, because it rouses inquiry into the meaning of words. To the sense of this is probably to be attributed the reserve on matters of doctrine and controversy which characterizes the present day, compared with the theological activity of twenty years ago [1].

These reflections bring us back to the question with which we began—'What effect will the critical interpretation of Scripture have on theology and on life?' Their tendency is to show that the result is beyond our control, and that the world is not unprepared for it. More things than at first sight appear are moving towards the same end. Religion often bids us think of ourselves, especially in later life, as, each one in his appointed place, carrying on a work

[1] [Written in 1860.]

which is fashioned within by unseen hands. The theologian, too, may have peace in the thought, that he is subject to the conditions of his age rather than one of its moving powers. When he hears theological inquiry censured as tending to create doubt and confusion, he knows very well that the cause of this is not to be sought in the writings of so-called rationalists or critics who are disliked partly because they unveil the age to itself; but in the opposition of reason and feeling, of the past and the present, in the conflict between the Calvinistic tendencies of an elder generation, and the influences which even in the same family naturally affect the young.

This distraction of the human mind between adverse influences and associations, is a fact which we should have to accept and make the best of, whatever consequences might seem to follow to individuals or Churches. It is not to be regarded as a merely heathen notion that 'truth is to be desired for its own sake even though no "good" result from it.' As a Christian paradox it may be said, 'What hast thou to do with "good?" follow thou Me.' But the Christian revelation does not require of us this Stoicism in most cases; it rather shows how good and truth are generally coincident. Even in this life, there are numberless links which unite moral good with intellectual truth. It is hardly too much to say that the one is but a narrower form of the other. Truth is to the world what holiness of life is to the individual—to man collectively the source of justice and peace and good.

There are many ways in which the connexion between truth and good may be traced in the Interpretation of Scripture. Is it a mere chimera that the different sections of Christendom may meet on the common ground of the New Testament? Or that the individual may be urged by the vacancy and unprofitableness of old traditions to make the Gospel his own—a life of Christ in the soul, instead of a theory of Christ which is in a book or written down? Or that in missions to the heathen Scripture may become the expression of universal truths rather than of the tenets of particular men or churches? That would remove many obstacles to the reception of Christianity. Or that the study of Scripture may have a more important place in a liberal education than hitherto? Or that the 'rational service' of interpreting Scripture may dry up the crude and dreamy vapours of religious excitement? Or, that in preaching, new sources of spiritual health may flow from a more natural use of Scripture? Or that the lessons of Scripture may have a nearer way to the hearts of the poor when disengaged from theological formulas? Let us consider more at length some of these topics.

I. No one casting his eye over the map of the Christian world can desire that the present lines of demarcation should always remain, any more than he will be inclined to regard the division of Christians to which he belongs himself, as in a pre-eminent or exclusive sense the Church of Christ. Those lines of demarcation seem to be political rather than religious; they are differences of nations, or governments, or ranks of society, more than of creeds or forms of faith. The feeling which gave rise to them has, in a great measure, passed away; no intelligent man seriously inclines to believe that salvation is to be found only in his own denomination. Examples of this 'sturdy orthodoxy,' in our own generation, rather provoke a smile than arouse serious disapproval. Yet many experiments show that these differences cannot be made up by any formal concordat or scheme of union; the parties cannot be brought to terms, and if they could, would cease to take an interest in the question at issue. The friction is too great when persons are invited to meet for a discussion of differences; such a process is like opening the doors and windows to put out a slumbering flame. But that is no reason for doubting that the divisions of the Christian world are beginning to pass away. The progress of politics, acquaintance with other countries, the growth of knowledge and of material greatness, changes of opinion in the Church of England, the present position of the Roman Communion—all these phenomena show that the ecclesiastical state of the world is not destined to be perpetual. Within the envious barriers which 'divide human nature into very little pieces' (Plato, *Rep.* iii. 395), a common sentiment is springing up of religious truth; the essentials of Christianity are contrasted with the details and definitions of it; good men of all religions find that they are more nearly agreed than heretofore. Neither is it impossible that this common feeling may so prevail over the accidental circumstances of Christian communities, that their political or ecclesiastical separation may be little felt. The walls which no adversary has scaled may fall down of themselves. We may perhaps figure to ourselves the battle against error and moral evil taking the place of one of sects and parties.

In this movement, which we should see more clearly but for the divisions of the Christian world which partly conceal it, the critical interpretation of Scripture will have a great influence. The Bible will be no longer appealed to as the witness of the opinions of particular sects, or of our own age; it will cease to be the battle-field of controversies. But as its true meaning is more clearly seen, its moral power will also be greater. If the outward and inward witness, instead of parting into two, as they once did, seem rather to blend and coincide in the Christian consciousness, that is not a source of weakness, but of strength. The Book itself, which links together the beginning and end of the human race, will not have a less inestimable value because the spirit has taken the place of the letter. Its discrepancies of fact, when we become familiar with them, will seem of little consequence in comparison with the truths which it unfolds. That these truths, instead of floating down the stream of tradition, or being lost in ritual observances, have been preserved for ever in a book, is one of the many blessings which the Jewish and Christian revelations have conferred on the world—a blessing not the less real, because it is not necessary to attribute it to miraculous causes.

Again, the Scriptures are a bond of union to the whole Christian world. No one denies their authority, and could all be brought to an intelligence of their true meaning, all might come to agree in matters of religion. That may seem to be a hope deferred, yet not altogether chimerical. If it is not held to be a thing impossible that there should be agreement in the meaning of Plato or Sophocles, neither is it to be regarded as absurd that there should be a like agreement in the interpretation of Scripture. The disappearance of artificial notions and systems will pave the way to such an agreement. The recognition of the fact, that many aspects and stages of religion are found in Scripture; that different, or even opposite parties existed in the Apostolic Church; that the first teachers of Christianity had a separate and individual mode of regarding the Gospel of Christ; that any existing communion is necessarily much more unlike the brotherhood of love in the New Testament than we are willing to suppose—Protestants in some respects, as much so as Catholics—that rival sects in our own day—Calvinists and Arminians—those who maintain and those who deny the final restoration of man—may equally find texts which seem to favour their respective tenets (Mark ix. 44-48; Romans xi. 32)—the recognition of these and similar facts will make us unwilling to impose any narrow rule of religious opinion on the ever-varying conditions of the human mind and Christian society.

II. Christian missions suggest another sphere in which a more enlightened use of Scripture might offer a great advantage to the teacher. The more he is himself penetrated with the universal spirit of Scripture, the more he will be able to resist the literal and servile habits of mind of Oriental nations. You cannot transfer English ways of belief, and almost the history of the Church of England itself, as the attempt is sometimes made—not to an uncivilized people, ready like children to receive new impressions, but to an ancient and decaying one, furrowed with the lines of thought, incapable of the principle of growth. But you may take the purer light or element of religion, of which Christianity is the expression, and make it shine on some principle in human nature which is the fallen image of it. You cannot give a people who have no history of their own, a sense of the importance of Christianity, as an historical fact; but, perhaps, that very peculiarity of their character may make them more impressible by the truths or ideas of Christianity. Neither is it easy to make them understand the growth of Revelation in successive ages—that there are precepts of the Old Testament which are reversed in the New—or that Moses allowed many things for the hardness of men's hearts. They are in one state of the world, and the missionary who teaches them is in another, and the Book through which they are taught does not altogether coincide with either. Many difficulties thus arise which we are most likely to be successful in meeting when we look them in the face. To one inference they clearly point, which is this: that it is not the Book of Scripture which we should seek to give them, to be reverenced like the Vedas or the Koran, and consecrated in its words and letters, but the truth of the Book, the mind of Christ and His Apostles, in which all lesser details and differences should be lost and absorbed. We want to awaken in them the sense that God is their Father, and they His children;—that is of more importance than any theory about the inspiration of Scripture. But to teach in this spirit, the missionary should himself be able to separate the accidents from the essence of religion; he should be conscious that the power of the Gospel resides not in the particulars of theology, but in the Christian life.

III. It may be doubted whether Scripture has ever been

sufficiently regarded as an element of liberal education. Few deem it worth while to spend in the study of it the same honest thought or pains which are bestowed on a classical author. Nor, as at present studied, can it be said always to have an elevating effect. It is not a useful lesson for the young student to apply to Scripture principles which he would hesitate to apply to other books; to make formal reconcilements of discrepancies which he would not think of reconciling in ordinary history; to divide simple words into double meanings; to adopt the fancies or conjectures of Fathers and Commentators as real knowledge. This laxity of knowledge is apt to infect the judgement when transferred to other subjects. It is not easy to say how much of the unsettlement of mind which prevails among intellectual young men is attributable to these causes; the mixture of truth and falsehood in religious education, certainly tends to impair, at the age when it is most needed, the early influence of a religious home.

Yet Scripture studied in a more liberal spirit might supply a part of education which classical literature fails to provide. 'The best book for the heart might also be made the best book for the intellect.' The noblest study of history and antiquity is contained in it; a poetry which is also the highest form of moral teaching; there, too, are lives of heroes and prophets, and especially of One whom we do not name with them, because He is above them. This history, or poetry, or biography, is distinguished from all classical or secular writings by the contemplation of man as he appears in the sight of God. That is a sense of things into which we must grow as well as reason ourselves, without which human nature is but a truncated, half-educated sort of being. But this sense or consciousness of a Divine presence in the world, which seems to be natural to the beginnings of the human race, but fades away and requires to be renewed in its after history, is not to be gathered from Greek or Roman literature, but from the Old and New Testament. And before we can make the Old and New Testament a real part of education, we must read them not by the help of custom or tradition, in the spirit of apology or controversy, but in accordance with the ordinary laws of human knowledge.

IV. Another use of Scripture is that in sermons, which seems to be among the tritest, and yet is far from being exhausted. If we could only be natural and speak of things as they truly are, with a real interest and not merely a conventional one! The words of Scripture come readily to hand, and the repetition of them requires no effort of thought in the writer or speaker. But, neither does it produce any effect on the hearer, which will always be in proportion to the degree of feeling or consciousness in ourselves. It may be said that originality is the gift of few; no Church can expect to have, not a hundred, but ten such preachers as Robertson or Newman. But, without originality, it seems possible to make use of Scripture in sermons in a much more living way than at present. Let the preacher make it a sort of religion, and proof of his reverence for Scripture, that he never uses its words without a distinct meaning; let him avoid the form of argument from Scripture, and catch the feeling and spirit. Scripture is itself a kind of poetry, when not overlaid with rhetoric. The scene and country has a freshness which may always be renewed; there is the interest of antiquity and the interest of home or common life as well. The facts and characters of Scripture might receive a new reading by being described simply as they are. The truths of Scripture again would have greater reality if divested of the scholastic form in which theology has cast them. The universal and spiritual aspects of Scripture might be more brought forward to the exclusion of questions of the Jewish law, or controversies about the sacraments, or exaggerated statements of doctrines which seem to be at variance with morality. The life of Christ, regarded quite naturally as of one 'who was in all points tempted like as we are, yet without sin,' is also the life and centre of Christian teaching. There is no higher aim which the preacher can propose to himself than to awaken what may be termed the feeling of the presence of God and the mind of Christ in Scripture; not to collect evidences about dates and books, or to familiarize metaphysical distinctions; but to make the heart and conscience of his hearers bear him witness that the lessons which are contained in Scripture—lessons of justice and truth—lessons of mercy and peace—of the need of man and the goodness of God to him, are indeed not human but divine.

V. It is time to make an end of this long disquisition—let the end be a few more words of application to the circumstances of a particular class in the present age. If any one who is about to become a clergyman feels, or thinks that he feels, that some of the preceding statements cast a shade of trouble or suspicion on his future walk of life, who, either from the influence of a stronger mind than his own, or from some natural tendency in himself, has been led to examine those great questions which lie on the threshold of the higher study of theology, and experiences a sort of shrinking or dizziness at the prospect which is opening upon him; let him lay to heart the following considerations:—First, that he may possibly not be the person who is called upon to pursue such inquiries. No man should busy himself with them who has not clearness of mind enough to see things as they are, and a faith strong enough to rest in that degree of knowledge which God has really given; or who is unable to separate the truth from his own religious wants and experiences. For the theologian as well as the philosopher has need of 'dry light,' 'unmingled with any tincture of the affections,' the more so as his conclusions are oftener liable to be disordered by them. He who is of another temperament may find another work to do, which is in some respects a higher one. Unlike philosophy, the Gospel has an ideal life to offer, not to a few only, but to all. There is one word of caution, however, to be given to those who renounce inquiry; it is, that they cannot retain the right to condemn inquirers. Their duty is to say with Nicodemus, 'Doth the Gospel condemn any man before it hear him?' although the answer may be only 'Art thou also of Galilee?' They have chosen the path of practical usefulness, and they should acknowledge that it is a narrow path. For any but a 'strong swimmer' will be insensibly drawn out of it by the tide of public opinion or the current of party.

Secondly, let him consider that the difficulty is not so great as imagination sometimes paints it. It is a difficulty which arises chiefly out of differences of education in different classes of society. It is a difficulty which tact, and prudence, and, much more, the power of a Christian life may hope to surmount. Much depends on the manner in which things are said; on the evidence in the writer or preacher of a real good will to his opponents, and a desire for the moral improvement of men. There is an aspect of truth which may always be put forward so as to find a way to the hearts of men. If there is danger and shrinking from one point of view, from another there is freedom and sense of relief. The wider contemplation of the religious world may enable us to adjust our own place in it. The acknowledgement of churches as political and national institutions is the basis of a sound government of them. Criticism itself is not only negative; if it creates some difficulties, it does away others. It may put us at variance with a party or section of Christians in our own neighbourhood. But, on the other hand, it enables us to look at all men as they are in the sight of God, not as they appear to human eye, separated and often interdicted from each other by lines of religious demarcation; it divides us from the parts to unite us to the whole. That is a great help to religious communion. It does away with the supposed opposition of reason and faith. It throws us back on the conviction that religion is a personal thing, in which certainty is to be slowly won and not assumed as the result of evidence or testimony. It places us, in some respects (though it be deemed a paradox to say so), more nearly in the position of the first Christians to whom the New Testament was not yet given, in whom the Gospel was a living word, not yet embodied in forms or supported by ancient institutions.

Thirdly, the suspicion or difficulty which attends critical inquiries is no reason for doubting their value. The Scripture nowhere leads us to suppose that the circumstance of all men speaking well of us is any ground for supposing that we are acceptable in the sight of God. And there is no reason why the condemnation of others should be witnessed to by our own conscience. Perhaps it may be true that, owing to the jealousy or fear of some, the reticence of others, the terrorism of a few, we may not always find it easy to regard these subjects with calmness and judgement. But, on the other hand, these accidental circumstances have nothing to do with the question at issue; they cannot have the slightest influence on the meaning of words, or on the truth of facts. No one can carry out the principle that public opinion or church authority is the guide to truth, when he goes beyond the limits of his own church or country. That is a consideration which may well make him pause before he accepts of such a guide in the journey to another world. All the arguments for repressing inquiries into Scripture in Protestant countries hold equally in Italy and Spain for repressing inquiries into matters of fact or doctrine, and so for denying the Scriptures to the common people.

Lastly, let him be assured that there is some nobler idea of truth than is supplied by the opinion of mankind in general, or the voice of parties in a church. Every one, whether a student of theology or not, has need to make war against his prejudices no less than against his passions;

and, in the religious teacher, the first is even more necessary than the last. For, while the vices of mankind are in a great degree isolated, and are, at any rate, reprobated by public opinion, their prejudices have a sort of communion or kindred with the world without. They are a collective evil, and have their being in the interest, classes, states of society, and other influences amid which we live. He who takes the prevailing opinions of Christians and decks them out in their gayest colours—who reflects the better mind of the world to itself—is likely to be its favourite teacher. In that ministry of the Gospel, even when assuming forms repulsive to persons of education, no doubt the good is far greater than the error or harm. But there is also a deeper work which is not dependent on the opinions of men, in which many elements combine, some alien to religion, or accidentally at variance with it. That work can hardly expect to win much popular favour, so far as it runs counter to the feelings of religious parties. But he who bears a part in it may feel a confidence, which no popular caresses or religious sympathy could inspire, that he has by a Divine help been enabled to plant his foot somewhere beyond the waves of time. He may depart hence before the natural term, worn out with intellectual toil; regarded with suspicion by many of his contemporaries; yet not without a sure hope that the love of truth, which men of saintly lives often seem to slight, is, nevertheless, accepted before God.

ON CONVERSION

AND

CHANGES OF CHARACTER

ROMANS VII.

Thus have we the image of the lifelong struggle gathered up in a single instant. In describing it we pass beyond the consciousness of the individual into a world of abstractions; we loosen the thread by which the spiritual faculties are held together, and view as objects what can, strictly speaking, have no existence, except in relation to the subject. The divided members of the soul are ideal, the combat between them is ideal, so also is the victory. What is real that corresponds to this is not a momentary, but a continuous conflict, which we feel rather than know—which has its different aspects of hope and fear, triumph and despair, the action and reaction of the Spirit of God in the depths of the human soul, awakening the sense of sin and conveying the assurance of forgiveness.

The language in which we describe this conflict is very different from that of the Apostle. Our circumstances are so changed that we are hardly able to view it in its simplest elements. Christianity is now the established religion of the civilized portion of mankind. In our own country it has become part of the law of the land; it speaks with authority, it is embodied in a Church, it is supported by almost universal opinion, and fortified by wealth and prescription. Those who know least of its spiritual life do not deny its greatness as a power in the world. Analogous to this relation in which it stands to our history and social state, is the relation in which it stands also to the minds of individuals. We are brought up in it, and unconsciously receive it as the habit of our thoughts and the condition of our life. It is without us, and we are within its circle; we do not become Christians, we are so from our birth. Even in those who suppose themselves to have passed through some sudden and violent change, and to have tasted once for all of the heavenly gift, the change is hardly ever in the form or substance of their belief, but in its quickening power; they feel not a new creed, but a new spirit within them. So that we might truly say of Christianity, that it is 'the daughter of time;' it hangs to the past, not only because the first century is the era of its birth, but because each successive century strengthens its form and adds to its external force, and entwines it with more numerous links in our social state. Not only may we say, that it is part and parcel of the law of the land, but part and parcel of the character of each one, which even the worst of men cannot wholly shake off.

But if with ourselves the influence of Christianity is almost always gradual and imperceptible, with the first believers it was almost always sudden. There was no interval which separated the preaching of Peter on the day of Pentecost, from the baptism of the three thousand. The eunuch of Candace paused for a brief space on a journey, and was then baptized into the name of Christ, which a few hours previously he had not so much as heard. There was no period of probation like that which, a century or two later, was appropriated to the instruction of the Catechumens. It was an impulse, an inspiration passing from the lips of one to a chosen few, and communicated by them to the ear and soul of listening multitudes. As the wind bloweth where it listeth, and we hear the sound thereof; as the lightning shineth from the one end of the heaven to the other; so suddenly, fitfully, simultaneously, new thoughts come into their minds, not to one only, but to many, to whole cities almost at once. They were pricked with the sense of sin; they were melted with the love of Christ; their spiritual nature 'came again like the flesh of a little child.' And some, like St. Paul, became the very opposite of their former selves; from scoffers, believers; from persecutors, preachers; the thing that they were was so strange to them, that they could no longer look calmly on the earthly scene, which they hardly seemed to touch, which was already lighted up with the wrath and mercy of God. There were those among them who 'saw visions and dreamed dreams,' who were 'caught up,' like St. Paul, 'into the third heaven,' or, like the twelve, 'spake with other tongues as the Spirit gave them utterance.' And sometimes, as in the Thessalonian Church, the ecstasy of conversion led to strange and wild opinions, such as the daily expectation of Christ's coming. The 'round world' itself began to reel before them, as they thought of the things that were shortly to come to pass.

But however sudden were the conversions of the earliest believers, however wonderful the circumstances which attended them, they were not for that reason the less lasting or sincere. Though many preached 'Christ of contention,' though 'Demas forsook the Apostle,' there were few who, having once taken up the cross, turned back from 'the love of this present world.' They might waver between Paul and Peter, between the circumcision and the uncircumcision; they might give ear to the strange and bewitching heresies of the East; but there is no trace that many returned to 'those that were no gods,' or put off Christ; the impression of the truth that they had received was everlasting on their minds. Even sins of fornication and uncleanness, which from the Apostle's frequent warnings against them we must suppose to have lingered, as a sort of remnant of heathenism in the early Church, did not wholly destroy their inward relation to God and Christ. Though 'their last state might be worse than the first,' they could never return again to live the life of all men after having tasted 'the heavenly gift and the powers of the world to come.'

Such was the nature of conversion among the early Christians, the new birth of which by spiritual descent we are ourselves the offspring. Is there anything in history like it? anything in our own lives which may help us to understand it? That which the Scripture describes from within, we are for a while going to look at from a different point of view, not with reference to the power of God, but to those secondary causes through which He works—the laws which experience shows that He himself imposes on the operations of His Spirit. Such an inquiry is not a mere idle speculation; it is not far from the practical question, 'How we are to become better.' Imperfect as any attempt to analyze our spiritual life must ever be, the changes which we ourselves experience or observe in others, compared with those greater and more sudden changes which took place in the age of the Apostle, will throw light upon each other.

In the sudden conversions of the early Christians we observe three things which either tend to discredit, or do not accompany, the working of a similar power among ourselves.—First, that conversion was marked by ecstatic and unusual phenomena; secondly, that, though sudden, it was permanent; thirdly, that it fell upon whole multitudes at once.

When we consider what is implied in such expressions as 'not many wise, not many learned' were called to the knowledge of the truth, we can scarcely avoid feeling that there must have been much in the early Church which would have been distasteful to us as men of education; much that must have worn the appearance of excitement and enthusiasm. Is the mean conventicle, looking almost like a private house, a better image of that first assembly of Christians which met in the 'large upper room,' or the Catholic church arrayed in all the glories of Christian art? Neither of them is altogether like in spirit perhaps, but in externals the first. Is the dignified hierarchy that occupy the seats around the altar, more like the multitudes of first believers, or the lowly crowd that kneel upon the pavement? If we try to embody in the mind's eye the forms of the first teachers, and still more of their followers, we cannot help reading the true lesson, however great may be the illusions of poetry or of art. Not St. Paul standing on Mars' hill in the fullness of manly strength, as we have him in the cartoon of Raphael, is the true image; but such a one as he himself would glory in, whose bodily presence was weak and speech feeble, who had an infirmity in his flesh, and bore in his body the marks of the Lord Jesus.

And when we look at this picture, 'full in the face,' however we might by nature be inclined to turn aside from it, or veil its details in general language, we cannot deny that many things that accompany the religion of the uneducated now, must then also have accompanied the Gospel preached to the poor. There must have been, humanly speaking, spiritual delusions where men lived so exclusively in the spiritual world; there were scenes which we know took place such as St. Paul says would make the unbeliever think that they were mad. The best and holiest persons among the poor and ignorant are not entirely free from superstition, according to the notions of the educated; at best they are apt to speak of religion in a manner not quite suited to our taste; they sing with a loud and excited voice; they imagine themselves to receive Divine oracles, even about the humblest cares of life. Is not this, in externals at least, very like the appearance which the first disciples must have presented, who obeyed the Apostle's injunction, 'Is any sad? let him pray; is any merry? let him sing psalms'? Could our nerves have borne to witness the speaking with tongues, or the administration of Baptism, or the love feasts as they probably existed in the early Church?

This difference between the feelings and habits of the first Christians and ourselves, must be borne in mind in relation to the subject of conversion. For as sudden changes are more likely to be met with amongst the poor and uneducated in the present day, it certainly throws light on the subject of the first conversions, that to the poor and uneducated the Gospel was first preached. And yet these sudden changes were as real, nay, more real than any gradual changes which take place among ourselves. The Stoic or Epicurean philosopher who had come into an assembly of believers speaking with tongues, would have remarked, that among the vulgar religious extravagances were usually short-lived. But it was not so. There was more there than he had eyes to see, or than was dreamed of in a philosophy like his. Not only was there the superficial appearance of poverty and meanness and enthusiasm, from a nearer view of which we are apt to shrink, but underneath this, brighter from its very obscurity, purer from the meanness of the raiment in which it was apparelled, was the life hidden with Christ and God. There, and there only, was the power which made a man humble instead of proud, self-denying instead of self-seeking, spiritual instead of carnal; which made him embrace, not only the brethren, but the whole human race in the arms of his love.

But it is a further difference between the power of the Gospel now and in the first ages, that it no longer converts whole multitudes at once. Perhaps this very individuality in its mode of working may not be without an advantage in awakening us to its higher truths and more entire spiritual freedom. Whether this be so or not; whether there be any spiritual law by which reason, in a measure, takes the place of faith, and the common religious impulse weakens as the power of reflection grows, we certainly observe a diminution in the collective force which religion exercises on the hearts of men. In our own days the preacher sees the seed which he has sown gradually spring up; first one, then another begins to lead a better life; then a change comes over the state of society, often from causes over which he has no control; he makes some steps forwards and a few backwards, and trusts far more, if he is wise, to the silent influence of religious education than to the power of preaching; and, perhaps, the result of a long life of ministerial labour is far less than that of a single discourse from the lips of the Apostles or their followers. Even in missions to the heathen the vital energies of Christianity cease to operate to any great extent, at least on the effete civilization of India and China; the limits of the kingdoms of light and darkness are nearly the same as heretofore. At any rate it cannot be said that Christianity has wrought any sudden amelioration of mankind by the immediate preaching of the word, since the conversion of the barbarians. Even within the Christian world there is a parallel retardation. The ebb and flow of reformation and counter-reformation have hardly changed the permanent landmarks. The age of spiritual crises is past. The growth of Christianity in modern times may be compared to the change of the body, when it has already arrived at its full stature. In one half-century so vast a progress was made, in a few centuries more the world itself seemed to 'have gone after Him,' and now for near a thousand years the voice of experience is repeating to us, 'Hitherto shalt thou go, but no further.'

Looking at this remarkable phenomenon of the conversion of whole multitudes at once, not from its Divine but from its human aspect (that is, with reference to that provision that God himself has made in human nature for the execution of His will), the first cause to which we are naturally led to attribute it is the power of sympathy. Why it is that men ever act together is a mystery of which our individual self-consciousness gives no account, any more than why we speak a common language, or form nations or societies, or merely in our physical nature are capable of taking diseases from one another. Nature and the Author of nature have made us thus dependent on each other both in body and soul. Whoever has seen human beings collected together in masses, and watched the movements that pass over them, like 'the trees of the forest moving in the wind,' will have no difficulty in imagining, if not in understanding, how the same voice might have found its way at the same instant to a thousand hearts, without our being able to say where the fire was first kindled, or by whom the inspiration was first caught. Such historical events as the Reformation, or the Crusades, or the French Revolution, are a sufficient evidence that a whole people, or almost, we may say, half a world, may be 'drunk into one spirit,' springing up, as it might seem, spontaneously in the breast of each, yet common to all. A parallel yet nearer is furnished by the history of the Jewish people, in whose sudden rebellion and restoration to God's favour, we recognize literally the momentary workings of, what is to ourselves a figure of speech, a national conscience.

In ordinary cases we should truly say that there must have been some predisposing cause of a great political or religious revolution ; some latent elements acting alike upon all, which, though long smouldering beneath, burst forth at last into a flame. Such a cause might be the misery of mankind, or the intense corruption of human society, which could not be quickened except it die, or the long-suppressed yearnings of the soul after something higher than it had hitherto known upon earth, or the reflected light of one religion or one movement of the human mind upon another. Such causes were actually at work, preparing the way for the diffusion of Christianity. The law itself was beginning to pass away in an altered world, the state of society was hollow, the chosen people were hopelessly under the Roman yoke. Good men refrained from the wild attempt of the Galilean Judas; yet the spirit which animated such attempts was slumbering in their bosoms. Looking back at their own past history, they could not but remember, even in an altered world, that there was One who ruled among the kingdoms of men, 'beside whom there was no God.' Were they to suppose that His arm was straitened to save? that He had forgotten His tender mercies to the house of David? that the aspirations of the prophets were vain? that the blood of the Maccabean heroes had sunk like water into the earth? This was a hard saying; who could bear it? It was long ere the nation, like the individual, put off the old man—that is, the temporal dispensation—and put on the new man—that is, the spiritual Israel. The very misery of the people seemed to forbid them to acquiesce in their present state. And with the miserable condition of the nation sprang up also the feeling, not only in individuals but in the race, that for their sins they were chastened, the feeling which their whole history seemed to deepen and increase. At last the scales fell from their eyes; the veil that was on the face of Moses was first transfigured before them, then removed; the thoughts of many hearts turned simultaneously to the Hope of Israel, 'Him whom the law and the prophets foretold.' As they listened to the preaching of the Apostles, they seemed to hear a truth both new and old; what many had thought, but none had uttered; which in its comfort and joyousness seemed to them new, and yet, from its familiarity and suitableness to their condition, not the less old.

Spiritual life, no less than natural life, is often the very opposite of the elements which seem to give birth to it. The preparation for the way of the Lord, which John the Baptist preached, did not consist in a direct reference to the Saviour. The words 'He shall baptize you with the Holy Ghost and with fire,' and 'He shall burn up the chaff with fire unquenchable,' could have given the Jews no exact conception of Him who 'did not break the bruised reed, nor quench the smoking flax.' It was in another way that John prepared for Christ, by quickening the moral sense of the people, and sounding in their ears the voice 'Repent, for the kingdom of heaven is at hand.' Beyond this useful lesson, there was a kind of vacancy in the preaching of John. He himself, as 'he was finishing his course,' testified that his work was incomplete, and that he was not the Christ. The Jewish people were prepared by his preaching for the coming of Christ, just as an individual might be prepared to receive Him by the conviction of sin and the conscious need of forgiveness.

Except from the Gospel history and the writings of Josephus and Philo, we know but little of the tendencies of the Jewish mind in the time of our Lord. Yet we cannot doubt that the entrance of Christianity into the world was not sudden and abrupt; that is an illusion which arises in the mind from our slender acquaintance with contemporary opinions. Better and higher and holier as it was, it was not absolutely distinct from the teaching of the doctors of the law either in form or substance; it was not unconnected with, but gave life and truth to, the mystic fancies of Alexandrian philosophy. Even in the counsels of perfection of the Sermon on the Mount, there is probably nothing which might not be found, either in letter or spirit, in Philo or some other Jewish or Eastern writer. The peculiarity of the Gospel is, not that it teaches what is wholly new, but that it draws out of the treasure-house of the human heart things new and old, gathering together in one the dispersed fragments of the truth. The common people would not have 'heard Him gladly,' but for the truth of what He said. The heart was its own witness to it. The better nature of man, though but for a moment, responded to it, spoken as it was with authority, and not as the scribes; with simplicity, and not as the great teachers of the law; and sanctified by the life and actions of Him from whose lips it came, and 'Who spake as never man spake.'

And yet, after reviewing the circumstances of the first preaching of the Gospel, there remains something which cannot be resolved into causes or antecedents; which eludes criticism, and can no more be explained in the world than the sudden changes of character in the individual. There are processes of life and organization about which we know nothing, and we seem to know that we shall never know anything. 'That which thou sowest is not quickened, except it die;' but the mechanism of this new life is too complex and yet too simple for us to untwist its fibres. The figure which St. Paul applies to the resurrection of the body is true also of the renewal of the soul, especially in the first ages of which we know so little, and in which the Gospel seems to have acted with such far greater power than among ourselves.

Leaving further inquiry into the conversion of the first Christians at the point at which it hides itself from us in mystery, we have now to turn to a question hardly less mysterious, though seemingly more familiar to us, which may be regarded as a question either of moral philosophy or of theology—the nature of conversion and changes of character among ourselves. What traces are there of a spiritual power still acting upon the human heart? What is the inward nature, and what are the outward conditions of changes in human conduct? Is our life a gradual and insensible progress from infancy to age, from birth to death, governed by fixed laws; or is it a miracle and mystery of thirty, or fifty, or seventy years' standing, consisting of so many isolated actions or portions knit together by no common principle?

Were we to consider mankind only from without, there could be no doubt of the answer which we should give to the last of these questions. The order of the world would scarcely even *seem* to be infringed by the free will of man.

In morals, no less than in physics, everything would appear to proceed by regular law. Individuals have certain capacities, which grow with their growth and strengthen with their strength; and no one by taking thought can add one cubit to his stature. As the poet says—'The boy is father to the man.' The lives of the great majority have a sort of continuity: as we know them by the same look, walk, manner; so when we come to converse with them, we recognize the same character as formerly. They may be changed; but the change in general is such as we expect to find in them from youth to maturity, or from maturity to decay. There is something in them which is not changed, by which we perceive them to be the same. If they were weak, they remain so still; if they were sensitive, they remain so still; if they were selfish or passionate, such faults are seldom cured by increasing age or infirmities. And often the same nature puts on many veils and disguises; to the outward eye it may have, in some instances, almost disappeared; when we look beneath, it is still there.

The appearance of this sameness in human nature has led many to suppose that no real change ever takes place. Does a man from a drunkard become sober? from a knight errant become a devotee? from a sensualist a believer in Christ? or a woman from a life of pleasure pass to a romantic and devoted religion? It has been maintained that they are the same still; and that deeper similarities remain than the differences which are a part of their new profession. Those who make the remark would say, that such persons exhibit the same vanity, the same irritability, the same ambition; that sensualism still lurks under the disguise of refinement, or earthly and human passion transfuses itself into devotion.

This 'practical fatalism,' which says that human beings can be what they are and nothing else, has a certain degree of truth, or rather, of plausibility, from the circumstance that men seldom change wholly, and that the part of their nature which changes least is the weakness and infirmity that shows itself on the surface. Few, comparatively, ever change their outward manner, except from the mere result of altered circumstances; and hence, to a superficial observer, they appear to change less than is really the fact. Probably St. Paul never lost that trembling and feebleness, which was one of the trials of his life. Nor, in so far as the mind is dependent on the body, can we pretend to be wholly free agents. Who can say that his view of life and his power of action are unaffected by his bodily state? or who expects to find a firm and decided character in the nervous and sensitive frame? The commonest facts of daily life sufficiently prove the connexion of mind and body; the more we attend to it the closer it appears. Nor, indeed, can it be denied that external circumstances fix for most men the path of life. They are the inhabitants of a particular country; they have a certain position in the world; they rise to their occupations as the morning comes round; they seldom get beyond the circle of ideas in which they have been brought up. Fearfully and wonderfully as they are made, though each one in his bodily frame, and even more in his thoughts and feelings, is a miracle of complexity, they seem, as they meet in society, to reunite into a machine, and society itself is the great automaton of which they are the parts. It is harder and more conventional than the individuals which compose it; it exercises a kind of regulating force on the wayward fancies of their wills; it says to them in an unmistakable manner that 'they shall not break their ranks.' The laws of trade, the customs of social life, the instincts of human nature, act upon us with a power little less than that of physical necessity.

If from this external aspect of human things we turn inward, there seems to be no limit to the changes which we deem possible. We are no longer the same, but different every hour. No physical fact interposes itself as an obstacle to our thoughts any more than to our dreams. The world and its laws have nothing to do with our free determinations. At any moment we can begin a new life; in idea at least, no time is required for the change. One instant we may be proud, the next humble; one instant sinning, at the next repenting; one instant, like St. Paul, ready to persecute, at another to preach the Gospel; full of malice and hatred one hour, melting into tenderness the next. As we hear the words of the preacher, there is a voice within telling us, that 'now, even now, is the day of salvation;' and if certain clogs and hindrances of earth could only be removed, we are ready to pass immediately into another state. And, at times, it seems as though we had actually passed into rest, and had a foretaste of the heavenly gift. Something more than imagination enables us to fashion a divine pattern to which we conform for a little while. The 'new man' unto which we become transformed, is so pleasant to us that it banishes the thought of 'the old.' In youth especially, when we are ignorant of the compass of our own nature, such frames of mind are perpetually recurring; perhaps, not without attendant evils; certainly, also, for good.

But besides such feelings as these, which we know to be partly true, partly illusive, every one's experience of himself appears to teach him, that he has gone through many changes and had many special providences vouchsafed to him; he says to himself that he has been led in a mysterious and peculiar way, not like the way of other men, and had feelings not common to others; he compares different times and places, and contrasts his own conduct here and there, now and then. In other men he remarks similarity of character; in himself he sees chiefly diversity. They seem to be the creatures of habit and circumstance; he alone is a free agent. The truth is, that he observes himself; he cannot equally observe them. He is not conscious of the inward struggles through which they have passed; he sees only the veil of flesh which conceals them from his view. He knows when he thinks about it, but he does not habitually remember, that, under that calm exterior, there is a like current of individual thoughts, feelings, interests, which have as great a charm and intensity for another as the workings of his own mind have for himself.

And yet it does not follow, that this inward fact is to be set aside as the result of egotism and illusion. It may be not merely the dreamy reflection of our life and actions in the mirror of self, but the subtle and delicate spring of the whole machine. To purify the feelings or to move the will, the internal sense may be as necessary to us as external observation is to regulate and sustain them. Even to the formula of the fatalist, that 'freedom is the consciousness of necessity,' it may be replied, that that very consciousness, as he terms it, is as essential as any other link in the chain in which 'he binds fast the world.' Human nature is beset by the contradiction, not of two rival theories, but of many apparently contradictory facts. If we cannot imagine how the world could go on without law and order in human actions, neither can we imagine how morality could subsist unless we clear a space around us for the freedom of the will.

But not in this place to get further into the meshes of the great question of freedom and necessity, let us rather turn aside for a moment to consider some practical aspects of the reflections which precede. Scripture and reason alike require that we should entirely turn to God, that we should obey the whole law. And hard as this may seem at first, there is a witness within us which pleads that it is possible. Our mind and moral nature are one; we cannot break ourselves into pieces in action any more than in thought. The whole man is in every part and in every act. This is not a mere mode of thought, but a truth of great practical importance. 'Easier to change many things than one,' is the common saying. Easier, we may add, in religion or morality, to change the whole than the part. Easier because more natural, more agreeable to the voice of conscience and the promises of Scripture. God himself deals with us as a whole; He does not forgive us in part any more than He requires us to serve Him in part. It may be true that, of the thousand hearers of the appeal of the preacher, not above one begins a new life. And some persons will imagine that it might be better to make an impression on them little by little, like the effect of the dropping of water upon stone. Not in this way is the Gospel written down on the fleshy tables of the heart. More true to our own experience of self, as well as to the words of Scripture, are such ideas as renovation, renewal, regeneration, taking up the cross and following Christ, dying with Christ that we may also live with Him.

Many a person will tease himself by counting minutes and providing small rules for his life, who would have found the task an easier and a nobler one, had he viewed it in its whole extent, and gone to God in a 'large and liberal spirit,' to offer up his life to Him. To have no *arrière pensée* in the service of God and virtue is the great source of peace and happiness. Make clean that which is within, and you have no need to purify that which is without. Take care of the little things of life, and the great ones will take care of themselves, is the maxim of the trader, which is sometimes, and with a certain degree of truth, applied to the service of God. But much more true is it in religion that we should take care of the great things, and the trifles of life will take care of themselves. 'If thine eye be single, thy whole body will be full of light.' Christianity is not acquired as an art by long practice; it does not carve and polish human nature with a graving tool; it makes the whole man; first pouring out his soul before God, and then 'casting him in a mould.' Its workings are not to be measured by time, even though among educated persons, and in modern times, sudden and momentary conversions can rarely occur.

For the doctrine of conversion the moralist substitutes the theory of habits. Good actions, he says, produce good habits; and the repetition of good actions makes them easier to perform, and 'fortifies us indefinitely against temptation.' There are bodily and mental habits—habits of reflection and habits of action. Practice gives skill or sleight of hand; constant attention, the faculty of abstraction; so the practice of virtue makes us virtuous, that of vice vicious. The more meat we eat, to use the illustration of Aristotle, in whom we find a cruder form of the same theory, the more we are able to eat meat; the more we wrestle, the more able we are to wrestle, and so forth. If a person has some duty to perform, say of common and trivial sort, to rise at a particular hour in the morning, to be at a particular place at such an hour, to conform to some rule about abstinence, we tell him that he will find the first occasion difficult, the second easy, and the difficulty is supposed to vanish by degrees until it wholly disappears. If a man has to march into a battle, or to perform a surgical operation, or to do anything else from which human nature shrinks, his nerves, we say, are gradually strengthened; his head, as was said of a famous soldier, clears up at the sound of the cannon; like the grave-digger in Hamlet, he has soon no 'feeling of his occupation.'

From a consideration of such instances as these, the rule has been laid down, that, 'as the passive impression weakens, the active habit strengthens.' But is not this saying of a great man founded on a narrow and partial contemplation of human nature? For, in the first place, it leaves altogether out of sight the motives of human action; it is equally suited to the most rigid formalist and to a moral and spiritual being. Secondly, it takes no account of the limitation of the power of habits, which neither in mind nor body can be extended beyond a certain point;

nor of the original capacity or peculiar character of individuals; nor of the different kinds of habits, nor of the degrees of strength and weakness in different minds; nor of the enormous difference between youth and age, childhood and manhood, in the capacity for acquiring habits. Old age does not move with accumulated force, either upwards or downwards; they are the lesser habits, not the great springs of life, that show themselves in it with increased power. Nor can the man who has neglected to form habits in youth, acquire them in mature life; like the body, the mind ceases to be capable of receiving a particular form. Lastly, such a description of human nature agrees with no man's account of himself; whatever moralists may say, he knows himself to be a spiritual being. 'The wind bloweth where it listeth,' and he cannot 'tell whence it cometh, or whither it goeth.'

All that is true in the theory of habits seems to be implied in the notion of order or regularity. Even this is inadequate to give a conception of the structure of human beings. Order is the beginning, but freedom is the perfection of our moral nature. Men do not live at random, or act one instant without reference to their actions just before. And in youth especially, the very sameness of our occupations is a sort of stay and support to us, as in age it may be described as a kind of rest. But no one will say that the mere repetition of actions until they constitute a habit, gives any explanation of the higher and nobler forms of human virtue, or the finer moulds of character. Life cannot be explained as the working of a mere machine, still less can moral or spiritual life be reduced to merely mechanical laws.

But if, while acknowledging that a great proportion of mankind are the creatures of habit, and that a great part of our actions are nothing more than the result of habit, we go on to ask ourselves about the changes of our life, and fix our minds on the critical points, we are led to view human nature, not only in a wider and more generous spirit, but also in a way more accordant with the language of Scripture. We no longer measure ourselves by days or by weeks; we are conscious that at particular times we have undergone great revolutions or emotions; and then, again, have intervened periods, lasting perhaps for years, in which we have pursued the even current of our way. Our progress towards good may have been in idea an imperceptible and regular advance; in fact, we know it to have been otherwise. We have taken plunges in life; there are many eras noted in our existence. The greatest changes are those of which we are the least able to give an account, and which we feel the most disposed to refer to a superior power. That they were simply mysterious, like some utterly unknown natural phenomena, is our first thought about them. But although unable to fathom their true nature, we are capable of analyzing many of the circumstances which accompany them, and of observing the impulses out of which they arise.

Every man has the power of forming a resolution, or, without previous resolution, in any particular instance, acting as he will. As thoughts come into the mind one cannot tell how, so too motives spring up, without our being able to trace their origin. Why we suddenly see a thing in a new light, is often hard to explain; why we feel an action to be right or wrong which has previously seemed indifferent, is not less inexplicable. We fix the passing dream or sentiment in action, the thought is nothing, the deed may be everything. That day after day, to use a familiar instance, the drunkard will find abstinence easier, is probably untrue; but that from once abstaining he will gain a fresh experience, and receive a new strength and inward satisfaction, which may result in endless consequences, is what every one is aware of. It is not the sameness of what we do, but its novelty, which seems to have such a peculiar power over us; not the repetition of many blind actions, but the performance of a single conscious one, that is the birth to a new life. Indeed, the very sameness of actions is often accompanied with a sort of weariness, which makes men desirous of change.

Nor is it less true, that by the commission, not of many, but a single act of vice or crime, an inroad is made into our whole moral constitution, which is not proportionably increased by its repetition. The first act of theft, falsehood, or other immorality, is an event in the life of the perpetrator which he never forgets. It may often happen that no account can be given of it; that there is nothing in the education, nor in the antecedents of the person, that would lead us, or even himself, to suspect it. In the weaker sort of natures, especially, suggestions of evil spring up we cannot tell how. Human beings are the creatures of habit; but they are the creatures of impulse too; and from the greater variableness of the outward circumstances of life, and especially of particular periods of life, and the greater freedom of individuals, it may, perhaps, be found that human actions, though less liable to wide-spread or sudden changes, have also become more capricious, and less reducible to simple causes, than formerly.

Changes in character come more often in the form of feeling than of reason, from some new affection or attachment, or alienation of our former self, rather than from the slow growth of experience, or a deliberate sense of right and duty. The meeting with some particular person, the remembrance of some particular scene, the last words of a parent or friend, the reading of a sentence in a book, may call forth a world within us of the very existence of which we were previously unconscious. New interests arise such as we never before knew, and we can no longer lie grovelling in the mire, but must be up and doing; new affections seem to be drawn out, such as warm our inmost soul and make action and exertion a delight to us. Mere human love at first sight, as we say, has been known to change the whole character and produce an earthly effect, analogous to that heavenly love of Christ and the brethren, of which the New Testament speaks. Have we not seen the passionate become calm, the licentious pure, the weak strong, the scoffer devout? We may not venture to say with St. Paul, 'This is a great mystery, but I speak concerning Christ and the church.' But such instances serve, at least, to quicken our sense of the depth and subtlety of human nature.

Of many of these changes no other reason can be given than that nature and the Author of nature have made men capable of them. There are others, again, which we seem to trace, not only to particular times, but to definite actions, from which they flow in the same manner that other effects follow from their causes. Among such causes none are more powerful than acts of self-sacrifice and devotion. A single deed of heroism makes a man a hero; it becomes a part of him, and, strengthened by the approbation and sympathy of his fellow-men, a sort of power which he gains over himself and them. Something like this is true of the lesser occasions of life no less than of the greatest; provided in either case the actions are not of such a kind that the performance of them is a violence to our nature. Many a one has stretched himself on the rack of asceticism, without on the whole raising his nature; often he has seemed to have gained in self-control only what he has lost in the kindlier affections, and by his very isolation to have wasted the opportunities which nature offered him of self-improvement. But no one with a heart open to human feelings, loving not man the less, but God more, sensitive to the happiness of this world, yet aiming at a higher—no man of such a nature ever made a great sacrifice, or performed a great act of self-denial, without impressing a change on his character, which lasted to his latest breath. No man ever took his besetting sin, it may be lust, or pride, or love of rank and position, and, as it were, cut it out by voluntarily placing himself where to gratify it was impossible, without sensibly receiving a new strength of character. In one day, almost in an hour, he may become an altered man; he may stand, as it were, on a different stage of moral and religious life; he may feel himself in new relations to an altered world.

Nor, in considering the effects of action, must the influence of impressions be lost sight of. Good resolutions are apt to have a bad name; they have come to be almost synonymous with the absence of good actions. As they get older, men deem it a kind of weakness to be guilty of making them; so often do they end in raising 'pictures of virtue, or going over the theory of virtue in our minds.' Yet this contrast between passive impression and active habit is hardly justified by our experience of ourselves or others. Valueless as they are in themselves, good resolutions are suggestive of great good; they are seldom wholly without effect on our conduct; in the weakest of men they are still the embryo of action. They may meet with a concurrence of circumstances in which they take root and grow, coinciding with some change of place, or of pursuits, or of companions, or of natural constitution, in which they acquire a peculiar power. They are the opportunities of virtue, if not virtue itself. At the worst they make us think; they give us an experience of ourselves; they prevent our passing our lives in total unconsciousness. A man may go on all his life making and not keeping them; miserable as such a state appears, he is perhaps not the worse, but something the better for them. The voice of the preacher is not lost, even if he succeed but for a few instants in awakening them.

A further cause of sudden changes in the moral constitution is the determination of the will by reason and knowledge. Suppose the case of a person living in a narrow circle of ideas, within the limits of his early education, perplexed by difficulties, yet never venturing beyond the wall of prejudices in which he has been brought up, or changing only into the false position of a rebellion against them. A new view of his relation to the world and to God is presented to him; such, for example, as in St. Paul's day was the grand acknowledgement that God was 'not the God of the Jews only;' such as in our own age would be the clear vision of the truth and justice of God, high above the clouds of earth and time, and of His goodwill to man. Convinced of the reasonableness of the Gospel, it becomes to him at once a self-imposed law. No longer does the human heart rebel; no longer has he 'to pose his understanding' with that odd resolution of Tertullian—'certum quia impossibile.' He perceives that the perplexities of religion have been made, not by the appointment of God, but by the ingenuity of man.

Lastly. Among those influences, by the help of which the will of man learns to disengage itself from the power of habit, must not be omitted the influence of circumstances. If men are creatures of habit, much more are they creatures of circumstances. These two, nature without us, and 'the second nature' that is within, are the counterbalancing forces of our being. Between them (so we may figure to ourselves the working of the mind) the human will inserts itself, making the force of one a lever against the other, and seeming to rule both. We fall under the power of habit, and feel ourselves weak and powerless to shake off the almost physical influence which it exerts upon us. The enfeebled frame cannot rid itself of the malady; the palsied springs of action cannot be strengthened for good, nor fortified against evil. Transplanted into another soil, and in a different air, we renew our strength. In youth especially, the character seems to respond kindly to the influence of the external world. Providence has placed us in a state in which we have many aids in the battle with self; the greatest of these is change of circumstances.

We have wandered far from the subject of conversion in the early Church, into another sphere in which the words 'grace, faith, the spirit,' have disappeared, and notions of moral philosophy have taken their place. It is better, perhaps, that the attempt to analyze our spiritual nature should assume this abstract form. We feel that words cannot express the life hidden with Christ and God; we are afraid of declaring on the housetop, what may only be spoken in the closet. If the rites and ceremonies of the elder dispensation, which have so little in them of a spiritual character, became a figure of the true, much more may the moral world be regarded as a figure of the spiritual world of which religion speaks to us.

There is a view of the changes of the characters of men which begins where this ends, which reads human nature by a different light, and speaks of it as the seat of a great struggle between the powers of good and evil. It would be untrue to identify this view with that which has preceded, and scarcely less untrue to attempt to interweave the two in a system of 'moral theology.' No addition of theological terms will transfigure Aristotle's Ethics into a 'Summa Theologiae.' When St. Paul says—'O wretched man that I am! who shall deliver me from the body of this death? I thank God through Jesus Christ our Lord;' he is not speaking the language of moral philosophy, but of religious feeling. He expresses what few have truly felt concentrated in a single instant, what many have deluded themselves into the belief of, what some have experienced accompanying them through life, what a great portion even of the better sort of mankind are wholly unconscious of. It seems as if Providence allowed us to regard the truths of religion and morality in many ways which are not wholly unconnected with each other, yet parallel rather than intersecting; providing for the varieties of human character, and not leaving those altogether without law, who are incapable in a world of sight of entering within the veil.

As we return to that 'hidden life' of which the Scripture speaks, our analysis of human nature seems to become more imperfect, less reducible to rule or measure, less capable of being described in a language which all men understand. What the believer recognizes as the record of his experience is apt to seem mystical to the rest of the world. We do not seek to thread the mazes of the human soul, or to draw forth to the light its hidden communion with its Maker, but only to present in general outline the power of religion among other causes of human action.

Directly, religious influences may be summed up under three heads:—The power of God; the love of Christ; the efficacy of prayer.

(1) So far as the influence of the first of these is capable of analysis, it consists in the practical sense that we are dependent beings, and that our souls are in the hands of God, who is acting through us, and ever present with us, in the trials of life and in the work of life. The believer is a minister who executes this work, hardly the partner in it; it is not his own, but God's. He does it with the greatest care, as unto the Lord and not to men, yet is indifferent as to the result, knowing that all things, even through his imperfect agency, are working together for good. The attitude of his soul towards God is such as to produce the strongest effects on his power of action. It leaves his faculties clear and unimpassioned; it places him above accidents; it gives him courage and freedom. Trusting in God only, like the Psalmist, 'he fears no enemy;' he has no want. There is a sort of absoluteness in his position in the world, which can neither be made better nor worse; as St. Paul says, 'All things are his, whether life or death, or things present, or things to come.'

In merely human things, the aid and sympathy of others increase our power to act: it is also the fact that we can work more effectually and think more truly, where the issue is not staked on the result of our thought and work.

The confidence of success would be more than half the secret of success, did it not also lead to the relaxation of our efforts. But in the life of the believer, the sympathy, if such a figure of speech may be allowed, is not human but Divine; the confidence is not a confidence in ourselves, but in the power of God, which at once takes us out of ourselves and increases our obligation to exertion. The instances just mentioned have an analogy, though but a faint one, with that which we are considering. They are shadows of the support which we receive from the Infinite and Everlasting. As the philosopher said that his theory of fatalism was absolutely required to insure the repose necessary for moral action, it may be said, in a far higher sense, that the consciousness of a Divine Providence is necessary to enable a rational being to meet the present trials of life, and to look without fear on his future destiny.

(2) But yet more strongly is it felt that the love of Christ has this constraining power over souls, that here, if anywhere, we are unlocking the twisted chain of sympathy, and reaching the inmost mystery of human nature. The sight, once for all, of Christ crucified, recalling the thought of what, more than 1800 years ago, He suffered for us, has ravished the heart and melted the affections, and made the world seem new, and covered the earth itself with a fair vision, that is, a heavenly one. The strength of this feeling arises from its being directed towards a person, a real being, an individual like ourselves, who has actually endured all this for our sakes, who was above us, and yet became one of us and felt as we did, and was like ourselves a true man. The love which He felt towards us, we seek to return to Him; the unity which He has with the Divine nature, He communicates to us; His Father is our Father, His God our God. And as human love draws men onwards to make sacrifices, and to undergo sufferings for the good of others, Divine love also leads us to cast away the interests of this world, and rest only in the noblest object of love. And

this love is not only a feeling or sentiment, or attachment, such as we may entertain towards a parent, a child, or a wife, in which, pure and disinterested as it may be, some shadow of earthly passion unavoidably mingles; it is also the highest exercise of the reason, which it seems to endow with the force of the affections, making us think and feel at once. And although it begins in gentleness, and tenderness, and weakness, and is often supposed to be more natural to women than men, yet it grows up also to 'the fulness of the stature of the perfect man.' The truest note of the depth and sincerity of our feelings towards our fellow creatures is a manly—that is, a self-controlled—temper: still more is this true of the love of the soul towards Christ and God.

Every one knows what it is to become like those whom we admire or esteem; the impress which a disciple may sometimes have received from his teacher, or the servant from his Lord. Such devotion to a particular person can rarely be thought to open our hearts to love others also; it often tends to weaken the force of individual character. But the love of Christ is the conducting medium to the love of all mankind; the image which He impresses upon us is the image not of any particular individual, but of the Son of Man. And this image, as we draw nearer to it, is transfigured into the image of the Son of God. As we become like Him, we see Him as He is; and see ourselves and all other things with true human sympathy. Lastly, we are sensible that more than all we feel towards Him, He feels towards us, and that it is He who is drawing us to Him, while we seem to be drawing to Him ourselves. This is a part of that mystery of which the Apostle speaks, 'of the length, and depth, and breadth of the love of Christ,' which passeth knowledge. Mere human love rests on instincts, the working of which we cannot explain, but which nevertheless touch the inmost springs of our being. So, too, we have spiritual instincts, acting towards higher objects, still more suddenly and wonderfully capturing our souls in an instant, and making us indifferent to all things else. Such instincts show themselves in the weak no less than in the strong; they seem to be not so much an original part of our nature as to fulfil our nature, and add to it, and draw it out, until they make us different beings to ourselves and others. It was the quaint fancy of a sentimentalist to ask whether any one who remembers the first sight of a beloved person, could doubt the existence of magic. We may ask another question, Can any one who has ever known the love of Christ, doubt the existence of a spiritual power?

(3) The instrument whereby, above all others, we realize the power of God, and the love of Christ, which carries us into their presence, and places us within the circle of a Divine yet personal influence, is prayer. Prayer is the summing up of the Christian life in a definite act, which is at once inward and outward, the power of which on the character, like that of any other act, is proportioned to its intensity. The imagination of doing rightly adds little to our strength; even the wish to do so is not necessarily accompanied by a change of heart and conduct. But in prayer we imagine, and wish, and perform all in one. Our imperfect resolutions are offered up to God; our weakness becomes strength, our words deeds. No other action is so mysterious; there is none in which we seem, in the same manner, to renounce ourselves that we may be one with God.

Of what nature that prayer is which is effectual to the obtaining of its requests is a question of the same kind as what constitutes a true faith. That prayer, we should reply, which is itself most of an act, which is most immediately followed by action, which is most truthful, manly, self-controlled, which seems to lead and direct, rather than to follow, our natural emotions. That prayer which is its own answer because it asks not for any temporal good, but for union with God. That prayer which begins with the confession, 'We know not what to pray for as we ought;' which can never by any possibility interfere with the laws of nature, because even in extremity of danger or suffering, it seeks only the fulfilment of His will. That prayer which acknowledges that our enemies, or those of a different faith, are equally with ourselves in the hands of God; in which we never unwittingly ask for our own good at the expense of others. That prayer in which faith is strong enough to submit to experience; in which the soul of man is nevertheless conscious not of any self-produced impression, but of a true communion with the Author and Maker of his being.

In prayer, as in all religion, there is something that it is impossible to describe, and that seems to be untrue the moment it is expressed in words. In the relations of man with God, it is vain to attempt to separate what belongs to the finite and what to the infinite. We can feel, but we cannot analyze it. We can lay down practical rules for it, but can give no adequate account of it. It is a mystery which we do not need to fathom. In all religion there is an element of which we are conscious—which is no mystery, which ought to be and is on a level with reason and experience. There is something besides, which, in those who give way to every vague spiritual emotion, may often fall below reason (for to them it becomes a merely physical state); which may also raise us above ourselves, until reason and feeling meet in one, and the life on earth even of the poor and ignorant answers to the description of the Apostle, 'Having your conversation in heaven.'

This partial indistinctness of the subject of religion, even independently of mysticism or superstition, may become to intellectual minds a ground for doubting the truth of that which will not be altogether reduced to the rules of human knowledge, which seems to elude our grasp, and retires into the recesses of the soul the moment we ask for the demonstration of its existence. Against this natural suspicion let us set two observations: first, that if the Gospel had spoken to the reason only, and not to the feelings—if 'the way to the blessed life' had to be won by clearness of ideas, then it is impossible that 'to the poor the Gospel should have been first preached.' It would have begun at the other end of society, and probably remained, like Greek philosophy, the abstraction of educated men. Secondly, let us remark that even now, judged by its effects, the power of religion is of all powers the greatest. Knowledge itself is a weak instrument to stir the soul compared with religion; morality has no way to the heart of man; but the Gospel reaches the feelings and the intellect at once. In nations as well as individuals, in barbarous times as well as civilized, in the great crises of history especially, even in the latest ages, when the minds of men seem to wax cold, and all things remain the same as at the beginning, it has shown itself to be a reality without which human nature would cease to be what it is. Almost every one has had the witness of it in himself. No one, says Plato, ever passed from youth to age in unbelief of the gods, in heathen times. Hardly any educated person in a Christian land has passed from youth to age without some aspiration after a better life, some thought of the country to which he is going.

As a fact, it would be admitted by most, that, at some period of their lives, the thought of the world to come and of future judgement, the beauty and loveliness of the truths of the Gospel, the sense of the shortness of our days here, have wrought a more quickening and powerful effect than any moral truths or prudential maxims. Many a one would acknowledge that he has been carried whither he knew not; and had nobler thoughts, and felt higher aspirations, than the course of his ordinary life seemed to allow. These were the most important moments of his life for good or for evil; the critical points which have made him what he is, either as he used or neglected them. They came he knew not how, sometimes with some outward and apparent cause, at other times without—the result of affliction or sickness, or 'the wind blowing where it listeth.'

And if such changes and such critical points should be found to occur in youth more often than in age, in the poor and ignorant rather than in the educated, in women more often than in men—if reason and reflection seem to weaken as they regulate the springs of human action, this very fact may lead us to consider that reason, and reflection, and education, and the experience of age, and the force of manly sense, are not the links which bind us to the communion of the body of Christ; that it is rather to those qualities which we have, or may have, in common with our fellow-men, that the Gospel is promised; and that it is with the weak, the poor, the babes in Christ—not with the strong-minded, the resolute, the consistent—that we shall sit down in the kingdom of heaven.

ESSAY

ON

CONTRASTS OF PROPHECY

ROMANS XI.

EVERY reader of the Epistles must have remarked the opposite and apparently inconsistent uses, which the Apostle St. Paul makes of the Old Testament. This appearance of inconsistency arises out of the different and almost conflicting statements, which may be read in the Old Testament itself. The law and the prophets are their own witnesses, but they are witnesses also to a truth which is beyond them. Two spirits are found in them, and the Apostle sets aside the one, that he may establish the other. When he says that 'the man that doeth these things shall live in them,' x. 5, and again two verses afterwards, 'the word is very nigh unto thee, even in thy mouth and in thy heart,' he is using the authority of the law, first, that out of its own mouth he may condemn the law; secondly, that he may confirm the Gospel by the authority of that which he condemns. Still more striking are the contrasts of prophecy in which he reads, not only the rejection of Israel, but its restoration; the over-ruling providence of God, as well as the free agency of man; not only as it is written, 'God gave unto them a spirit of heaviness,' but, 'who hath believed our report;' nor only, 'all day long I have stretched forth my hand to a disobedient and gainsaying people,' but 'there shall come out of Sion a deliverer and he shall turn away iniquities from Jacob.' Experience and faith seem to contend together in the Apostle's own mind, and alike to find an echo in the two voices of prophecy.

It were much to be wished that we could agree upon a chronological arrangement of the Old Testament, which would approach more nearly to the true order in which the books were written, than that in which they have been handed down to us. Such an arrangement would throw great light on the interpretation of prophecy. At present, we scarcely resist the illusion exercised upon our minds by 'four prophets the greater, followed by twelve prophets the less;' some of the latter being of a prior date to any of the former. Even the distinction of the law and the prophets as well as of the Psalms and the prophets leads indirectly to a similar error. For many elements of the prophetical spirit enter into the law, and legal precepts are repeated by the prophets. The continuity of Jewish history is further broken by the Apocrypha. The four centuries before Christ were as fruitful of hopes and struggles and changes of thought and feeling in the Jewish people as any preceding period of their existence as a nation, perhaps more so. And yet we piece together the Old and New Testament as if the interval were blank leaves only. Few, if any, English writers have ever attempted to form a conception of the growth of the spirit of prophecy, from its first beginnings in the law itself, as it may be traced in the lives and characters of Samuel and David, and above all, of Elijah and his immediate successor; as it reappears a few years later, in the written prophecies respecting the house of Israel, and the surrounding nations (not even in the oldest of the prophets, without reference to Messiah's kingdom); or again after the carrying away of the ten tribes, as it concentrates itself in Judah, uttering a sadder and more mournful cry in the hour of captivity, yet in the multitude of sorrows increasing the comfort; the very dispersion of the people widening the prospect of Christ's kingdom, as the nation 'is cut short in righteousness,' God being so much the nearer to those who draw near to Him.

The fulfilment of prophecy has been sought for in a series of events which have been sometimes bent to make them fit, and one series of events has frequently taken the place of another. Even the passing circumstances of to-day or yesterday, at the distance of about two thousand years, and as many miles, which are but shadows flitting on the mountains compared with the deeper foundations of human history, are thought to be within the range of the prophet's eye. And it may be feared that, in attempting to establish a claim which, if it could be proved, might be made also for heathen oracles and prophecies, commentators have sometimes lost sight of those great characteristics which distinguish Hebrew prophecy from all other professing revelations of other religions: (1) the sense of the truthfulness, and holiness, and loving-kindness of the Divine Being, with which the prophet is as one possessed, which he can no more forget or doubt than he can cease to be himself; (2) their growth, that is, their growing perception of the moral nature of the revelation of God to man, apart from the commandments of the law or the privileges of the house of Israel.

There are some prophecies more national, of which the fortunes of the Jewish people are the only subject; others more individual, seeming to enter more into the recesses of the human soul, and which are, at the same time, more universal, rising above earthly things, and passing into the distant heaven. At one time the prophet embodies 'these thoughts of many hearts' as present, at another as future; in some cases as following out of the irrevocable decree of God, in others as dependent on the sin or repentance of man. At one moment he is looking for the destruction of Israel, at another for its consolation; going from one of these aspects of the heavenly vision to another, like St. Paul himself in successive verses. And sometimes he sees the Lord's house exalted in the top of the mountains, and the image of the 'Wonderful, Counsellor, the Mighty Prince, the Everlasting God.' At other times, his vision is of the Servant whom it 'pleased the Lord to bruise,' whose form was 'marred more than that of the sons of men,' who was 'led as a lamb to the slaughter.'

National, individual, — spiritual, temporal, — present, future,—rejection, restoration,—faith, the law,—Providence, freewill,—mercy, sacrifice,—Messiah suffering and triumphant,—are so many pairs of opposites with reference to which the structure of prophecy admits of being examined. It is true that such an examination is nothing more than a translation or decomposition of prophecy into the modes of thought of our own time, and is far from reproducing the living image which presented itself to the eyes of the prophet. But, like all criticism, it makes us think; it enables us to observe fresh points of connexion between the Old Testament and the New; it keeps us from losing our way in the region of allegory or of modern history. Many things are unlearnt as well as learnt by the aid of criticism; it clears the mind of conventional interpretations, teaching us to look amid the symbols of time and place for the higher and universal meaning.

Prophecy has a human as well as a Divine element: that is to say, it partakes of the ordinary workings of the mind. There is also something beyond which the analogy of human knowledge fails to explain. Could the prophet himself have been asked what was the nature of that impulse by which he was carried away, he would have replied that 'the God of Israel was a living God' who had 'ordained him a prophet before he came forth from the womb.' Of the Divine element no other account can be given—'it pleased God to raise up individuals in a particular age and country, who had a purer and loftier sense of truth than their fellow men.' Prophecy would be no longer prophecy if we could untwist its soul. But the human part admits of being analyzed like poetry or history, of which it is a kind of union; it is written with a man's pen in a known language; it is cast in the imaginative form of early language itself. The truth of God comes into contact with the world, clothing itself in human feelings, revealing the lesson of historical events. But human feelings and the lesson of events vary, and in this sense the prophetic lesson varies too. Even in the workings of our own minds we may perceive this; those who think much about themselves and God cannot but be conscious of great changes and transitions of feeling at different periods of life. We are the creatures of impressions and associations; and although Providence has not made our knowledge of himself dependent on these impressions, He has allowed it to be coloured by them. We cannot say that in the hours of prosperity and adversity, in health and sickness, in poverty and wealth, our sense of God's dealings with us is absolutely the same; still less, that all our prayers and aspirations have received the answer that we wished or expected. And sometimes the thoughts of our own hearts go before to God; at other times, the power of God seems to anticipate the thoughts of our hearts. And sometimes, in looking back at our past lives, it seems as if God had done everything; at other times, we are conscious of the movement of our own will. The wide world itself also, and the political fortunes of our country, have been enveloped in the light or darkness which rested on our individual soul.

Especially are we liable to look at religious truth under many aspects, if we live amid changes of religious opinions, or are witnesses of some revival or reaction in religion, or supposing our lot to be cast in critical periods of history, such as extend the range and powers of human nature, or certainly enlarge our experience of it. Then the germs of new truths will subsist side by side with the remains of old ones; and thoughts, that are really inconsistent, will have a place together in our minds, without our being able to perceive their inconsistency. The inconsistency will be traced by posterity; they will remark that up to a particular point we saw clearly; but that no man is beyond his age—there was a circle which we could not pass. And some one living in our own day may look into the future with 'eagle eye;' he may weigh and balance with a sort of omniscience the moral forces of the world, perhaps with something too much of confidence that the right will ultimately prevail even on earth; and after ages may observe that his predictions were not always fulfilled or not fulfilled at the time he said.

Such general reflections may serve as an introduction to what at first appears an anomaly in prophecy—that it has not one, but many lessons; and that the manner in which it teaches those lessons is through the alternations of the human soul itself. There are failings of prophecy, just as there are failings in our own anticipations of the future. And sometimes when we had hoped to be delivered it has seemed good to God to afflict us still. But it does not follow that religion is therefore a cunningly devised fable, either now or then. Neither the faith of the people, nor of the prophet, in the God of their fathers is shaken because the prophecies are not realized before their eyes; because 'the vision,' as they said, 'is delayed;' because in many cases events seem to occur which make it impossible that it should be accomplished. A true instinct still enables them to separate the prophets of Jehovah from the numberless false prophets with whom the land swarmed; they are gifted with the 'same discernment of spirits' which distinguished Micaiah from the four hundred whom Ahab called. The internal evidence of the true prophet we are able to recognize in the written prophecies also. In the earliest as well as the latest of them there is the same spirit one and continuous, the same witness of the invisible God, the same character of the Jewish people, the same law of justice and mercy in the dealings of Providence with respect to them, the same 'walking with God' in the daily life of the prophet himself.

'Novum Testamentum in vetere latet,' has come to be a favourite word among theologians, who have thought they saw in the truths of the Gospel the original design as well as the evangelical application of the Mosaical law. With a deeper meaning, it may be said that prophecy grows out of itself into the Gospel. Not, as some extreme critics have conceived, that the facts of the Gospel history are but the crystallization of the imagery of prophecy. Say, rather, that the river of the water of life is beginning again to flow. The Son of God himself is 'that prophet'—the prophet, not of one nation only, but of all mankind, in whom the particularity of the old prophets is finally done away, and the ever-changing form of the 'servant in whom my soul delighteth' at last finds rest. St. Paul, too, is a prophet who has laid aside the poetical and authoritative garb of old times, and is wrapped in the rhetorical or dialectical one of his own age. The language of the old prophets comes unbidden into his mind; it seems to be the natural expression of his own thoughts. Separated from Joel, Amos, Hosea, Micah, and Isaiah by an interval of about eight hundred years, he finds their words very near to him 'even in his mouth and his heart;' that is the word which he preached. When they spoke of forgiveness of sins, of non-imputation of sins, of a sudden turning to God, what did this mean but righteousness by faith? when they said 'I will have mercy, and not sacrifice,' here also was imaged the great truth, that salvation was not of the law. If St. Paul would have 'no man judged for a new moon or sabbath,' the prophets of old time had again and again said in the name of Jehovah 'Your new moons and sabbaths I cannot away with.' Like the elder prophets, he came not 'to build up a temple made with hands,' but to teach a moral truth; like them he went forth alone, and not in connexion with the

Church at Jerusalem. His calling is to be Apostle of the Gentiles; they also sometimes pass beyond the borders of Israel, to receive Egypt and Assyria into covenant with God.

It is not, however, this deeper unity between St. Paul and the prophets of the old dispensation that we are about to consider further, but a more superficial parallelism, which is afforded by the alternation or successive representation of the purposes of God towards Israel, which we meet with in the Old Testament, and which recurs in the Epistle to the Romans. Like the elder prophets, St. Paul also 'prophesies in part,' feeling after events rather than seeing them, and divided between opposite aspects of the dealings of Providence with mankind. This changing feeling often finds an expression in the words of Isaiah or the Psalmist, or the author of the book of Deuteronomy. Hence a kind of contrast springs up in the writings of the Apostle, which admits of being traced to its source in the words of the prophets. Portions of his Epistles are the *disjecta membra* of prophecy. Oppositions are brought into view by him, and may be said to give occasion to a struggle in his own mind, which were unobserved by the prophets themselves. For so far from prophecy setting forth one unchanging purpose of God, it seems rather to represent a succession of purposes conditional on men's actions; speaking as distinctly of the rejection as of the restoration of Israel; and of the restoration almost as the correlative of the rejection; often, too, making a transition from the temporal to the spiritual. Some of these contrasts it is proposed to consider in detail as having an important bearing on St. Paul's Epistles, especially on the Epistles to the Thessalonians, and on chapters x.–xii. of the Epistle to the Romans.

(1) All the prophets are looking for and hastening to 'the day of the Lord,' the 'great day,' 'which there is none like,' 'the day of the Lord's sacrifice,' the 'day of visitation,' of 'the great slaughter,' in which the Lord shall judge 'in the

valley of Jehoshaphat,' in which 'they shall go into the clefts of the rocks, and into the tops of the ragged rocks, for fear of the Lord, and for the glory of his majesty, when he ariseth to shake terribly the earth.' That day is the fulfilment and realization of prophecy, without which it would cease to have any meaning, just as religion itself would cease to have any meaning to ourselves, were there no future life, or retribution of good and evil. All the prophets are in spirit present at it; living alone with God, and hardly mingling with men on earth, they are fulfilled with its terrors and its glories. For the earth is not to go on for ever as it is, the wickednesses of the house of Israel are not to last for ever. First, the prophet sees the pouring out of the vials of wrath upon them; then, more at a distance, follows the vision of mercy, in which they are to be comforted, and their enemies, the ministers of God's vengeance on them, in turn punished. And evil and oppression everywhere, so far as it comes within the range of the prophet's eye, is to be punished in that day, and good is to prevail.

In these 'terrors of the day of the Lord,' of which the prophets speak, the fortunes of the Jewish people mingle with another vision of a more universal judgement, and it has been usual to have recourse to the double senses of prophecy to separate the one from the other, an instrument of interpretation which has also been applied to the New Testament for the same purpose. Not in this way could the prophet or apostle themselves have conceived them. To them they were not two, but one; not 'double one against the other,' or separable into the figure and the thing signified. For the figure is in early ages the mode of conception also. More true would it be to say that the judgements of God on the Jewish people were an anticipation or illustration of His dealings with the world generally. If a separation is made at all, let us rather separate the accidents of time and place from that burning sense of the righteousness of God, which somewhere we cannot tell where, at some time we cannot tell when, must and will have retribution on evil; which has this other note of its Divine character, that in judgement it remembers mercy, pronouncing no endless penalty or irreversible doom, even upon the house of Israel. This twofold lesson of goodness and severity speaks to us as well as to the Jews. Better still to receive the words of prophecy as we have them, and to allow the feeling which it utters to find its way to our hearts, without stopping to mark out what was not separated in the prophet's own mind and cannot therefore be divided by us.

Other contrasts are traceable in the teaching of the prophets respecting the day of the Lord. In that day the Lord is to judge Israel, and He is to punish Egypt and Assyria; and yet it is said also, the Lord shall heal Egypt, and Israel shall be the third with Egypt and Assyria whom the Lord shall bless (Is. xix. 25). In many of the prophecies also the judgement is of two kinds; it is a judgement on Israel, which is executed by the heathen; it is a judgement against the heathen, and in favour of Israel, in which God himself is sometimes said to be their advocate as well as their judge 'in that day.' A singular parallel with the New Testament is presented by another contrast which occurs in a single passage. That the day of the Lord is near, 'it cometh, it cometh,' is the language of all the prophets; and yet there were those who said also in Ezekiel's time, 'The days are prolonged, and every vision faileth. Tell them therefore, Thus saith the Lord God; I will make this proverb to cease, and they shall no more use it as a proverb in Israel; but say unto them, The days are at hand, and the effect of every vision' (xii. 22). (Compare 2 Pet. iii. 4, 'Where is the promise of his coming?') On the other hand, in the later chapters of Isaiah (xl. seq.) we seem to trace the same feeling as in the New Testament itself: the anticipation of prophecy has ceased; the hour of its fulfilment has arrived; men seem to be conscious that they are living during the restoration of Israel as the disciples at the day of Pentecost felt that they were living amid the things spoken of by the prophet Joel.

(2) A closer connexion with the Epistle to the Romans is furnished by the double and, on the surface, inconsistent language of prophecy respecting the rejection and restoration of Israel. These seem to follow one another often in successive verses. It is true that the appearance of inconsistency is greater than the reality, owing to the lyrical and concentrated style of prophecy (some of its greatest works being not much longer than this 'cobweb[1]' of an essay); and this leads to opposite feelings and trains of thought being presented to us together, without the preparations and joinings which would be required in the construction of a modern poem. Yet, after making allowance for this peculiarity of the ancient Hebrew style, it seems as if there were two thoughts ever together in the prophet's mind: captivity, restoration,—judgement, mercy,—sin, repentance, —'the people sitting in darkness, and the great light.'

There are portions of prophecy in which the darkness is deep and enduring, 'darkness that may be felt,' in which the prophet is living amid the sins and sufferings of the people; and hope is a long way off from them—when they need to be awakened rather than comforted; and things must be worse, as men say, before they can become better. Such is the spirit of the greater part of the book of Jeremiah. But the tone of prophecy is on the whole that of alternation; God deals with the Israelites as with children; he cannot bear to punish them for long; his heart comes back to them when they are in captivity; their very helplessness gives them a claim on him. Vengeance may endure for a time, but soon the full tide of His mercy returns upon them. Another voice is heard, saying, 'Comfort ye, comfort ye, my people.' 'Speak ye comfortably to Jerusalem, and say unto her that she hath received of the Lord's hand

[1] Carlyle.

double for all her sins.' So from the vision of God on Mount Sinai, at the giving of the Law amid storms and earthquakes, arises that tender human relation in which the Gospel teaches that He stands, not merely to His Church as a body, but to each one of us.

Naturally this human feeling is called forth most in the hour of adversity. As the affliction deepens, the hope also enlarges, seeming often to pass beyond the boundaries of this life into a spiritual world. Though their sins are as scarlet, they shall be white as snow; when Jerusalem is desolate, there shall be a tabernacle on Mount Sion. The formula in which this enlargement of the purposes of God is introduced, is itself worthy of notice. 'It shall be no more said, The Lord liveth, that brought up the children of Israel out of the land of Egypt; but, The Lord liveth, that brought up the children of Israel from the land of the North, and from all the lands whither he had driven them.' Their old servitude in Egypt came back to their minds now that they were captives in a strange land, and the remembrance that they had already been delivered from it was an earnest that they were yet to return. Deeply rooted in the national mind, it had almost become an attribute of God himself that He was their deliverer from the house of bondage.

With this narrower view of the return of the children of Israel from captivity, not without a remembrance of that great empire which had once extended from the River of Egypt to the Euphrates, there blended also the hope of another kingdom in which dwelt righteousness—the kingdom of Solomon 'become the kingdom of Christ and God.' The children of Israel had been in their origin 'the fewest of all people,' and the most alien to the nations round about. The Lord their God was a jealous God, who would not suffer them to mingle with the idolatries of the heathen. And in that early age of the world, when national life was so strong and individuals so feeble, we cannot conceive how the worship of the true God could have been otherwise preserved. But the day had passed away when the nation could be trusted with the preservation of the faith of Jehovah; 'it had never been good for much at any time.' The prophets, too, seem to withdraw from the scenes of political events; they are no longer the judges and leaders of Israel; it is a part of their mission to commit to writing for the use of after ages the predictions which they utter. We pass into another country, to another kingdom in which the prospect is no more that which Moses saw from Mount Pisgah, but in which the 'Lord's horn is exalted in the top of the mountains and all nations flock to it.'

In this kingdom the Gentiles have a place, still on the outskirts, but not wholly excluded from the circle of God's providence. Sometimes they are placed on a level with Israel, the 'circumcised with the uncircumcised,' as if only to teach the Apostle's lesson, 'that there is no respect of persons with God' (Jer. ix. 25, 26; compare Rom. ii. 12-28). At other times they are themselves the subjects of promises and threatenings (Jer. xii. 14-17). It is to them that God will turn when His patience is exhausted with the rebellions of Israel; for whom it shall be 'more tolerable' than for Israel and Judah in the day of the Lord. They are those upon whom, though at a distance, the brightness of Jehovah must overflow; who, in the extremities of the earth, are bathed with the light of His presence. Helpers of the joy of Israel, they pour with gifts and offerings through the open gates of the city of God. They have a part in Messiah's kingdom, not of right, but because without them it would be imperfect and incomplete. In one passage only, which is an exception to the general spirit of prophecy, Israel 'makes the third' with Egypt and Assyria, 'whom the Lord of Hosts shall bless' (Is. xix. 18-25).

It was not possible that such should be the relation of the Gentiles to the people of God in the Epistles of St. Paul. Experience seemed to invert the natural order of Providence —the Jew first and afterwards the Gentile. Accordingly, what is subordinate in the prophets, becomes of principal importance in the application of the Apostle. The dark sayings about the Gentiles had more meaning than the utterers of them were aware of. Events connected them with the rejection of the Jews, of which the same prophets spoke. Not only had the Gentiles a place on the outskirts of the people of God, gathering up the fragments of promises 'under the table;' they themselves were the spiritual Israel. When the prophets spoke of the Mount Sion, and all nations flowing to it, they were not expecting literally the restoration of the kingdom to Israel. They spoke of they knew not what—of something that had as yet no existence upon the earth. What that was, the vision on the way to Damascus, no less than the history of the Church and the world, revealed to the Apostle of the Gentiles.

(3) Another characteristic of Hebrew prophecy is the transition from the nation to the individual. That is to say, first the nation becomes an individual; it is spoken of, thought of, dealt with, as a person, it 'makes the third' with God and the prophet. Almost a sort of drama is enacted between them, the argument of which is the mercy and justice of God; and the Jewish nation itself has many parts assigned to it. Sometimes she is the 'adulterous sister,' the 'wife of whoredoms,' who has gone astray with Chaldean and Egyptian lovers. In other passages, still retaining the same personal relation to God, the 'daughter of my people' is soothed and comforted; then a new vision rises before the prophet's mind—not the same with that of the Jewish people, but not wholly distinct from it, in which the suffering prophet himself, or Cyrus the prophet king, have a part—the vision of 'the servant of God,' 'the Saviour with dyed garments' from Bosra—'he shall grow up before him as a tender plant;' 'he is led as a lamb to the slaughter' (Is. liii. 2, 7; compare Jer. xi. 19). Yet there is a kind of glory even on earth in this image of gentleness and suffering: 'A bruised reed shall he not

break, and smoking flax shall he not quench, until he hath brought forth judgement unto victory.' We feel it to be strange, and yet it is true. So we have sometimes seen the image of the kingdom of God among ourselves, not in noble churches or scenes of ecclesiastical power or splendour, but in the face of some child or feeble person, who, after overcoming agony, is about to depart and be with Christ.

Analogies from Greek philosophy may seem far-fetched in reference to Hebrew prophecy, yet there are particular points in which subjects the most dissimilar receive a new light from one another. In the writings of Plato and Aristotle, and the philosophers who were their successors, moral truths gradually separate from politics, and the man is acknowledged to be different from the mere citizen: and there arises a sort of ideal of the individual, who has a responsibility to himself only. The growth of Hebrew prophecy is so different; its figures and modes of conception are so utterly unlike; there seems such a wide gulf between morality which almost excludes God, and religion which exists only in God, that at first sight we are unwilling to allow any similarity to exist between them. Yet an important point in both of them is really the same. For the transition from the nation to the individual is also the more perfect revelation of God himself, the change from the temporal to the spiritual, from the outward glories of Messiah's reign to the kingdom of God which is within. Prophets as well as apostles teach the near intimate personal relation of man to God. The prophet and psalmist, who is at one moment inspired with the feelings of a whole people, returns again to God to express the lowliest sorrows of the individual Christian. The thought of the Israel of God is latent in prophecy itself, not requiring a great nation or company of believers; 'but where one is' there is God present with him.

There is another way also in which the individual takes the place of the nation in the purposes of God; 'a remnant shall be saved.' In the earlier books of the Old Testament, the whole people is bound up together for good or for evil. In the law especially, there is no trace that particular tribes or individuals are to be singled out for the favour of God. Even their great men are not so much individuals as representatives of the whole people. They serve God as a nation; as a nation they go astray. If, in the earlier times of Jewish history, we suppose an individual good man living 'amid an adulterous and crooked generation,' we can scarcely imagine the relation in which he would stand to the blessings and cursings of the law. Would the righteous perish with the wicked? That be 'far from thee, O Lord.' Yet 'prosperity, the blessing of the Old Testament,' was bound up with the existence of the nation. Gradually the germ of the new dispensation begins to unfold itself; the bands which held the nation together are broken in pieces; a fragment only is preserved, a branch, in the Apostle's language, cut off from the patriarchal stem, to be the beginning of another Israel.

The passage quoted by St. Paul in the eleventh chapter of the Romans is the first indication of this change in God's mode of dealing with His people. The prophet Elijah wanders forth into the wilderness to lay before the Lord the iniquities of the people: 'The children of Israel have forsaken thy covenant, thrown down thine altars, and slain thy prophets with the sword.' 'But what,' we may ask with the Apostle, 'saith the answer of God to him?' Not 'They are corrupt, they are altogether become abominable,' but 'Yet I have seven thousand men who have not bowed the knee to Baal.' The whole people were not to be regarded as one; there were a few who still preserved, amid the general corruption, the worship of the true God.

The marked manner in which the answer of God is introduced, the contrast of the 'still small voice' with the thunder, the storm, and the earthquake, the natural symbols of the presence of God in the law—the contradiction of the words spoken to the natural bent of the prophet's mind, and the greatness of Elijah's own character—all tend to stamp this passage as marking one of the epochs of prophecy. The solitude of the prophet and his separation in 'the mount of God,' from the places in which 'men ought to worship,' are not without meaning. There had not always 'been this proverb in the house of Israel;' but from this time onwards it is repeated again and again. We trace the thought of a remnant to be saved in captivity, or to return from captivity, through a long succession of prophecies—Hosea, Amos, Micah, Isaiah, Jeremiah, Ezekiel; —it is the text of almost all the prophets, passing, as a familiar word, from the Old Testament to the New. The voice uttered to Elijah was the beginning of this new Revelation.

(4) Coincident with the promise of a remnant is the precept, 'I will have mercy and not sacrifice,' which, in modern language, opposes the moral to the ceremonial law. It is another and the greatest step onward towards the spiritual dispensation. Moral and religious truths hang together; no one can admit one of them in the highest sense, without admitting a principle which involves the rest. He who acknowledged that God was a God of mercy and not of sacrifice, could not long have supposed that He dealt with nations only, or that He raised men up for no other end but to be vessels of His wrath or monuments of His vengeance. For a time there might be 'things too hard for him,' clouds resting on his earthly tabernacle, when he 'saw the ungodly in such prosperity;' yet had he knowledge enough, as he 'went into the sanctuary of God,' and confessed himself to be 'a stranger and pilgrim upon the earth.'

It is in the later prophets that the darkness begins to be dispelled and the ways of God justified to man. Ezekiel is above all others the teacher of this 'new commandment.' The familiar words, 'when the wicked man turneth away from his wickedness, and doeth that which is lawful and right, he shall save his soul alive,' are the theme of a great part of this wonderful book. Other prophets have more of poetical beauty, a deeper sense of Divine things, a tenderer feeling of the mercies of God to His people; none teach so simply this great moral lesson, to us the first of all lessons. On the eve of the captivity, and in the midst of it, when the hour of mercy is past, and no image is too loathsome to describe the iniquities of Israel, still the prophet does not forget that the Lord will not destroy the righteous with the wicked: 'Though Noah, Daniel, and Job were in the land, as I live, saith the Lord, they shall deliver neither son nor daughter; they shall deliver but their own souls by their righteousness' (xiv. 20). 'Yet, behold, therein shall be left a remnant; and they shall know that I have not done without cause all that I have done, saith the Lord' (ver. 22, 23).

It is observable that, in the Book of Ezekiel as well as of Jeremiah, this new principle on which God deals with mankind, is recognized as a contradiction to the rule by which he had formerly dealt with them. At the commencement of chap. xviii, as if with the intention of revoking the words of the second commandment, 'visiting the sins of the fathers upon the children,' it is said:—

'The word of the Lord came unto me again, saying,

'What mean ye, that ye use this proverb concerning the land of Israel, saying, The fathers have eaten sour grapes, and the children's teeth are set on edge?

'*As* I live, saith the Lord GOD, ye shall not have *occasion* any more to use this proverb in Israel.

'Behold, all souls are mine; as the soul of the father, so also the soul of the son is mine: the soul that sinneth, it shall die.'

Similar language occurs also in Jer. xxxi. 29, in a connexion which makes it still more remarkable, as the new truth is described as a part of that fuller revelation which God will give of himself, when He makes a new covenant with the house of Israel. And yet the same prophet, as if not at all times conscious of his own lesson, says also in his prayer to God (Lam. v. 7), 'Our fathers have sinned and are not, and we have borne their iniquities.' The truth which he felt was not one and the same always, but rather two opposite truths, like the Law and the Gospel, which, for a while, seemed to struggle with one another in the teaching of the prophet and the heart of man.

And yet this opposition was not necessarily conscious to the prophet himself. Isaiah, who saw the whole nation going before to judgement, did not refrain from preaching the lessons, 'If ye be willing and obedient,' and 'Let the wicked forsake his way, and the unrighteous man his thoughts.' Ezekiel, the first thought and spirit of whose prophecies might be described in modern language as the responsibility of man, like Micaiah in the Book of Kings, seemed to see the false prophets inspired by Jehovah himself to their own destruction. As in the prophet, so in the Apostle, there was no sense that the two lessons were in any degree inconsistent with each other. It is an age of criticism and philosophy, which, in making the attempt to conceive the relation of God to the world in a more abstract way, has invented for itself the perplexity, or, may we venture to say, by the very fact of acknowledging it, has also found its solution. The intensity with which the prophet felt the truths that he revealed, the force with which he uttered them, the desire with which he yearned after their fulfilment, have passed from the earth; but the truths themselves remain an everlasting possession. We seem to look upon them more calmly, and adjust them more truly. They no longer break through the world of sight with unequal power; they can never again be confused with the accidents of time and place. The history of the Jewish people has ceased to be the only tabernacle in which they are enshrined; they have an independent existence, and a light and order of their own.

ESSAY

ON

CASUISTRY

ROMANS XIV.

———◆———

RELIGION and morality seem often to become entangled in circumstances. The truth which came, not 'to bring peace upon earth, but a sword,' could not but give rise to many new and conflicting obligations. The kingdom of God had to adjust itself with the kingdoms of this world; though 'the children were free,' they could not escape the fulfilment of duties to their Jewish or Roman governors; in the bosom of a family there were duties too; in society there were many points of contact with the heathen. A new element of complexity had been introduced in all the relations between man and man, giving rise to many new questions, which might be termed, in the phraseology of modern times, 'cases of conscience.'

Of these the one which most frequently recurs in the Epistles of St. Paul, is the question respecting meats and drinks, which appears to have agitated both the Roman and Corinthian Churches, as well as those of Jerusalem and Antioch, and probably, in a greater or less degree, every other Christian community in the days of the Apostle. The scruple which gave birth to it was not confined to

Christianity; it was Eastern rather than Christian, and originated in a feeling into which entered, not only Oriental notions of physical purity and impurity, but also those of caste and of race. With other Eastern influences it spread towards the West, in the flux of all religions, exercising a peculiar power on the susceptible temper of mankind.

The same tendency exhibited itself in various forms. In one form it was the scruple of those who ate herbs, while others 'had faith' to eat anything. The Essenes and Therapeutae among the Jews, and the Pythagoreans in the heathen world, had a similar feeling respecting the use of animal food. It was a natural association which led to such an abstinence. In the East, ever ready to connect, or rather incapable of separating, ideas of moral and physical impurity—where the heat of the climate rendered animal food unnecessary, if not positively unhealthful; where corruption rapidly infected dead organized matter; where, lastly, ancient tradition and ceremonies told of the sacredness of animals and the mysteriousness of animal life— nature and religion alike seemed to teach the same lesson, it was safer to abstain. It was the manner of such a scruple to propagate itself. He who revolted at animal food could not quietly sit by and see his neighbour partake of it. The ceremonialism of the age was the tradition of thousands of years, and passed by a sort of contagion from one race to another, from Paganism or Judaism to Christianity. How to deal with this 'second nature' was a practical difficulty among the first Christians. The Gospel was not a gospel according to the Essenes, and the church could not exclude those who held the scruples, neither could it be narrowed to them; it would not pass judgement on them at all. Hence the force of the Apostle's words: 'Him that is weak in the faith receive, not to the decision of his doubts.'

There was another point in reference to which the same spirit of ceremonialism propagated itself, viz. meats offered to idols. Even if meat in general were innocent and a creature of God, it could hardly be a matter of indifference to partake of that which had been 'sacrificed to devils;' least of all, to sit at meat in the idol's temple. True, the idol was 'nothing in the world'—a block of stone, to which the words good or evil were misapplied; 'a graven image' which the workman made, 'putting his hand to the hammer,' as the old prophets described in their irony. And such is the Apostle's own feeling (1 Cor. viii. 4; x. 19). But he has also the other feeling which he himself regards as not less true (1 Cor. x. 20), and which was more natural to the mind of the first believers. When they saw the worshippers of the idol revelling in impurity, they could not but suppose that a spirit of some kind was there. Their warfare, as the Apostle had told them, was not 'against flesh and blood, but against principalities, against powers, against the rulers of the darkness of this world.' Evil angels were among them; where would they more naturally take up their abode than around the altars and in the temples of the heathen? And if they had been completely free from superstition, and could have regarded the heathen religions which they saw enthroned over the world simply with contempt, still the question would have arisen, What connexion were they to have with them and with their worshippers? a question not easy to be answered in the bustle of Rome and Corinth, where every circumstance of daily life, every amusement, every political and legal right, was in some way bound up with the heathen religions. Were they to go out of the world? if not, what was to be their relation to those without?

A third instance of the same ceremonialism so natural to that age, and to ourselves so strange and unmeaning, is illustrated by the words of the Jerusalem Christians to the Apostle—'Thou wentest in unto men uncircumcised, and didst eat with them;' a scruple so strong that, probably, St. Peter himself was never entirely free from it, and at any rate yielded to the fear of it in others when withstood by St. Paul at Antioch. This scruple may be said in one sense to be hardly capable of an explanation, and in another not to need one. For, probably, nothing can give our minds any conception of the nature of the feeling, the intense hold which it exercised, the concentration which it was of every national and religious prejudice, the constraint which was required to get rid of it as a sort of *horror naturalis* in the minds of Jews; while, on the other hand, feelings at the present day not very dissimilar exist, not only in Eastern countries, but among ourselves. There is nothing strange in human nature being liable to them, or in their long lingering and often returning, even when reason and charity alike condemn them. We ourselves are not insensible to differences of race and colour, and may therefore be able partially to comprehend (allowing for the difference of East and West) what was the feeling of Jews and Jewish Christians towards men uncircumcised.

On the last point St. Paul maintains but one language:—
'In Christ Jesus there is neither circumcision nor uncircumcision.' No compromise could be allowed here, without destroying the Gospel that he preached. But the other question of meats and drinks, when separated from that of circumcision, admitted of various answers and points of view. Accordingly there is an appearance of inconsistency in the modes in which the Apostle resolves it. All these modes have a use and interest for ourselves; though our difficulties are not the same as those of the early Christians, the words speak to us, so long as prudence, and faith, and charity are the guides of Christian life. It is characteristic of the Apostle that his answers run into one another, as though each of them to different individuals, and all in their turn, might present the solution of the difficulty.

We may begin with 1 Cor. x. 25, which may be termed the rule of Christian prudence: 'Whatsoever is sold in the shambles, that eat, asking no question for conscience sake.' That is to say: 'Buy food as other men do; perhaps what you purchase has come from the idol's temple, perhaps not. Do not encourage your conscience in raising scruples, life will become impossible if you do. One question involves another and another and another without end. The manly and the Christian way is to cut them short; both as tending to weaken the character and as inconsistent with the very nature of spiritual religion.'

So we may venture to amplify the Apostle's precept, which breathes the same spirit of moderation as his decisions respecting celibacy and marriage. Among ourselves the remark is often made that 'extremes are practically untrue.' This is another way of putting the same lesson:—If I may not sit in the idol's temple, it may be plausibly argued, neither may I eat meats offered to idols; and if I may not eat meats offered to idols, then it logically follows that I ought not to go into the market where idols' meat is sold. The Apostle snaps the chain of this misapplied logic: there must be a limit somewhere; we must not push consistency where it is practically impossible. A trifling scruple is raised to the level of a religious duty, and another and another, until religion is made up of scruples, and the light of life fades, and the ways of life narrow themselves.

It is not hard to translate the Apostle's precept into the language of our time. Instances occur in politics, in theology, in our ordinary occupations, in which beyond a certain point consistency is impossible. Take for example the following: A person feels that he would be wrong in carrying on his business, or going to public amusements, on a Sunday. He says: If it be wrong for me to work, it is wrong to make the servants in my house work; or if it be wrong to go to public amusements, it is wrong to enjoy the recreation of walking on a Sunday. So it may be argued that, because slavery is wrong, therefore it is not right to purchase the produce of slavery, or that of which the produce of slavery is a part, and so on without end, until we are forced out of the world from a remote fear of contagion with evil. Or I am engaged in a business which may be in some degree deleterious to the health or injurious to the morals of those employed in it, or I trade in some articles of commerce which are unwholesome or dangerous, or I let a house or a ship to another whose employment is of this description. Numberless questions of the same kind relating to the profession of a clergyman, an advocate, or a soldier, have been pursued into endless consequences. Is the mind of any person so nicely balanced that 'every one of six hundred disputed propositions' is the representative of his exact belief? or can every word in a set form of prayer at all times reflect the feeling of those who read or follow it? There is no society to which we can belong, no common act of business or worship in which two or three are joined together, in which such difficulties are not liable to arise. Three editors conduct a newspaper, can it express equally the conviction of all the three? Three lawyers sign an opinion in common, is it the judgement of all or of one or two of them? High-minded men have often got themselves into a false position by regarding these questions in too abstract a way. The words of the Apostle are a practical answer to them which may be paraphrased thus: 'Do as other men do in a Christian country,' Conscience will say, 'He who is guilty of the least, is guilty of all.' In the Apostle's language it then becomes 'the strength of sin,' encouraging us to despair of all, because in that mixed condition of life in which God has placed us we cannot fulfil all.

In accordance with the spirit of the same principle of doing as other men do, the Apostle further implies that believers are to accept the hospitality of the heathen (1 Cor. x. 27). But here a modification comes in, which may be termed the law of Christian charity or courtesy:— Avoid giving offence, or, as we might say, 'Do not defy opinion.' Eat what is set before you; but if a person sitting at meat pointedly says to you, 'This was offered to idols,' do not eat. 'All things are lawful, but all things are not expedient,' and this is one of the not-expedient class. There appears to be a sort of inconsistency in this advice, as there must always be inconsistency in the rules of practical life which are relative to circumstances. It might be said: 'We cannot do one thing at one time, and another thing at another; now be guided by another man's conscience, now by our own.' It might be retorted, 'Is not this the dissimulation which you blame in St. Peter?' To which it may be answered in turn: 'But a man may do one thing at one time, another thing at another time, "becoming to the Jews a Jew," if he do it in such a manner as to avoid the risk of misconstruction.' And this again admits of a retort: 'Is it possible to avoid misconstruction? Is it not better to dare to be ourselves, to act like ourselves, to speak like ourselves, to think like ourselves?' We seem to have lighted unawares on two varieties of human disposition; the one harmonizing and adapting itself to the perplexities of life, the other rebelling against them, and seeking to disentangle itself from them. Which side of this argument shall we take; neither or both? The Apostle appears to take both sides; for in the abrupt transition that follows, he immediately adds, 'Why is my liberty to be judged of another man's conscience? what right has another man to attack me for what I do in the innocency of my heart?' It is good advice to say, 'Regard the opinions of others;' and equally good advice to say, 'Do not regard the opinions of others.' We must balance between the two; and over all, adjusting the scales, is the law of Christian love.

Both in 1 Cor. viii. and Rom. xiv. the Apostle adds another principle, which may be termed the law of individual conscience, which we must listen to in ourselves and regard in others. 'He that doubteth is damned; whatsoever is not of faith is sin.' All things are lawful to him who feels them to be lawful, but the conscience may be polluted by the most indifferent things. When we eat, we should remember that the consequence of following our example may be serious to others. For not only may our brother be offended at us, but also by our example be drawn into sin; that is, to do what, though indifferent in itself, is sin to him. And so the weak brother, for whom Christ died, may perish through our fault; that is, he may lose his peace and harmony of soul and conscience void of offence, and all through our heedlessness in doing some unnecessary thing, which were far better left undone.

Cases may be readily imagined, in which, like the preceding, the rule of conduct here laid down by the Apostle would involve dissimulation. So many thousand scruples and opinions as there are in the world, we should have 'to go out of the world' to fulfil it honestly. All reserve, it may be argued, tends to break up the confidence between man and man; and there are times in which concealment of our opinions, even respecting things indifferent, would be treacherous and mischievous; there are times, too, in which things cease to be indifferent, and it is our duty to speak out respecting the false importance which they have acquired. But, after all qualifications of this kind have been made, the secondary duty yet remains, of consideration for others, which should form an element in our conduct. If truth is the first principle of our speech and action, the good of others should, at any rate, be the second. 'If any man (not see thee who hast knowledge sitting in the idol's temple, but) hear thee discoursing rashly of the Scriptures and the doctrines of the Church, shall not the faith of thy younger brother become confused? and his conscience being weak shall cease to discern between good and evil. And so thy weak brother shall perish for whom Christ died.'

The Apostle adds a fourth principle, which may be

termed the law of Christian freedom, as the last solution of the difficulty: 'Therefore, whether ye eat or drink, do all to the glory of God.' From the perplexities of casuistry, and the conflicting rights of a man's own conscience and that of another, he falls back on the simple rule, 'Whatever you do, sanctify the act.' It cannot be said that all contradictory obligations vanish the moment we try to act with simplicity and truth; we cannot change the current of life and its circumstances by a wish or an intention; we cannot dispel that which is without, though we may clear that which is within. But we have taken the first step, and are in the way to solve the riddle. The insane scruple, the fixed idea, the ever-increasing doubt begins to pass away; the spirit of the child returns to us; the mind is again free, and the road of life open. 'Whether ye eat or drink, do all to the glory of God;' that is, determine to seek only the will of God, and you may have a larger measure of Christian liberty allowed to you; things, perhaps wrong in others, may be right for you.

Questions of meats and drinks, of eating with washen or unwashen hands, and the like, have passed from the stage of religious ordinances to that of proprieties and decencies of life. The purifications of the law of Moses are no longer binding upon Christians. Nature herself teaches all things necessary for health and comfort. But the spirit of casuistry in every age finds fresh materials to employ itself upon, laying hold of some question of a new moon or a sabbath, some fragment of antiquity, some inconsistency of custom, some subtlety of thought, some nicety of morality, analyzing and dividing the actions of daily life; separating the letter from the spirit, and words from things; winding its toils around the infirmities of the weak, and linking itself to the sensibility of the intellect.

Out of this labyrinth of the soul the believer finds his way, by keeping his eye fixed on that landmark which the Apostle himself has set up: 'In Christ Jesus neither circumcision availeth anything, nor uncircumcision, but a new creature.'

There is no one probably, of any religious experience, who has not at times felt the power of a scrupulous conscience. In speaking of a scrupulous conscience, the sense of remorse for greater offences is not intended to be included. These may press more or less heavily on the soul; and the remembrance of them may ingrain itself, with different degrees of depth, on different temperaments; but whether deep or shallow, the sorrow for them cannot be brought under the head of scruples of conscience. There are 'many things in which we offend all,' about which there can be no mistake, the impression of which on our minds it would be fatal to weaken or do away. Nor is it to be denied that there may be customs almost universal among us which are so plainly repugnant to morality. that we can never be justified in acquiescing in them; or that individuals of clear head and strong will have been led on by feelings which other men would deride as conscientious scruples into an heroic struggle against evil. But quite independently of real sorrows for sin, or real protests against evil, most religious persons in the course of their lives have felt unreal scruples or difficulties, or exaggerated real but slight ones; they have abridged their Christian freedom, and thereby their means of doing good; they have cherished imaginary obligations, and artificially hedged themselves in a particular course of action. Honour and truth have seemed to be at stake about trifles light as air, or conscience has become a burden too heavy for them to bear in some doubtful matter of conduct. Scruples of this kind are ever liable to increase; as one vanishes, another appears; the circumstances of the world and of the Church, and the complication of modern society, have a tendency to create them. The very form in which they come is of itself sufficient to put us on our guard against them; for we can give no account of them to ourselves; they are seldom affected by the opinion of others : they are more often put down by the exercise of authority than by reasoning or judgement. They gain hold on the weaker sort of men, or on those not naturally weak, in moments of weakness. They often run counter to our wish or interest, and for this very reason acquire a kind of tenacity. They seem innocent, mistakes, at worst, on the safe side, characteristic of the ingenuousness of youth, or indicative of a heart uncorrupted by the world. But this is not so. Creatures as we are of circumstances, we cannot safely afford to give up things indifferent, means of usefulness, instruments of happiness to ourselves, which may affect our lives and those of our children to the latest posterity. There are few greater dangers in religion than the indulgence of such scruples, the consequences of which can rarely be seen until too late, and which affect the moral character of a man at least as much as his temporal interests.

Strange as it may appear, it is nevertheless true, that scruples about lesser matters almost always involve some dereliction of duty in greater or more obvious ones. A tender conscience is a conscience unequal to the struggles of life. At first sight it seems as if, when lesser duties were cared for, the greater would take care of themselves. But this is not the lesson which experience teaches. In our moral as in our physical nature, we are finite beings, capable only of a certain degree of tension, ever liable to suffer disorder and derangement, to be over-exercised in one part and weakened in another. No one can fix his mind intently on a trifling scruple or become absorbed in an eccentric fancy, without finding the great principles of truth and justice insensibly depart from him. He has been looking through a microscope at life, and cannot take in its general scope. The moral proportions of things are lost to him : the question of a new moon or a Sabbath has taken the place of diligence or of honesty. There is no limit to the illusions which he may practise on himself. There are those, all whose interests and prejudices at once take the form of duties and scruples, partly from dishonesty, but also from weakness, and because that is the form in which they can with the best grace maintain them against other men, and conceal their true nature from themselves.

Scruples are dangerous in another way, as they tend to drive men into a corner in which the performance of our duty becomes so difficult as to be almost impossible. A virtuous and religious life does not consist merely in abstaining from evil, but in doing what is good. It has to find opportunities and occasions for itself, without which it languishes. A man has a scruple about the choice of a profession: as a Christian, he believes war to be unlawful; in familiar language, he has doubts respecting orders, difficulties about the law. Even the ordinary ways of conducting trade appear deficient to his nicer sense of honesty; or perhaps he has already entered on one of these lines of life, and finds it necessary to quit it. At last, there comes the difficulty of 'how he is to live.' There cannot be a greater mistake than to suppose that a good resolution is sufficient in such a case to carry a man through a long life.

But even if we suppose the case of one who is endowed with every earthly good and instrument of prosperity, who can afford, as is sometimes said, to trifle with the opportunities of life, still the mental consequences will be hardly less injurious to him. For he who feels scruples about the ordinary enjoyments and occupations of his fellows, does so far cut himself off from his common nature. He is an isolated being, incapable of acting with his fellow-men. There are plants which, though the sun shine upon them, and the dews water them, peak and pine from some internal disorder, and appear to have no sympathy with the influences around them. So is the mind corroded by scruples of conscience. It cannot expand to sun or shower: it belongs not to the world of light: it has no intelligence of or harmony with mankind around. It is insensible to the great truth, that though we may not do evil that good may come, yet that good and evil, truth and falsehood, are bound together on earth, and that we cannot separate ourselves from them.

It is one of the peculiar dangers of scruples of conscience, that the consequence of giving way to them is never felt at the time that they press upon us. When the mind is worried by a thought secretly working in it, and its trial becomes greater than it can bear, it is eager to take the plunge in life that may put it out of its misery; to throw aside a profession it may be, or to enter a new religious communion. We shall not be wrong in promising ourselves a few weeks of peace and placid enjoyment. The years that are to follow we are incapable of realizing; whether the weary spirit will require some fresh pasture, will invent for itself some new doubt; whether its change is a return to nature or not, it is impossible for us to anticipate. Whether it has in itself that hidden strength which, under every change of circumstances, is capable of bearing up, is a question which we are the least able to determine for ourselves. In general we may observe, that the weakest minds, and those least capable of enduring such consequences, are the most likely to indulge the scruples. We know beforehand the passionate character, hidden often under the mask of reserve, the active yet half-reasoning intellect, which falls under the power of such illusions.

In the Apostolic Church 'cases of conscience' arose out of religious traditions, and what may be termed the ceremonial cast of the age; in modern times the most frequent source of them may be said to be the desire of logical or practical consistency, such as is irreconcilable with the mixed state of human affairs and the feebleness of the human intellect. There is no lever like the argument from consistency, with which to bring men over to our opinions. A particular system or view, Calvinism perhaps, or Catholicism, has taken possession of the mind. Shall we stop short of pushing its premises to their conclusions? Shall we stand in the midway, where we are liable to be overridden by the combatants on either side in the struggle? Shall we place ourselves between our reason and our affections; between our practical duties and our intellectual convictions? Logic would have us go forward, and take our stand at the most advanced point—we are there already, it is urged, if we were true to ourselves—but feeling, and habit, and common sense bid us stay where we are, unable to give an account of ourselves, yet convinced that we are right. We may listen to the one voice, we may listen also to the other. The true way of guiding either is to acknowledge both; to use them for a time against each other, until experience of life and of ourselves has taught us to harmonize them in a single principle.

So, again, in daily life cases often occur, in which we must do as other men do, and act upon a general understanding, even though unable to reconcile a particular practice to the letter of truthfulness or even to our individual conscience. It is hard in such cases to lay down a definite rule. But in general we should be suspicious of any conscientious scruples in which other good men do not share. We shall do right to make a large allowance for the perplexities and entanglements of human things; we shall observe that persons of strong mind and will brush away our scruples; we shall consider that not he who has most, but he who has fewest scruples approaches most nearly the true Christian. The man whom we emphatically call 'honest,' 'able,' 'upright,' who is a religious as well as a sensible man, seems to have no room for them; from which we are led to infer that such scruples are seldom in the nature of things themselves, but arise out of some peculiarity or eccentricity in those who indulge them. That they are often akin to madness, is an observation not without instruction even to those whom God has blest with the full use of reason.

So far we arrive at a general conclusion like St. Paul's:—

'Whether ye eat or drink, do all to the glory of God;' and, 'Blessed is he who condemneth not himself in that which he alloweth.' 'Have the Spirit of truth, and the truth shall make you free;' and the entanglements of words and the perplexities of action will disappear. But there is another way in which such difficulties have been resolved, which meets them in detail; viz., the practice of confession and the rules of casuistry, which are the guides of the confessor. When the spirit is disordered within us, it may be urged that we ought to go out of ourselves, and confess our sins one to another. But he who leads, and he who is led, alike require some rules for the examination of conscience, to quicken or moderate the sense of sin, to assist experience, to show men to themselves as they really are, neither better nor worse. Hence the necessity for casuistry.

It is remarkable, that what is in idea so excellent that it may be almost described in St. Paul's language as 'holy, just, and good,' should have become a byword among mankind for hypocrisy and dishonesty. In popular estimation, no one is supposed to resort to casuistry, but with the view of evading a duty. The moral instincts of the world have risen up and condemned it. It is fairly put down by the universal voice, and shut up in the darkness of the tomes of the casuists. A kind of rude justice has been done upon the system, as in most cases of popular indignation, probably with some degree of injustice to the individuals who were its authors. Yet, hated as casuistry has deservedly been, it is fair also to admit that it has an element of truth which was the source of its influence. This element of truth is the acknowledgement of the difficulties which arise in the relations of a professing Christian world to the Church and to Christianity. How, without lowering the Gospel, to place it on a level with daily life is a hard question. It will be proper for us to consider the system from both sides—in its origin and in its perversion. Why it existed, and why it has failed, furnish a lesson in the history of the human mind of great interest and importance.

The unseen power by which the systems of the casuists were brought into being, was the necessity of the Roman Catholic Church. Like the allegorical interpretation of Scripture, they formed a link between the present and the past. At the time of the Reformation the doctrines of the ancient, no less than of the Reformed, faith awakened into life. But they required to be put in a new form, to reconcile them to the moral sense of mankind. Luther ended the work of self-examination by casting all his sins on Christ. But the casuists could not thus meet the awakening of men's consciences and the fearful looking for of judgement. They had to deal with an altered world, in which nevertheless the spectres of the past, purgatory, penance, mortal sin, were again rising up; hallowed as they were by authority and antiquity they could not be cast aside; the preacher of the Counter-reformation could only explain them away. If he had placed distinctly before men's eyes, that for some one act of immorality or dishonesty they were in a state of mortal sin, the heart true to itself would have recoiled from such a doctrine, and the connexion between the Church and the world would have been for ever severed. And yet the doctrine was a part of ecclesiastical tradition; it could not be held, it could not be given up. The Jesuits escaped the dilemma by holding and evading it.

So far it would not be untrue to say that casuistry had originated in an effort to reconcile the Roman Catholic faith with nature and experience. The Roman system was, if strictly carried out, horrible and impossible; a doctrine not, as it has been sometimes described, of salvation made easy, but of universal condemnation. From these fearful conclusions of logic the subtilty of the human intellect was now to save it. The analogy of law, as worked out by jurists and canonists, supplied the means. What was repugnant to human justice could not be agreeable to Divine.

The scholastic philosophy, which had begun to die out and fade away before the light of classical learning, was to revive in a new form, no longer hovering between heaven and earth, out of the reach of experience, yet below the region of spiritual truth, but, as it seemed, firmly based in the life and actions of mankind. It was the same sort of wisdom which defined the numbers and order of the celestial hierarchy, which was now to be adapted to the infinite modifications of which the actions of men are capable.

It is obvious that there are endless points of view in which the simplest duties may be regarded. Common sense says—'A man is to be judged by his acts,' 'there can be no mistake about a lie,' and so on. The casuists proceed by a different road. Fixing the mind, not on the simplicity, but on the intricacy of human action, they study every point of view, and introduce every conceivable distinction. A first most obvious distinction is that of the intention and the act: ought the one to be separated from the other? The law itself seems to teach that this may hardly be; rather the intention is held to be that which gives form and colour to the act. Then the act by itself is nothing, and the intention by itself almost innocent. As we play between the two different points of view, the act and the intention together evanesce. But, secondly, as we consider the intention, must we not also consider the circumstances of the agent? For plainly a being deprived of free will cannot be responsible for his actions. Place the murderer in thought under the conditions of a necessary agent, and his actions are innocent; or under an imperfect necessity, and he loses half his guilt. Or suppose a man ignorant, or partly ignorant, of what is the teaching of the Church, or the law of the land—here another abstract point of view arises, leading us out of the region of common sense to difficult and equitable considerations, which may be determined fairly, but which we have the greatest motive to decide in favour of ourselves. Or again, try to conceive an act without reference to its consequences, or in reference to some single consequence, without regarding it as a violation of morality or of nature, or in reference solely to the individual conscience. Or imagine the will half consenting to, half withdrawing from its act; or acting by another, or in obedience to another, or with some good object, or under the influence of some imperfect obligation, or of opposite obligations. Even conscience itself may be at last played off against the plainest truths.

By the aid of such distinctions the simplest principles of morality multiply to infinity. An instrument has been introduced of such subtilty and elasticity that it can accommodate the canons of the Church to any consciences, to any state of the world. Sin need no longer be confined to the dreadful distinction of moral and venial sin; it has lost its infinite and mysterious character; it has become a thing of degrees, to be aggravated or mitigated in idea, according to the expediency of the case or the pliability of the confessor. It seems difficult to perpetrate a perfect sin. No man need die of despair; in some page of the writings of the casuists will be found a difference suited to his case. And this without in any degree interfering with a single doctrine of the Church, or withdrawing one of its anathemas against heresy.

The system of casuistry, destined to work such great results, in reconciling the Church to the world and to human nature, like a torn web needing to be knit together, may be regarded as a science or profession. It is a classification of human actions, made in one sense without any reference to practice. For nothing was further from the mind of the casuist than to inquire whether a particular distinction would have a good or bad effect, was liable to perversion or not. His object was only to make such distinctions as the human mind was capable of perceiving and acknowledging. As to the physiologist objects in themselves loathsome and disgusting may be of the deepest interest, so to the casuist

the foulest and most loathsome vices of mankind are not
matters of abhorrence, but of science, to be arranged and
classified, just like any other varieties of human action. It
is true that the study of the teacher was not supposed to be
also open to the penitent. But it inevitably followed that
the spirit of the teacher communicated itself to the taught.
He could impart no high or exalted idea of morality or
religion, who was measuring it out by inches, not deepening
men's idea of sin, but attenuating it; 'mincing into non-
sense' the first principles of right and wrong.

The science was further complicated by the 'doctrine of
probability,' which consisted in making anything approved
or approvable that was confirmed by authority; even, as
was said by some, of a single casuist. That could not be
very wrong which a wise and good man had once thought
to be right—a better than ourselves perhaps, surveying the
circumstances calmly and impartially. Who would wish
that the rule of his daily life should go beyond that of
a saint and doctor of the Church? Who would require
such a rule to be observed by another? Who would refuse
another such an escape out of the labyrinth of human
difficulties and perplexities? As in all the Jesuit distinctions, there was a kind of reasonableness in the theory of
this; it did but go on the principle of cutting short scruples
by the rule of common sense.

And yet, what a door was here opened for the dishonesty
of mankind! The science itself had dissected moral action
until nothing of life or meaning remained in it. It had
thrown aside, at the same time, the natural restraint which
the moral sense itself exercises in determining such questions. And now for the application of this system, so
difficult and complicated in itself, so incapable of receiving
any check from the opinions of mankind, the authority not
of the Church, but of individuals, was to be added as a new
lever to overthrow the last remains of natural religion and
morality.

The marvels of this science are not yet ended. For the same changes admit of being rung upon speech as well as upon action, until truth and falsehood become alike impossible. Language itself dissolves before the decomposing power; oaths, like actions, vanish into air when separated from the intention of the speaker; the shield of custom protects falsehood. It would be a curious though needless task to follow the subject into further details. He who has read one page of the casuists has read all. There is nothing that is not right in some particular point of view—nothing that is not true under some previous supposition.

Such a system may be left to refute itself. Those who have strayed so far away from truth and virtue are self-condemned. Yet it is not without interest to trace by what false lights of philosophy or religion good men, revolting themselves at the commission of evil, were led step by step to the unnatural result. We should expect to find that such a result originated not in any settled determination to corrupt the morals of mankind, but in an intellectual error; and it is suggestive of strange thoughts respecting our moral nature, that an intellectual error should have had the power to produce such consequences. Such appears to have been the fact. The conception of moral action on which the system depends, is as erroneous and imperfect as that of the scholastic philosophy respecting the nature of ideas. The immediate reduction of the error to practice through the agency of an order made the evil greater than that of other intellectual errors on moral and religious subjects, which, springing up in the brain of an individual, are often corrected and purified in the course of nature before they find their way into the common mind.

1. Casuistry ignores the difference between thought and action. Actions are necessarily external. The spoken word constitutes the lie; the outward performance the crime. The Highest Wisdom, it is true, has identified the two: 'He that looketh on a woman to lust after her hath already

committed adultery with her in his heart.' But this is not the rule by which we are to judge our past actions, but to guard our future ones. He who has thoughts of lust or passion is not innocent in the sight of God, and is liable to be carried on to perform the act on which he suffers himself to dwell. And, in looking forward, he will do well to remember this caution of Christ: but in looking backward, in thinking of others, in endeavouring to estimate the actual amount of guilt or trespass, if he begins by placing thought on the level of action, he will end by placing action on the level of thought. It would be a monstrous state of mind in which we regarded mere imagination of evil as the same with action; hatred as the same with murder; thoughts of impurity as the same with adultery. It is not so that we must learn Christ. Actions are one thing and thoughts another in the eye of conscience, no less than of the law of the land; of God as well as man. However important it may be to remember that the all-seeing eye of God tries the reins, it is no less important to remember also that morality consists in definite acts, capable of being seen and judged of by our fellow-creatures, impossible to escape ourselves.

2. What may be termed the frame of casuistry was supplied by law, while the spirit is that of the scholastic philosophy. Neither afforded any general principle which might correct extravagancies in detail, or banish subtilties, or negative remote and unsafe inferences. But the application of the analogy of law to subjects of morality and religion was itself a figment which, at every step, led deeper into error. The object was to realize and define, in every possible stage, acts which did not admit of legal definition, either because they were not external, but only thoughts or suggestions of the mind, or because the external part of the action was not allowed to be regarded separately from the motives of the agent. The motive or intention which law takes no account of, except as indicating the nature of the act, becomes the principal subject of the casuist's art.

Casuistry may be said to begin where law ends. It goes where law refuses to follow with legal rules and distinctions into the domain of morality. It weighs in the balance of precedent and authority the impalpable acts of a spiritual being. Law is a real science which has its roots in history, which grasps fact; seeking, in idea, to rest justice on truth only, and to reconcile the rights of individuals with the well-being of the whole. But casuistry is but the ghost or ape of a science; it has no history and no facts corresponding to it; it came into the world by the ingenuity of man; its object is to produce an artificial disposition of human affairs, at which nature rebels.

3. The distinctions of the casuist are far from equalling the subtilty of human life, or the diversity of its conditions. It is quite true that actions the same in name are, in the scale of right and wrong, as different as can be imagined; varying with the age, temperament, education, circumstances of each individual. The casuist is not in fault for maintaining this difference, but for supposing that he can classify or distinguish them so as to give any conception of their innumerable shades and gradations. All his folios are but the weary effort to abstract or make a brief of the individuality of man. The very actions which he classifies change their meaning as he writes them down, like the words of a sentence torn away from their context. He is ever idealizing and creating distinctions, splitting straws, dividing hairs; yet any one who reflects on himself will idealize and distinguish further still, and think of his whole life in all its circumstances, with its sequence of thoughts and motives, and, withal, many excuses. But no one can extend this sort of idealism beyond himself; no insight of the confessor can make him clairvoyant of the penitent's soul. Know ourselves we sometimes truly may, but we cannot know others, and no other can know us. No other can know or understand us in the same wonderful or mysterious way; no other can be conscious of the spirit

in which we have lived; no other can see us as a whole or get within. God has placed a veil of flesh between ourselves and other men, to screen the nakedness of our soul. Into the secret chamber He does not require that we should admit any other judge or counsellor but himself. Two eyes only are upon us—the eye of our own soul—the eye of God, and the one is the light of the other. That is the true light, on the which if a man look he will have a knowledge of himself, different in kind from that which the confessor extracts from the books of the casuists.

4. There are many cases in which our first thoughts, or, to speak more correctly, our instinctive perceptions, are true and right; in which it is not too much to say, that he who deliberates is lost. The very act of turning to a book, or referring to another, enfeebles our power of action. Works of art are produced we know not how, by some simultaneous movement of hand and thought, which seem to lend to each other force and meaning. So in moral action, the true view does not separate the intention from the act, or the act from the circumstances which surround it, but regards them as one and absolutely indivisible. In the performance of the act and in the judgement of it, the will and the execution, the hand and the thought are to be considered as one. Those who act most energetically, who in difficult circumstances judge the most truly, do not separately pass in review the rules, and principles, and counter principles of action, but grasp them at once, in a single instant. Those who act most truthfully, honestly, firmly, manfully, consistently, take least time to deliberate. Such should be the attitude of our minds in all questions of right and wrong, truth and falsehood: we may not inquire, but act.

5. Casuistry not only renders us independent of our own convictions, it renders us independent also of the opinion of mankind in general. It puts the confessor in the place of ourselves, and in the place of the world. By making the actions of men matters of science, it cuts away the supports

and safeguards which public opinion gives to morality; the confessor in the silence of the closet easily introduces principles from which the common sense or conscience of mankind would have shrunk back. Especially in matters of truth and falsehood, in the nice sense of honour shown in the unwillingness to get others within our power, his standard will probably fall short of that of the world at large. Public opinion, it is true, drives men's vices inwards; it teaches them to conceal their faults from others, and if possible from themselves, and this very concealment may sink them in despair, or cover them with self-deceit. And the soul—whose 'house is its castle'—has an enemy within, the strength of which may be often increased by communications from without. Yet the good of this privacy is on the whole greater than the evil. Not only is the outward aspect of society more decorous, and the confidence between man and man less liable to be impaired; the mere fact of men's sins being known to themselves and God only, and the support afforded even by the undeserved opinion of their fellows, are of themselves great helps to a moral and religious life. Many a one by being thought better than he was has become better; by being thought as bad or worse has become worse. To communicate our sins to those who have no claim to know them is of itself a diminution of our moral strength. It throws upon others what we ought to do for ourselves; it leads us to seek in the sympathy of others a strength which no sympathy can give. It is a greater trust than is right for us commonly to repose in our fellow-creatures; it places us in their power; it may make us their tools.

To conclude, the errors and evils of casuistry may be summed up as follows:—It makes that abstract which is concrete, scientific which is contingent, artificial which is natural, positive which is moral, theoretical which is intuitive and immediate. It puts the parts in the place of the whole, exceptions in the place of rules, system in the place of experience, dependence in the place of responsibility, reflection in the place of conscience. It lowers the heavenly to the earthly, the principles of men to their practice, the tone of the preacher to the standard of ordinary life. It sends us to another for that which can only be found in ourselves. It leaves the highway of public opinion to wander in the labyrinths of an imaginary science; the light of the world for the darkness of the closet. It is to human nature what anatomy is to our bodily frame; instead of a moral and spiritual being, preserving only 'a body of death.'

ESSAY

ON

NATURAL RELIGION

THE revelation of righteousness by faith in the Epistle to the Romans is relative to a prior condemnation of Jew and Gentile, who are alike convicted of sin. If the world had not been sitting in darkness and the shadow of death, there would have been no need of the light. And yet this very darkness is a sort of contradiction, for it is the darkness of the soul, which, nevertheless, sees itself and God. Such 'darkness visible' St. Paul had felt in himself, and, passing from the individual to the world, he lifts up the veil partially, and lets the light of God's wrath shine upon the corruption of man. What he himself in the searchings of his own spirit had become conscious of was 'written in large letters' on the scene around. To all Israelites at least, the law stood in the same relation as it had once done to himself; it placed them in a state of reprobation. Without law 'they had not had sin,' and now, the only way to do away with sin is to do away the law itself.

But, if 'sin is not imputed where there is no law,' it might seem as though the heathen could not be brought within the sphere of the same condemnation. Could we suppose men to be like animals, 'nourishing a blind life within the brain,' 'the seed that is not quickened except it die' would have no existence in them. Common sense tells us that all evil implies a knowledge of good, and that no man can be responsible for the worship of a false God who has no means of approach to the true. But this was not altogether the case of the Gentile; 'without the law sin was in the world;' as the Jew had the law, so the Gentile had the witness of God in creation. Nature was the Gentile's law, witnessing against his immoral and degraded state, leading him upward through the visible things to the unseen power of God. He knew God, as the Apostle four times repeats, and magnified Him not as God; so that he was without excuse, not only for his idolatry, but because he worshipped idols in the presence of God himself.

Such is the train of thought which we perceive to be working in the Apostle's mind, and which leads him, in accordance with the general scope of the Epistle to the Romans, to speak of natural religion. In two passages in the Acts he dwells on the same subject. It was one that found a ready response in the age to which St. Paul preached. Reflections of a similar kind were not uncommon among the heathen themselves. If at any time in the history of mankind natural religion can be said to have had a real and independent existence, it was in the twilight of heathenism and Christianity. 'Seeking after God, if haply they might feel after him and find him,' is a touching description of the efforts of philosophy in its later period. That there were principles in Nature higher and purer than the creations of mythology was a reflection made by those who would have deemed 'the cross of Christ foolishness,' who 'mocked at the resurrection of the dead.' The Olympic heaven was no longer the air which men breathed, or the sky over their heads. The better mind of the world was turning from 'dumb idols.' Ideas about God and man were taking the place of the old heathen rites. Religions, like nations, met and mingled. East and West were learning of each other, giving and receiving spiritual and political elements; the objects of Gentile worship fading into a more distant and universal God; the Jew also travelling in thought into regions which his fathers knew not, and beginning to form just conceptions of the earth and its inhabitants.

While we remain within the circle of Scripture language, or think of St. Paul as speaking only to the men of his own age in words that were striking and appropriate to them, there is no difficulty in understanding his meaning. The Old Testament denounced idolatry as hateful to God. It was away from Him, out of His sight; except where it touched the fortunes of the Jewish people, hardly within the range either of His judgements or of His mercies. No Israelite, in the elder days of Jewish history, supposed the tribes round about, or the individuals who composed them, to be equally with himself the objects of God's care. The Apostle brings the heathen back before the judgement seat of God. He sees them sinking into the condition of the old Canaanitish nations. He regards this corruption of Nature as a consequence of their idolatry. They knew, or might have known, God, for creation witnesses of Him. This is the hinge of the Apostle's argument: 'If they had not known God they had not had sin;' but now they know Him, and sin in the light of knowledge. Without this consciousness of sin there would be no condemnation of the heathen, and therefore no need of justification for him—no parallelism or coherence between the previous states of Jew and Gentile, or between the two parts of the scheme of redemption.

But here philosophy, bringing into contrast the Scriptural view of things and the merely historical or human one, asks the question, 'How far was it possible for the heathen to have seen God in Nature?' Could a man anticipate the true religion any more than he could anticipate discoveries in science or in art? Could he pierce the clouds of mythology, or lay aside language as it were a garment? Three or four in different ages, who have been the heralds of great religious revolutions, may have risen above their natural state under the influence of some divine impulse. But men in general do as others do; single persons in India or China do not dislocate themselves from the customs, traditions, prejudices, rites, in which they have been brought up. The mind of a nation has its own structure, which receives and also idealizes in various degrees the forms of outward Nature. Religions, like languages, conform to this mental structure; they are prior to the thoughts of individuals; no one is responsible for them. Homer is not to blame for his conception of the Grecian gods; it is natural and adequate to his age. For no one in primitive times could disengage himself from that world of sense which grew to him and enveloped him; we might as well imagine that he could invent a new language, or change the form which he inherited from his race into some other type of humanity.

The question here raised is one of the most important, as it is perhaps one that has been least considered, out of the many questions in which reason and faith, historical fact and religious belief, come into real or apparent conflict with each other. Volumes have been written on the connexion of geology with the Mosaic account of the creation—a question which is on the outskirts of the great difficulty—a sort of advanced post, at which theologians go out to meet the enemy. But we cannot refuse seriously to consider the other difficulty, which affects us much more nearly, and in the present day almost forces itself upon us, as the spirit of the ancient religions is more understood, and the forms of religion still existing among men become better known.

It sometimes seems as if we lived in two, or rather many distinct worlds—the world of faith and the world of experience—the world of sacred and the world of profane history. Between them there is a gulf; it is not easy to pass from one to the other. They have a different set of words and ideas, which it would be bad taste to intermingle;

and of how much is this significant? They present themselves to us at different times, and call up a different train of associations. When reading Scripture we think only of the heavens 'which are made by the word of God,' of 'the winds and waves obeying his will,' of the accomplishment of events in history by the interposition of His hand. But in the study of ethnology or geology, in the records of our own or past times, a curtain drops over the Divine presence; human motives take the place of spiritual agencies; effects are not without causes; interruptions of Nature repose in the idea of law. Race, climate, physical influences, states of the human intellect and of society, are among the chief subjects of ordinary history; in the Bible there is no allusion to them; to the inspired writer they have no existence. Were men different, then, in early ages, or does the sacred narrative show them to us under a different point of view? The being of whom Scripture gives one account, philosophy another—who has a share in Nature and a place in history, who partakes also of a hidden life, and is the subject of an unseen power—is he not the same? This is the difficulty of our times, which presses upon us more and more, both in speculation and practice, as different classes of ideas come into comparison with each other. The day has passed in which we could look upon man in one aspect only, without interruption or confusion from any other. And Scripture, which uses the language and ideas of the age in which it was written, is inevitably at variance with the new modes of speech, as well as with the real discoveries of later knowledge.

Yet the Scriptures lead the way in subjecting the purely supernatural and spiritual view of human things to the laws of experience. The revocation in Ezekiel of the 'old proverb in the house of Israel,' is the assertion of a moral principle, and a return to fact and Nature. The words of our Saviour —'Think ye that those eighteen on whom the tower of Siloam fell, were sinners above all the men who dwelt in

Jerusalem?' and the parallel passage respecting the one born blind—'Neither this man did sin, nor his parents,' are an enlargement of the religious belief of the time in accordance with experience. When it is said that faith is not to look for wonders; or 'the kingdom of God cometh not with observation,' and 'neither will they be persuaded though one rose from the dead,' here, too, is an elevation of the order of Nature over the miraculous and uncommon. The preference of charity to extraordinary gifts is another instance, in which the Spirit of Christ speaks by the lips of Paul, of a like tendency. And St. Paul himself, in recognizing a world without the Jewish, as responsible to God, and subject to His laws, is but carrying out, according to the knowledge of his age, the same principle which a wider experience of the world and of antiquity compels us to extend yet further to all time and to all mankind.

It has been asked: 'How far, in forming a moral estimate of an individual, are we to consider his actions simply as good or evil; or how far are we to include in our estimate education, country, rank in life, physical constitution, and so forth?' Morality is rightly jealous of our resolving evil into the influence of circumstances: it will no more listen to the plea of temptation as the excuse for vice, than the law will hear of the same plea in mitigation of the penalty for crime. It requires that we should place ourselves within certain conditions before we pass judgement. Yet we cannot deny a higher point of view also—of 'him that judged not as a man judgeth,' in which we fear to follow only because of the limitation of our faculties. And in the case of a murderer or other great criminal, if we were suddenly made aware, when dwelling on the enormity of his crime, that he had been educated in vice and misery, that his act had not been unprovoked, perhaps that his physical constitution was such as made it nearly impossible for him to resist the provocation which was offered to him, the knowledge of these and similar circumstances would alter our estimate of the complexion of his guilt. We might think him guilty, but we should also think him unfortunate. Stern necessity might still require that the law should take its course, but we should feel pity as well as anger. We should view his conduct in a larger and more comprehensive way, and acknowledge that, had we been placed in the same circumstances, we might have been guilty of the same act.

Now the difference between these two views of morality is analogous to the difference between the way in which St. Paul regards the heathen religions, and the way in which we ourselves regard them, in proportion as we become better acquainted with their true nature. St. Paul conceives idolatry separate from all the circumstances of time, of country, of physical or mental states by which it is accompanied, and in which it may be almost said to consist. He implies a deliberate knowledge of the good, and choice of the evil. He supposes each individual to contrast the truth of God with the error of false religions, and deliberately to reject God. He conceives all mankind, 'creatures as they are one of another,' and

'Moving all together if they move at all,'

to be suddenly freed from the bond of nationality, from the customs and habits of thought of ages. The moral life which is proper to the individual, he breathes into the world collectively. Speaking not of the agents and their circumstances, but of their acts, and seeing these reflected in what may be termed in a figure the conscience, not of an individual but of mankind in general, he passes on all men everywhere the sentence of condemnation. We can hardly venture to say what would have been his judgement on the great names of Greek and Roman history, had he familiarly known them. He might have felt as we feel, that there is a certain impropriety in attempting to determine, with a Jesuit writer, or even in the spirit of love and admiration which the great Italian poet shows for them, the places of the philosophers and heroes of antiquity in the world to come. More in his own spirit, he would have spoken of them as a part of 'the mystery which was not then revealed as it now is.' But neither can we imagine how he could have become familiar with them at all without ceasing to be St. Paul.

Acquainted as we are with Greek and Roman literature from within, lovers of its old heroic story, it is impossible for us to regard the religions of the heathen world in the single point of view which they presented to the first believers. It would be a vain attempt to try and divest ourselves of the feelings towards the great names of Greek and Roman history which a classical education has implanted in us; as little can we think of the deities of the heathen mythology in the spirit of a Christian of the first two centuries. Looking back from the vantage ground of ages, we see more clearly the proportions of heathenism and Christianity, as of other great forms or events of history, than was possible for contemporaries. Ancient authors are like the inhabitants of a valley who know nothing of the countries beyond: they have a narrow idea either of their own or other times; many notions are entertained by them respecting the past history of mankind which a wider prospect would have dispelled. The horizon of the sacred writers too is limited; they do not embrace the historical or other aspects of the state of man to which modern reflection has given rise; they are in the valley still, though with the 'light of the world' above. The Apostle sees the Athenians from Mars' Hill 'wholly given to idolatry:' to us, the same scene would have revealed wonders of art and beauty, the loss of which the civilized nations of Europe still seem with a degree of seriousness to lament. He thinks of the heathen religions in the spirit of one of the old prophets; to us they are subjects of philosophy also. He makes no distinction between their origin and their decline, the dreams of the childhood of the human race and

the fierce and brutal lusts with which they afterwards
became polluted ; we note many differences between Homer
and the corruption of later Greek life, between the rustic
simplicity of the old Roman religion and the impurities
of the age of Clodius or Tiberius. More and more, as they
become better known to us, the original forms of all religions
are seen to fall under the category of nature and less under
that of mind, or free will. There is nothing to which they
are so much akin as language, of which they are a sort of
after-growth—in their fantastic creations the play or sport
of the same faculty of speech ; they seem to be also based
on a spiritual affection, which is characteristic of man
equally with the social ones. Religions, like languages, are
inherent in all men everywhere, having a close sympathy
or connexion with political and family life. It would be
a shallow and imaginary explanation of them that they are
corruptions of some primaeval revelation, or impostures
framed by the persuasive arts of magicians or priests. There
are many other respects in which our first impressions
respecting the heathen world are changed by study and
experience. There was more of true greatness in the conceptions of heathen legislators and philosophers than we
readily admit, and more of nobility and disinterestedness
in their character. The founders of the Eastern religions
especially, although indistinctly seen by us, appear to be
raised above the ordinary level of mortality. The laws of
our own country are an inheritance partly bequeathed to
us by a heathen nation ; many of our philosophical and
most of our political ideas are derived from a like source.
What shall we say to these things ? Are we not under-
going, on a wider scale and in a new way, the same change
which the Fathers of Alexandria underwent, when they
became aware that heathenism was not wholly evil, and
that there was as much in Plato and Aristotle which was
in harmony with the Gospel as of what was antagonistic
to it.

Among the many causes at present in existence which will influence 'the Church of the future,' none is likely to have greater power than our increasing knowledge of the religions of mankind. The study of them is the first step in the philosophical study of revelation itself. For Christianity or the Mosaic religion, standing alone, is hardly a subject for scientific inquiry: only when compared with other forms of faith do we perceive its true place in history, or its true relation to human nature. The glory of Christianity is not to be as unlike other religions as possible, but to be their perfection and fulfilment. Those religions are so many steps in the education of the human race. One above another, they rise or grow side by side, each nation, in many ages, contributing some partial ray of a divine light, some element of morality, some principle of social life, to the common stock of mankind. The thoughts of men, like the productions of Nature, do not endlessly diversify; they work themselves out in a few simple forms. In the fullness of time, philosophy appears, shaking off, yet partly retaining, the nationality and particularity of its heathen origin. Its top 'reaches to heaven,' but it has no root in the common life of man. At last, the crown of all, the chief corner-stone of the building, when the impressions of Nature and the reflections of the mind upon itself have been exhausted, Christianity arises in the world, seeming to stand in the same relation to the inferior religions that man does to the inferior animals.

When, instead of painting harsh contrasts between Christianity and other religions, we rather draw them together as nearly as truth will allow, many thoughts come into our minds about their relation to each other which are of great speculative interest as well as of practical importance. The joyful words of the Apostle: 'Is he the God of the Jews only, is he not also of the Gentiles?' have a new meaning for us. And this new application the Apostle himself may be regarded as having taught us, where he says: 'When the Gentiles which know not the law do by nature the things contained in the law, these not having the law are a law unto themselves.' There have been many schoolmasters to bring men to Christ, and not the law of Moses only. Ecclesiastical history enlarges its borders to take in the preparations for the Gospel, the anticipations of it, the parallels with it; collecting the scattered gleams of truth which may have revealed themselves even to single individuals in remote ages and countries. We are no longer interested in making out a case against the heathen religions in the spirit of party—the superiority of Christianity will appear sufficiently without that—we rather rejoice that, at sundry times and in divers manners, by ways more or less akin to the methods of human knowledge, 'God spake in time past to the fathers,' and that in the darkest ages, amid the most fanciful aberrations of mythology, He left not himself wholly without a witness between good and evil in the natural affections of mankind.

Some facts also begin to appear, which have hitherto been unknown or concealed. They are of two kinds, relating partly to the origin or development of the Jewish or Christian religion; partly also independent of them, yet affording remarkable parallels both to their outward form and to their inner life. Christianity is seen to have partaken much more of the better mind of the Gentile world than the study of Scripture only would have led us to conjecture: it has received, too, many of its doctrinal terms from the language of philosophy. The Jewish religion is proved to have incorporated with itself some elements which were not of Jewish origin; and the Jewish history begins to be explained by the analogy of other nations. The most striking fact of the second kind is found in a part of the world which Christianity can be scarcely said to have touched, and is of a date some centuries anterior to it. That there is a faith [1] which has a greater number of

---
[1] Buddhism.

worshippers than all sects of Christians put together, which originated in a reformation of society, tyrannized over by tradition, spoiled by philosophy, torn asunder by caste—which might be described, in the words of Scripture, as a 'preaching of the Gospel to the poor;' that this faith, besides its more general resemblance to Christianity, has its incarnation, its monks, its saints, its hierarchy, its canonical books, its miracles, its councils, the whole system being 'full blown' before the Christian era; that the founder of this religion descended from a throne to teach the lesson of equality among men—('there is no distinction of' Chinese or Hindoo, Brahmin or Sudra, such at least was the indirect consequence of his doctrine)—that, himself contented with nothing, he preached to his followers the virtues of poverty, self-denial, chastity, temperance, and that once, at least, he is described as 'taking upon himself the sins of mankind:'—these are facts which, when once known, are not easily forgotten; they seem to open an undiscovered world to us, and to cast a new light on Christianity itself. And it 'harrows us with fear and wonder,' to learn that this vast system, numerically the most universal or catholic of all religions, and, in many of its leading features, most like Christianity, is based, not on the hope of eternal life, but of complete annihilation.

The Greek world presents another parallel with the Gospel, which is also independent of it; less striking, yet coming nearer home, and sometimes overlooked because it is general and obvious. That the political virtues of courage, patriotism, and the like, have been received by Christian nations from a classical source is commonly admitted. Let us ask now the question, Whence is the love of knowledge? who first taught men that the pursuit of truth was a religious duty? Doubtless the words of one greater than Socrates come into our minds: 'For this end was I born, and for this cause came I into the world, that they might know the truth.' But the truth here spoken of is of another and more mysterious kind; not truth in the logical or speculative sense of the word, nor even in its ordinary use. The earnest inquiry after the nature of things, the devotion of a life to such an inquiry, the forsaking all other good in the hope of acquiring some fragment of true knowledge,—this is an instance of human virtue not to be found among the Jews, but among the Greeks. It is a phenomenon of religion, as well as of philosophy, that among the Greeks too there should have been those who, like the Jewish prophets, stood out from the world around them, who taught a lesson, like them, too exalted for the practice of mankind in general; who anticipated out of the order of nature the knowledge of future ages; whose very chance words and misunderstood modes of speech have moulded the minds of men in remote times and countries. And that these teachers of mankind, 'as they were finishing their course' in the decline of Paganism, like Jewish prophets, though unacquainted with Christianity, should have become almost Christian, preaching the truths which we sometimes hold to be 'foolishness to the Greek,' as when Epictetus spoke of humility, or Seneca told of a God who had made of one blood all nations of the earth,—is a sad and touching fact.

But it is not only the better mind of heathenism in East or West that affords parallels with the Christian religion: the corruptions of Christianity, its debasement by secular influences, its temporary decay at particular times or places, receive many illustrations from similar phenomena in ancient times and heathen countries. The manner in which the Old Testament has taken the place of the New; the tendency to absorb the individual life in the outward church; the personification of the principle of separation from the world in monastic orders; the accumulation of wealth with the profession of poverty; the spiritualism, or childlike faith, of one age, and the rationalism or formalism of another; many of the minute controversial disputes which exist between Christians respecting doctrines both of natural and revealed religion ;—all these errors or corruptions of Christianity admit of being compared with similar appearances either in Buddhism or Mahomedanism. Is not the half-believing half-sceptical attitude in which Socrates and others stood to the 'orthodox' pagan faith very similar to that in which philosophers, and in some countries educated men, generally have stood to established forms of Christianity? Is it only in Christian times that men have sought to consecrate art in the service of religion? Did not Paganism do so far more completely? or was it Plato only to whom moral ideas represented themselves in sensual forms? Has not the whole vocabulary of art, in modern times, become confused with that of morality? The modern historian of Greece and Rome draws our attention to other religious features in the ancient world, which are not without their counterpart in the modern,—'old friends with new faces,'—which a few words are enough to suggest. The aristocratic character of Paganism, the influence which it exerted over women, its galvanic efforts to restore the past, the ridicule with which the sceptic assails its errors, and the manner in which the antiquarians Pausanias and Dionysius contemptuously reply; also the imperfect attempts at reconcilement of old and new, found in such writers as Plutarch, and the obscure sense of the real connexion of the Pagan worship with political and social life, the popularity of its temporary hierophants; its panics, wonders, oracles, mysteries,—these features make us aware that however unlike the true life of Christianity may have been even to the better mind of heathenism, the corruptions and weaknesses of Christianity have never been without a parallel under the sun.

Those religions which possess sacred books furnish some other curious, though exaggerated, likenesses of the use which has been sometimes made of the Jewish or Christian Scriptures. No believer in organic or verbal inspiration has applied more high-sounding titles to the Bible than the Brahmin or Mussulman to the Koran or the Vedas. They have been loaded with commentaries—buried under the accumulations of tradition ; no care has been thought too great of their words and letters, while the original meaning has been lost, and even the language in which they were written ceased to be understood. Every method of interpretation has been practised upon them ; logic and mysticism have elicited every possible sense ; the aid of miracles has been called in to resolve difficulties and reconcile contradictions. And still, notwithstanding the perverseness with which they are interpreted, these half-understood books exercise a mighty spell ; single verses, misapplied words, disputed texts, have affected the social and political state of millions of mankind during a thousand or many thousand years. Even without reference to their contents, the mere name of these books has been a power in the Eastern world. Facts like these would be greatly misunderstood if they were supposed to reduce the Old and New Testament to the level of other sacred books, or Christianity to the level of other religions. But they may guard us against some forms of superstition which insensibly, almost innocently, spring up among Christians ; and they reveal weaknesses of human nature, from which we can scarcely hope that our own age or country is exempt.

Let us conclude this digression by summing up the use of such inquiries ; as a touchstone and witness of Christian truth ; as bearing on our relations with the heathens themselves.

Christianity, in its way through the world, is ever taking up and incorporating with itself Jewish, secular, or even Gentile elements. And the use of the study of the heathen religions is just this : it teaches us to separate the externals or accidents of Christianity from its essence ; its local, temporary type from its true spirit and life. These externals, which Christianity has in common with other religions of the East, may be useful, may be necessary, but they are not the truths which Christ came on earth to reveal. The fact of the possession of sacred books, and the claim which is made for them, that they are free from all error or imperfection, if admitted, would not distinguish the Christian from the Mahomedan faith. Most of the Eastern religions, again, have had vast hierarchies and dogmatic systems; neither is this a note of divinity. Also, they are witnessed to by signs and wonders; we are compelled to go further to find the characteristics of the Gospel of Christ. As the Apostle says: 'And yet I show you a more excellent way,'—not in the Scriptures, nor in the church, nor in a system of doctrines, nor in miracles, does Christianity consist, though some of these may be its necessary accompaniments or instruments, but in the life and teaching of Christ.

The study of 'comparative theology' not only helps to distinguish the accidents from the essence of Christianity; it also affords a new kind of testimony to its truth; it shows what the world was aiming at through many cycles of human history—what the Gospel alone fulfilled. The Gentile religions, from being enemies, became witnesses of the Christian faith. They are no longer adverse positions held by the powers of evil, but outworks or buttresses, like the courts of the Temple on Mount Sion, covering the holy place. Granting that some of the doctrines and teachers of the heathen world were nearer the truth than we once supposed, such resemblances cause no alarm or uneasiness; we have no reason to fable that they are the fragments of some primaeval revelation. We look forwards, not backwards; to the end, not to the beginning; not to the garden of Eden, but to the life of Christ. There is no longer any need to maintain a thesis; we have the perfect freedom and real peace which is attained by the certainty that we know all, and that nothing is kept back. Such was the position of Christianity in former ages; it was on a level with the knowledge of mankind. But in later years unworthy fear has too often paralyzed its teachers: instead of seeking to readjust its relations to the present state of history and science, they have clung in agony to the past. For the Gospel is the child of light; it lives in the light of this world; it has no shifts or concealments; there is no kind of knowledge which it needs to suppress; it allows us to see the good in all things; it does not forbid us to observe also the evil which has incrusted upon itself. It is willing that we should look calmly and steadily at all the facts of the history of religion. It takes no offence at the remark, that it has drawn into itself the good of other religions; that the laws and institutions of the Roman Empire have supplied the outer form, and heathen philosophy some of the inner mechanism which was necessary to its growth in the world. No violence is done to its spirit by the enumeration of the causes which have led to its success. It permits us also to note, that while it has purified the civilization of the West, there are soils of earth on which it seems hardly capable of living without becoming corrupt or degenerate. Such knowledge is innocent and a 'creature of God.' And considering how much of the bitterness of Christians against one another arises from ignorance and a false conception of the nature of religion, it is not chimerical to imagine that the historical study of religions may be a help to Christian charity. The least differences seem often to be the greatest; the perception of the greater differences makes the lesser insignificant. Living within the sphere of Christianity, it is good for us sometimes to place ourselves without; to turn away from 'the weak and beggarly elements' of worn-out controversies to contemplate the great phases of human existence. Looking at the religions of mankind, succeeding one another in a wonderful order, it is hard to narrow our minds to party or sectarian views in our own age or country. Had it been known that a dispute about faith and works existed among Buddhists, would not this knowledge have modified the great question of the Reformation? Such studies have also a philosophical value as well as a Christian use. They may, perhaps, open to us a new page in the history of our own minds, as well as in the history of the human race. Mankind, in primitive times, seem at first sight very unlike ourselves : as we look upon them with sympathy and interest, a likeness begins to appear ; in us too there is a piece of the primitive man ; many of his wayward fancies are the caricatures of our errors or perplexities. If a clearer light is ever to be thrown either on the nature of religion or of the human mind, it will come, not from analyses of the individual or from inward experience, but from a study of the mental history of mankind, and especially of those ages in which human nature was fusile, still not yet cast in a mould, and rendered incapable of receiving new creations or impressions.

The study of the religions of the world has also a bearing on the present condition of the heathen. We cannot act upon men unless we understand them ; we cannot raise or elevate their moral character unless we are able to draw from its concealment the seed of good which they already contain. It is a remarkable fact, that Christianity, springing up in the East, should have conquered the whole western world, and that in the East itself it should have scarcely extended its border, or even retained its original hold. 'Westward the course of Christianity has taken its way ; ' and now it seems as if the two ends of the world would no longer meet ; as if differences of degree had extended to differences of kind in human nature, and that we cannot pass from one species to another. Whichever way we look, difficulties appear such as had no existence in the first ages : either barbarism, paling in the presence of a superior race, so that it can hardly be kept alive to receive Christianity, or the mummy-like civilization of China, which seems as though it could never become instinct with a new life, or Brahminism, outlasting in its pride many conquerors of the soil, or the nobler form of Mahomedanism ; the religion of the patriarchs, as it were, overliving itself, preaching to the sons of Ishmael the God of Abraham, who had not yet revealed himself as man. These great systems of religious belief have been subject to some internal changes in a shifting world: the effect produced upon them from without is as yet scarcely perceptible. The attempt to move them is like a conflict between man and nature. And in some places it seems as if the wave had receded again after its advance, and some conversions have been dearly bought, either by the violence of persecution or the corruption or accommodation of the truth. Each sect of Christians has been apt to lend itself to the illusion that the great organic differences of human nature might be bridged over, could the Gospel of Christ be preached to the heathen in that precise form in which it is received by themselves; 'if we could but land in remote countries, full armed in that particular system or way after which we in England worship the God of our Fathers.' And often the words have been repeated, sometimes in the spirit of delusion, sometimes in that of faith and love: 'Lift up your eyes, and behold the fields, that they are already white for harvest,' when it was but a small corner of the field that was beginning to whiten, a few ears only which were ready for the reapers to gather.

And yet the command remains: 'Go forth and preach the Gospel to every creature.' Nor can any blessing be conceived greater than the spread of Christianity among heathen nations, nor any calling nobler or higher to which Christians can devote themselves. Why are we unable to fulfil this command in any effectual manner? Is it that the Gospel has had barriers set to it, and that the stream no longer overflows on the surrounding territory; that we have enough of this water for ourselves, but not enough for us and them? or that the example of nominal Christians, who are bent on their own trade or interest, destroys the lesson which has been preached by the ministers of religion? Yet the lives of believers did not prevent the spread of

Christianity at Corinth and Ephesus. And it is hard to suppose that the religion which is true for ourselves has lost its vital power in the world.

The truth seems to be, not that Christianity has lost its power, but that we are seeking to propagate Christianity under circumstances which, during the eighteen centuries of its existence, it has never yet encountered. Perhaps there may have been a want of zeal, or discretion, or education in the preachers; sometimes there may have been too great a desire to impress on the mind of the heathen some peculiar doctrine, instead of the more general lesson of 'righteousness, temperance, judgement to come.' But however this may be, there is no reason to believe that even if a saint or apostle could rise from the dead, he would produce by his preaching alone, without the use of other means, any wide or deep impression on India or China. To restore life to those countries is a vast and complex work, in which many agencies have to co-operate—political, industrial, social; and missionary efforts, though a blessed, are but a small part; and the Government is not the less Christian because it seeks to rule a heathen nation on principles of truth and justice only. Let us not measure this great work by the number of communicants or converts. Even when wholly detached from Christianity, the true spirit of Christianity may animate it. The extirpation of crime, the administration of justice, the punishment of falsehood, may be regarded, without a figure of speech, as 'the word of the Lord' to a weak and deceitful people. Lessons of purity and love too flow insensibly out of improvement in the relations of social life. It is the disciple of Christ, not Christ himself, who would forbid us to give these to the many, because we can only give the Gospel to a very few. For it is of the millions, not of the thousands, in India that we must first give an account. Our relations to the heathen are different from those of Christians in former ages, and our progress in their conversion slower. The success which attends our efforts may be disparagingly compared with that of Boniface or Augustine; but if we look a little closer, we shall see no reason to regret that Providence has placed in our hands other instruments for the spread of Christianity besides the zeal of heroes and martyrs. The power to convert multitudes by a look or a word has passed away; but God has given us another means of ameliorating the condition of mankind, by acting on their circumstances, which works extensively rather than intensively, and is in some respects safer and less liable to abuse. The mission is one of governments rather than of churches or individuals. And if, in carrying it out, we seem to lose sight of some of the distinctive marks of Christianity, let us not doubt that the increase of justice and mercy, the growing sense of truth, even the progress of industry, are in themselves so many steps towards the kingdom of heaven.

In the direct preaching of the Gospel, no help can be greater than that which is gained from a knowledge of the heathen religions. The resident in heathen countries readily observes the surface of the world; he has no difficulty in learning the habits of the natives; he avoids irritating their fears or jealousies. It requires a greater effort to understand the mind of a people; to be able to rouse or calm them; to sympathize with them, and yet to rule them. But it is a higher and more commanding knowledge still to comprehend their religion, not only in its decline and corruption, but in its origin and idea,—to understand that which they misunderstand, to appeal to that which they reverence against themselves, to turn back the currents of thought and opinion which have flowed in their veins for thousands of years. Such is the kind of knowledge which St. Paul had when to the Jews he became as a Jew, that he might win some; which led him while placing the new and old in irreconcilable opposition, to bring forth the new out of the treasure-house of the old. No religion, at present existing in the world, stands in the same relation to Christianity that Judaism once did; there is no other religion which is prophetic or anticipatory of it. But neither is there any religion which does not contain some idea of truth, some notion of duty or obligation, some sense of dependence on God and brotherly love to man, some human feeling of home or country. As in the vast series of the animal creation, with its many omissions and interruptions, the eye of the naturalist sees a kind of continuity—some elements of the higher descending into the lower, rudiments of the lower appearing in the higher also—so the Christian philosopher, gazing on the different races and religions of mankind, seems to see in them a spiritual continuity, not without the thought crossing him that the God who has made of one blood all the nations of the earth may yet renew in them a common life, and that our increasing knowledge of the present and past history of the world, and the progress of civilization itself, may be the means which He has provided, working not always in the way which we expect—'that his banished ones be not expelled from him.'

§ 2.

Natural religion, in the sense in which St. Paul appeals to its witness, is confined within narrower limits. It is a feeling rather than a philosophy; and rests not on arguments, but on impressions of God in nature. The Apostle, in the first chapter of the Romans, does not reason from first causes or from final causes; abstractions like these would not have been understood by him. Neither is he taking an historical survey of the religions of mankind: he touches, in a word only, on those who changed the glory of God into the 'likeness of man, and birds, and four-footed beasts, and creeping things' (Rom. i. 23), as on the differences of nations, in Acts xviii. 26. More truly may we describe him in the language of the Psalmist, the very vacancy of which has a peculiar meaning: 'He lifts up his eyes to the hills from whence cometh his salvation.' He wishes to inspire other men with that consciousness of God in all things which he himself feels: 'in a dry and thirsty land where no water is,' he would raise their minds to think of Him 'who gave them rain from heaven and fruitful seasons;' in the city of Pericles and Phidias he bids them turn from gilded statues and temples formed with hands, to the God who made of one blood all the nations of the earth, 'who is not far from every one of us.' Yet it is observable that he also begins by connecting his own thoughts with theirs, quoting 'their own poets,' and taking occasion, from an inscription which he found in their streets, to declare 'the mystery which was once hidden, but now revealed.'

The appeal to the witness of God in nature has passed from the Old Testament into the New; it is one of the many points which the Epistles of St. Paul and the Psalms and Prophets have in common. 'The invisible things from the creation of the world are clearly seen, being understood by the things that are made,' is another way of saying, 'The heavens declare the glory of God; and the firmament showeth his handywork.' Yet the conception of the Old Testament is not the same with that of the New: in the latter we seem to be more disengaged from the things of sense; the utterance of the former is more that of feeling, and less of reflection. One is the poetry of a primitive age, full of vivid immediate impressions; in the other nature is more distant—the freshness of the first vision of earth has passed away. The Deity himself, in the Hebrew Scriptures, has a visible form: as He appeared 'with the body of heaven in his clearness;' as He was seen by the prophet Ezekiel out of the midst of the fire and the whirlwind, 'full of eyes within and without, and the spirit of the living creature in the wheels.' But in the New Testament, 'No man hath seen God at any time; the only begotten Son, who is in the bosom of the Father, he hath declared him.' And this difference leads to a further difference in His relation to His works. In what we term nature, the prophet beheld only the covering cherubim that veil the face of God: as He moves, earth moves to meet Him; 'He maketh the winds his angels,' 'the heavens also bow before him.' His voice, as the Psalmist says, is heard in the storm: 'The Highest gives his thunder; at thy chiding, O Lord, the foundations of the round world are discovered.' The wonders of creation are not ornaments or poetical figures, strewed over the pages of the Old Testament by the hand of the artist, but the frame in which it consists. And yet in this material garb the moral and spiritual nature of God is never lost sight of: in the conflict of the elements He is the free Lord over them; at His breath—the least exertion of His power—'they come and flee away.' He is spirit, not light—a person, not an element or principle; though creating all things by His word, and existing without reference to them, yet also, in His condescension, the God of the Jewish nation, and of individuals who serve Him. The terrible imagery in which the Psalmist delights to array His power is not inconsistent with the gentlest feelings of love and trust, such as are also expressed in the passage just now quoted: 'I will love thee, O Lord, my strength.' God is in nature because He is near also to the cry of His servants. The heart of man expands in His presence; he fears to die lest he should be taken from it. There is nothing like this in any other religion in the world. No Greek or Roman ever had the consciousness of love towards his God. No other sacred books can show a passage displaying such a range of feeling as the eighteenth or twenty-ninth Psalm—so awful a conception of the majesty of God, so true and tender a sense of His righteousness and lovingkindness. It is the same God who wields nature, who also brought up Israel out of the land of Egypt; who, even though the mother desert 'her sucking child,' will not 'forget the work of his hands.'

But the God of nature in the Old Testament is not the God of storms or of battles only, but of peace and repose.

Sometimes a sort of confidence fills the breast of the Psalmist, even in that land of natural convulsions: 'He hath set the round world so fast that it cannot be moved.' At other times the same peace seems to diffuse itself over the scenes of daily life: 'The hills stand round about Jerusalem, even so is the Lord round about them that fear him.' 'He maketh me to lie down in green pastures: he leadeth me beside the still waters.' Then again the Psalmist wonders at the contrast between man and the other glories of creation: 'When I consider the heavens, the work of thy hands, the moon and the stars, that thou hast ordained; what is man, that thou art mindful of him? or the son of man, that thou visitest him?' Yet these 'glories' are the images also of a higher glory: Jerusalem itself is transfigured into a city in the clouds, and the tabernacle and temple become the pavilion of God on high. And the dawn of day in the prophecies, as well as in the Epistles, is the light which is to shine 'for the healing of the nations.' There are other passages in which the thought of the relation of God to nature calls forth a sort of exulting irony, and the prophet speaks of God, not so much as governing the world, as looking down upon it and taking His pastime in it: 'It is he that sitteth upon the circle of the heavens, and the inhabitants thereof are as grasshoppers;' or 'he measureth the waters in the hollow of his hand;' or 'he taketh up the isles as a very little thing:' the feeling of which may be compared with the more general language of St. Paul: 'We are the clay and he the potter.' The highest things on earth reach no farther than to suggest the reflection of their inferiority: 'Behold even the sun, and it shineth not; and the moon is not pure in his sight.'

It is hard to say how far such meditations belong only to particular ages, or to particular temperaments in our own. Doubtless, the influence of natural scenery differs with difference of climate, pursuits, education. 'The God of the hills is not the God of the valleys also;' that is to say, the aspirations of the human heart are roused more by the singular and uncommon, than by the quiet landscape which presents itself in our own neighbourhood. The sailor has a different sense of the vastness of the great deep and the infinity of the heaven above, from what is possible to another. Dwellers in cities, no less than the inhabitants of the desert, gaze upon the stars with different feelings from those who see the ever-varying forms of the seasons. What impression is gathered, or what lesson conveyed, seems like matter of chance or fancy. The power of these sweet influences often passes away when language comes between us and them. Yet they are not mere dreams of our own creation. He who has lost, or has failed to acquire, this interest in the beauty of the world around, is without one of the greatest of earthly blessings. The voice of God in nature calls us away from selfish cares into the free air and the light of day. There, as in a world the face of which is not marred by human passion, we seem to feel 'that the wicked cease from troubling, and the weary are at rest.'

It is impossible that our own feeling towards nature in the present day can be the same with that of the Psalmist; neither is that of the Psalmist the same with that of the Apostle; while, in the Book of Job and Ecclesiastes we seem to catch the echo of a strain different from either. To us, God is not in the whirlwind nor in the storm, nor in the earthquake, but in the still small voice. Is it not for the attempt to bring God nearer to us in the works of nature that we can truly conceive Him to be, that a poet of our own age has been subject to the charge of pantheism? God has removed himself out of our sight, that He may give us a greater idea of the immensity of His power. Perhaps it is impossible for us to have the wider and the narrower conception of God at the same time. We cannot see Him equally in the accidents of the world, when we think of Him as identified with its laws. But there is another way into His presence through our own hearts. He has given us the more circuitous path of knowledge; He has not closed against us the door of faith. He has enabled us, not merely to gaze with the eye on the forms and colours of Nature, but in a measure also to understand its laws, to wander over space and time in the contemplation of its mechanism, and yet to return again to 'the meanest flower that breathes,' for thoughts such as the other wonders of earth and sky are unable to impart.

It is a simpler, not a lower, lesson which we gather from the Apostle. First, he teaches that in Nature there is something to draw us from the visible to the invisible. The world to the Gentiles also had seemed full of innumerable deities; it is really full of the presence of Him who made it. Secondly, the Apostle teaches the universality of God's providence over the whole earth. He covered it with inhabitants, to whom He gave their times and places of abode, 'that they should seek the Lord, if haply they might feel after him, and find him.' They are one family, 'his offspring,' notwithstanding the varieties of race, language, religion. As God is one, even so man is one in a common human nature—in the universality of sin, no less than the universality of redemption. A third lesson is the connexion of immorality and idolatry. They who lower the nature of God lower the nature of man also. Greek philosophy fell short of these lessons. Often as Plato speaks of the myths and legends of the gods, he failed to perceive the immorality of a religion of sense. Still less had any Greek imagined a brotherhood of all mankind, or a dispensation of God reaching backwards and forwards over all time. Its limitation was an essential principle of Greek life; it was confined to a narrow spot of earth, and to small cities; it could not include others besides Greeks; its gods were not gods of the world, but of Greece.

Aspects of Nature in different ages have changed before the eye of man; at times fruitful of many thoughts; at other times either unheeded or fading into insignificance in comparison of the inner world. When the Apostle spoke of the visible things which 'witness of the divine power and glory,' it was not the beauty of particular spots which he recalled; his eye was not satisfied with seeing the fairness of the country any more than the majesty of cities. He did not study the flittings of shadows on the hills, or even the movements of the stars in their courses. The plainest passages of the book of nature were, equally with the sublimest, the writing of a Divine hand. Neither was it upon scenes of earth that he was looking when he spoke of the 'whole creation groaning together until now.' Whatever associations of melancholy or pity may attach to places or states of the heavens, or to the condition of the inferior animals who seem to suffer for our sakes; it is not in these that the Apostle traces the indications of a ruined world, but in the misery and distraction of the heart of man. And the prospect on which he loves to dwell is not that of the promised land, as Moses surveyed it far and wide from the top of Pisgah, but the human race itself, the great family in heaven and earth, of which Christ is the head, reunited to the God who made it, when 'there shall be neither barbarian, Scythian, bond nor free, but all one in Christ,' the Apostle himself also waiting for the fuller manifestation of the sons of God, and sometimes carrying his thoughts yet further to that mysterious hour, when 'the Son shall be subject to him that put all things under him, that God may be all in all.'

When thoughts like these fill the mind, there is little room for reflection on the world without. Even the missionary in modern times hardly cares to go out of his way to visit a picturesque country or the monuments of former ages. He is 'determined to know one thing only, Christ crucified.' Of the beauties of creation, his chief thought is that they are the work of God. He does not analyze them by rules of taste, or devise material out of them for literary discourse. The Apostle, too, in the abundance of his revelations, has an eye turned inward on another world. It is not that he is dead to Nature, but that it is out of his way; not as in the Old Testament, the veil or frame of the Divine presence, but only the background of human nature and of revelation. When speaking of the heathen, it comes readily into his thoughts; it never seems to occur to him in connexion with the work of Christ. He does not read mysteries in the leaves of the forest, or see the image of the cross in the forms of the tree, or find miracles of design in the complex structures of animal life. His thoughts respecting the works of God are simpler, and also deeper. The child and the philosopher alike hear a witness in the first chapter of the Romans, or in the discourse of the Apostle on Mars' Hill, or at Lystra, which the mystic fancies of Neoplatonism, and the modern evidences of natural theology, fail to convey to them.

§ 3.

In the common use of language natural religion is opposed to revealed. That which men know, or seem to know, of themselves, which if the written word were to be destroyed would still remain, which existed prior to revelation, and which might be imagined to survive it, which may be described as general rather than special religion, as Christianity rationalized into morality, which speaks of God, but not of Christ—of nature, but not of grace—has been termed natural religion. Philosophical arguments for the being of a God are comprehended under the same term. It is also used to denote a supposed primitive or patriarchal religion, whether based on a primaeval revelation or not, from which the mythologies or idolatries of the heathen world are conceived to be offshoots.

The line has been sometimes sharply drawn between natural and revealed religion; in other ages of the world, the two have been allowed to approximate, or be almost identified with each other. Natural religion has been often depressed with a view to the exaltation of revealed; the feebleness of the one seeming to involve a necessity for the other. Natural religion has sometimes been regarded as the invention of human reason; at other times, as the decaying sense of a primaeval revelation. Yet natural and revealed religion, in the sense in which it is attempted to oppose them, are contrasts rather of words than of ideas. For who can say where the one begins and the other ends? Who will determine how many elements of Scriptural truth enter into modern philosophy or the opinions of the world in general? Who can analyze how much, even in a Christian country, is really of heathen origin? Revealed religion is ever taking the form of the voice of Nature within; experience is ever modifying our application of the truths of Scripture. The ideal of Christian life is more easily distinguishable from the ideal of Greek and Roman, than the elements of opinion and belief which have come from a Christian source are from those which come from a secular or heathen one. Education itself tends to obliterate the distinction. The customs, laws, principles of a Christian nation may be regarded either as a compromise between the two, or as a harmony of them. We cannot separate the truths of Christianity from Jewish or heathen anticipations of them; nor can we say how far the common sense or morality of the present day is indirectly dependent on the Christian religion.

And if, turning away from the complexity of human life in our own age to the beginning of things, we try to conceive revelation in its purity before it came into contact with other influences, or mingled in the great tide of political and social existence, we are still unable to distinguish between natural and revealed religion. Our difficulty is like the old Aristotelian question, how to draw the line between the moral and intellectual faculties. Let us imagine a first moment at which revelation came into the world; there must still have been some prior state which made revelation possible : in other words, revealed religion presupposes natural. The mind was not a *tabula rasa*, on which the characters of truth had to be inscribed; that is a mischievous notion, which only perplexes our knowledge of the origin of things, whether in individuals or in the race. If we say that this prior state is a Divine preparation for the giving of the Law of Moses, or the spread of Christianity, the difference becomes one of degree which admits of no sharp contrast. Revealed religion has already taken the place of natural, and natural religion extended itself into the province of revealed. Many persons who are fond of discovering traces of revelation in the religions of the Gentile world, resent the intrusion of natural elements into Scripture or Christianity. Natural religion they are willing to see identified with revealed, but not revealed with natural; all Nature may be a miracle, but miracles are not reducible to the course of Nature. But here is only a play between words which derive their meaning from contrast; the phenomena are the same, but we read them by a different light. And sometimes it may not be without advantage to lay aside the two modes of expression, and think only of that 'increasing purpose which through the ages ran.' Religious faith strikes its roots deeper into the past, and wider over the world, when it acknowledges Nature as well as Scripture.

But although the opposition of natural and revealed religion is an opposition of abstractions, to which no facts really correspond, the term natural religion may be conveniently used to describe that aspect or point of view in which religion appears when separated from Judaism or Christianity. It will embrace all conceptions of religion or morality which are not consciously derived from the Old or New Testament. The favourite notion of a common or patriarchal religion need not be excluded. Natural religion, in this comprehensive sense, may be divided into two heads, which the ambiguity of the word nature has sometimes helped to confuse. First, (i.) the religion of nature before revelation, such as may be supposed to have existed among the patriarchs, or to exist still among primitive peoples, who have not yet been enlightened by Christianity, or debased by idolatry; such (ii.) more truly, as the religions of the Gentile world were and are. Secondly, the religion of nature in a Christian country; either the evidences of religion which are derived from a source independent of the written word, or the common sense of religion and morality, which affords a rule of life to those who are not the subjects of special Christian influences.

i. Natural religion in the first sense is an idea and not a fact. The same tendency in man which has made him look fondly on a golden age, has made him look back also to a religion of nature. Like the memory of childhood, the thought of the past has a strange power over us; imagination lends it a glory which is not its own. What can be more natural than that the shepherd, wandering over the earth beneath the wide heavens, should ascend in thought to the throne of the Invisible? There is a refreshment to the fancy in thinking of the morning of the world's day, when the sun arose pure and bright, ere the clouds of error darkened the earth. Everywhere, as a fact, the first inhabitants of earth of whom history has left a memorial are sunk in helpless ignorance. Yet there must have been a time, it is conceived, of which there are no memorials, earlier still; when the Divine image was not yet lost, when men's wants were few and their hearts innocent, ere cities had taken the place of fields, or art of nature. The revelation of God to the first father of the human race must have spread itself in an ever-widening circle to his posterity. We pierce through one layer of superstition to another, in the hope of catching the light beyond, like children digging to find the sun in the bosom of the earth.

The origin of an error so often illustrates the truth, that it is worth while to pause for an instant and consider the source of this fallacy, which in all ages has exerted a great influence on mankind, reproducing itself in many different forms among heathen as well as Christian writers. In technical language, it might be described as the fallacy of putting what is intelligible in the place of what is true. It is easy to draw an imaginary picture of a golden or pastoral age, such as poetry has always described it. The mode of thought is habitual and familiar, the phrases which delineate it are traditional, handed on from one set of poets to another, repeated by one school of theologians to the next. It is a different task to imagine the old world as it truly was, that is, as it appears to us, dimly yet certainly, by the unmistakable indications of language and of mythology. It is hard to picture scenes of external nature unlike what we have ever beheld: but it is harder far so to lay aside ourselves as to imagine an inner world unlike our own, forms of belief, not simply absurd, but indescribable and unintelligible to us. No one, probably, who has not realized the differences of the human mind in different ages and countries, either by contact with heathen nations or the study of old language and mythology, with the help of such a parallel as childhood offers to the infancy of the world, will be willing to admit them in their full extent.

Instead of this difficult and laborious process, we readily conceive of man in the earliest stages of society as not different, but only less than we are. We suppose him deprived of the arts, unacquainted with the truths of Christianity, without the knowledge obtained from books, and yet only unlike us in the simplicity of his tastes and habitudes. We generalize what we are ourselves, and drop out the particular circumstances and details of our lives, and then suppose ourselves to have before us the dweller in Mesopotamia in the days of Abraham, or the patriarchs going down to gather corn in Egypt. This imaginary picture of a patriarchal religion has had such charms for some minds, that they have hoped to see it realized on the wreck of Christianity itself. They did not perceive that they were deluding themselves with a vacant dream which has never yet filled the heart of man.

Philosophers have illustrated the origin of government by a picture of mankind meeting together in a large plain, to determine the rights of governors and subjects; in like manner we may assist imagination, by conceiving the multitude of men with their tribes, races, features, languages, convoked in the plains of the East, to hear from some inspired legislator as Moses, or from the voice of God himself, a revelation about God and nature, and their future destiny; such a revelation in the first day of the world's history as the day of judgement will be at the last. Let us fix our minds, not on the Giver of the revelation, but on the receivers of it. Must there not have been in them some common sense, or faculty, or feeling, which made them capable of receiving it? Must there not have been an apprehension which made it a revelation to them? Must they not all first have been of one language and one speech? And, what is implied by this, must they not all have had one mental structure, and received the same impressions from external objects, the same lesson from nature? Or, to put the hypothesis in another form, suppose that by some electric power the same truth could have been made to sound in the ears and flash before the eyes of all, would they not have gone their ways, one to tents, another to cities; one to be a tiller of the ground, another to be a feeder of sheep; one to be a huntsman, another to be a warrior; one to dwell in woods and forests, another in boundless plains; one in valleys, one on mountains, one beneath the liquid heaven of Greece and Asia, another in the murky regions of the north? And amid all this diversity of habits, occupations, scenes, climates, what common truth of religion could we expect to remain while man was man, the creature in a great degree of outward circumstances? Still less reason would there be to expect the preservation of a primaeval truth throughout the world, if we imagine the revelation made, not to the multitude of men, but to a single individual, and not committed to writing for above two thousand years.

ii. The theory of a primitive tradition, common to all mankind, has only to be placed distinctly before the mind, to make us aware that it is the fabric of a vision. But, even if it were conceivable, it would be inconsistent with facts. Ancient history says nothing of a general religion, but of particular national ones; of received beliefs about places and persons, about animal life, about the sun, moon, and stars, about the Divine essence permeating the world, about gods in the likeness of men appearing in battles and directing the course of states, about the shades below, about sacrifices, purifications, initiations, magic, mysteries. These were the religions of nature, which in historical times have received from custom also a second nature. Early poetry shows us the same religions in a previous stage, while they are still growing, and fancy is freely playing around the gods of its own creation. Language and mythology carry us a step further back, into a mental world yet more distant and more unlike our own. That world is a prison of sense, in which outward objects take the place of ideas; in which morality is a fact of nature, and 'wisdom at one entrance quite shut out.' Human beings in that pre-historic age seem to have had only a kind of limited intelligence; they were the slaves, as we should say, of association. They were rooted in particular spots, or wandered up and down upon the earth, confusing themselves and God and nature, gazing timidly on the world around, starting at their very shadows, and seeing in all things a superhuman power at the mercy of which they were. They had no distinction of body and soul, mind and matter, physical and moral. Their conceptions were neither here nor there; neither sensible objects, nor symbols of the unseen. Their gods were very near; the neighbouring hill or passing stream, brute matter as we regard it, to them a divinity, because it seemed inspired with a life like their own. They could not have formed an idea of the whole earth, much less of the God who made it. Their mixed modes of thought, their figures of speech, which are not figures, their personifications of nature, their reflections of the individual upon the world, and of the world upon the individual, the omnipresence to them of the sensuous and visible, indicate an intellectual state which it is impossible for us, with our regular divisions of thought, even to conceive. We must raze from the table of the mind their language, ere they could become capable of a universal religion.

But although we find no vestiges of a primaeval revelation, and cannot imagine how such a revelation could have been possible consistently with those indications of the state of man which language and mythology supply, it is true, nevertheless, that the primitive peoples of mankind have a religious principle common to all. Religion, rather than reason, is the faculty of man in the earliest stage of his existence. Reverence for powers above him is the first principle which raises the individual out of himself; the germ of political order, and probably also of social life. It is the higher necessity of nature, as hunger and the animal passions are the lower. 'The clay' falls before the rising dawn; it may stumble over stocks and stones; but it is struggling upwards into a higher day. The worshipper is drawn as by a magnet to some object out of himself. He is weak and must have a god; he has the feeling of a slave towards his master, of a child towards its parents, of the lower animals towards himself. The being whom he serves is, like himself, passionate and capricious; he sees him starting up everywhere in the unmeaning accidents of life. The good which he values himself he attributes to him; there is no proportion in his ideas; the great power of nature is the lord also of sheep and oxen. Sometimes, with childish joy, he invites the god to drink of his beverage or eat of his food; at other times, the orgies which he enacts before him, lead us seriously to ask the question 'whether religion may not in truth have been a kind of madness.' He propitiates him and is himself soothed and comforted; again he is at his mercy, and propitiates him again. So the dream of life is rounded to the poor human creature: incapable as he is of seeing his true Father, religion seems to exercise over him a fatal overpowering influence; the religion of nature we cannot call it, for that would of itself lead to a misconception, but the religion of the place in which he lives, of the objects which he sees, of the tribe to which he belongs, of the animal forms which range in the wilds around him, mingling strangely with the witness of his own spirit that there is in the world a being above him.

Out of this troubled and perplexed state of the human fancy the great religions of the world arose, all of them in different degrees affording a rest to the mind, and reducing to rule and measure the wayward impulses of human nature. All of them had a history in antecedent ages; there is no stage in which they do not offer indications of an earlier religion which preceded them. Whether they came into being, like some geological formations, by slow deposits, or, like others, by the shock of an earthquake, that is, by some convulsion and settlement of the human mind, is a question which may be suggested, but cannot be answered. The Hindoo Pantheon, even in the antique form in which the world of deities is presented in the Vedas, implies a growth of fancy and ceremonial which may have continued for thousands of years. Probably at a much earlier period than we are able to trace them, religions, like languages, had their distinctive characters with corresponding differences in the first rude constitution of society. As in the case of languages, it is a fair subject of inquiry, whether they do not all mount up to some elementary type in which they were more nearly allied to sense; a primaeval religion, in which we may imagine the influence of nature was analogous to the first impressions of the outward world on the infant's wandering eyesight, and the earliest worship may be compared with the first use of signs or stammering of speech. Such a religion we may conceive as springing from simple instinct; yet an instinct higher, even in its lowest degree, than the instinct of the animal creation; in which the fear of nature combined with the assertion of sway over it, which had already a law of progress, and was beginning to set bounds to the spiritual chaos. Of this aboriginal state we only 'entertain conjecture;' it is beyond the horizon, even when the eye is strained to the uttermost.

But if the first origin of the heathen religions is in the clouds, their decline, though a phenomenon with which we are familiar in history, of which in some parts of the world we are living witnesses, is also obscure to us. The kind of knowledge that we have of them is like our knowledge of the ways of animals; we see and observe, but we cannot get inside them; we cannot think or feel with their worshippers. Most or all of them are in a state of decay; they have lost their life or creative power; once adequate to the wants of man, they have ceased to be so for ages. Naturally we should imagine that the religion itself would pass away when its meaning was no longer understood; that with the spirit, the letter too would die; that when the circumstances of a nation changed, the rites of worship to which they had given birth would be forgotten. The reverse is the fact. Old age affords examples of habits which become insane and inveterate at a time when they have no longer an object; that is an image of the antiquity of religions. Modes of worship, rules of purification, set forms of words, cling with a greater tenacity when they have no meaning or purpose. The habit of a week or a month may be thrown off; not the habit of a thousand years. The hand of the past lies heavily on the present in all religions; in the East it is a yoke which has never been shaken off. Empire, freedom, among the educated classes belief may pass away, and yet the routine of ceremonial continues; the political glory of a religion may be set at the time when its power over the minds of men is most ineradicable.

One of our first inquiries in reference to the elder religions of the world is how we may adjust them to our own moral and religious ideas. Moral elements seem at first sight to be wholly wanting in them. In the modern sense of the term, they are neither moral nor immoral, but natural; they have no idea of right and wrong, as distinct from the common opinion or feeling of their age and country. No action in Homer, however dishonourable or treacherous, calls forth moral reprobation. Neither gods nor men are expected to present any ideal of justice or virtue; their power or splendour may be the theme of the poet's verse, not their truth or goodness. The only principle on which the Homeric deities reward mortals, is in return for gifts and sacrifices, or from personal attachment. A later age made a step forwards in morality and backwards at the same time; it acquired clearer ideas of right and wrong, but found itself encumbered with conceptions of fate and destiny. The vengeance of the Eumenides has but a rude analogy with justice; the personal innocence of the victim whom the gods pursued is a part of the interest, in some instances, of Greek tragedy. Higher and holier thoughts of the Divine nature appear in Pindar and Sophocles, and philosophy sought to make religion and mythology the vehicles of moral truth. But it was no part of their original meaning.

Yet, in a lower sense, it is true that the heathen religions, even in their primitive form, are not destitute of morality. Their morality is unconscious morality, not 'man a law to himself,' but 'man bound by the will of a superior being.' Ideas of right and wrong have no place in them, yet the first step has been made from sense and appetite into the ideal world. He who denies himself something, who offers up a prayer, who practises a penance, performs an act, not of necessity, nor of choice, but of duty; he does not simply follow the dictates of passion, though he may not be able to give a reason for the performance of his act. He whose God comes first in his mind has an element within him which in a certain degree sanctifies his life by raising him above himself. He has some common interest with other men, some unity in which he is comprehended with them. There is a preparation for thoughts yet higher; he contrasts the permanence of divine and the fleeting nature of human things; while the generations of men pass away 'like leaves,' the form of his God is unchanging, and grows not old.

Differences in modes of thought render it difficult for us to appreciate what spiritual elements lurked in disguise among the primitive peoples of mankind. Many allowances must be made before we judge them by our own categories. They are not to be censured for indecency because they had symbols which to after ages became indecent and obscene. Neither were they mere fetish worshippers because they use sensuous expressions. Religion, like language, in early ages takes the form of sense, but that form of sense is also the embodiment of thought. The stream and the animal are not adored by man in heathen countries because they are destitute of life or reason, but because they seem to him full of mystery and power. It was with another feeling than that of a worshipper of matter that the native of the East first prostrated himself before the rising sun, in whose beams his nature seemed to revive, and his soul to be absorbed. The most childish superstitions are often nothing more than misunderstood relics of antiquity. There are the remains of fetishism in the charms and cures of Christian countries; no one regards the peasant who uses them as a fetish worshipper. Many other confusions have their parallel among ourselves; if we only knew it. For indeed our own ideas in religion, as in everything else, seem clearer to us than they really are, because they are our own. To expect the heathen religions to conform to other modes of thought, is as if the inhabitant of one country were to complain of the inhabitant of another for not speaking the same language with him. Our whole attitude towards nature is different from theirs: to us all is 'law;' to them it was all life and fancy, inconsecutive as a dream. Nothing is more deeply fixed to us than the dualism of body and soul, mind and matter; they knew of no such distinction. But we cannot infer from this a denial of the existence of mind or soul; because they use material images, it would be ridiculous to describe the Psalmist or the prophet Isaiah as materialists; whether in heathen poets or in the Jewish Scriptures, such language belongs to an intermediate state, which has not yet distinguished the spheres of the spiritual and the sensuous. Childhood has been often used as the figure of such a state, but the figure is only partially true, for the childhood of the human race is the childhood of grown up men, and in the child of the nineteenth century there is a piece also of the man of the nineteenth century. Less obvious differences in speech and thought are more fallacious. The word 'God' means something as dissimilar among ourselves and the Greeks as can possibly be imagined; even in Greek alone the difference of meaning can hardly be exaggerated. It includes beings as unlike each other as the muscular, eating and drinking deities of Homer, and the abstract Being of Parmenides, or the Platonic idea of good. All religions of the world use it, however different their conceptions of God may be—polytheistic, pantheistic, monotheistic: it is universal, and also individual; or rather, from being universal, it has become individual, a logical process which has quickened and helped to develop the theological one. Other words, such as prayer, sacrifice, expiation, in like manner vary in meaning with the religion of which they are the expression. The Homeric sacrifice is but a feast of gods and men, destitute of any sacrificial import. Under expiations for sin are included two things which to us are distinct, atonement for moral guilt and accidental pollution. Similar ambiguities occur in the ideas of a future life. The sapless ghosts in Homer are neither souls nor bodies, but a sort of shadowy beings. A like uncertainty extends in the Eastern religions to some of the first principles of thought and being: whether the negative is not also a positive; whether the mind of man is not also God; whether this world is not another; whether privation of existence may not in some sense be existence still.

These are a few of the differences for which we have to allow in a comparison of our own and other times and countries. We must say to ourselves, at every step, human nature in that age was unlike the human nature with which we are acquainted, in language, in modes of thought, in morality, in its conception of the world. Yet it was more like than these differences alone would lead us to suppose. The feelings of men draw nearer than their thoughts; their natural affections are more uniform than their religious systems. Marriage, burial, worship, are at least common to all nations. There never has been a time in which the human race was absolutely without social laws; in which there was no memory of the past; no reverence for a higher power. More defined religious ideas, where the understanding comes into play, grow more different; it is by comparison they are best explained; like natural phenomena, they derive their chief light from analogy with each other. Travelling in thought from China, by way of India, Persia, and Egypt, to the northern shores of the Mediterranean Sea, we distinguish a succession of stages in which the worship of nature is developed; in China as the rule or form of political life, almost grovelling on the level of sense; in India rising into regions of thought and fancy, and allowing a corresponding play in the institutions and character of the people; in Egypt wrapping itself in the mystery of antiquity, becoming the religion of death and of the past; in Persia divided between light and darkness, good and evil, the upper and the under world; in Phoenicia, fierce and licentious, imbued with the spirit of conquest and colonization. These are the primary strata of the religions of mankind, often shifting their position, and sometimes overlapping each other; they are distinguished from the secondary strata, as the religions of nations from the inspirations of individuals. Thrown into the form of abstraction, they express the various degrees of distinctness with which man realizes his own existence or that of a Divine Being and the relations between them. But they are also powers which have shaped the course of events in the world. The secret is contained in them, why one nation has been free, another a slave; why one nation has dwelt like ants upon a hillock, another has swept over the earth; why one nation has given up its life almost without a struggle, while another has been hewn limb from limb in the conflict with its conquerors. All these religions contributed to the polytheism of Greece; some elements derived from them being absorbed in the first origin of the Greek religion and language, others acting by later contact, some also by contrast.

> 'Nature through five cycles ran,
> And in the sixth she moulded man.'

We may conclude this portion of our subject with a few remarks on the Greek and Roman religions, which have a peculiar interest to us for several reasons: first, because they have exercised a vast influence on modern Europe, the one through philosophy, the other through law, and both through literature and poetry; secondly, because, almost alone of the heathen religions, they came into contact with early Christianity; thirdly, because they are the religions of ancient, as Christianity is of modern civilization.

The religion of Greece is remarkable for being a literature as well as a religion. Its deities are 'nameless' to us before

Homer; to the Greek himself it began with the Olympic family. Whatever dim notions existed of chaos and primaeval night—of struggles for ascendency between the elder and younger gods, these fables are buried out of sight before Greek mythology begins. The Greek came forth at the dawn of day, himself a youth in the youth of the world, drinking in the life of nature at every pore. The form which his religion took was fixed by the Homeric poems, which may be regarded as standing in the same relation to the religion of Greece as sacred books to other forms of religion. It cannot be said that they aroused the conscience of men; the more the Homeric poems are considered, the more evident it becomes that they have no inner life of morality like Hebrew prophecy, no Divine presence of good slowly purging away the mist that fills the heart of man. What they implanted, what they preserved in the Greek nation, was not the sense of truth or right, but the power of conception and expression—harmonies of language and thought which enabled man to clothe his ideas in forms of everlasting beauty. They stamped the Greek world as the world of art; its religion became the genius of art. And more and more in successive generations, with the co-operation of some political causes, the hand of art impressed itself on religion; in poetry, in sculpture, in architecture, in festivals and dramatic contests, until in the artistic phase of human life the religious is absorbed. And the form of man, and the intellect of man, as if in sympathy with this artistic development, attained a symmetry and power of which the world has never seen the like.

And yet the great riddle of existence was not answered: its deeper mysteries were not explored. The strife of man with himself was healed only superficially; there was beauty and proportion everywhere, but no 'true being.' The Jupiter Olympius of Phidias might seem worthy to preside over the Greek world which he summoned before him; the Olympic victor might stand godlike in the fullness of manly vigour; but where could the weak and mean appear? what place was found for the slave or captive? Could bereaved parents acquiesce in the 'sapless shades' of Homer, or the moral reflections of Thucydides? Was there not some deeper intellectual or spiritual want which man felt, some taste of immortality which he had sometimes experienced, which made him dissatisfied with his earthly state?

No religion that failed to satisfy these cries of nature could become the religion of mankind. Greek art and Greek literature, losing something of their original refinement, spread themselves over the Roman world; except Christianity, they have become the richest treasure of modern Europe. But the religion of Greece never really grew in another soil, or beneath another heaven; it was local and national: dependent on the fine and subtle perceptions of the Greek race; though it amalgamated its deities with those of Egypt and Rome, its spirit never swayed mankind. It has a truer title to permanence and universality in the circumstance that it gave birth to philosophy.

The Greek mind passed, almost unconsciously to itself, from polytheism to monotheism. While offering up worship to the Dorian Apollo, performing vows to Esculapius, panic-stricken about the mutilation of the Hermae, the Greek was also able to think of God as an idea, Θεός not Ζεύς. In this generalized or abstract form the Deity presided over daily life. Not a century after Anaxagoras had introduced the distinction of mind and matter, it was the belief of all philosophic inquirers that God was mind, or the object of mind. The Homeric gods were beginning to be out of place; philosophy could not distinguish Apollo from Athene, or Leto from Here. Unlike the saints of the middle ages, they suggested no food for meditation; they were only beautiful forms, without individual character. By the side of religion and art, speculation had arisen and waxed strong, or rather it might be described as the inner life which sprang from their decay. The clouds of mythology hung around it; its youth was veiled in forms of sense; it was itself a new sort of poetry or religion. Gradually it threw off the garment of sense; it revealed a world of ideas. It is impossible for us to conceive the intensity of these ideas in their first freshness; they were not ideas, but gods, penetrating into the soul of the disciple, sinking into the mind of the human race; objects, not of speculation only, but of faith and love. To the old Greek religion, philosophy might be said to stand in a relation not wholly different from that which the New Testament bears to the Old; the one putting a spiritual world in the place of a temporal, the other an intellectual in the place of a sensuous; and to mankind in general it taught an everlasting lesson, not indeed that of the Gospel of Christ, but one in a lower degree necessary for man, enlarging the limits of the human mind itself, and providing the instruments of every kind of knowledge.

What the religion of Greece was to philosophy and art, that the Roman religion may be said to have been to political and social life. It was the religion of the family; the religion also of the empire of the world. Beginning in rustic simplicity, the traces of which it ever afterwards retained, it grew with the power of the Roman state, and became one with its laws. No fancy or poetry moulded the forms of the Roman gods; they are wanting in character and hardly distinguishable from one another. Not what they were, but their worship, is the point of interest about them. Those inanimate beings occasionally said a patriotic word at some critical juncture of the Roman affairs, but they had no attributes or qualities; they are the mere impersonation of the needs of the state. They were easily identified in civilized and literary times with the Olympic deities, but the transformation was only superficial. Greece never conquered the religion of its masters. Great as was the readiness in later times to admit the worship of foreign deities, endless as were the forms of private superstition, these intrusions never weakened or broke the legal hold of the Roman religion. It was truly the 'established' religion. It represented the greatness and power of Rome. The deification of the Emperor, though disagreeable to the more spiritual and intellectual feelings of that age of the world, was its natural development. While Rome lasted the Roman religion lasted; like some vast fabric which the destroyers of a great city are unable wholly to demolish, it continued, though in ruins, after the irruption of the Goths, and has exercised, through the medium of the civil law, a power over modern Europe.

More interesting for us than the pursuit of this subject into further details is the inquiry, in what light the philosopher regarded the religious system within the circle of which he lived; the spirit of which animated Greek and Roman poetry, the observance of which was the bond of states. In the age of the Antonines, more than six hundred years had passed away since the Athenian people first became conscious of the contrariety of the two elements; and yet the wedge which philosophy had inserted in the world seemed to have made no impression on the deeply rooted customs of mankind. The ever-flowing stream of ideas was too feeble to overthrow the intrenchments of antiquity. The course of individuals might be turned by philosophy; it was not intended to reconstruct the world. It looked on and watched, seeming, in the absence of any real progress, to lose its original force. Paganism tolerated; it had nothing to fear. Socrates and Plato in an earlier, Seneca and Epictetus in a later age, acquiesced in this heathen world, unlike as it was to their own intellectual conceptions of a divine religion. No Greek or Roman philosopher was also a great reformer of religion. Some, like Socrates, were punctual in the observance of religious rites, paying their vows to the gods, fearful of offending against the letter as well as the spirit of divine commands; they thought it was hardly worth while to rationalize the Greek mythology, when there were so many things nearer home to do. Others, like the Epicureans, transferred the gods into a distant heaven, where they were no more heard of; some, like the Stoics, sought to awaken a deeper sense of moral responsibility. There were devout men, such as Plutarch, who thought with reverence of the past, seeking to improve the old heathen faith, and also lamenting its decline; there were scoffers, too, like Lucian, who found inexhaustible amusement in the religious follies of mankind. Others, like Herodotus in earlier ages, accepted with childlike faith the more serious aspect of heathenism, or contented themselves, like Thucydides, with ignoring it. The world, 'wholly given to idolatry,' was a strange inconsistent spectacle to those who were able to reflect, which was seen in many points of view. The various feelings with which different classes of men regarded the statues, temples, sacrifices, oracles, and festivals of the gods, with which they looked upon the conflict of religions meeting on the banks of the Tiber, are not exhausted in the epigrammatic formula of the modern historian: 'All the heathen religions were looked upon by the vulgar as equally true, by the philosopher as equally false, by the magistrate as equally useful.'

Such was the later phase of the religion of nature, with which Christianity came into conflict. It had supplied some of the needs of men by assisting to build up the fabric of society and law. It had left room for others to find expression in philosophy or art. But it was a world divided against itself. It contained two nations or opinions 'struggling in its womb;' the nation or opinion of the many, and the nation or opinion of the few. It was bound together in the framework of law or custom, yet its morality fell below the natural feelings of mankind, and its religious spirit was confused and weakened by the admixture of foreign superstitions. It was a world of which it is not difficult to find traces that it was self-condemned. It might be compared to a fruit, the rind of which was hard and firm, while within it was soft and decaying. Within this outer rind or circle, for two centuries and a half, Christianity was working; at last it appeared without, itself the seed or kernel of a new organization. That when the conflict was over, and the world found itself Christian, many elements of the old religion still remained, and reasserted themselves in Christian forms; that the 'ghost of the dead Roman Empire' lingered 'about the grave thereof;' that Christianity accomplished only imperfectly what heathenism failed to do at all, is a result unlike pictures that are sometimes drawn, but sadly in accordance with what history teaches of mankind and of human nature.

§ 4.

Natural religion is not only concerned with the history of the religions of nature, nor does it only reflect that 'light of the Gentiles' which philosophy imparted; it has to do with the present as well as with the past, with Christian as well as heathen countries. Revealed religion passes into natural, and natural religion exists side by side with revealed; there is a truth independent of Christianity; and the daily life of Christian men is very different from the life of Christ. This general or natural religion may be compared to a wide-spread lake, shallow and motionless, rather than to a living water—the overflowing of the Christian faith over a professing Christian world, the level of which may be at one time higher or lower; it is the religion of custom or prescription, or rather the unconscious influence of religion on the minds of men in general; it includes also the speculative idea of religion when taken off the Christian foundation. Natural religion, in this modern sense, has a relation both to philosophy and life. That is to say (1), it is a theory of religion which appeals to particular evidences for the being of a God, though resting, perhaps more safely, on the general conviction that 'this universal frame cannot want a mind.' But it has also a relation to life and practice (2), for it is the religion of the many; the average, as it may be termed, of religious feeling in a Christian land, the leaven of the Gospel hidden in the world. St. Paul speaks of those 'who knowing not the law are a law unto themselves.' Experience seems to show that something of the same kind must be acknowledged in Christian as well as in heathen countries; which may be conveniently considered under the head of natural religion.

Arguments for the being of a God are of many kinds. There are arguments from final causes, and arguments from first causes, and arguments from ideas; logical forms, as they appear to be, in which different metaphysical schools mould their faith. Of the first sort the following may be taken as an instance:—A person walking on the seashore finds a watch or other piece of mechanism; he observes its parts, and their adaptation to each other; he sees the watch in motion, and comprehends the aim of the whole. In the formation of that senseless material he perceives that which satisfies him that it is the work of intelligence, or, in other words, the marks of design. And looking from the watch to the world around him, he seems to perceive innumerable ends, and innumerable actions tending to them, in the composition of the world itself, and in the structure of plants and animals. Advancing a step further, he asks himself the question, why he should not acknowledge the like marks of design in the moral world also; in passions and actions, and in the great end of life. Of all there is the same account to be given— 'the machine of the world,' of which God is the Maker.

This is the celebrated argument from final causes for the being of a God, the most popular of the arguments of natural religion, partly because it admits of much ingenious illustration, and also because it is tangible and intelligible. Ideas of a Supreme Being must be given through something.

for it is impossible that we should know Him as He is. And the truest representation that we can form of God is, in one sense, that which sets forth His nature most vividly; yet another condition must also be remembered, viz. that this representation ought not only to be the most distinct, but the highest and holiest possible. Because we cannot see Him as He is, that is no reason for attributing to Him the accidents of human personality. And, in using figures of speech, we are bound to explain to all who are capable of understanding, that we speak in a figure only, and to remind them that names by which we describe the being or attributes of God need a correction in the silence of thought. Even logical categories may give as false a notion of the Divine nature in our own age, as graven images in the days of the patriarchs. However legitimate or perhaps necessary the employment of them may be, we must place ourselves not below, but above them.

(α) In the argument from final causes, the work of the Creator is compared to a work of art. Art is a poor figure of nature; it has no freedom or luxuriance. Between the highest work of art and the lowest animal or vegetable production, there is an interval which will never be spanned. The miracle of life derives no illustration from the handicraftsman putting his hand to the chisel, or anticipating in idea the form which he is about to carve. More truly might we reason, that what the artist is, the God of nature is not. For all the processes of nature are unlike the processes of art. If, instead of a watch, or some other piece of curious and exquisite workmanship, we think of a carpenter and a table, the force of the argument seems to vanish, and the illustration becomes inappropriate and unpleasing. The ingenuity and complexity of the structure, and not the mere appearance of design, makes the watch a natural image of the creation of the world.

(3) But not only does the conception of the artist supply no worthy image of the Creator and His work; the idea of

design which is given by it requires a further correction before it can be transferred to nature. The complication of the world around us is quite different from the complexity of the watch. It is not a regular and finite structure, but rather infinite in irregularity; which instead of design often exhibits absence of design, such as we cannot imagine any architect of the world contriving; the construction of which is far from appearing, even to our feeble intelligence, the best possible, though it, and all things in it, are very good. If we fix our minds on this very phrase 'the machine of the world,' we become aware that it is unmeaning to us. The watch is separated and isolated from other matter; dependent indeed on one or two general laws of nature, but otherwise cut off from things around. But nature, the more we consider it, the more does one part appear to be linked with another; there is no isolation here; the plants grow in the soil which has been preparing for them through a succession of geological eras, they are fed by the rain and nourished by light and air; the animals depend for their life on all inferior existences.

(γ) This difference between art and nature leads us to observe another defect in the argument from final causes—that, instead of putting the world together, it takes it to pieces. It fixes our minds on those parts of the world which exhibit marks of design, and withdraws us from those in which marks of design seem to fail. There are formations in nature, such as the hand, which have a kind of mechanical beauty, and show in a striking way, even to an uneducated person, the wonder and complexity of creation. In like manner we feel a momentary surprise in finding out, through the agency of a microscope, that the minutest creatures have their fibres, tissues, vessels. And yet the knowledge of this is but the most fragmentary and superficial knowledge of nature; it is the wonder in which philosophy begins, very different from the comprehension of this universal frame in all its complexity and in all its minuteness. And from this elementary notion of nature, we seek to form an idea of the Author of nature. As though God were in the animal frame and not also in the dust to which it turns; in the parts, and not equally in the whole; in the present world, and not also in the antecedent ages which have prepared for its existence.

(δ) Again, this teleological argument for the being of God gives an erroneous idea of the moral government of the world. For it leads us to suppose that all things are tending to some end; that there is no prodigality or waste, but that all things are, and are made, in the best way possible. Our faith must be tried to find a use for barren deserts, for venomous reptiles, for fierce wild beasts, nay, for the sins and miseries of mankind. Nor does 'there seem to be any resting place,' until the world and all things in it are admitted to have some end impressed upon them by the hand of God, but unseen to us. Experience is cast aside while our meditations lead us to conceive the world under this great form of a final cause. All that is in nature is best; all that is in human life is best. And yet every one knows instances in which nature seems to fail of its end—in which life has been cut down like a flower, and trampled under foot of man.

(ε) There is another way in which the argument from final causes is suggestive of an imperfect conception of the Divine Being. It presents God to us exclusively in one aspect, not as a man, much less as a spirit holding communion with our spirit, but only as an artist. We conceive of Him, as in the description of the poet, standing with compasses over sea and land, and designing the wondrous work. Does not the image tend to make the spiritual creation an accident of the material? For although it is possible, as Bishop Butler has shown, to apply the argument from final causes, as a figure of speech, to the habits and feelings, this adaptation is unnatural, and open even to greater objections than its application to the physical world.

For how can we distinguish true final causes from false ones ? how can we avoid confusing what ought to be with what is—the fact with the law ?

(ζ) If we look to the origin of the notion of a final cause, we shall feel still further indisposed to make it the category under which we sum up the working of the Divine Being in creation. As Aristotle, who probably first made a philosophical use of the term, says, it is transferred from mind to matter ; in other words, it clothes facts in our ideas. Lord Bacon offers another warning against the employment of final causes in the service of religion : 'they are like the vestals consecrated to God, and are barren.' They are a figure of speech which adds nothing to our knowledge. When applied to the Creator, they are a figure of a figure ; that is to say, the figurative conception of the artist embodied or idealized in his work, is made the image of the Divine Being. And no one really thinks of God in nature under this figure of human skill. As certainly as the man who found a watch or piece of mechanism on the seashore would conclude, 'here are marks of design, indications of an intelligent artist,' so certainly, if he came across the meanest or the highest of the works of nature, would he infer, 'this was not made by man, nor by any human art.' He sees in a moment that the seaweed beneath his feet is something different in kind from the productions of man. What should lead him to say, that in the same sense that man made the watch, God made the seaweed ? For the seaweed grows by some power of life, and is subject to certain physiological laws, like all other vegetable or animal substances. But if we say that God created this life, or that where this life ends there His creative power begins, our analogy again fails, for God stands in a different relation to animal and vegetable life from what the artist does to the work of His hands. And, when we think further of God, as a Spirit without body, creating all things by His word, or rather by His thought, in an instant of time, to whom the plan and execution are all one, we become absolutely bewildered in the attempt to apply the image of the artist to the Creator of the world.

These are some of the points in respect of which the argument from final causes falls short of that conception of the Divine nature which reason is adequate to form. It is the beginning of our knowledge of God, not the end. It is suited to the faculties of children rather than of those who are of full age. It belongs to a stage of metaphysical philosophy, in which abstract ideas were not made the subject of analysis; to a time when physical science had hardly learnt to conceive the world as a whole. It is a devout thought which may well arise in the grateful heart when contemplating the works of creation, but must not be allowed to impair that higher intellectual conception which we are able to form of a Creator, any more than it should be put in the place of the witness of God within.

Another argument of the same nature for the being of a God is derived from first causes, and may be stated as follows:—All things that we see are the results or effects of causes, and these again the effects of other causes, and so on through an immense series. But somewhere or other this series must have a stop or limit; we cannot go back from cause to cause without end. Otherwise the series will have no basis on which to rest. Therefore there must be a first cause, that is, God. This argument is sometimes strengthened by the further supposition that the world must have had a beginning, whence it seems to follow, that it must have a cause external to itself which made it begin; a principle of rest, which is the source of motion to all other things, as ancient philosophy would have expressed it—hovering in this as in other speculations intermediate between the physical and metaphysical world.

The difficulty about this argument is much the same as that respecting the preceding. So long as we conceive the world under the form of cause and effect, and suppose the first link in the chain to be the same with those that succeed it, the argument is necessary and natural; we cannot escape from it without violence to our reason. Our only doubt will probably be, whether we can pass from the notion of a first cause to that of an intelligent Creator. But when, instead of resting in the word 'cause,' we go on to the idea, or rather the variety of ideas which are signified by the word 'cause,' the argument begins to dissolve. When we say, 'God is the cause of the world,' in what sense of the word cause is this? Is it as life or mind is a cause, or the hammer or hand of the workman, or light or air, or any natural substance? Is it in that sense of the word cause, in which it is almost identified with the effect? or in that sense in which it is wholly external to it? Or when we endeavour to imagine or conceive a common cause of the world and all things in it, do we not perceive that we are using the word in none of these senses; but in a new one, to which life, or mind, or many other words, would be at least equally applicable? 'God is the life of the world.' That is a poor and somewhat unmeaning expression to indicate the relation of God to the world; yet life is a subtle and wonderful power, pervading all things, and in various degrees animating all things. 'God is the mind of the world.' That is still inadequate as an expression, even though mind can act where it is not, and its ways are past finding out. But when we say, 'God is the cause of the world,' that can be scarcely said to express more than that God stands in some relation to the world touching which we are unable to determine whether He is in the world or out of it, 'immanent' in the language of philosophy, or 'transcendent.'

There are two sources from which these and similar proofs of the being of a God are derived: first, analogy; secondly, the logical necessity of the human mind. Analogy supplies an image, an illustration. It wins for us an imaginary world from the void and formless infinite. But whether it does more than this must depend wholly on the nature of the analogy. We cannot argue from the seen to the unseen, unless we previously know their relation to each other. We cannot say at random that another life is the double or parallel of this, and also the development of it; we cannot urge the temporary inequality of this world as a presumption of the final injustice of another. Who would think of arguing from the vegetable to the animal world, except in those points where he had already discovered a common principle? Who would reason that animal life must follow the laws of vegetation in those points which were peculiar to it? Yet many theological arguments have this fundamental weakness; they lean on faith for their own support; they lower the heavenly to the earthly, and may be used to prove anything.

The other source of these and similar arguments is the logical necessity of the human mind. A first cause, a beginning, an infinite Being limiting our finite natures, is necessary to our conceptions. 'We have an idea of God, there must be something to correspond to our idea,' and so on. The flaw here is equally real, though not so apparent. While we dwell within the forms of the understanding and acknowledge their necessity, such arguments seem unanswerable. But once ask the question, Whence this necessity? was there not a time when the human mind felt no such necessity? is the necessity really satisfied? or is there not some further logical sequence in which I am involved which still remains unanswerable? the whole argument vanishes at once, as the chimera of a metaphysical age. The seventeenth and eighteenth centuries have been peculiarly fertile in such arguments; the belief in which, whether they have any value or not, must not be imposed upon us as an article of faith.

If we say again, 'that our highest conception must have a true existence,' which is the well-known argument of Anselm and Des Cartes for the being of God, still this is no more than saying, in a technical or dialectical form, that we cannot imagine God without imagining that He is. Of no other conception can it be said that it involves existence; and hence no additional force is gained by such a mode of statement. The simple faith in a Divine Being is cumbered, not supported, by evidences derived from a metaphysical system which has passed away. It is a barren logic that elicits the more meagre conception of existence from the higher one of Divinity. Better for philosophy, as well as faith, to think of God at once and immediately as 'Perfect Being.'

Arguments from first and final causes may be regarded as a kind of poetry of natural religion. There are some minds to whom it would be impossible to conceive of the relation of God to the world under any more abstract form. They, as well as all of us, may ponder in amazement on the infinite contrivances of creation. We are all agreed that none but a Divine power framed them. We differ only as to whether the Divine power is to be regarded as the hand that fashioned, or the intelligence that designed them, or an operation inconceivable to us which we dimly trace and feebly express in words.

That which seems to underlie our conception both of first and final causes, is the idea of law which we see not broken or intercepted, or appearing only in particular spots of nature, but everywhere and in all things. All things do not equally exhibit marks of design, but all things are equally subject to the operation of law. The highest mark of intelligence pervades the whole; no one part is better than another; it is all 'very good.' The absence of design, if we like so to turn the phrase, is a part of the design. Even the less comely parts, like the plain spaces in a building, have elements of use and beauty. He who has ever thought in the most imperfect manner of the universe which modern science unveils, needs no evidence that the details of it are incapable of being framed by anything short of a Divine power. Art, and nature, and science, these three—the first giving us the conception of the relation of parts to a whole; the second, of endless variety and intricacy, such as no art has ever attained; the third, of uniform laws which amid all the changes of created things remain fixed as at the first, reaching even to the heavens—are the witnesses of the Creator in the external world.

Nor can it weaken our belief in a Supreme Being, to observe that the same harmony and uniformity extend also to the actions of men. Why should it be thought a thing incredible that God should give law and order to the spiritual, no less than the natural creation? That human beings do not 'thrust or break their ranks;' that the life of nations, like that of plants or animals, has a regular growth; that the same strata or stages are observable in the religions, no less than the languages of mankind, as in the structure of the earth, are strange reasons for doubting the Providence of God. Perhaps it is even stranger, that those who do not doubt should eye with jealousy the accumulation of such facts. Do we really wish that our conceptions of God should only be on the level of the ignorant; adequate to the passing emotions of human feeling, but to reason inadequate? That Christianity is the confluence of many channels of human thought does not interfere with its Divine origin. It is not the less immediately the word of God because there have been preparations for it in all ages, and in many countries.

The more we take out of the category of chance in the world either of nature or of mind, the more present evidence we have of the faithfulness of God. We do not need to have a chapter of accidents in life to enable us to realize the existence of a personal God, as though events which we can account for were not equally His work. Let not use or custom so prevail in our minds as to make this higher notion of God cheerless or uncomfortable to us. The rays of His presence may still warm us, as well as enlighten us. Surely

He, in whom we live and move and have our being, is nearer to us than He would be if He interfered occasionally for our benefit.

'The curtain of the physical world is closing in upon us:' What does this mean but that the arms of His intelligence are embracing us on every side? We have no more fear of nature; for our knowledge of the laws of nature has cast out fear. We know Him as He shows himself in them, even as we are known of Him. Do we think to draw near to God by returning to that state in which nature seemed to be without law, when man cowered like the animals before the storm, and in the meteors of the skies and the motions of the heavenly bodies sought to read the purposes of God respecting himself? Or shall we rest in that stage of the knowledge of nature which was common to the heathen philosophers and to the Fathers of the Christian Church? or in that of two hundred years ago, ere the laws of the heavenly bodies were discovered? or of fifty years ago, before geology had established its truths on sure foundations? or of thirty years ago, ere the investigation of old language had revealed the earlier stages of the history of the human mind. At which of these resting-places shall we pause to renew the covenant between Reason and Faith? Rather at none of them, if the first condition of a true faith be the belief in all true knowledge.

To trace our belief up to some primitive revelation, to entangle it in a labyrinth of proofs or analogies, will not infix it deeper or elevate its character. Why should we be willing to trust the convictions of the father of the human race rather than our own, the faith of primitive rather than of civilized times? Or why should we use arguments about the Infinite Being, which, in proportion as they have force, reduce him to the level of the finite; and which seem to lose their force in proportion as we admit that God's ways are not as our ways, nor His thoughts as our thoughts? The belief is strong enough without those fictitious supports;

it cannot be made stronger with them. While nature still presents to us its world of unexhausted wonders; while sin and sorrow lead us to walk by faith, and not by sight; while the soul of man departs this life not knowing whither it goes; so long will the belief endure of an Almighty Creator, from whom we came, to whom we return.

Why, again, should we argue for the immortality of the soul from the analogy of the seed and the tree, or the state of human beings before and after birth, when the ground of proof in the one case is wanting in the other, namely, experience? Because the dead acorn may a century hence become a spreading oak, no one would infer that the corrupted remains of animals will rise to life in new forms. The error is not in the use of such illustrations as figures of speech, but in the allegation of them as proofs or evidences after the failure of the analogy is perceived. Perhaps it may be said that in popular discourse they pass unchallenged; it may be a point of honour that they should be maintained, because they are in Paley or Butler. But evidences for the many which are not evidences for the few are treacherous props to Christianity. They are always liable to come back to us detected, and to need some other fallacy for their support.

Let it be considered, whether the evidences of religion[7] should be separated from religion itself. The Gospel has a truth perfectly adapted to human nature; its origin and diffusion in the world have a history like any other history. But truth does not need evidences of the truth, nor does history separate the proof of facts from the facts themselves. It was only in the decline of philosophy the Greeks began to ask about the criterion of knowledge. What would be thought of an historian who should collect all the testimonies on one side of some disputed question, and insist on their reception as a political creed? Such evidences do not require the hand of some giant infidel to pull them down; they fall the moment they are touched. But the Christian faith is in its holy place, uninjured by the fall; the truths of the existence of God, or of the immortality of the soul, are not periled by the observation that some analogies on which they have been supposed to rest are no longer tenable. There is no use in attempting to prove by the misapplication of the methods of human knowledge, what we ought never to doubt.

'There are two things,' says a philosopher of the last century; 'of which it may be said, that the more we think of them, the more they fill the soul with awe and wonder—the starry heaven above, and the moral law within. I may not regard either as shrouded in darkness, or look for or guess at either in what is beyond, out of my sight. I see them right before me, and link them at once with the consciousness of my own existence. The former of the two begins with place, which I inhabit as a member of the outward world, and extends the connexion in which I stand with it into immeasurable space; in which are worlds upon worlds, and systems upon systems; and so on into the endless times of their revolutions, their beginning and continuance. The second begins with my invisible self; that is to say, my personality, and presents me in a world which has true infinity, but which the lower faculty of the soul can hardly scan; with which I know myself to be not only as in the world of sight, in an accidental connexion, but in a necessary and universal one. The first glance at innumerable worlds annihilates any importance which I may attach to myself as an animal structure; whilst the matter out of which it is made must again return to the earth (itself a mere point in the universe), after it has been endued, one knows not how, with the power of life for a little season. The second glance exalts me infinitely as an intelligent being, whose personality involves a moral law, which reveals in me a life distinct from that of the animals, independent of the world of sense. So much at least I may infer from the regular determination of my being by this law, which is itself infinite, free from the limitations and conditions of this present life.'

So, in language somewhat technical, has Kant described two great principles of natural religion. 'There are two witnesses,' we may add in a later strain of reflection, 'of the being of God; the order of nature in the world, and the progress of the mind of man. He is not the order of nature, nor the progress of mind, nor both together; but that which is above and beyond them; of which they, even if conceived in a single instant, are but the external sign, the highest evidences of God which we can conceive, but not God himself. The first to the ancient world seemed to be the work of chance, or the personal operation of one or many Divine beings. We know it to be the result of laws endless in their complexity, and yet not the less admirable for their simplicity also. The second has been regarded, even in our own day, as a series of errors capriciously invented by the ingenuity of individual men. We know it to have a law of its own, a continuous order which cannot be inverted; not to be confounded with, yet not wholly separate from, the law of nature and the will of God. Shall we doubt the world to be the creation of a Divine power, only because it is more wonderful than could have been conceived by "them of old time;" or human reason to be in the image of God, because it too bears the marks of an overruling law or intelligence?'

§ 5.

Natural religion, in the last sense in which we are to consider it, carries us into a region of thought more practical, and therefore more important, than any of the preceding; it comes home to us; it takes in those who are near and dear to us; even ourselves are not excluded from it. Under this name, or some other, we cannot refuse to consider a subject which involves the religious state of the greater portion of mankind, even in a Christian country. Every Sunday the ministers of religion set before us the ideal of

Christian life; they repeat and expand the words of Christ and his Apostles; they speak of the approach of death, and of this world as a preparation for a better. It is good to be reminded of these things. But there is another aspect of Christianity which we must not ignore, the aspect under which experience shows it, in our homes and among our acquaintance, on the level of human things; the level of education, habit, and circumstances on which men are, and on which they will probably remain while they live. This latter phase of religion it is our duty to consider, and not narrow ourselves to the former only.

It is characteristic of this subject that it is full of contradictions; we say one thing at one time about it, another thing at another. Our feelings respecting individuals are different in their lifetime, and after their death, as they are nearly related to us, or have no claims on our affections. Our acknowledgement of sin in the abstract is more willing and hearty than the recognition of particular sins in ourselves, or even in others. We readily admit that 'the world lieth in wickedness;' where the world is, or of whom it is made up, we are unable to define. Great men seem to be exempt from the religious judgement which we pass on our fellows; it does not occur to persons of taste to regard them under this aspect; we deal tenderly with them, and leave them to themselves and God. And sometimes we rest on outward signs of religion; at other times we guard ourselves and others against trusting to such signs. And commonly we are ready to acquiesce in the standard of those around us, thinking it a sort of impertinence to interfere with their religious concerns; at other times we go about the world as with a lantern, seeking for the image of Christ among men, and are zealous for the good of others, out of season or in season. We need not unravel further this tangled web of thoughts and feelings, which religion, and affection, and habit, and opinion weave. A few words will describe the fact out of which these contradictions arise.

It is a side of the world from which we are apt to turn away, perhaps hoping to make things better by fancying them so, instead of looking at them as they really are.

It is impossible not to observe that innumerable persons—shall we say the majority of mankind?—who have a belief in God and immortality, have nevertheless hardly any consciousness of the peculiar doctrines of the Gospel. They seem to live away from them in the routine of business or of society, 'the common life of all men,' not without a sense of right, and a rule of truth and honesty, yet insensible to what our Saviour meant by taking up the cross and following Him, or what St. Paul meant by 'being one with Christ.' They die without any great fear or lively faith; to the last more interested about concerns of this world than about the hope of another. In the Christian sense they are neither proud nor humble; they have seldom experienced the sense of sin, they have never felt keenly the need of forgiveness. Neither on the other hand do they value themselves on their good deeds, or expect to be saved by their own merits. Often they are men of high moral character; many of them have strong and disinterested attachments, and quick human sympathies; sometimes a stoical feeling of uprightness, or a peculiar sensitiveness to dishonour. It would be a mistake to say they are without religion. They join in its public acts; they are offended at profaneness or impiety; they are thankful for the blessings of life, and do not rebel against its misfortunes. Such persons meet us at every turn. They are those whom we know and associate with; honest in their dealings, respectable in their lives, decent in their conversation. The Scripture speaks to us of two classes represented by the Church and the world, the wheat and the tares, the sheep and the goats, the friends and enemies of God. We cannot say in which of these two divisions we should find a place for them.

The picture is a true one, and, if we turn the light round, some of us may find in it a resemblance of ourselves no less than of other men. Others will include us in the same circle in which we are including them. What shall we say to such a state, common as it is to both us and them? The fact that we are considering is not the evil of the world, but the neutrality of the world, the indifference of the world, the inertness of the world. There are multitudes of men and women everywhere, who have no peculiarly Christian feelings, to whom, except for the indirect influence of Christian institutions, the life and death of Christ would have made no difference, and who have, nevertheless, the common sense of truth and right almost equally with true Christians. You cannot say of them 'there is none that doeth good; no, not one.' The other tone of St. Paul is more suitable, 'When the Gentiles that know not the law do by nature the things contained in the law, these not knowing the law are a law unto themselves.' So of what we commonly term the world, as opposed to those who make a profession of Christianity, we must not shrink from saying. 'When men of the world do by nature whatsoever things are honest, whatsoever things are lovely, whatsoever things are of good report, these not being conscious of the grace of God, do by nature what can only be done by His grace.' Why should we make them out worse than they are? We must cease to speak evil of them, ere they will judge fairly of the characters of religious men. That, with so little recognition of His personal relation to them, God does not cast them off, is a ground of hope rather than of fear—of thankfulness, not of regret.

Many strange thoughts arise at the contemplation of this intermediate world, which some blindness, or hardness, or distance in nature, separates from the love of Christ. We ask ourselves 'what will become of them after death?' 'For what state of existence can this present life be a preparation?' Perhaps they will turn the question upon us; and we may answer for ourselves and them, 'that we throw ourselves on the mercy of God.' We cannot deny that in the sight of God they may condemn us; their moral worth may be more acceptable to Him than our Christian feeling. For we know that God is not like some earthly sovereign, who may be offended at the want of attention which we show to him. He can only estimate us always by our fulfilment of moral and Christian duties. When the balance is struck, it is most probable, nay, it is quite certain, that many who are first will be last, and the last first. And this transfer will take place, not only among those who are within the gates of the Christian Church, but from the world also into the Church. There may be some among us who have given the cup of cold water to a brother, 'not knowing it was the Lord.' Some again may be leading a life in their own family which is 'not far from the kingdom of heaven.' We do not say that for ourselves there is more than one way; that way is Christ. But, in the case of others, it is right that we should take into account their occupation, character, circumstances, the manner in which Christianity may have been presented to them, the intellectual or other difficulties which may have crossed their path. We shall think more of the unconscious Christianity of their lives, than of the profession of it on their lips. So that we seem almost compelled to be Christian and Unchristian at once: Christian in reference to the obligations of Christianity upon ourselves; Unchristian—if indeed it be not a higher kind of Christianity—in not judging those who are unlike ourselves by our own standard.

Other oppositions have found their way into statements of Christian truth, which we shall sometimes do well to forget. Mankind are not simply divided into two classes; they pass insensibly from one to the other. The term world is itself ambiguous, meaning the world very near to us, and yet a long way off from us; which we contrast with the Church, and which we nevertheless feel to be one with the Church, and incapable of being separated. Sometimes the Church bears a high and noble witness against the world, and at other times, even to the religious mind, the balance seems to be even, and the world in its turn begins to bear witness against the Church. There are periods of history in which they both grow together. Little cause as there may be for congratulation in our present state, yet we cannot help tracing, in the last half-century, a striking amelioration in our own and some other countries, testified to by changes in laws and manners. Many reasons have been given for this change: the efforts of a few devoted men in the last, or the beginning of the present, century; a long peace; diffusion of education; increase of national wealth; changes in the principles of government; improvement in the lives of the ministers of religion. No one who has considered this problem will feel that he is altogether able to solve it. He cannot venture to say that the change springs from any bold aggression which the Church has made upon the vices of mankind; nor is it certain that any such effort would have produced the result. In the Apostle's language it must still remain a mystery 'why mankind collectively often become better;' and not less so, 'why, when deprived of all the means and influences of virtue and religion, they do not always become worse.' Even for evil, Nature, that is, the God of nature, has set limits; men do not corrupt themselves endlessly. Here, too, it is, 'Hitherto shalt thou go, but no further.'

Reflections of this kind are not a mere speculation; they have a practical use. They show us the world as it is, neither lighted up with the aspirations of hope and faith, nor darkened beneath the shadow of God's wrath. They teach us to regard human nature in a larger and more kindly way, which is the first step towards amending and strengthening it. They make us think of the many as well as of the few; as ministers of the Gospel, warning us against preaching to the elect only, instead of seeking to do good to all men. They take us out of the straits and narrownesses of religion, into wider fields in which the analogy of faith is still our guide. They help us to reconcile nature with grace; they prevent our thinking that Christ came into the world for our sakes only, or that His words have no meaning when they are scattered beyond the limits of the Christian Church. They remind us that the moral state of mankind here, and their eternal state hereafter, are not wholly dependent on our poor efforts for their religious improvement; and that the average of men who seem often to be so careless about their own highest interest, are not when they pass away uncared for in His sight.

Doubtless, the lives of individuals that rise above this average are the salt of the earth. They are not to be confounded with the many, because for these latter a place may be found in the counsels of Providence. Those who add the love of their fellow-creatures to the love of God, who make the love of truth the rule of both, bear the image of Christ until His coming again. And yet, probably, they would be the last persons to wish to distinguish themselves from their fellow-creatures. The Christian life makes all things kin; it does not stand out 'angular' against any part of mankind. And that humble spirit which the best of men have ever shown in reference to their brethren, is also the true spirit of the Church towards the world. If a tone of dogmatism and exclusiveness is unbecoming in individual Christians, is it not equally so in Christian communities? There is no need, because men will not listen to one motive, that we should not present them with another; there is no reason, because they will not hear the voice of the preacher, that they should be refused the blessings of education; or that we should cease to act upon their circumstances, because we cannot awaken the heart and conscience. We are too apt to view as hostile to religion that which only takes a form different from religion, as trade, or politics, or professional life. More truly may religious men regard the world, in its various phases, as in many points a witness against themselves. The exact appreciation of the good as well as the evil of the world is a link of communion with our fellow-men; may it not also be, too, with the body of

Christ? There are lessons of which the world is the keeper no less than the Church. Especially have earnest and sincere Christians reason to reflect, if ever they see the moral sentiments of mankind directed against them.

The God of peace rest upon you, is the concluding benediction of most of the Epistles. How can He rest upon us, who draw so many hard lines of demarcation between ourselves and other men; who oppose the Church and the world, Sundays and working days, revelation and science, the past and present, the life and state of which religion speaks and the life which we ordinarily lead? It is well that we should consider these lines of demarcation rather as representing aspects of our life than as corresponding to classes of mankind. It is well that we should acknowledge that one aspect of life or knowledge is as true as the other. Science and revelation touch one another: the past floats down in the present. We are all members of the same Christian world; we are all members of the same Christian Church. Who can bear to doubt this of themselves or of their family? What parent would think otherwise of his child?—what child of his parent? Religion holds before us an ideal which we are far from reaching; natural affection softens and relieves the characters of those we love; experience alone shows men what they truly are. All these three must so meet as to do violence to none. If, in the age of the Apostles, it seemed to be the duty of the believers to separate themselves from the world and take up a hostile position, not less marked in the present age is the duty of abolishing in a Christian country what has now become an artificial distinction, and seeking by every means in our power, by fairness, by truthfulness, by knowledge, by love unfeigned, by the absence of party and prejudice, by acknowledging the good in all things, to reconcile the Church to the world, the one half of our nature to the other; drawing the mind off from speculative difficulties, or matters of party and opinion, to that which almost all equally acknowledge and almost equally rest short of—the life of Christ.

ESSAY

ON

RIGHTEOUSNESS BY FAITH

———••———

No doctrine in later times has been looked at so exclusively through the glass of controversy as that of justification. From being the simplest it has become the most difficult; the language of the heart has lost itself in a logical tangle. Differences have been drawn out as far as possible, and then taken back and reconciled. The extreme of one view has more than once produced a reaction in favour of the other. Many senses have been attributed to the same words, and simple statements carried out on both sides into endless conclusions. New formulas of conciliation have been put in the place of old-established phrases, and have soon died away, because they had no root in language or in the common sense or feeling of mankind. The difficulty of the subject has been increased by the different degrees of importance attached to it: while to some it is an *articulus stantis aut cadentis ecclesiae*, others have never been able to see in it more than a verbal dispute.

This perplexity on the question of righteousness by faith is partly due to the character of the age in which it began to revive. Men felt at the Reformation the need of a spiritual religion, and could no longer endure the yoke which had been put upon their fathers. The heart rebelled against the burden of ordinances; it wanted to take a nearer way to reconciliation with God. But when the struggle was over, and individuals were seeking to impart to others the peace which they had found themselves, they had no simple or natural expression of their belief. They were alone in a world in which the human mind had been long enslaved. It was necessary for them to go down into the land of the enemy, and get their weapons sharpened before they could take up a position and fortify their camp.

In other words, the Scholastic Logic had been for six centuries previous the great instrument of training the human mind; it had grown up with it, and become a part of it. Neither would it have been more possible for the Reformers to have laid it aside than to have laid aside the use of language itself. Around theology it lingers still, seeming reluctant to quit a territory which is peculiarly its own. No science has hitherto fallen so completely under its power: no other is equally unwilling to ask the meaning of terms; none has been so fertile in reasonings and consequences. The change of which Lord Bacon was the herald has hardly yet reached it; much less could the Reformation have anticipated the New Philosophy.

The whole mental structure of that time rendered it necessary that the Reformers, no less than their opponents, should resort to the scholastic methods of argument. The difference between the two parties did not lie here. Perhaps it may be said with truth that the Reformers were even more schoolmen than their opponents, because they dealt more with abstract ideas, and were more concentrated on a single topic. The whole of Luther's teaching was summed up in a single article, 'Righteousness by Faith.' That was to him the Scriptural expression of a Spiritual religion. But this, according to the manner of that time, could not be left in the simple language of St. Paul. It was to be proved from Scripture first, then isolated by definition; then it might be safely drawn out into remote consequences.

And yet, why was this? Why not repeat, with a slight alteration of the words rather than the meaning of the Apostle, Neither justification by faith nor justification by works, but 'a new creature'? Was there not yet 'a more excellent way' to oppose things to words—the life, and spirit, and freedom of the Gospel, to the deadness, and powerlessness, and slavery of the Roman Church? So it seems natural to us to reason, looking back after an interval of three centuries on the weary struggle; so absorbing to those who took part in it once, so distant now either to us or them. But so it could not be. The temper of the times, and the education of the Reformers themselves, made it necessary that one dogmatic system should be met by another. The scholastic divinity had become a charmed circle, and no man could venture out of it, though he might oppose or respond within it.

And thus justification by faith, and justification by works, became the watchword of two parties. We may imagine ourselves at that point in the controversy when the Pelagian dispute had been long since hushed, and that respecting Predestination had not yet begun; when men were not differing about original sin, and had not begun to differ about the Divine decrees. What Luther sought for was to find a formula which expressed most fully the entire, unreserved, immediate dependence of the believer on Christ. What the Catholic sought for was so to modify this formula as not to throw dishonour on the Church by making religion a merely personal matter; or on the lives of holy men of old, who had wrought out their salvation by asceticism; or endanger morality by appearing to undervalue good works. It was agreed by all, that men are saved through Christ— [that men are saved] not of themselves, but of the grace of God, was equally agreed since the condemnation of Pelagius —that faith and works imply each other, was not disputed by either. A narrow space is left for the combat, which has to be carried on within the outworks of an earlier creed, in which, nevertheless, great subtlety of human thought and differences of character admit of being displayed.

On this narrow ground the first question that naturally arises is, how faith is to be defined? is it to include love and holiness, or to be separated from them? If the former, it seems to lose its apprehensive dependent nature, and to be scarcely distinguishable from works; if the latter, the statement is too refined for the common sense of mankind; though made by Luther, it could scarcely be retained even by his immediate followers. Again, is it an act or a state? are we to figure it as a point, or as a line? Is the whole of our spiritual life anticipated in the beginning, or may faith no less than works, justification equally with sanctification, be conceived of as going on to perfection? Is justification an objective act of Divine mercy, or a subjective state of which the believer is conscious in himself? Is the righteousness of faith imputed or inherent, an attribution of the merits of Christ, or a renewal of the human heart itself? What is the test of a true faith? And is it possible for those who are possessed of it to fall away? How can we exclude the doctrine of human merit consistently with Divine justice? How do we account for the fact that some have this faith, and others are without it, this difference being apparently independent of their moral state? If faith comes by grace, is it imparted to few or to all? And in what relation does the whole doctrine stand to Predestinarianism on the one hand, and to the Catholic or Sacramental theory on the other?

So at many points the doctrine of righteousness by faith touches the metaphysical questions of subject and object, of necessity and freedom, of habits and actions, and of human consciousness, like a magnet drawing to itself philosophy, as it has once drawn to itself the history of Europe. There were distinctions also of an earlier date, with which it had to struggle, of deeper moral import than their technical form would lead us to suppose, such as that of congruity and condignity, in which the analogy of Christianity is transferred to heathenism, and the doer of good works before justification is regarded as a shadow of the perfected believer. Neither must we omit to observe that, as the doctrine of justification by faith had a close connexion with the Pelagian controversy, carrying the decision of the Church a step further, making Divine Grace not only the source of human action, but also requiring the consciousness or assurance of grace in the believer himself: so it put forth its roots in another direction, attaching itself to Anselm as well as Augustine, and comprehending the idea of satisfaction; not now, as formerly, of Christ offered in the sacrifice of the mass, but of one sacrifice, once offered for the sins of men, whether considered as an expiation by suffering, or implying only a reconciliation between God and man, or a mere manifestation of the righteousness of God.

Such is the whole question, striking deep, and spreading far and wide with its offshoots. It is not our intention to enter on the investigation of all these subjects, many of which are interesting as phases of thought in the history of the Church, but have no bearing on the interpretation of St. Paul's Epistles, and would be out of place here. Our inquiry will embrace two heads: (1) What did St. Paul mean by the expression 'righteousness of faith,' in that age ere controversies about his meaning arose? and (2) What do we mean by it, now that such controversies have died away, and the interest in them is retained only by the theological student, and the Church and the world are changed, and there is no more question of Jew or Gentile, circumcision or uncircumcision, and we do not become Christians, but are so from our birth? Many volumes are not required to explain the meaning of the Apostle; nor can the words of eternal life be other than few and simple to ourselves.

There is one interpretation of the Epistles of St. Paul which is necessarily in some degree false; that is, the interpretation put upon them by later controversy. When the minds of men are absorbed in a particular circle of ideas they take possession of any stray verse, which becomes the centre of their world. They use the words of Scripture, but are incapable of seeing that they have another meaning and are used in a different connexion from that in which they employ them. Sometimes there is a degree of similarity in the application which tends to conceal the difference. Thus Luther and St. Paul both use the same term, 'justified by faith;' and the strength of the Reformer's words is the authority of St. Paul. Yet, observe how far this agreement is one of words: how far of things. For Luther is speaking solely of individuals, St. Paul also of nations; Luther of faith absolutely, St. Paul of faith as relative to the law. With St. Paul faith is the symbol of the universality of the Gospel. Luther excludes this or any analogous point of view. In St. Paul there is no opposition of faith and love; nor does he further determine righteousness by faith as meaning a faith in the blood or even in the death of Christ; nor does he suppose consciousness or assurance in the person justified. But all these are prominent features of the Lutheran doctrine. Once more: the faith of St. Paul has reference to the evil of the world of sight; which was soon to vanish away, that the world in which faith walks might be revealed; but no such allusion is implied in the language of the Reformer. Lastly: the change in the use of the substantive 'righteousness' to 'justification' is the indication of a wide difference between St. Paul and Luther; the natural, almost accidental, language of St. Paul having already passed into a technical formula.

These contrasts make us feel that St. Paul can only be interpreted by himself, not from the systems of modern theologians, nor even from the writings of one who had so much in common with him as Luther. It is the spirit and feeling of St. Paul which Luther represents, not the meaning of his words. A touch of nature in both 'makes them kin.' And without bringing down one to the level of the other, we can imagine St. Paul returning that singular affection, almost like an attachment to a living friend, which the great Reformer felt towards the Apostle. But this personal attachment or resemblance in no way lessens the necessary difference between the preaching of Luther and of St. Paul, which arose in some degree perhaps from their individual character, but chiefly out of the different circumstances and modes of thought of their respective ages. At the Reformation we are at another stage of the human mind, in which system and logic and the abstractions of Aristotle have a kind of necessary force, when words have so completely taken the place of things, that the minutest distinctions appear to have an intrinsic value.

It has been said (and the remark admits of a peculiar application to theology), that few persons know sufficient of things to be able to say whether disputes are merely verbal or not. Yet, on the other hand, it must be admitted that, whatever accidental advantage theology may derive from system and definition, mere accurate statements can never form the substance of our belief. No one doubts that Christianity could be in the fullest sense taught to a child or a savage, without any mention of justification or satisfaction or predestination. Why should we not receive the Gospel as 'little children?' Why should we not choose the poor man's part in the inheritance of the kingdom of heaven? Why elaborate doctrinal abstractions which are so subtle in their meaning as to be in great danger of being lost in their translation from one language to another? which are always running into consequences inconsistent with our moral nature, and the knowledge of God derived from it? which are not the prevailing usage of Scripture, but technical terms which we have gathered from one or two passages, and made the key-notes of our scale? The words satisfaction and predestination nowhere occur in Scripture; the word regeneration only twice, and but once in a sense at all similar to that which it bears among ourselves; the word justification twice only, and nowhere as a purely abstract term.

But although language and logic have strangely transfigured the meaning of Scripture, we cannot venture to say that all theological controversies are questions of words. If from their winding mazes we seek to retrace our steps, we still find differences which have a deep foundation in the opposite tendencies of the human mind, and the corresponding division of the world itself. That men of one temper of mind adopt one expression rather than another may be partly an accident; but the adoption of an expression by persons of marked character makes the difference of words a reality also. That can scarcely be thought a matter of words which cut in sunder the Church, which overthrew princes, which made the line of demarcation between Jewish and Gentile Christians in the Apostolic age, and is so, in another sense, between Protestant and Catholic at the present day. And in a deeper way of reflection than this, if we turn from the Church to the individual, we seem to see around us opposite natures and characters, whose lives really exhibit a difference corresponding to that of which we are speaking. The one incline to morality, the other to religion; the one to the sacramental, the other to the spiritual; the one to multiplicity in outward ordinances, the other to simplicity; the one consider chiefly the means, the other the end; the one desire to dwell upon doctrinal statements, the other need only the name of Christ; the one turn to ascetic practices, to lead a good life, and to do good to others, the other to faith, humility, and dependence on God. We may sometimes find the opposite attributes combine with each other (there have ever been cross-divisions on this article of belief in the Christian world; the great body of the Reformed Churches, and a small minority of Roman Catholics before the Reformation, being on the one side ; and the whole Roman Catholic Church since the Reformation, and a section of the Protestant Episcopalians, and some lesser communions, on the other); still, in general, the first of these characters answers to that doctrine which the Roman Church sums up in the formula of justification by works; the latter is that temper of mind which finds its natural dogmatic expression in the words 'We are justified by faith.'

These latter words have been carried out of their original circle of ideas into a new one by the doctrines of the Reformation. They have become hardened, stiffened, sharpened by the exigencies of controversy, and torn from what may be termed their context in the Apostolical age. To that age we must return ere we can think in the Apostle's language. His conception of faith, although simpler than our own, has nevertheless a peculiar relation to his own day; it is at once wider, and also narrower, than the use of the word among ourselves—wider in that it is the symbol of the admission of the Gentiles into the Church, but narrower also in that it is the negative of the law. Faith is the proper technical term which excludes the law ; being what the law is not, as the law is what faith is not. No middle term connects the two, or at least none which the Apostle admits, until he has first widened the breach between them to the uttermost. He does not say, 'Was not Abraham our father justified by works (as well as by faith), when he had offered up Isaac his son on the altar?' but only, 'What saith the Scripture? Abraham believed God, and it was counted to him for righteousness.'

The Jewish conception of righteousness was the fulfilment of the Commandments. He who walked in all the precepts of the law blameless, like Daniel in the old Testament, or Joseph and Nathanael in the New, was righteous before God. 'What shall I do to inherit eternal life? Thou knowest the commandments. Do not commit adultery, do not steal, do not bear false witness. All these have I kept from my youth up.' This is a picture of Jewish righteousness as it presents itself in its most favourable light. But it was a righteousness which comprehended the observance of ceremonial details as well as moral precepts, which confused questions of a new moon or a sabbath with the weightier matters of common honesty or filial duty. It might be nothing more than an obedience to the law as such, losing itself on the surface of religion, in casuistical distinctions about meats and drinks, or vows or forms of oaths, or purifications, without any attempt to make clean that which is within. It might also pierce inward to the dividing asunder of the soul. Then was heard the voice of conscience crying, 'All these things cannot make the doers thereof perfect.' When every external obligation was fulfilled, the internal began. Actions must include thoughts and intentions—the Seventh Commandment extends to the adultery of the heart; in one word, the law must become a spirit.

But to the mind of St. Paul the spirit presented itself not so much as a higher fulfilment of the law, but as antagonistic to it. From this point of view, it appeared not that man could never fulfil the law perfectly, but that he could never fulfil it at all. What God required was something different in kind from legal obedience. What man needed was a return to God and nature. He was burdened, straitened, shut out from the presence of his Father— a servant, not a son; to whom, in a spiritual sense, the heaven was become as iron, and the earth brass. The new righteousness must raise him above the burden of ordinances, and bring him into a living communion with God. It must be within, and not without him—written not on tables of stone, but on fleshy tables of the heart. But inward righteousness was no peculiar privilege of the Israelites; it belonged to all mankind. And the revelation of it, as it satisfied the need of the individual soul, vindicated also the ways of God to man; it showed God to be equal in justice and mercy to all mankind.

As the symbol of this inward righteousness, St. Paul found an expression—righteousness by faith—derived from those passages in the Old Testament which spoke of Abraham being justified by faith. It was already in use among the Jews; but it was the Apostle who stamped it first with a permanent and universal import. The faith of St. Paul was not the faith of the Patriarchs only, who believed in the promises made to their descendants; it entered within the veil—out of the reach of ordinances—beyond the evil of this present life; it was the instrument of union with Christ, in whom all men were one; whom they were expecting to come from heaven. The Jewish nation itself was too far gone to be saved as a nation: individuals had a nearer way. The Lord was at hand; there was no time for a long life of laborious service. As at the last hour, when we have to teach men rather how to die than how to live, the Apostle could only say to those who would receive it, 'Believe; all things are possible to him that believes.'

Such are some of the peculiar aspects of the Apostle's doctrine of righteousness by faith. To our own minds it has become a later stage or a particular form of the more general doctrine of salvation through Christ, of the grace of God to man, or of the still more general truth of spiritual religion. It is the connecting link by which we appropriate these to ourselves—the hand which we put out to apprehend the mercy of God. It was not so to the Apostle. To him grace and faith and the Spirit are not parts of a doctrinal system, but different expressions of the same truth. 'Beginning in the Spirit' is another way of saying 'Being justified by faith.' He uses them indiscriminately, and therefore we cannot suppose that he could have laid any stress on distinctions between them. Even the apparently precise antithesis of the prepositions $\ἐν$, $διά$ varies in different passages. Only in reference to the law, faith, rather than grace, is the more correct and natural expression. It was Christ or not Christ, the Spirit or not the Spirit, faith and the law, that were the dividing principles: not Christ through faith, as opposed to Christ through works; or the Spirit as communicated through grace, to the Spirit as independent of grace.

Illusive as are the distinctions of later controversies as guides to the interpretation of Scripture, there is another help, of which we can hardly avail ourselves too much—the interpretation of fact. To read the mind of the Apostle, we must read also the state of the world and the Church by which he was surrounded. Now, there are two great facts which correspond to the doctrine of righteousness by faith, which is also the doctrine of the universality of the Gospel: first, the vision which the Apostle saw on the way to Damascus; secondly, the actual conversion of the Gentiles by the preaching of the Apostle. Righteousness by faith, admission of the Gentiles, even the rejection and restoration of the Jews, are—himself under so many different points of view. The way by which God had led him was the way also by which he was leading other men. When he preached righteousness by faith, his conscience also bore him witness that this was the manner in which he had himself passed from darkness to light, from the burden of ordinances to the power of an endless life. In proclaiming the salvation of the Gentiles, he was interpreting the world as it was; their admission into the Church had already taken place before the eyes of all mankind; it was a purpose of God that was actually fulfilled, not waiting for some future revelation. Just as when doubts are raised respecting his Apostleship, he cut them short by the fact that he was an Apostle, and did the work of an Apostle; so, in adjusting the relations of Jew and Gentile, and justifying the ways of God, the facts, read aright, are the basis of the doctrine which he teaches. All that he further shows is, that these facts were in accordance with the Old Testament, with the words of the Prophets, and the dealings of God with the Jewish people. And the Apostles at Jerusalem, equally with himself, admitted the success of his mission as an evidence of its truth.

But the faith which St. Paul preached was not merely the evidence of things not seen, in which the Gentiles also had part, nor only the reflection of 'the violence' of the world around him, which was taking the kingdom of heaven by force. The source, the hidden life, from which justification flows, in which it lives, is—Christ. It is true that we nowhere find in the Epistles the expression 'justification by Christ' exactly in the sense of modern theology. But, on the other hand, we are described as dead with Christ, we live with Him, we are members of His body, we follow Him in all the stages of His being. All this is another way of expressing 'We are justified by faith.' That which takes us out of ourselves and links us with Christ, which anticipates in an instant the rest of life, which is the door of every heavenly and spiritual relation, presenting us through a glass with the image of Christ crucified, is faith. The difference between our own mode of thinking and that of the Apostle is mainly this—that to him Christ is set forth more as in a picture, and less through the medium of ideas or figures of speech; and that while we conceive the Saviour more naturally as an object of faith, to St. Paul He is rather the indwelling power of life which is fashioned in him, the marks of whose body he bears, the measure of whose sufferings he fills up.

When in the Gospel it is said, 'Believe on the Lord Jesus Christ, and thou shalt be saved,' this is substantially the same truth as 'We are justified by faith.' It is another way of expressing 'Therefore being justified by faith, we have peace with God through our Lord Jesus Christ.' Yet we may note two points of difference, as well as two of resemblance, in the manner in which the doctrine is set forth in the Gospel as compared with the manner of the Epistles of St. Paul. First, in the omission of any connexion between the doctrine of faith in Christ, and the admission of the Gentiles. The Saviour is within the borders of Israel; and accordingly little is said of the 'sheep not of this fold,' or the other husbandmen who shall take possession of the vineyard. Secondly, there is in the words of Christ no antagonism or opposition to the law, except so far as the law itself represented an imperfect or defective morality, or the perversions of the law had become inconsistent with every moral principle. Two points of resemblance have also to be remarked between the faith of the Gospels and of the Epistles. In the first place, both are accompanied by forgiveness of sins. As our Saviour to the disciple who affirms his belief says, 'Thy sins be forgiven thee;' so St. Paul, when seeking to describe, in the language of the Old Testament, the state of justification by faith, cites the words of David, 'Blessed is the man to whom the Lord will not impute sin.' Secondly, they have both a kind of absoluteness which raises them above earthly things. There is a sort of omnipotence attributed to faith, of which the believer is made a partaker. 'Whoso hath faith as a grain of mustard seed, and should say unto this mountain, Be thou removed, and be thou cast into the sea, it shall be done unto him,' is the language of our Lord. 'I can do all things through Christ that strengtheneth me,' are the words of St. Paul.

Faith, in the view of the Apostle, has a further aspect, which is freedom. That quality in us which in reference to God and Christ is faith, in reference to ourselves and our fellow-men is Christian liberty. 'With this freedom Christ has made us free;' 'where the spirit of the Lord is, there is liberty.' It is the image also of the communion of the world to come. 'The Jerusalem that is above is free,' and 'the creature is waiting to be delivered into the glorious liberty of the children of God.' It applies to the Church as now no longer confined in the prison-house of the Jewish dispensation; to the grace of God, which is given irrespectively to all; to the individual, the power of whose will is now loosed; to the Gospel, as freedom from the law, setting the conscience at rest about questions of meats and drinks, and new moons and sabbaths; and, above all, to the freedom from the consciousness of sin: in all these senses the law of the spirit of life is also the law of freedom.

In modern language, assurance has been deemed necessary to the definition of a true faith. There is a sense, too, in which final assurance entered into the conception of the faith of the Epistles. Looking at men from without, it was possible for them to fall away finally; it was possible also to fall without falling away; as St. John says, there is a sin unto death, and there is a sin not unto death. But looking inwards into their hearts and consciences, their salvation was not a matter of probability; they knew whom they had believed, and were confident that He who had begun the good work in them would continue it unto the end. All calculations respecting the future were to them lost in the fact that they were already saved; to use a homely expression, they had no time to inquire whether the state to which they were called was permanent and final. The same intense faith which separated them from the present world, had already given them a place in the world to come. They had not to win the crown—it was already won: this life, when they thought of themselves in relation to Christ, was the next; as their union with Him seemed to them more true and real than the mere accidents of their temporal existence.

A few words will briefly recapitulate the doctrine of righteousness by faith as gathered from the Epistles of St. Paul.

Faith, then, according to the Apostle, is the spiritual principle whereby we go out of ourselves to hold communion with God and Christ; not like the faith of the Epistle to the Hebrews, clothing itself in the shadows of the law; but opposed to the law, and of a nature purely moral and spiritual. It frees man from the flesh, the law, the world, and from himself also; that is, from his sinful nature, which is the meeting of these three elements in his spiritual consciousness. And to be 'justified' is to pass into a new state; such as that of the Christian world when compared with the Jewish or Pagan; such as that which St. Paul had himself felt at the moment of his conversion; such as that which he reminds the Galatian converts they had experienced, 'before whose eyes Jesus Christ was evidently set forth crucified;' an inward or subjective state, to which the outward or objective act of calling, on God's part, through the preaching of the Apostle, corresponded; which, considered on a wider scale, was the acceptance of the Gentiles and of every one who feared God; corresponding in like manner to the eternal purpose of God; indicated in the case of the individual by his own inward assurance; in the case of the world at large, testified by the fact; accompanied in the first by the sense of peace and forgiveness, and implying to mankind generally the last final principle of the Divine Government—'God concluded all under sin that he might have mercy upon all.'

We acknowledge that there is a difference between the meaning of justification by faith to St. Paul and to ourselves. Eighteen hundred years cannot have passed away, leaving the world and the mind of man, or the use of language, the same as it was. Times have altered, and Christianity, partaking of the social and political progress of mankind, receiving, too, its own intellectual development, has inevitably lost its simplicity. The true use of philosophy is to restore this simplicity; to undo the perplexities which the love of system or past philosophies, or the imperfection of language or logic, have made; to lighten the burden which the traditions of ages have imposed upon us. To understand St. Paul we found it necessary to get rid of definitions and deductions, which might be compared to a mazy undergrowth of some noble forest, which we must clear away ere we can wander in its ranges. And it is necessary for ourselves also to return from theology to Scripture; to seek a truth to live and die in—not to be the subject of verbal disputes, which entangle the religious sense in scholastic refinements. The words of eternal life are few and simple, 'Believe on the Lord Jesus Christ, and thou shalt be saved.'

Remaining, then, within the circle of the New Testament, which we receive as a rule of life for ourselves, no less than for the early Church, we must not ignore the great differences by which we are distinguished from those for whom it was written. Words of life and inspiration, heard by them with ravishment for the first time, are to us words of fixed and conventional meaning; they no longer express feelings of the heart, but ideas of the head. Nor is the difference less between the state of the world then and now; not only of the outward world in which we live, but of that inner world which we ourselves are. The law is dead to us, and we to the law; and the language of St. Paul is relative to what has passed away. The transitions of meaning in the use of the word law tend also to a corresponding variation in the meaning of faith. We are not looking for the immediate coming of Christ, and do not anticipate, in a single generation, the end of human things, or the history of a life in the moment of baptism or conversion. To us time and eternity have a fixed boundary, between them there is a gulf which we cannot pass; we do not mingle in our thoughts earth and heaven. Last of all, we are in a professing Christian world, in which religion, too, has become a sort of business; moreover, we see a long way off truths of which the first believers were eye-witnesses. Hence it has become difficult for us to conceive the simple force of such expressions as 'dead with Christ,' 'if ye then be risen with Christ,' which are repeated in prayers or sermons, but often convey no distinct impression to the minds of the hearers.

The neglect of these differences between ourselves and the first disciples has sometimes led to a distortion of doctrine and a perversion of life; where words had nothing to correspond to them, views of human nature have been invented to suit the supposed meaning of St. Paul. Thus, for example, the notion of legal righteousness is indeed a fiction as applied to our own times. Nor, in truth, is the pride of human nature, or the tendency to rebel against the will of God, or to attach an undue value to good works, better founded. Men are evil in all sorts of ways: they deceive themselves and others; they walk by the opinion of others, and not by faith; they give way to their passions: they are imperious and oppressive to one another. But if we look closely, we perceive that most of their sins are not consciously against God; the pride of rank, or wealth, or power, or intellect, may be shown towards their brethren, but no man is proud towards God. No man does wrong for the sake of rebelling against God. The evil is not that men are bound under a curse by the ever-present consciousness of sin, but that sins pass unheeded by: not that they wantonly offend God, but that they know Him not. So, again, there may be a false sense of security towards God, as is sometimes observed on a death-bed, when mere physical weakness seems to incline the mind to patience and resignation; yet this more often manifests itself in a mistaken faith, than in a reliance on good works. Or, to take another instance, we are often surprised at the extent to which men who are not professors of religion seem to practise Christian virtues; yet their state, however we may regard it, has nothing in common with legal or self-righteousness.

And besides theories of religion at variance with experience, which have always a kind of unsoundness, the attempt of men to apply Scripture to their own lives in the letter rather than in the spirit, has been very injurious in other ways to the faith of Christ. Persons have confused the accidental circumstances or language of the Apostolic times with the universal language of morality and truth. They have reduced human nature to very great straits; they have staked salvation upon the right use of a word; they have enlisted the noblest feelings of mankind in opposition to their 'Gospel.' They have become mystics in the attempt to follow the Apostles, who were not mystics. Narrowness in their own way of life has led to exclusiveness in their judgements on other men. The undue stress which they have laid on particular precepts or texts of Scripture has closed their minds against its general purpose; the rigidness of their own rules has rendered it impossible that they should grow freely to 'the stature of the perfect man.' They have ended in a verbal Christianity, which has preserved words when the meaning of them had changed, taking the form, while it quenched the life, of the Gospel.

Leaving the peculiar and relative aspect of the Pauline doctrine, as well as the scholastic and traditional one, we have again to ask the meaning of justification by faith. We may divide the subject, first, as it may be considered in the abstract; and, secondly, as personal to ourselves.

I. Our justification may be regarded as an act on God's part. It may be said that this act is continuous, and commensurate with our whole lives; that although 'known unto God are all his works from the beginning,' yet that, speaking as men, and translating what we term the acts of God into human language, we are ever being more and more justified, as in theological writers we are said also to be more and more sanctified. At first sight it seems that to deny this involves an absurdity; it may be thought a contradiction to maintain that we are justified at once, but sanctified all our life long. Yet perhaps this latter mode of statement is better than the other, because it presents two aspects of the truth instead of one only; it is also a nearer expression of the inward consciousness of the soul itself. For must we not admit that it is the unchangeable will of God that all mankind should be saved? Justification in the mind of the believer is the perception of this fact, which always was. It is not made more a fact by our knowing it for many years or our whole life. And this is the witness of experience. For he who is justified by faith does not go about doubting in himself or his future destiny, but trusting in God. From the first moment that he turns earnestly to God he believes that he is saved; not from any confidence in himself, but from an overpowering sense of the love of God and Christ.

II. It is an old problem in philosophy, What is the beginning of our moral being? What is that prior principle which makes good actions produce good habits? Which of those actions raises us above the world of sight? Plato would have answered, the contemplation of the idea of good. Some of ourselves would answer, by the substitution of a conception of moral growth for the mechanical theory of habits. Leaving out of sight our relation to God, we can only say, that we are fearfully and wonderfully made, with powers which we are unable to analyze. It is a parallel difficulty in religion which is met by the doctrine of righteousness by faith. We grow up spiritually, we cannot tell how; not by outward acts, nor always by energetic effort, but stilly and silently, by the grace of God descending upon us, as the dew falls upon the earth. When a person is apprehensive and excited about his future state, straining every nerve lest he should fall short of the requirements of God, overpowered with the memory of his past sins, that is not the temper of mind in which he can truly serve God, or work out his own salvation. Peace must go before as well as follow after; a peace, too, not to be found in the necessity of law (as philosophy has sometimes held), but in the sense of the love of God to His creatures. He has no right to this peace, and yet he has it; in the consciousness of his new state there is more than he can reasonably explain. At once and immediately the Gospel tells him that he is justified by faith, that his pardon is simultaneous with the moment of his belief, that he may go on his way rejoicing to fulfil the duties of life; for, in human language, God is no longer angry with him.

III. Thus far, in the consideration of righteousness by faith, we have obtained two points of view, in which, though regarded in the abstract only, the truth of which these words are the symbol has still a meaning; first, as expressing the unchangeableness of the mercy of God; and, secondly, the mysteriousness of human action. As we approach nearer, we are unavoidably led to regard the gift of righteousness rather in reference to the subject than to the object, in relation to man rather than God. What quality, feeling, temper, habit in ourselves answers to it? It may be more or less conscious to us, more of a state and less of a feeling, showing itself rather in our lives than our lips. But for these differences we can make allowance. It is the same faith still, under various conditions and circumstances, and sometimes taking different names.

IV. The expression 'righteousness by faith' indicates the personal character of salvation; it is not the tale of works that we do, but we ourselves who are accepted of God. Who can bear to think of his own actions as they are seen by the eye of the Almighty? Looking at their defective performance, or analyzing them into the secondary motives out of which they have sprung, do we seem to have any ground on which we can stand; is there anything which satisfies ourselves? Yet, knowing that our own works cannot abide the judgement of God, we know also that His love is not proportioned to them. He is a Person who deals with us as persons over whom He has an absolute right, who have nevertheless an endless value to Him. When He might exact all, He forgives all; 'the kingdom of heaven' is like not only to a Master taking account with his servants, but to a Father going out to meet his returning son. The symbol and mean of this personal relation of man to God is faith; and the righteousness which consists not in what we do, but in what we are, is the righteousness of faith.

V. Faith may be spoken of, in the language of the Epistle to the Hebrews, as the substance of things unseen. But what are the things unseen? Not only an invisible world ready to flash through the material at the appearance of Christ; not angels, or powers of darkness, or even God Himself 'sitting,' as the Old Testament described, 'on the circle of the heavens;' but the kingdom of truth and justice, the things that are within, of which God is the centre, and with which men everywhere by faith hold communion. Faith is the belief in the existence of this kingdom; that is, in the truth and justice and mercy of God, who disposes all things—not, perhaps, in our judgement for the greatest happiness of His creatures, but absolutely in accordance with our moral notions. And that this is not seen to be the case here, makes it a matter of faith that it will be so in some way that we do not at present comprehend. He that believes on God believes, first, that He is; and, secondly, that He is the Rewarder of them that seek Him.

VI. Now, if we go on to ask what gives this assurance of the truth and justice of God, the answer is, the life and death of Christ, who is the Son of God, and the Revelation of God. We know what He himself has told us of God, and we cannot conceive perfect goodness separate from perfect truth; nay, this goodness itself is the only conception we can form of God, if we confess what the mere immensity of the material world tends to suggest, that the Almighty is not a natural or even a supernatural power, but a Being of whom the reason and conscience of man have a truer conception than imagination in its highest flights. He is not in the storm, nor in the thunder, nor in the earthquake, but 'in the still small voice.' And this image of God as He reveals himself in the heart of man is 'Christ in us the hope of glory;' Christ as He once was upon earth in His sufferings rather than His miracles—the image of goodness and truth and peace and love.

We are on the edge of a theological difficulty; for who can deny that the image of that goodness may fade from the mind's eye after so many centuries, or that there are those who recognize the idea and may be unable to admit the fact? Can we say that this error of the head is also a corruption of the will? The lives of such unbelievers in the facts of Christianity would sometimes refute our explanation. And yet it is true that Providence has made our spiritual life dependent on the belief in certain truths, and those truths run up into matters of fact, with the belief in which they have ever been associated; it is true, also, that the most important moral consequences flow from unbelief. We grant the difficulty: no complete answer can be given to it on this side the grave. Doubtless God has provided a way that the sceptic no less than the believer shall receive his due; He does not need our timid counsels for the protection of the truth. If among those who have rejected the facts of the Gospel history some have been rash, hypercritical, inflated with the pride of intellect, or secretly alienated by sensuality from the faith of Christ—there have been others, also, upon whom we may conceive to rest a portion of that blessing which comes to such as 'have not seen and yet have believed.'

VII. In the Epistles of St. Paul, and yet more in the Epistle to the Hebrews, the relation of Christ to mankind is expressed under figures of speech taken from the Mosaic dispensation: He is the Sacrifice for the sins of men, 'the Lamb of God that taketh away the sins of the world;' the Antitype of all the types, the fulfilment in His own person of the Jewish law. Such words may give comfort to those who think of God under human imagery, but they seem to require explanation when we rise to the contemplation of Him as the God of truth, without parts or passions, who knows all things, and cannot be angry with any, or see them other than they truly are. What is indicated by them, to us 'who are dead to the law,' is, that God has manifested himself in Christ as the God of mercy; who is more ready to hear than we to pray ; who has forgiven us almost before we ask Him ; who has given us His only Son, and how will He not with Him also give us all things? They intimate, on God's part, that He is not extreme to mark what is done amiss ; in human language, 'he is touched with the feeling of our infirmities :' on our part, that we say to God, ' Not of ourselves, but of thy grace and mercy, O Lord.' Not in the fullness of life and health, nor in the midst of business, nor in the schools of theology; but in the sick chamber, where are no more earthly interests, and in the hour of death, we have before us the living image of the truth of justification by faith, when man acknowledges, on the confines of another world, the unprofitableness of his own good deeds, and the goodness of God even in afflicting him, and his absolute reliance not on works of righteousness that he has done, but on the Divine mercy.

VIII. A true faith has been sometimes defined to be not a faith in the unseen merely, or in God or Christ, but a personal assurance of salvation. Such a feeling may be only the veil of sensualism ; it may be also the noble confidence of St. Paul. 'I am persuaded that neither death, nor life, nor angels, nor principalities, nor powers, nor things present, nor things to come, nor height, nor death, nor any other creature, shall be able to separate us from the love of God which is in Christ Jesus our Lord.' It may be an emotion, resting on no other ground except that we believe ; or, a conviction deeply rooted in our life and character. Scripture and reason alike seem to require this belief in our own salvation : and yet to assume that we are at the end of the race may make us lag in our course. Whatever danger there is in the doctrine of the Divine decrees, the danger is nearer home, and more liable to influence practice, when our faith takes the form of personal assurance. How, then, are we to escape from the dilemma, and have a rational confidence in the mercy of God?

IX. This confidence must rest, first, on a sense of the truth and justice of God, rising above perplexities of fact in the world around us, or the tangle of metaphysical or theological difficulties. But although such a sense of the truth or justice of God is the beginning of our peace, yet a link of connexion is wanting before we can venture to apply to ourselves that which we acknowledge in the abstract. The justice of God may lead to our condemnation as well as to our justification. Are we then, in the language of the ancient tragedy, to say that no one can be counted happy before he dies, or that salvation is only granted when the end of our course is seen? Not so; the Gospel encourages us to regard ourselves as already saved; for we have communion with Christ and appropriate His work by faith. And this appropriation means nothing short of the renunciation of self and the taking up of the cross of Christ in daily life. Whether such an imitation or appropriation of Christ is illusive or real, a new mould of nature or only an outward and superficial impression, is a question not to be answered by any further theological distinction, but by an honest and good heart searching into itself. Then only, when we surrender ourselves into the hands of God, when we ask Him to show us to ourselves as we truly are, when we allow ourselves in no sin, when we attribute nothing to our own merits, when we test our faith, not by the sincerity of an hour, but of months and years, we learn the true meaning of that word in which, better than any other, the nature of righteousness by faith is summed up—peace.

'And now abideth faith, hope, and love, these three; but the greatest of these is love.' There seems to be a contradiction in love being the 'greatest,' when faith is the medium of acceptance. Love, according to some, is preferred to faith, because it reaches to another life; when faith and hope are swallowed up in sight, love remains still.

Love, according to others, has the first place, because it is Divine as well as human; it is the love of God to man, as well as of man to God. Perhaps, the order of precedence is sufficiently explained by the occasion; to a Church torn by divisions the Apostle says, 'that the first of Christian graces is love.' Another thought, however, is suggested by these words, which has a bearing on our present subject. It is this, that in using the received terms of theology, we must also acknowledge their relative and transient character. Christian truth has many modes of statement; love is the more natural expression to St. John, faith to St. Paul. The indwelling of Christ or of the Spirit of God, grace, faith, hope, love, are not parts of a system, but powers or aspects of the Christian life. Human minds are different, and the same mind is not the same at different times; and the best of men nowadays have but a feeble consciousness of spiritual truths. We ought not to dim that consciousness by insisting on a single formula; and therefore while speaking of faith as the instrument of justification, because faith indicates the apprehensive, dependent character of the believer's relation to Christ, we are bound also to deny that the Gospel is contained in any word, or the Christian life inseparably linked to any one quality. We must acknowledge the imperfection of language and thought, and seek rather to describe than to define the work of God in the soul, which has as many forms as the tempers, capacities, circumstances, and accidents of our nature.

ESSAY

ON

THE LAW AS THE STRENGTH OF SIN

'The strength of sin is the law.'—1 Cor. xv. 56.

THESE words occur parenthetically in the fifteenth chapter of the First Epistle to the Corinthians. They may be regarded as a summary of the seventh chapter of the Romans. The thought contained in them is also the undercurrent of several other passages in the Epistles of St. Paul, as, for example, Rom. v. 20; xiv. 22, 23; Gal. ii. 17-21; Col. ii. 14. The Apostle is speaking of that prior state out of which he passed into the liberty of the Gospel. When he asked himself what preceded Christ in his own life and in the dispensations of Providence, what he had once felt within warring against his soul, what he saw without contending against the cross, the answer to all was given in the same word, 'the Law.'

But the singular description of the law as the strength of sin goes further, and has a deeper meaning; for it seems to make the law the cause of sin. Here is the difficulty. The law may have been defective adapted, as we should say, to a different state of society, enforcing in some passages the morality of a half-civilized age, such as could never render the practisers thereof perfect, powerless to create a new life either in the Jewish nation collectively, or in the individuals who composed the nation; yet this imperfection and 'unprofitableness' of the law are not what the Apostle means by the strength of sin. If we say, in the words of James, quoted in the Acts, that it was a burden too heavy for men to bear, still language like this falls short of the paradox, as it appears to us, of St. Paul. There is no trace that the law was regarded by him as given 'because of the hardness of men's hearts,' as our Saviour says; or that he is speaking of the law as corrupted by the Pharisee, or overlaid by Jewish traditions. The Apostle is not contrasting, as we are apt to do, Moses and the prophets with the additions of those who sat in Moses' seat. The same law which is holy, and good, and just, is also the strength of sin.

There is another kind of language used respecting the law in Scripture which is very familiar, and seems to be as natural to our preconceived notions as the passage which we are now considering is irreconcilable with them. The law is described as the preparation of the Gospel; the first volume of the book, the other half of Divine Revelation. It is the veil on the face of Moses which obscured the excess of light, as the Apostle himself says in the Epistle to the Corinthians; or the schoolmaster to bring men to Christ, as in the Galatians; or the shadow of good things to come, as in the Hebrews. But all these figures of speech can only be cited here to point out how different the conception in them is from that which is implied in such words as 'The strength of sin is the law.' In these latter we have not the light shining more and more unto the perfect day, but the light and darkness; that is, the Gospel and the law opposed, as it were two hemispheres, dividing time and the world and the human heart.

Nor, again, if we consider the law in its immediate workings on the mind, as it might seem to be struggling within for mastery over the Gospel, as we may imagine Catholicism and Protestantism in the mind of Luther or of a modern convert, do we make a nearer approach to the solution of our difficulty. Even Luther, when denouncing the Pope as Antichrist, would not have spoken of the Catholic faith as the strength of sin. Still less would he have one instant described it as 'holy, just, and good,' and in the next as deceiving and slaying him. The struggle between one religion and another, or, even without any conflict of creeds, between hope and despair, may trouble the conscience, may enfeeble the will, may darken the intellect; still no sober-minded man would think of attributing his sins to having passed through such a struggle.

Once more, parallels from heathen authors, such as 'Nitimur in vetitum semper,' and the witness of the heart against itself, 'that it is evil continually,' have been quoted in illustration of the verse placed at the beginning of this Essay. The aphorisms alluded to are really metaphorical expressions, intended by satirists and moralists to state forcibly that men are prone to err, not that law is provocative or the cause of sin. Mankind offend in various ways, and from different motives—ambition, vanity, selfishness, passion—but not simply from the desire to break the law, or to offend God. So, again, as we multiply laws, we may seem to multiply offences: the real truth is, that as offences multiply the laws multiply also. To break the law for the sake of doing so, is not crime or sin, but madness. Nor, again, will it do to speak of the perversity of the human will—of men like children, doing a thing because, as we say in familiar language, they are told not to do it. This perversity consists simply in knowing the better and choosing the worse, in passion prevailing over reason. The better is not the cause of their choosing the worse, nor is reason answerable for the dictates of passion, which would be the parallel required.

All these, then, we must regard as half-explanations, which fail to reach the Apostle's meaning. When we ask what he can mean by saying that 'the law is the strength of sin,' it is no answer to reply, that the law was imperfect or transient, that it could not take away sin, that it had been made of none effect by tradition, that its ceremonial observances were hypocritical and unmeaning; or that we, too, use certain metaphorical expressions, which, however different in sense, have a sound not unlike the words of the Apostle. We require an explanation that goes deeper, which does not pare away the force of the expression, such as can be gathered only from the Apostle himself, and the writings of his time. The point of view from which we regard things may begin to turn round; to understand the meaning of the law, we may have to place ourselves within the circle of its influences; to understand the nature of sin, we may be compelled to imagine ourselves in the very act of sinning: this inversion of our ordinary modes of thought may be the only means of attaining the true and natural sense of the Apostle's words.

We are commencing an inquiry which lacks the sustaining interest of controversy, the data of which are metaphysical reasonings and points of view which cannot be even imagined without a considerable effort of mind, and which there will be the more indisposition to admit, as they run counter to the popular belief that the Bible is a book easily and superficially intelligible. Such feelings are natural; we are jealous of those who wrap up in mystery the Word of life, who carry us into an atmosphere which none else can breathe. We cannot be too jealous of Kant or Fichte, Schelling or Hegel, finding their way into the interpretation of Scripture. As jealous should we be also of any patristic or other system which draws away its words from their natural meaning. Still the Scripture has difficulties not brought but found there, a few words respecting which will pave the way for the inquiry on which we are entering.

The Bible is at once the easiest and the hardest of books. The easiest, in that it gives us plain rules for moral and religious duties which he that runs can read, an example that every one can follow, a work that any body may do. But it is the hardest also, in that it is fragmentary, written in a dead language, and referring to times and actions of which in general we have no other record, and, above all, using modes of thought and often relating to spiritual states, which amongst ourselves have long ceased to exist, or the influence of institutions which have passed away. Who can supply the external form of the primitive Church of the first century, whether in its ritual or discipline, from the brief allusions of the Gospels and Epistles? Who can imagine the mind of the first believers, as they sat 'with their lamps lighted and their loins girded,' waiting for the reappearance of the Lord? Who describe the prophesyings or speaking with tongues, or interpretation of tongues? Who knows the spirit of a man who consciously recognizes in his ordinary life the inward workings of a Divine power? The first solution of such difficulties is to admit them, to acknowledge that the world in which we live is not the world of the first century, and that the first Christians were not like ourselves.

Nor is this difficulty less, but greater, in reference to words which are common to us and to them, which are used by both with a certain degree of similarity, and with a sort of analogy to other words which puts us off our guard, and prevents our perceiving the real change of meaning. Such is the case with the words church, priest, sacrifice, and in general with words taken from the Mosaic dispensation; above all, with the word 'law.' Does not common sense teach us that whatever St. Paul meant by law, he must have meant something hard to us to understand, to whom the law has no existence, who are Europeans, not Orientals? to whom the law of the land is no longer the immediate direct law of God, and who can form no idea of the entanglements and perplexities which the attempt to adapt the law of Mount Sinai to an altered world must have caused to the Jew? Is it not certain that whenever we use the word 'law' in its theological acceptation, we shall give it a meaning somewhat different from that of the Apostle? We cannot help doing so. Probably we may sum it up under the epithet 'moral or ceremonial,' or raise the question to which of these the Apostle refers, forgetting that they are distinctions which belong to us, but do not belong to him. The study of a few pages of the Mischna, which mounts up nearly to the time of the Apostles, would reveal to us how very far our dim indefinite notion of the 'law' falls short of that intense life and power and sacredness which were attributed to it by a Jew of the first century; as well as how little conception he had of the fundamental distinctions which theologians have introduced respecting it.

But the consideration of these difficulties does not terminate with themselves; they lead us to a higher idea of Scripture; they compel us to adapt ourselves to Scripture, instead of adapting Scripture to ourselves. In the ordinary study of the sacred volume, the chief difficulty is the accurate perception of the connexion. The words lie smoothly on the page; the road is trite and worn. Only just here and there we stumble over an impediment; as it were a stone lying not loose, but deeply embedded in the soil; which is the indication of a world below just appearing on the surface. Such are many passages in the Epistles of St. Paul. There is much that we really understand, much that we appear to understand, which has, indeed, a deceitful congruity with words and thoughts of our own day. Some passages remain intractable. From these latter we obtain the pure ore; here, if anywhere, are traces of the peculiar state and feelings of the Church of the Apostles, such as no after age could invent, or even understand. It is to these we turn, not for a rule of conduct, but for the inner life of Apostles and Churches; rejecting nothing as designedly strange or mysterious, satisfied with no explanation that does violence to the language, not suffering our minds to be diverted from the point of the difficulty, comparing one difficulty with another; seeking the answer, not in ourselves and in the controversies of our own day, but in the Scripture and the habits of thought of the age; collecting every association that bears upon it, and gathering up each fragment that remains, that nothing be lost; at the same time acknowledging how defective our knowledge really is, not merely in that general sense in which all human knowledge is feeble and insufficient, but in the particular one of our actual ignorance of the facts and persons and ways of thought of the age in which the Gospel came into the world.

The subject of the present Essay is suggestive of the following questions:—'What did St. Paul mean by the law, and what by sin?' 'Is the Apostle speaking from the experience of his own heart and the feelings of his age and country, or making an objective statement for mankind in general, of what all men do or ought to feel?' 'Is there anything in his circumstances, as a convert from the law to the Gospel, that gives the words a peculiar force?' And lastly, we may inquire what application may be made of them to ourselves: whether, 'now that the law is dead to us, and we to the law,' the analogy of faith suggests anything, either in our social state or in our physical constitution or our speculative views, which stands in the same relation to us that the law did to the first converts?

First, then, as has been elsewhere remarked, the law includes in itself different and contradictory aspects. It is at once the letter of the book of the law, and the image of law in general. It is alive, and yet dead; it is holy, just, and good, and yet the law of sin and death. It is without and within at the same time; a power like that of conscience is ascribed to it, and yet he who is under its power feels that he is reaching towards something without him which can never become a part of his being. In its effect on individuals it may be likened to a sword entering into the soul, which can never knit together with flesh and blood. In relation to the world at large, it is a prison in which men are shut up. As the Jewish nation is regarded also as an individual; as the kingdom of heaven is sometimes outward and temporal, sometimes inward and spiritual, used in reference either to the spread of the Gospel, or the second coming of Christ; as the parables of Christ admit of a similar double reference; in like manner, the law has its 'double senses.' It is national and individual at once; the law given on Mount Sinai, and also a rule of conduct. It is the schoolmaster unto Christ, and yet the great enemy of the Gospel; added to make men transgress, and yet affording the first knowledge of truth and holiness; applying to the whole people and to the world of the past, and also to each living man; though a law, and therefore concerned with actions only, terrible to the heart and conscience, requiring men to perform all things, and enabling them to accomplish nothing.

This ambiguity in the use of the word 'law' first occurs in the Old Testament itself. In the prophecies and psalms, as well as in the writings of St. Paul, the law is in a great measure ideal. When the Psalmist spoke of 'meditating in the law of the Lord,' he was not thinking of the five books of Moses. The law which he delighted to contemplate was not written down (as well might we imagine that the Platonic idea was a treatise on philosophy); it was the will of God, the truth of God, the justice and holiness of God. In later ages the same feelings began to gather around the volume of the law itself. The law was ideal still; but with this idealism were combined the reference to its words, and the literal enforcement of its precepts. That it was the law of God was a solemn thought to those who violated the least of its commandments; and yet its commandments were often such as in a changed world it was impossible to obey. It needed interpreters before it could be translated into the language of daily life. Such a law could have little hold on practice; but it had the greatest on ideas. It was the body of truth, the framework of learning and education, the only and ultimate appeal in all controversies. Even its entire disuse did not prevent the Rabbis from discussing with animosity nice questions of minute detail. In Alexandria especially, which was far removed from Jerusalem and the scenes of Jewish history, such an idealizing tendency was carried to the uttermost. Whether there was a temple or not, whether there were sacrifices or not, whether there were feasts or not, mattered little; there was the idea of a temple, the idea of feasts, the idea of sacrifices. Whether the Messiah actually came or not mattered little, while he was discernible to the mystic in every page of the law. The Jewish religion was beginning to rest on a new basis which, however visionary it may seem to us, could not be shaken any more than the clouds of heaven, even though one stone were not left upon another.

This idealizing tendency of his age we cannot help tracing in St. Paul himself. As to the Jew of Alexandria the law became an ideal rule of truth and right, so to St. Paul after his conversion it became an ideal form of evil. As there were many Antichrists, so also there were many laws, and none of them absolutely fallen away from their Divine original. In one point of view, the fault was all with the law; in another point of view, it was all with human nature; the law ideal and the law actual, the law as it came from God and the law in its consequences to man, are ever crossing each other. It was the nature of the law to be good and evil at once; evil, because it was good; like the pillar of cloud and fire, which was its image, light by night and darkness by day—light and darkness in successive instants.

But, as the law seems to admit of a wider range of meaning than we should at first sight have attributed to it, so also the word 'sin' has a more extended sense than our own use of it implies. Sin with us is a definite act or state. Any crime or vice considered in reference to God may be termed sin; or, according to another use of it, which is more general and abstract, sin is the inherent defect of human nature, or that evil state in which, even without particular faults or vices, we live. None of these senses includes that peculiar aspect in which it is regarded by St. Paul. Sin is with him inseparable from the consciousness of sin. It is not only the principle of evil, working blindly in the human heart, but the principle of discord and dissolution piercing asunder the soul and spirit. He who has felt its power most is not the perpetrator of the greatest crimes, a Caligula or Nero; but he who has suffered most deeply from the spiritual combat, who has fallen into the abyss of despair, who has the sentence of death in himself, who is wringing his hands and crying aloud in his agony, 'O wretched man that I am!' Sin is not simply evil, but intermediate between evil and good, implying always the presence of God within, light revealing darkness, life in the corruption of death; it is the soul reflecting upon itself in the moment of commission of sin. If we are surprised at St. Paul regarding the law—holy, just, and good as it was—as almost sin, we must remember that sin itself, if the expression may be excused, as a spiritual state, has a good element in it. It is the voice of despair praying to God, 'Who shall deliver me from the body of this death!' It approximates to the law at the very instant in which it is repelled from it.

There are physical states in which the body is exquisitely sensitive to pain, which are not the sign of health, but of disease. So also there are mental states in which the sense of sin and evil, and the need of forgiveness, press upon us with an unusual heaviness. Such is the state which the Scriptures describe by the words, 'they were pricked to the heart,' when whole multitudes in sympathy with each other felt the need of a change, and in the extremity of their suffering were saved, looking on the Lord Jesus. No such spiritual agonies occur in the daily life of all men. Crimes and vices and horrid acts there are, but not that of which the Apostle speaks. That which he sums up in a moment of time, which may be compared to the last struggle when we are upon the confines of two worlds, of which we are so intensely conscious that it is impossible for us permanently to retain the consciousness of it, is 'Sin.'

As there could be no sin if we were wholly unconscious of it, as children or animals are in a state of innocence, as the heathen world we ourselves regard as less guilty or responsible than those who have a clearer light in the dispensation of the Gospel, so in a certain point of view sin may be regarded as the consciousness of sin. It is this latter which makes sin to be what it is, which distinguishes it from crime or vice, which links it with our personality. The first state described by the Roman satirist—

> 'At stupet hic vitio et fibris increvit opimum
> Pingue; caret culpâ; nescit quid perdat,'—

is the reverse of what the Apostle means by the life of sin. In ordinary language, vices, regarded in reference to God, are termed sins; and we attempt to arouse the child or the savage to a right sense of his unconscious acts by so terming them. But, in the Apostle's language, consciousness is presupposed in the sin itself; not reflected on it from without. That which gives it the nature of sin is *conscientia peccati*. As Socrates, a little inverting the ordinary view and common language of mankind, declared all virtue to be knowledge; so the language of St. Paul implies all sin to be the knowledge of sin. *Conscientia peccati peccatum ipsum est.*

It is at this point the law enters, not to heal the wounded soul, but to enlarge its wound. The law came in that the offence might abound. Whatever dim notion of right and wrong pre-existed; whatever sense of physical impurity may have followed, in the language of the Book of Job, one born in sin; whatever terror the outpouring of the vials of

God's wrath, in the natural world, may have infused into the soul—all this was heightened and defined by the law of God. In comparison with this second state, it might be said of the previous one, 'Sin is not imputed where there is no law,' and man 'was alive without the law once ; but when the law came, sin revived, and he died.' The soul condemned itself, it was condemned by the law, it is in the last stage of decay and dissolution.

If from the Apostle's ideal point of view we regard the law, not as the tables given on Mount Sinai, or the books of Moses, but as the law written on the heart, the difficulty is, not how we are to identify the law with the consciousness of sin, but how we are to distinguish them. They are different aspects of the same thing, related to each other as positive and negative, two poles of human nature turned towards God, or away from Him. In the language of metaphysical philosophy, we say that 'the subject is identical with the object;' in the same way sin implies the law. The law written on the heart, when considered in reference to the subject, is simply the conscience. The conscience, in like manner, when conceived of objectively, as words written down in a book, as a rule of life which we are to obey, becomes the law. For the sake of clearness we may express the whole in a sort of formula. 'Sin=the consciousness of sin=the law.' From this last conclusion the Apostle only stops short from the remembrance of the Divine original of the law, and the sense that what made it evil to him was the fact that it was in its own nature good.

Wide, then, as might at first have seemed to be the interval between the law and sin, we see that they have their meeting point in the conscience. Yet their opposition and identity have a still further groundwork or reflection in the personal character and life of the Apostle.

I. The spiritual combat, in the seventh chapter of the Epistle to the Romans, which terminates with the words, 'O wretched man that I am ! who shall deliver me from the body of this death? I thank God, through Jesus Christ our Lord,' is the description, in a figure, of the Apostle's journey to Damascus. Almost in a moment he passed from darkness to light. Nothing could be more different or contrasted than his after life and his former life. In his own language he might be described as cut in two by the sword of the Spirit; his present and previous states were like good and evil, light and darkness, life and death. It accords with what we know of human feelings, that this previous state should have a kind of terror for him, and should be presented to his mind, not as it appeared at the time when he 'thought, verily, that he ought to do many things against Jesus of Nazareth,' but as it afterwards seemed, when he counted himself to be the least of the Apostles, because twenty years before he had persecuted the Church of God; when he was amazed at the goodness of God in rescuing the chief of sinners. The life which he had once led was 'the law.' He thought of it, indeed, sometimes as the inspired word, the language of which he was beginning to invest with a new meaning; but more often as an ideal form of evil, the chain by which he had been bound, the prison in which he was shut up. And long after his conversion the shadow of the law seemed to follow him at a distance, and threatened to overcast his heaven; when, with a sort of inconsistency for one assured of 'the crown,' he speaks of the trouble of spirit which overcame him, and of the sentence of death in himself.

II. In another way the Apostle's personal history gives a peculiar aspect to his view of the law. On every occasion, at every turn of his life, on his first return to Jerusalem, when preaching the Gospel in Asia and Greece, in the great struggle between Jewish and Gentile Christians—his persecutors were the Jews, his great enemy the law. Is it surprising that this enmity should have been idealized by him? that the law within and the law without should have blended in one? that his own remembrances of the past should be identified with that spirit of hatred and fanaticism which he saw around him? Not only when he looked back to his past life, and 'the weak and beggarly elements' to which he had been in bondage, but also when he saw the demoniac spirit which, under the name of Judaism, arrayed itself against the truth, might he repeat the words—'the strength of sin is the law.' And, placing these words side by side with other expressions of the Apostle's, such as, 'We wrestle not against flesh and blood, but against principalities, against powers, against spiritual wickedness in heavenly places,' we can understand how heretics of the second century, who regarded the law and the Old Testament as the work of an evil principle, were induced to attach themselves specially to St. Paul.

III. The Gospel of St. Paul was a spirit, not a law; it nowhere enjoined the observance of feasts and sacrifices, and new moons and sabbaths, but was rather antagonistic to them; it was heedless of externals of any kind, except as matter of expediency and charity. It was a Gospel which knew of no distinction of nations or persons; in which all men had the offer of 'grace, mercy, and peace from the Lord Jesus Christ;' which denounced the oldness of the letter; which contrasted 'the tables of stone with fleshy tables of the heart;' which figured Christ taking the handwriting of ordinances and nailing them to His cross; which put faith in the place of works, and even prohibited circumcision. Such a Gospel was in extreme antagonism to the law. Their original relation was forgotten; the opposition between them insensibly passed into an opposition of good and evil. And yet a new relation sprang up also. For the law, too, witnessed against itself; and, to the Apostle interpreting its words after the manner of his age, became the allegory of the Gospel.

IV. Once more: it may be observed (see note on the *Imputation of the Sin of Adam*), that the place which the law occupies in the teaching of St. Paul is analogous to that which the doctrine of original sin holds in later writings. It represents the state of wrath and bondage out of which men pass into the liberty of the children of God. It is the state of nature to the Jew; it is also a law of sin to him; he cannot help sinning, and this very impotency is the extremity of guilt and despair. Similar expressions respecting original sin are sometimes used among ourselves; though not wholly parallel, they may nevertheless assist in shadowing forth the Apostle's meaning.

V. It is not, however, to the life of the Apostle, or to the circle of theological doctrines, that we need confine ourselves for illustration of the words, 'the strength of sin is the law.' Morality also shows us many ways in which good and evil meet together, and truth and error seem inseparable from each other. We cannot do any thing good without some evil consequences indirectly flowing from it; we cannot express any truth without involving ourselves in some degree of error, or occasionally conveying an impression to others wholly erroneous. Human characters and human ideas are always mixed and limited; good and truth ever drag evil and error in their train. Good itself may be regarded as making evil to be what it is, if, as we say, they are relative terms, and the disappearance of the one would involve the disappearance of the other. And there are many things, in which not only may the old adage be applied — 'Corruptio optimi pessima,' but in which the greatest good is seen to be linked with the worst evil, as, for example, the holiest affections with the grossest sensualities, or a noble ambition with crime and unscrupulousness; even religion seems sometimes to have a dark side, and readily to ally itself with immorality or with cruelty.

Plato's kingdom of evil (Rep. I.) is not unlike the state into which the Jewish people passed during the last few years before the taking of the city. Of both it might be said, in St. Paul's language, 'the law is the strength of sin.' A kingdom of pure evil, as the Greek philosopher observed, there could not be; it needs some principle of good to be the minister of evil; it can only be half wicked, or it would destroy itself. We may say the same of the Jewish people. Without the law it never could have presented an equally signal example either of sin or of vengeance. The nation, like other nations, would have yielded quietly to the power of Rome; 'it would have died the death of all men.' But the spirit which said, 'We have a law, and by our law he ought to die,' recoiled upon itself; the intense fanaticism which prevented men from seeing the image of love and goodness in that Divine form, bound together for destruction a whole people, to make them a monument to after ages of a religion that has outlived itself.

VI. The law and the Gospel may be opposed, according to a modern distinction, as positive and moral. 'Moral precepts are distinguished from positive, as precepts the reasons of which we see from those the reasons of which we do not see.' Moral precepts may be regarded as the more general, while positive precepts fill up the details of the general principle, and apply it to circumstances. Every positive precept involves not merely a moral obligation to obey it so far as it is just, but a moral law, which is its ultimate basis. It will often happen that what was at first just and right may in the course of ages become arbitrary and tyrannical, if the enforcement of it continue after the reason for it has ceased. Or, as it may be expressed more generally, the positive is ever tending to become moral, and the moral to become positive; the positive to become moral, in so far as that which was at first a mere external command has acquired such authority, and so adapted itself to the hearts of men, as to have an internal witness to it, as in the case of the fourth commandment; the moral to become positive, where a law has outlived itself, and the state of society to which it was adapted and the feelings on which it rested have passed away.

The latter was the case with the Jewish law. It had once

been moral, and it had become positive. Doubtless, for the minutest details, the colours of the sanctuary, the victims offered in sacrifice, there had once been reasons; but they had been long since forgotten, and if remembered would have been unintelligible. New reasons might be given for them; the oldness of the letter might be made to teach a new lesson after the lapse of a thousand years; but in general the law was felt to be 'a burden that neither they nor their fathers were able to bear.' Side by side with it another religion had sprung up, the religion of the prophets first, and of the zealots afterwards; religions most different indeed from each other, yet equally different from the law; in the first of which the voice of God in man seemed to cry aloud against sacrifice and offering, and to proclaim the only true offering, to do justice and to love mercy, and to walk humbly with God; while in the second of them the national faith took the form of a fanatical patriotism. And yet the law still remained as a body of death, with its endless routine of ceremonial, its numberless disputes, its obsolete commands, never suffering the worshipper to be free, and enforcing its least detail with the curses of the book of the law and the terrors of Mount Sinai.

Much of this burden would have been taken off, had there existed among the Jews the distinction which is familiar to ourselves of a moral and ceremonial law. They would then have distinguished between the weightier matters of the law and the 'tithe of mint, anise, and cumin.' Such distinctions are great 'peace-makers;' they mediate between the present and the past. But in Judaism all was regarded as alike of Divine authority, all subjected the transgressor to the same penalty. 'He who offended in one point was guilty of all;' the least penalty was, in a figure, 'death,' and there was no more for the greatest offences. The infringement of any positive command tortured the conscience with a fearful looking for of judgement; the deepest moral guilt could do no more. Such a religion could only end in hypocrisy and inhumanity, in verily believing that the law demanded His death, in whom only 'the law was fulfilled.'

Let us imagine, in contrast with this, the Gospel with its spiritualizing humanizing influences, soothing the soul of man, the source of joy, and love, and peace. It is a supernatural power, with which the elements themselves bear witness, endowed with a fullness of life, and imparting life to all who receive it. It is not a law to which the will must submit, but an inward principle which goes before the will; it is also a moral principle to which the heart and conscience instantly assent, which gives just what we want, and seems to set us right with the world, with ourselves, and with God. Yet, in a figure, it is a law also; but in a very different sense from that of Moses: a law within, and not without us; a law of the Spirit of life, not of death; of freedom, not of slavery; of blessing, not of cursing; of mercy, not of vengeance: a law which can be obeyed, not one to which, while it exacts punishment, obedience is impossible. When we look upon this picture, and upon that, is it strange that one who was filled with the mind of Christ should have regarded the law as the strength of sin?

Of what has been said, the sum is as follows:—When St. Paul speaks of 'the law as the strength of sin,' he uses the term law partly for law in general, but more especially for the burden of the Jewish law on the conscience; when he speaks of sin, he means chiefly the consciousness of sin, of which it may be truly said, 'Where there is no law, there is no transgression; and sin is not imputed where there is no law.' Thirdly, he speaks of the law from his own spiritual experience of 'fears within, and of fightings without;' and from a knowledge of his own countrymen, who 'please not God, but are contrary to all men.' Fourthly, he conceives the law as an ideal form of evil, analogous to original sin in the language of a later theology. Lastly, if there be anything apparently contradictory or to us unintelligible in his manner of speaking of the law, we must attribute this to the modes of thought of his age, which blended many things that are to us separate. Had St. Paul distinguished between the law and conscience, or between the law and morality, or between the moral and ceremonial portions of the law itself, or between the law in its first origin and in the practice of his own age, he would perhaps have confined the law to a good sense, or restricted its use to the books of Moses, and not have spoken of it in one verse as 'holy, just, and good,' and in the next as being the means of deceiving and slaying him.

In another sense than that in which the Apostle employs the words, 'the law is dead to us, and we to the law.' The lapse of ages has but deepened the chasm which separates Judaism from Christianity. Between us and them there is a gulf fixed, so that few are they who pass from them to us, nor do any go from us to them. The question remains, What application is it possible for us to make of that which has preceded? Is there anything in the world around standing in the same relation to us that the law did to the contemporaries of St. Paul?

One answer that might be given is, 'the Roman Catholic Church.' The experience of Luther seems indeed not unlike that struggle which St. Paul describes. But whatever resemblance may be found between Romanism and the ancient Jewish religion—whether in their ceremonial or sacrificial character, or in the circumstance of their both resting on outward and visible institutions, and so limiting the worship of Spirit and truth—it cannot be said that Romanism stands in the same relation to us individually that the law did to the Apostle St. Paul. The real parallels are more general, though less obvious. The law St. Paul describes as without us, but not in that sense in which an object of sense is without us: though without us it exercises an inward power; it drives men to despair; it paralyzes human nature; it causes evil by its very justice and holiness. It is like a barrier which we cannot pass; a chain wherewith a nation is bound together; a rule which is not adapted to human feelings, but which guides them into subjection to itself.

It has been already remarked that a general parallel to 'the law as the strength of sin' is to be found in that strange blending of good and evil, of truth and error, which is the condition of our earthly existence. But there seem also to be cases in which the parallel is yet closer; in which good is not only the accidental cause of evil, but the limiting principle which prevents man from working out to the uttermost his individual and spiritual nature. In some degree, for example, society may exercise the same tyranny over us, and its conventions be stumbling-blocks to us of the same kind as the law to the contemporaries of St. Paul; or, in another way, the thought of self and the remembrance of our past life may 'deceive and slay us.' As in the description of the seventh chapter of the Romans—'It was I, and it was not I; and who can deliver me from the influence of education and the power of my former self?' Or faith and reason, reason and faith may seem mutually to limit each other, and to make the same opposition in speculation that the law and the flesh did to the Apostle in practice. Or, to seek the difficulty on a lower level, while fully assured of the truths of the Gospel, we may seem to be excluded from them by our mental or bodily constitution, which no influences of the Spirit or power of habit may be capable of changing.

1. The society even of a Christian country—and the same remark applies equally to a Church—is only to a certain extent based upon Christian principle. It rests neither on the view that all mankind are evil, nor that they are all good, but on certain motives, supposed to be strong enough to bind mankind together; on institutions handed down from former generations; on tacit compacts between opposing

parties and opinions. Every government must tolerate, and therefore must to a certain degree sanction, contending forms of faith. Even in reference to those more general principles of truth and justice which, in theory at least, equally belong to all religions, the government is limited by expediency, and seeks only to enforce them so far as is required for the preservation of society. Hence arises a necessary opposition between the moral principles of the individual and the political principles of a state. A good man may be sensitive for his faith, zealous for the honour of God, and for every moral and spiritual good; the statesman has to begin by considering the conditions of human society. Aristotle raises a famous question, whether the good citizen is the good man? We have rather to raise the question, whether the good man is the good citizen? If matters of state are to be determined by abstract principles of morality and religion—if, for the want of such principles, whole nations are to be consigned to the vengeance of heaven—if the rule is to be not 'my kingdom is not of this world,' but, 'we ought to obey God rather than man'—there is nothing left but to supersede civil society, and found a religious one in its stead.

It is no imaginary spectre that we are raising, but one that acts powerfully on the minds of religious men. Is it not commonly said by many, that the government is unchristian, that the legislature is unchristian, that all governments and all legislatures are the enemies of Christ and His Church? Herein to them is the fixed evil of the world; not in vice, or in war, or in injustice, or in falsehood; but simply in the fact that the constitution of their country conforms to the laws of human society. It is not necessary to suppose that they will succeed in carrying out their principles, or that a civilized nation will place its liberties in the keeping of a religious party. But, without succeeding, they do a great deal of harm to themselves and to the world. For they draw the mind away from the simple truths of the Gospel to manifestations of opinion and party spirit; they waste their own power to do good; some passing topic of theological controversy drains their life. We may not 'do evil that good may come,' they say; and 'what is morally wrong cannot be politically right;' and with this misapplied 'syllogism of the conscience' they would make it impossible, in the mixed state of human affairs, to act at all, either for good or evil. He who seriously believes that not for our actual sins, but for some legislative measure of doubtful expediency, the wrath of God is hanging over his country, is in so unreal a state of mind as to be scarcely capable of discerning the real evils by which we are surrounded. The remedies of practical ills sink into insignificance compared with some point in which the interests of religion appear to be, but are not, concerned.

But it is not only in the political world that imaginary forms of evil present themselves, and we are haunted by ideas which can never be carried out in practice; the difficulty comes nearer home to most of us in our social life. If governments and nations appear unchristian, the appearance of society itself is in a certain point of view still more unchristian. Suppose a person acquainted with the real state of the world in which we live and move, and neither morosely depreciating nor unduly exalting human nature, to turn to the image of the Christian Church in the New Testament, how great would the difference appear! How would the blessing of poverty contrast with the real, even the moral advantages of wealth! the family of love, with distinctions of ranks! the spiritual, almost supernatural, society of the first Christians, with our world of fashion, of business, of pleasure! the community of goods, with our meagre charity to others! the prohibition of going to law before the heathen, with our endless litigation before judges of all religions! the cross of Christ, with our ordinary life! How little does the world in which we live seem to be designed for the tabernacle of immortal souls! How large a portion of mankind, even in a civilized country, appears to be sacrificed to the rest, and to be without the means of moral and religious improvement! How fixed, and steadfast, and regular do dealings of money and business appear! how transient and passing are religious objects! Then, again, consider how society, sometimes in self-defence, sets a false stamp on good and evil; as in the excessive punishment of the errors of women, compared with Christ's conduct to the woman who was a sinner. Or when men are acknowledged to be in the sight of God equal, how strange it seems that one should heap up money for another, and be dependent on him for his daily life. Susceptible minds, attaching themselves, some to one point some to another, may carry such reflections very far, until society itself appears evil, and they desire some primitive patriarchal mode of life. They are tired of conventionalities; they want, as they say, to make the Gospel a reality; to place all men on a religious, social, and political equality. In this, as in the last case, 'they are kicking against the pricks;' what they want is a society which has not the very elements of a social state; they do not perceive that the cause of the evil is human nature itself, which will not cohere without mixed motives and received forms and distinctions, and that Providence has been pleased to rest the world on a firmer basis than is supplied by the fleeting emotions of philanthropy, viz. self-interest. We are not, indeed, to sit with our arms folded, and acquiesce in human evil. But we must separate the accidents from the essence of this evil: questions of taste, things indifferent, or customary, or necessary, from the weightier matters of oppression, falsehood, vice. The ills of society are to be struggled against in such a manner as not to violate the conditions of society; the precepts of Scripture are to be applied, but not without distinctions of times and countries; Christian duties are to be enforced, but not identified with political principles.

To see the world—not as it ought to be, but as it is—to be on a level with the circumstances in which God has placed them, to renounce the remote and impossible for what is possible and in their reach; above all, to begin within— these are the limits which enthusiasts should set to their aspirations after social good. It is a weary thing to be all our life long warring against the elements, or, like the slaves of some eastern lord, using our hands in a work which can only be accomplished by levers and machines. The physician of society should aid nature instead of fighting against it; he must let the world alone as much as he can; to a certain degree, he will even accept things as they are in the hope of bettering them.

II. Mere weakness of character will sometimes afford an illustration of the Apostle's words. If there are some whose days are 'bound each to each by natural piety,' there are others on whom the same continuous power is exercised for evil as well as good; they are unable to throw off their former self; the sins of their youth lie heavy on them; the influence of opinions which they have ceased to hold discolours their minds. Or it may be that their weakness takes a different form, viz. that of clinging to some favourite resolve, or of yielding to some fixed idea which gets dominion over them, and becomes the limit of all their ideas. A common instance of this may be found in the use made by many persons of conscience. Whatever they wish or fancy, whatever course of action they are led to by some influence obvious to others, though unobserved by themselves, immediately assumes the necessary and stereotyped form of the conscientious fulfilment of a duty. To every suggestion of what is right and reasonable, they reply only with the words—'their consciences will not allow it.' They do what they think right; they do not observe that they never seem to themselves to do otherwise. No voice of authority, no opinion of others, weighs with them when put in the scale against the dictates of what they term conscience. As they get older, their narrow ideas of right acquire a greater tenacity; the world is going on, and they are as they were. A deadening influence lies on their moral nature, the peculiarity of which is, that, like the law, it assumes the appearance of good, differing from the law only in being unconscious. Conscience, one may say, putting their own character into the form of a truth or commandment, 'has deceived and slain them.'

Another form of conscience yet more closely resembles the principle described in the seventh chapter of the Romans. There is a state in which man is powerless to act, and is, nevertheless, clairvoyant of all the good and evil of his own nature. He places the good and evil principle before him, and is ever oscillating between them. He traces the labyrinth of conflicting principles in the world, and is yet further perplexed and entangled. He is sensitive to every breath of feeling, and incapable of the performance of any duty. Or take another example: it sometimes happens that the remembrance of past suffering, or the consciousness of sin, may so weigh a man down as fairly to paralyze his moral power. He is distracted between what he is and what he was; old habits and vices, and the new character which is being fashioned in him. Sometimes the balance seems to hang equal; he feels the earnest wish and desire to do rightly, but cannot hope to find pleasure and satisfaction in a good life; he desires heartily to repent, but can never think it possible that God should forgive. 'It is I, and it is not I, but sin that dwelleth in me.' 'I have, and have never ceased to have, the wish for better things, even amid haunts of infamy and vice.' In such language, even now, though with less fervour than in 'the first spiritual chaos of the affections,' does the soul cry out to God—'O wretched man that I am, who shall deliver me from the body of this death?'

III. There is some danger of speculative difficulties presenting the same hindrance and stumbling-block to our own generation, that the law is described as doing to the contemporaries of St. Paul. As the law was holy, just, and good, so many of these difficulties are true, and have real grounds: all of them, except in cases where they spring from hatred and opposition to the Gospel, are at least innocent. And yet, by undermining received opinions, by increasing vanity and egotism, instead of strengthening the will and fixing the principles, their promulgation may become a temporary source of evil; so that, in the words of the Apostle, it may be said of them that, taking occasion by the truth, they deceive and slay men. What then? is the law sin? is honest inquiry wrong? God forbid! it is we ourselves who are incapable of receiving the results of inquiry; who will not believe unless we see; who demand a proof that we cannot have; who begin with appeals to authority, and tradition, and consequences, and, when dissatisfied with these, imagine that there is no other foundation on which life can repose but the loose and sandy structure of our individual opinions. Persons often load their belief in the hope of strengthening it; they escape doubt by assuming certainty. Or they believe 'under an hypothesis;' their worldly interests lead them to acquiesce; their higher intellectual convictions rebel. Opinions, hardly won from study and experience, are found to be at variance with early education, or natural temperament. Opposite tendencies grow together in the mind; appearing and reappearing at intervals. Life becomes a patchwork of new and old cloth, or like a garment which changes colour in the sun.

It is true that the generation to which we belong has difficulties to contend with, perhaps greater than those of any former age; and certainly different from them. Some of those difficulties arise out of the opposition of reason and faith; the critical inquiries of which the Old and New Testament have been the subject, are a trouble to many; the circumstance that, while the Bible is the word of life for all men, such inquiries are open only to the few, increases the irritation. The habit of mind which has been formed in the study of Greek or Roman history may be warned off the sacred territory, but cannot really be prevented from trespassing; still more impossible is it to keep the level of knowledge at one point in Germany, at another in England. Geology, ethnology, historical and metaphysical criticism, assail in succession not the Scriptures themselves, but notions and beliefs which in the minds of many good men are bound up with them. The eternal strain to keep theology where it is while the world is going on, specious reconcilements, political or ecclesiastical exigencies, recent attempts to revive the past, and the reaction to which they have given birth, the contrast that everywhere arises of old and new, all add to the confusion. Probably no other age has been to the same extent the subject of cross and contradictory influences. What can be more unlike than the tone of sermons and of newspapers? or the ideas of men on art, politics, and religion, now, and half a generation ago? The thoughts of a few original minds, like wedges, pierce into all received and conventional opinions and are almost equally removed from either. The destruction of 'shams,' that is, the realization of things as they are amid all the conventions of thought and speech and action, is also an element of unsettlement. The excess of self-reflection, again, is not favourable to strength or simplicity of character. Every one seems to be employed in decomposing the world, human nature, and himself. The discovery is made that good and evil are mixed in a far more subtle way than at first sight would have appeared possible; and that even extremes of both meet in the same person. The mere analysis of moral and religious truth, the fact that we know the origin of many things which the last generation received on authority, is held by some to destroy their sacredness. Lastly, there are those who feel that all the doubts of sceptics put together, fall short of that great doubt which has insinuated itself into their minds, from the contemplation of mankind—saying one thing and doing another.

It is foolish to lament over these things; it would be still more foolish to denounce them. They are the mental trials of the age and country in which God has placed us. If they seem at times to exercise a weakening or unsettling influence, may we not hope that increasing love of truth, deeper knowledge of ourselves and other men, will, in the end, simplify and not perplex the path of life. We may leave off in mature years where we began in youth, and receive not only the kingdom of God, but the world also, as 'little children.' The analysis of moral and religious truth may correct its errors without destroying its obligations. Experience of the illusions of religious feeling at a particular time should lead us to place religion on a foundation which is independent of feeling. Because the Scripture is no longer held to be a book of geology or ethnology, or a supernatural revelation of historical facts, it will not cease to be the law of our lives, exercising an influence over us, different in kind from the ideas of philosophical systems, or the aspirations of poetry or romance. Because the world (of which we are a part) is hypocritical and deceitful, and individuals go about dissecting their neighbours' motives and lives, that is a reason for cherishing a simple and manly temper of mind, which does not love men the less because it knows human nature more; which pierces the secrets of the heart, not by any process of anatomy, but by the light of an eye from which the mists of selfishness are dispersed.

IV. The relation in which science stands to us may seem to bear but a remote resemblance to that in which the law stood to the Apostle St. Paul. Yet the analogy is not fanciful, but real. Traces of physical laws are discernible everywhere in the world around us; in ourselves also, whose souls are knit together with our bodies, whose bodies are a part of the material creation. It seems as if nature came so close to us as to leave no room for the motion of our will: instead of the inexhaustible grace of God enabling us to say, in the language of the Apostle, 'I can do all things through Christ that strengtheneth me,' we become more and more the slaves of our own physical constitution. Our state is growing like that of a person whose mind is over sensitive to the nervous emotions of his own bodily frame. And as the self-consciousness becomes stronger and the contrast between faith and experience more vivid, there arises a conflict between the spirit and the flesh, nature and grace, not unlike that of which the Apostle speaks. No one who, instead of hanging to the past, will look forward to the future, can expect that natural science should stand in the same attitude towards revelation fifty years hence as at present. The faith of mankind varies from age to age; it is weaker, or it may be stronger, at one time than at another. But that which never varies or turns aside, which is always going on and cannot be driven back, is knowledge based on the sure ground of observation and experiment, the regular progress of which is itself matter of observation. The stage at which the few have arrived is already far in advance of the many, and if there were nothing remaining to be discovered, still the diffusion of the knowledge that we have, without new addition, would exert a great influence on religious and social life. Still greater is the indirect influence which science exercises through the medium of the arts. In one century a single invention has changed the face of Europe; three or four such inventions might produce a gulf between us and the future far greater than the interval which separates ancient from modern civilization. Doubtless God has provided a way that the thought of Him should not be banished from the hearts of men. And habit, and opinion, and prescription may 'last our time,' and many motives may conspire to keep our minds off the coming change. But if ever our present knowledge of geology, of languages, of the races and religions of mankind, of the human frame itself, shall be regarded as the starting-point of a goal which has been almost reached, supposing too the progress of science to be accompanied by a corresponding development of the mechanical arts, we can hardly anticipate, from what we already see, the new relation that will then arise between reason and faith. Perhaps the very opposition between them may have died away. At any rate experience shows that religion is not stationary when all other things are moving onward.

Changes of this kind pass gradually over the world; the mind of man is not suddenly thrown into a state for which it is unprepared. No one has more doubts than he can carry; the way of life is not found to stop and come to an end in the midst of a volcano, or on the edge of a precipice. Dangers occur, not from the disclosure of any new, or hitherto unobserved, facts, for which, as for all other blessings, we have reason to be thankful to God; but from our concealment or denial of them, from the belief that we can make them other than they are; from the fancy that some *a priori* notion, some undefined word, some intensity of personal conviction, is the weapon with which they are to be met. New facts, whether bearing on Scripture, or on religion generally, or on morality, are sure to win their way; the tide refuses to recede at any man's bidding. And there are not wanting signs that the increase of secular knowledge is beginning to be met by a corresponding progress in religious ideas. Controversies are dying out; the lines of party are fading into one another; niceties of doctrine are laid aside. The opinions respecting the inspiration of Scripture, which are held in the present day by good and able men, are not those of fifty years ago; a change may be observed on many points, a reserve on still more. Formulas of reconciliation have sprung up: 'the Bible is not a book of science,' 'the inspired writers were not taught supernaturally what they could have learned from ordinary sources,' resting-places in the argument at which travellers are the more ready to halt, because they do not perceive that they are only temporary. For there is no real resting-place but in the entire faith, that all true knowledge is a revelation of the will of God. In the case of the poor and suffering, we often teach resignation to the accidents of life; it is not less plainly a duty of religious men, to submit to the progress of knowledge. That is a new kind of resignation, in which many Christians have to school themselves. When the difficulty may seem, in anticipation, to be greatest, they will find, with the Apostle, that there is a way out: 'The truth has made them free.'

ESSAY

ON

THE OLD TESTAMENT

ROMANS IV.

'Ηνίκα δ' ἂν ἐπιστρέψῃ πρὸς κύριον, περιαιρεῖται τὸ κάλυμμα.—2 Cor. iii. 16.

Thus we have reached another stage in the development of the great theme. The new commandment has become old; faith is taught in the Book of the Law. 'Abraham had faith in God, and it was counted to him for righteousness.' David spoke of the forgiveness of sins in the very spirit of the Gospel. The Old Testament is not dead, but alive again. It refers not to the past, but to the present. The truths which we daily feel, are written in its pages. There are the consciousness of sin and the sense of acceptance. There is the veiled remembrance of a former world, which is also the veiled image of a future one.

To us the Old and New Testaments are two books, or two parts of the same book, which fit into one another, and can never be separated or torn asunder. They are double one against the other, and the New Testament is the revelation of the Old. To the first believers it was otherwise: as yet there was no New Testament; nor is there any trace that the authors of the New Testament ever expected their own writings to be placed on a level with the Old. We can scarcely imagine what would have been the feeling of St. Paul, could he have foreseen that later ages would look not to the faith of Abraham in the law, but to the Epistle to the Romans, as the highest authority on the doctrine of justification by faith; or that they would have regarded the allegory of Hagar and Sarah, in the Epistle to the Galatians, as a difficulty to be resolved by the inspiration of the Apostle. Neither he who wrote, nor those to whom he wrote, could ever have thought that words which were meant for a particular Church were to give life also to all mankind; and that the Epistles in which they occurred were one day to be placed on a level with the Books of Moses themselves.

But if the writings of the New Testament were regarded by the contemporaries of the Apostle in a manner different from that of later ages, there was a difference, which it is far more difficult for us to appreciate, in their manner of reading the Old Testament. To them it was not half, but the whole, needing nothing to be added to it or to counteract it, but containing everything in itself. It seemed to come home to them; to be meant specially for their age; to be understood by them, as its words had never been understood before. 'Did not their hearts burn within them?' as the Apostles expounded to them the Psalms and Prophets. The manner of this exposition was that of the age in which they lived. They brought to the understanding of it, not a knowledge of the volume of the New Testament, but the mind of Christ. Sometimes they found the lesson which they sought in the plain language of Scripture; at other times, coming round to the same lesson by the paths of allegory, or seeming even in the sound of a word to catch an echo of the Redeemer's name. Various as are the writings of the Old Testament, composed by such numerous authors, at so many different times, so diverse in style and subject, in them all they read only—the truth of Christ. They read without distinctions of moral and ceremonial, type and antitype, history and prophecy, without inquiries into the original meaning or connexion of passages, without theories of the relation of the Old and New Testaments. Whatever contrast existed was of another kind, not of the parts of a book, but of the law and faith;

of the earlier and later dispensations. The words of the book were all equally for their instruction; the whole volume lighted up with new meaning.

What was then joined cannot now be divided or put asunder. The New Testament will never be unclothed of the Old. No one in later ages can place himself in the position of the heathen convert who learnt the name of Christ first, afterwards the Law and the Prophets. Such instances were probably rare even in the first days of the Christian Church. No one can easily imagine the manner in which St. Paul himself sets the Law over against the Gospel, and at the same time translates one into the language of the other. Time has closed up the rent which the law made in the heart of man; and the superficial resemblances on which the Apostle sometimes dwells, have not the same force to us which they had to his contemporaries. But a real unity remains to ourselves as well as to the Apostle, the unity not of the letter, but of the spirit, like the unity of life or of a human soul, which lasts on amid the changes of our being. The Old Testament and the New do not dovetail into one another like the parts of an indenture; it is a higher figure than this, which is needed to describe the continuity of the Divine work. Or rather, the simple fact is above all figures, and can receive no addition from philosophical notions of design, or the observation of minute coincidences. What we term the Old and New dispensation is the increasing revelation of God, amid the accidents of human history: first, in himself; secondly, in His Son, gathering not one nation only, but all mankind into His family. It is the vision of God himself, true and just, and remembering mercy in one age of the world; not ceasing to be true and just, but softening also into human gentleness, and love, and forgiveness, and making His dwelling in the human heart in another. The wind, and the earthquake, and the fire pass by first, and after that 'the still small voice.' This is the great fulfilment of the Law and the Prophets in the Gospel. No other religion has anything like it. And the use of language, and systems of theology, and the necessity of 'giving ideas through something,' and the prayers and thoughts of eighteen hundred years, have formed another connexion between the Old and New Testament, more accidental and outward, and also more intricate and complex, which is incapable of being accurately drawn out, and ought not to be imposed as an article of faith; which yet seems to many to supply a want in human nature, and gives expression to feelings which would otherwise be unuttered.

It is not natural, nor perhaps possible, to us to cease to use the figures in which 'holy men of old' spoke of that which belonged to their peace. But it is well that we should sometimes remind ourselves, that 'all these things are a shadow, but the body is of Christ.' Framed as our minds are, we are ever tending to confuse that which is accidental with that which is essential, to substitute the language of imagery for the severity of our moral ideas, to entangle Divine truths in the state of society in which they came into the world or in the ways of thought of a particular age. 'All these things are a shadow;' that is to say, not only the temple and tabernacle, and the victim laid on the altar, and the atonement offered once a year for the sins of the nation; but the conceptions which later ages express by these words, so far as anything human or outward or figurative mingles with them, so far as they cloud the Divine nature with human passions, so far as they imply, or seem to imply, anything at variance with our notions of truth and right, are as much, or even more a shadow than that outward image which belonged to the elder dispensation. The same Lord who compared the scribe instructed in the kingdom of heaven to a householder who brought forth out of his treasure things new and old, said also in a figure, that 'new cloth must not be put on an old garment' or 'new wine into old bottles.'

ESSAY

ON THE

IMPUTATION OF THE SIN OF ADAM

ROMANS V.

THAT so many opposite systems of Theology seek their authority in Scripture is a fair proof that Scripture is different from them all. That is to say, Scripture often contains in germ what is capable of being drawn to either side; it is indistinct, where they are distinct; it presents two lights, where they present only one; it speaks inwardly, while they clothe themselves in the forms of human knowledge. That indistinct, intermediate, inward point of view at which the truth exists but in germ, they have on both sides tended to extinguish and suppress. Passing allusions, figures of speech, rhetorical oppositions, have been made the foundation of doctrinal statements, which are like a part of the human mind itself, and seem as if they could never be uprooted, without uprooting the very sentiment of religion. Systems of this kind exercise a constraining power, which makes it difficult for us to see anything in Scripture but themselves.

For example, how slender is the foundation in the New Testament for the doctrine of Adam's sin being imputed to his posterity—two passages in St. Paul at most, and these of uncertain interpretation. The little cloud, no bigger than a man's hand, has covered the heavens. To reduce such subjects to their proper proportions, we should consider :—first, what space they occupy in Scripture ; secondly, how far the language used respecting them is literal or figurative; thirdly, whether they agree with the more general truths of Scripture and our moral sense, or are not 'rather repugnant thereto ;' fourthly, whether their origin may not be prior to Christianity, or traceable in the after history of the Church ; fifthly, whether the words of Scripture may not be confused with logical inferences which are appended to them ; sixthly, in the case of this and of some other doctrines, whether even poetry has not lent its aid to stamp them in our minds in a more definite and therefore different form from that in which the Apostles taught them ; lastly, how far in our own day they are anything more than words.

The two passages alluded to are Rom. v. 12–21 ; 1 Cor. xv. 21, 22, 45–49, in both of which parallels are drawn between Adam and Christ. In both the sin of Adam is spoken of, or seems to be spoken of, as the source of death to man : 'As by one man's transgression sin entered into the world, and death by sin,' and 'As in Adam all die.' Such words appear plain at first sight ; that is to say, we find in them what we bring to them : let us see what considerations modify their meaning. If we accept the Pelagian view of the passage, which refers the death of each man to actual sin, there is an end of the controversy. But it does not equally follow that, if what is termed the received interpretation is given to the words, the doctrine which it has been attempted to ground upon them would have any real foundation.

We will suppose, then, that no reference is contained in either passage to 'actual sin.' In some other sense than this mankind are identified with Adam's transgression. But the question still remains, whether Adam's sin and death are merely the type of the sin and death of his posterity, or, more than this, the cause. The first explanation quite satisfies the meaning of the words, 'As in Adam all die;' the second seems to be required by the parallel passage in the Romans: 'As by one man sin came into the world,' and 'As by one man many were made sinners,' if taken literally.

The question involves the more general one, whether the use of language by St. Paul makes it necessary that we should take his words literally in this passage. Is he speaking of Adam's sin being the cause of sin and death to his posterity, in any other sense than he spoke of Abraham being a father of circumcision to the uncircumcised? (chap. iv.) Yet no one has ever thought of basing a doctrine on these words. Or is he speaking of all men dying in Adam in any other sense than he says in 2 Cor. v. 15, that if one died for all, then all died? Yet in this latter passage, while Christ died literally, it was only in a figure that all died. May he be arguing in the same way as when he infers from the word 'seed' being used in the singular, that 'thy seed is Christ'? Or, if we confine ourselves to the passage under consideration—Is the righteousness of Christ there imputed to believers, independently of their own inward holiness? and if so, should the sin of Adam be imputed independently of the actual sins of men?

I. A very slight difference in the mode of expression would make it impossible for us to attribute to St. Paul the doctrine of the imputation of the sin of Adam. But we have seen before how varied, and how different from our own, are his modes of thought and language. Compare i. 4; iv. 25. To him, it was but a slight transition, from the identification of Adam with the sins of all mankind, to the representation of the sin of Adam as the cause of those sins. To us, there is the greatest difference between the two statements. To him, it was one among many figures of the same kind, to oppose the first and second Adam, as elsewhere he opposes the old and new man. With us, this figure has been singled out to be made the foundation of a most exact statement of doctrine. We do not remark that there is not even the appearance of attributing Adam's sin to his posterity, in any part of the Apostle's writings in which he is not drawing a parallel between Adam and Christ.

II. The Apostle is not speaking of Adam as fallen from a state of innocence. He could scarcely have said, 'The first man is of the earth, earthy,' if he had had in his mind that Adam had previously existed in a pure and perfect state. He is only drawing a parallel between Adam and Christ. The moment we leave this parallel, all is uncertain and undetermined. What was the nature of that innocent life? or of the act of Adam which forfeited it? and how was the effect of that act communicated to his posterity? The minds of men in different ages of the world have strayed into these and similar inquiries. Difficulties about 'fate, predestination, and free-will' (not food for angels' thoughts) cross our path in the garden of Eden itself. But neither the Old or New Testament give any answer to them. Imagination has possessed itself of the vacant spot, and been busy, as it often is, in proportion to the slenderness of knowledge.

III. There are other elements of St. Paul's teaching, which are either inconsistent with the imputation of Adam's sin to his posterity, or at any rate are so prominent as to make such a doctrine if held by him comparatively unimportant. According to St. Paul, it is not the act of Adam, but the law that

> 'Brought sin into the world and all our woe.'

And the law is almost equivalent to 'the knowledge of sin.' But original sin is, or may be, wholly unconscious—the fault of nature in the infant equally with the man. Not so the sin of which St. Paul speaks, which is inseparable from consciousness, as he says himself: 'I was alive without the law once,' that is, before I came to the consciousness of sin.

IV. It will be admitted that we ought to feel still greater reluctance to press the statement of the Apostle to its strict logical consequences, if we find that the language which he here uses is that of his age and country. From the circumstance of our first reading the doctrine of the imputation of Adam's sin to his posterity in the Epistles of St. Paul, we can hardly persuade ourselves that this is not its original source. The incidental manner in which it is alluded to might indeed lead us to suppose that it would scarcely have been intelligible, had it not been also an opinion of his time. But if this inference should seem doubtful, there is direct evidence to show that the Jews connected sin and death, and the sins and death of mankind, with the sin of Adam, in the same way as the Apostle. The earliest trace of such a doctrine is found in the apocryphal Book of Wisdom, ii. 24: 'But God created man to be immortal, and made him to be an image of his own eternity. Nevertheless, through envy of the devil came death into the world; and they that do hold of his side do find it.' And Eccles. xxv. 24: 'Of the woman came the beginning of sin, and through her we all die.' It was a further refinement of some of their teachers, that when Adam sinned the whole world sinned; because, at that time, Adam was the whole world, or because the soul of Adam comprehended the souls of all, so that Adam's sin conveyed a hereditary taint to his posterity. It was a confusion of a half physical, half logical or metaphysical notion, arising in the minds of men who had not yet learnt the lesson of our Saviour—'That which is from without defileth not a man.' That human nature or philosophy sometimes rose up against such inventions is certainly true; but it seems to be on the whole admitted, that the doctrine of Augustine is in substance generally agreed to by the Rabbis, and that there is no trace of their having derived it from the writings of St. Paul. Compare the passages quoted in Fritzsche, vol. i. pp. 293-296, and Schoettgen.

But not only is the connexion of sin and death with each other, and with the sin of Adam, found in the Rabbinical writings; the type and antitype of the first and second Adam are also contained in them. In reading the first chapters of Genesis, the Jews made a distinction between the higher Adam, who was the light of the world, and had control over all things, who was mystically referred to where it is said, 'they two shall be one flesh;' and the inferior Adam, who was Lord only of the creation; who had 'the breath of life,' but not 'the living soul.' (Schoettgen, i. 512–514, 670–673.) By some, indeed, the latter seems to have been identified with the Messiah. By Philo, on the other hand, the λόγος is identified with the πρῶτος 'Aδάμ, who is without sex, while the ἄνθρωπος χοικός is created afterwards by the help of the angels (De Creat. Mund. p. 30). It is not the object of this statement to reconcile these variations, but merely to indicate, first, that the idea of a first and second Adam was familiar to the Jews in the time of St. Paul, and that one or other of them was regarded by them as the Word and the Messiah.

V. A slighter, though not less real foundation of the doctrine has been what may be termed the logical symmetry of the imputation of the righteousness of Christ and of the sin of Adam. The latter half is the correlative of the former; they mutually support each other. We place the first and second Adam in juxtaposition, and seem to see a fitness or reason in the one standing in the same relation to the fallen as the other to the saved.

VI. It is hardly necessary to ask the further question, what meaning we can attach to the imputation of sin and guilt which are not our own, and of which we are unconscious. God can never see us other than we really are, or judge us without reference to all our circumstances and antecedents. If we can hardly suppose that He would allow a fiction of mercy to be interposed between ourselves and Him, still less can we imagine that He would interpose a fiction of vengeance. If He requires holiness before He will save, much more, may we say in the Apostle's form of speech, will He require sin before He dooms us to perdition. Nor can anything be in spirit more contrary to the living consciousness of sin of which the Apostle everywhere speaks, than the conception of sin as dead unconscious evil, originating in the act of an individual man, in the world before the flood.

VII. A small part of the train of consequences which have been drawn out by divines can be made to hang even upon the letter of the Apostle's words, though we should not take into account the general temper and spirit of his writings. Logical inferences often help to fill up the aching void in our knowledge of the spiritual world. They seem necessary; in time they receive a new support from habit and tradition. They hide away and conceal the nature of the original premisses. They may be likened to the superstructure of a building which the foundation has not strength to bear; or, rather, perhaps, when compared to the serious efforts of human thought, to the plaything of the child who places one brick upon another in wondering suspense, until the whole totters and falls, or his childish fancy pleases itself with throwing it down. So, to apply these remarks to our present subject, we are contented to repeat the simple words of the Apostle, 'As in Adam all die, even so in Christ shall all be made alive.' Perhaps we may not be able to recall all the associations which they conveyed to his mind. But neither are we willing to affirm his meaning to be that the sin of one man was the cause of other men's sins, or that God condemned one part of the human race for a fault not their own, because He was going to save another part; or that original sin, as some say, or the guilt of original sin, as is the opinion of others, is washed away in baptism. There is a terrible explicitness in such language touching the realities of a future life which makes us shrink from trusting our own faculties amid far-off deductions like these.

We feel that we are undermining, not strengthening, the foundations of the Gospel. We fear to take upon ourselves a burden which neither 'we nor our fathers are able to bear.' Instead of receiving such statements only to explain them away, or keep them out of sight, it is better to answer boldly in the words of the Apostle, 'God forbid! for how shall God judge the world.'

On the whole, then, we are led to infer that in the Augustinian interpretation of this passage, even if it agree with the letter of the text, too little regard has been paid to the extent to which St. Paul uses figurative language, and to the manner of his age in interpretations of the Old Testament. The difficulty of supposing him to be allegorizing the narrative of Genesis is slight, in comparison with the difficulty of supposing him to countenance a doctrine at variance with our first notions of the moral nature of God.

But when the figure is dropped, and allowance is made for the manner of the age, the question once more returns upon us—'What is the Apostle's meaning?' He is arguing, we see, κατ' ἄνθρωπον, and taking his stand on the received opinions of his time. Do we imagine that his object is no other than to set the seal of his authority on these traditional beliefs? The whole analogy, not merely of the writings of St. Paul, but of the entire New Testament, would lead us to suppose that his object was not to reassert them, but to teach, through them, a new and nobler lesson. The Jewish Rabbis would have spoken of the first and second Adam; but which of them would have made the application of the figure to all mankind? Which of them would have breathed the quickening Spirit into the dry bones? The figure of the Apostle bears the impress of his own age and country; the interpretation of the figure is for every age, and for the whole world. A figure of speech it remains still, an allegory after the manner of that age and country, but yet with no uncertain or ambiguous signification. It means that 'God hath made of one blood all the nations of the earth;' and that 'he hath concluded all under sin, that he may have mercy upon all.' It means a truth deep yet simple—the fact which we recognize in ourselves and trace everywhere around us—that we are one in a common evil nature, which, if it be not derived from the sin of Adam, exists as really as if it were. It means that we shall be made one in Christ, by the grace of God, in a measure here, more fully and perfectly in another world. It means that Christ is the natural head of the human race, the author of its spiritual life. It shows Him to us as He enters within the veil, in form as a man, the 'first fruits of them which sleep.' It is a sign or intimation which guides our thoughts in another direction also, beyond the world of which religion speaks, to observe what science tells us of the interdependence of soul and body—what history tells of the chain of lives and events. It leads us to reflect on ourselves not as isolated, independent beings;—not such as we appear to be to our own narrow consciousness; but as we truly are—the creatures of antecedents which we can never know, fashioned by circumstances over which we have no control. The infant, coming into existence in a wonderful manner, inherits something, not from its parents only, but from the first beginning of the human race. He too is born into a family of which God in Christ is the Father. There is enough here to meditate upon—'a mystery since the world was'—without the 'weak and beggarly' elements of Rabbinical lore. We may not encumber St. Paul 'with the things which he destroyed.'

ESSAY

ON

ATONEMENT AND SATISFACTION

'Sacrifice and offering thou wouldest not . . . Then said I, Lo, I come to do thy will, O God.'—Ps. xl. 6-8.

———

THE doctrine of the Atonement has often been explained in a way at which our moral feelings revolt. God is represented as angry with us for what we never did; He is ready to inflict a disproportionate punishment on us for what we are; He is satisfied by the sufferings of His Son in our stead. The sin of Adam is first imputed to us; then the righteousness of Christ. The imperfection of human law is transferred to the Divine; or rather a figment of law which has no real existence. The death of Christ is also explained by the analogy of the ancient rite of sacrifice. He is a victim laid upon the altar to appease the wrath of God. The institutions and ceremonies of the Mosaical religion are applied to Him. He is further said to bear the infinite punishment of infinite sin. When He had suffered or paid the penalty, God is described as granting Him the salvation of mankind in return.

I shall endeavour to show, 1. that these conceptions of the work of Christ have no foundation in Scripture; 2. that their growth may be traced in ecclesiastical history; 3. that the only sacrifice, atonement, or satisfaction, with which the Christian has to do, is a moral and spiritual one; not the pouring out of blood upon the earth, but the living sacrifice 'to do thy will, O God;' in which the believer has part as well as his Lord; about the meaning of which there can be no more question in our day than there was in the first ages.

§ 1.

It is difficult to concentrate the authority of Scripture on points of controversy. For Scripture is not doctrine but teaching; it arises naturally out of the circumstances of the writers; it is not intended to meet the intellectual refinements of modern times. The words of our Saviour, 'My kingdom is not of this world,' admit of a wide application, to systems of knowledge, as well as to systems of government and politics. The 'bread of life' is not an elaborate theology. The revelation which Scripture makes to us of the will of God, does not turn upon the exact use of language. ('Lo, O man, he hath showed thee what he required of thee; to do justly and to love mercy, and to walk humbly with thy God.') The books of Scripture were written by different authors, and in different ages of the world; we cannot, therefore, apply them with the minuteness and precision of a legal treatise. The Old Testament is not on all points the same with the New; for 'Moses allowed of some things for the hardness of their hearts;' nor the Law with the Prophets, for there were 'proverbs in the house of Israel' that were reversed; nor does the Gospel, which is simple and universal, in all respects agree with the Epistles which have reference to the particular state of the first converts; nor is the teaching of St. James, who admits works as a coefficient with faith in the justification of man, absolutely identical with that of St. Paul, who asserts righteousness by faith only; nor is the character of all the Epistles of St. Paul, written as they were at different times amid the changing scenes of life, precisely the same; nor does he himself claim an equal authority for all his precepts. No theory of inspiration can obliterate these differences; or rather none can be true which does not admit them. The neglect of them reduces the books of Scripture to an unmeaning unity, and effectually seals up their true sense. But if we acknowledge this natural diversity of form, this perfect humanity of Scripture, we must, at any rate in some general way, adjust the relation of the different parts to one another before we apply its words to the establishment of any doctrine.

Nor again is the citation of a single text sufficient to prove a doctrine; nor must consequences be added on, which are not found in Scripture, nor figures of speech reasoned about, as though they conveyed exact notions. An accidental similarity of expression is not to be admitted as an authority; nor a mystical allusion, which has been gathered from Scripture, according to some method which in other writings the laws of language and logic would not justify. When engaged in controversy with Roman Catholics, about the doctrine of purgatory, or transubstantiation, or the authority of the successors of St. Peter, we are willing to admit these principles. They are equally true when the subject of inquiry is the atoning work of Christ. We must also distinguish the application of a passage in religious discourse from its original meaning. The more obvious explanation which is received in our own day, or by our own branch of the Church, will sometimes have to be set aside for one more difficult, because less familiar, which is drawn from the context. Nor is it allowable to bar an interpretation of Scripture from a regard to doctrinal consequences. Further, it is necessary that we should make allowance for the manner in which ideas were represented in the ages at which the books of Scripture were written which cannot be so lively to us as to contemporaries. Nor can we deny that texts may be quoted on both sides of a controversy, as for example, in the controversy respecting predestination.

For in religious, as in other differences, there is often truth on both sides.

The drift of the preceding remarks is not to show that there is any ambiguity or uncertainty in the witness of Scripture to the great truths of morality and religion. Nay, rather the universal voice of the Old Testament and the New proclaims that there is one God of infinite justice, goodness, and truth : and the writers of the New Testament agree in declaring that Jesus Christ, the Son of God, is the Saviour of the world. There can never, by any possibility, be a doubt that our Lord and St. Paul taught the doctrine of a future life, and of a judgement, at which men would give an account of the deeds done in the body. It is no matter for regret that the essentials of the Gospel are within the reach of a child's understanding. But this clearness of Scripture about the great truths of religion does not extend to the distinctions and developments of theological systems; it rather seems to contrast with them. It is one thing to say that 'Christ is the Saviour of the world,' or that 'we are reconciled to God through Christ,' and another thing to affirm that the Levitical or heathen sacrifices typified the death of Christ; or that the death of Christ has a sacrificial import, and is an atonement or satisfaction for the sins of men. The latter positions involve great moral and intellectual difficulties; many things have to be considered, before we can allow that the phraseology of Scripture is to be caught up and applied in this way. For we may easily dress up in the externals of the New Testament a doctrine which is really at variance with the Spirit of Christ and His Apostles, and we may impart to this doctrine, by the help of living tradition, that is to say, custom and religious use, a sacredness yet greater than is derived from such a fallacious application of Scripture language. It happens almost unavoidably (and our only chance of guarding against the illusion is to be aware of it) that we are more under the influence of rhetoric in theology than in other branches of knowledge; our minds are so constituted that what we often hear we are ready to believe, especially when it falls in with previous convictions or wants. But he who desires to know whether the statements above referred to have any real objective foundation in the New Testament, will carefully weigh the following considerations:—Whether there is any reason for interpreting the New Testament by the analogy of the Old? Whether the sacrificial expressions which occur in the New Testament, and on which the question chiefly turns, are to be interpreted spiritually or literally? Whether the use of such expressions may not be a figurative mode of the time, which did not necessarily recall the thing signified any more than the popular use of the term 'Sacrifice' among ourselves? He will consider further whether this language is employed vaguely, or definitely? Whether it is the chief manner of expressing the work of Christ, or one among many? Whether it is found to occur equally in every part of the New Testament; for example, in the Gospels, as well as in the Epistles? Whether the more frequent occurrence of it in particular books, as for instance, in the Epistle to the Hebrews, may not be explained by the peculiar object or circumstances of the writer? Whether other figures of speech, such as death, life, resurrection with Christ, are not equally frequent, which have never yet been made the foundation of any doctrine? Lastly, whether this language of sacrifice is not applied to the believer as well as to his Lord, and whether the believer is not spoken of as sharing the sufferings of his Lord?

I. All Christians agree that there is a connexion between the Old Testament and the New: 'Novum Testamentum in vetere latet; Vetus Testamentum in novo patet:' 'I am not come to destroy the law and the prophets, but to fulfil.' But, respecting the nature of the revelation or fulfilment which is implied in these expressions, they are not equally agreed. Some conceive the Old and New Testaments to be 'double one against the other;' the one being the type, and the other the antitype, the ceremonies of the Law, and the symbols and imagery of the Prophets, supplying to them the forms of thought and religious ideas of the Gospel. Even the history of the Jewish people has been sometimes thought to be an anticipation or parallel of the history of the Christian world; many accidental circumstances in the narrative of Scripture being likewise taken as an example of the Christian life. The relation between the Old and New Testaments has been regarded by others from a different point of view, as a continuous one, which may be described under some image of growth or development; the facts and ideas of the one leading on to the facts and ideas of the other; and the two together forming one record of 'the increasing purpose which through the ages ran.' This continuity, however, is broken at one point, and the parts separate and reunite like ancient and modern civilization, though the connexion is nearer, and of another kind; the Messiah, in whom the hopes of the Jewish people centre, being the first-born of a new creation, the Son of Man and the Son of God. It is necessary, moreover, to distinguish the connexion of fact from that of language and idea; because the Old Testament is not only the preparation for the New, but also the figure and expression of it. Those who hold the first of these two views, viz. the reduplication of the Old Testament in the New, rest their opinion chiefly on two grounds. First, it seems incredible to them, and repugnant to their conception of a Divine revelation, that the great apparatus of rites and ceremonies, with which, even at this distance of time, they are intimately acquainted, should have no inner and symbolical meaning; that the Jewish nation for many ages should have carried with it a load of forms only; that the words of Moses which they 'still hear read in the synagogue every sabbath-day,' and which they often read in their own households, should relate only to matters of outward observance; just as they are unwilling to believe that the prophecies, which they also read, have no reference to the historical events of modern times. And, secondly, they are swayed by the authority of the Epistle to the Hebrews, the writer of which has made the Old Testament the allegory of the New.

It will be considered hereafter what is to be said in answer to the last of these arguments. The first is perhaps sufficiently answered by the analogy of other ancient religions. It would be ridiculous to assume a spiritual meaning in the Homeric rites and sacrifices; although they may be different in other respects, have we any more reason for inferring such a meaning in the Mosaic? Admitting the application which is made of a few of them by the author of the Epistle to the Hebrews to be their original intention, the great mass would still remain unexplained, and yet they are all alike contained in the same Revelation. It may seem natural to us to suppose that God taught His people like children by the help of outward objects. But no *a priori* supposition of this kind, no fancy, however natural, of a symmetry or coincidence which may be traced between the Old Testament and the New, nor the frequent repetition of such a theory in many forms, is an answer to the fact. That fact is the silence of the Old Testament itself. If the sacrifices of the Mosaical religion were really symbolical of the death of Christ, how can it be accounted for that no trace of this symbolism appears in the books of Moses themselves? that prophets and righteous men of old never gave this interpretation to them? that the lawgiver is intent only on the sign, and says nothing of the thing signified? No other book is ever supposed to teach truths about which it is wholly silent. We do not imagine the Iliad and Odyssey to be a revelation of the Platonic or Socratic philosophy. The circumstances that these poems received this or some other allegorical explanation from a school of Alexandrian critics, does not incline us to believe that such an explanation is a part of their original meaning. The human mind does not work in this occult manner; language was not really given men to conceal their thoughts; plain precepts or statements do not contain hidden mysteries.

It may be said that the Levitical rites and offerings had a meaning, not for the Jews, but for us, 'on whom the ends of the world are come.' Moses, David, Isaiah were unacquainted with this meaning; it was reserved for those who lived after the event to which they referred had taken place to discover it. Such an afterthought may be natural to us, who are ever tracing a literary or mystical connexion between the Old Testament and the New; it would have been very strange to us, had we lived in the ages before the coming of Christ. It is incredible that God should have instituted rites and ceremonies, which were to be observed as forms by a whole people throughout their history, to teach mankind fifteen hundred years afterwards, uncertainly and in a figure, a lesson which Christ taught plainly and without a figure. Such an assumption confuses the application of Scripture with its original meaning; the use of language in the New Testament with the facts of the Old. Further, it does away with all certainty in the interpretation of Scripture. If we can introduce the New Testament into the Old, we may with equal right introduce Tradition or Church History into the New.

The question here raised has a very important bearing on the use of the figures of atonement and sacrifice in the New Testament. For if it could be shown that the sacrifices which were offered up in the Levitical worship were anticipatory only; that the law too declared itself to be 'a shadow of good things to come;' that Moses had himself spoken 'of the reproach of Christ;' in that case the slightest allusion in the New Testament to the customs or words of the law would have a peculiar interest. We should be justified in referring to them as explanatory of the work of Christ, in studying the Levitical distinctions respecting offerings with a more than antiquarian interest, in 'disputing about purifying' and modes of expiation. But if not; if, in short, we are only reflecting the present on the past, or perhaps confusing both together, and interpreting Christianity by Judaism, and Judaism by Christianity; then the sacrificial language of the New Testament loses its depth and significance, or rather acquires a higher, that is, a spiritual one.

II. Of such an explanation, if it had really existed when the Mosaic religion was still a national form of worship, traces would occur in the writings of the Psalmists and the Prophets; for these furnish a connecting link between the Old Testament and the New. But this is not the case; the Prophets are, for the most part, unconscious of the law, or silent respecting its obligations.

In many places, their independence of the Mosaical religion passes into a kind of opposition to it. The inward and spiritual truth asserts itself, not as an explanation of the ceremonial observance, but in defiance of it. The 'undergrowth of morality' is putting forth shoots in spite of the deadness of the ceremonial hull. Isaiah i. 13 : 'Bring no more vain oblations; incense is an abomination unto me; the new moons and sabbaths, the calling of assemblies, I cannot away with; it is iniquity, even the solemn meeting.' Micah vi. 6 : 'Wherewith shall I come before the Lord, or bow myself before the high God? shall I come before him with burnt offerings, with calves of a year old? Will the Lord be pleased with thousands of rams, or with ten thousands of rivers of oil?' Psalm l. 10 : 'All the beasts of the forests are mine, and so are the cattle upon a thousand hills: If I were hungry I would not tell thee.' We cannot doubt that in passages like these we are bursting the bonds of the Levitical or ceremonial dispensation.

The spirit of prophecy, speaking by Isaiah, does not say 'I will have mercy as well as sacrifice,' but 'I will have mercy and not (or rather than) sacrifice.' In the words of the Psalmist, 'Sacrifice and offering thou wouldest not; Then said I, Lo, I come to do thy will, O God;' 'The sacrifices of God are a broken spirit:' or again, 'A bruised reed shall he not break, and smoking flax shall he not quench; he shall bring forth judgement unto truth:' or again, according to the image both of Isaiah and Jeremiah (Isa. liii. 7; Jer. xi. 19), which seems to have passed before the vision of John the Baptist (John i. 36), 'He is brought as a lamb to the slaughter, and as a sheep before her shearers is dumb.' These are the points at which the Old and New Testaments most nearly touch, the ($τύποι$) types or ensamples of the one which we find in the other, the pre-notions or preparations with which we pass from Moses and the Prophets to the Gospel of Christ.

III. It is hard to imagine that there can be any truer expression of the Gospel than the words of Christ himself, or that any truth omitted by Him is essential to the Gospel. 'The disciple is not above his master, nor the servant greater than his lord.' The philosophy of Plato was not better understood by his followers than by himself, nor can we allow that the Gospel is to be interpreted by the Epistles, or that the Sermon on the Mount is only half Christian and needs the fuller inspiration or revelation of St. Paul or the author of the Epistle to the Hebrews. There is no trace in the words of our Saviour of any omission or imperfection; there is no indication in the Epistles of any intention to complete or perfect them. How strange would it have seemed in the Apostle St. Paul, who thought himself unworthy 'to be called an Apostle because he persecuted the Church of God,' to find that his own words were preferred in after ages to those of Christ himself!

There is no study of theology which is likely to exercise a more elevating influence on the individual, or a more healing one on divisions of opinion, than the study of the words of Christ himself. The heart is its own witness to them; all Christian sects acknowledge them; they seem to escape or rise above the region or atmosphere of controversy. The form in which they exhibit the Gospel to us is the simplest and also the deepest; they are more free from details than any other part of Scripture, and they are absolutely independent of personal and national influences. In them is contained the expression of the inner life, of mankind, and of the Church; there, too, the individual beholds, as in a glass, the image of a goodness which is not of this world. To rank their authority below that of Apostles and Evangelists is to give up the best hope of reuniting Christendom in itself, and of making Christianity a universal religion.

And Christ himself hardly even in a figure uses the word 'sacrifice;' never with the least reference to His own life or death. There are many ways in which our Lord describes His relation to His Father and to mankind. His disciples are to be one with Him, even as He is one with the Father; whatsoever things He seeth the Father do He doeth. He says, 'I am the resurrection and the life;' or, 'I am the way, the truth, and the life;' and, 'No man cometh unto the Father but by me;' and again, 'Whatsoever things ye shall ask in my name shall be given you;' and once again, 'I will pray the Father, and he shall give you another comforter.' Most of His words are simple, like 'a man talking to his friends;' and their impressiveness and beauty partly flow from this simplicity. He speaks of His 'decease too which he should accomplish at Jerusalem,' but not in sacrificial language. 'And now I go my way to him that sent me;' and 'Greater love hath no man than this, that a man lay down his life for his friends.' Once indeed He says, 'The bread that I give is my flesh, which I give for the salvation of the world;' to which He himself adds, 'The words that I speak unto you they are spirit and they are truth,' a commentary which should be applied not only to these but to all other figurative expressions which occur in the New Testament. In the words of institution of the Lord's supper, He also speaks of His death as in some way connected with the remission of sins. But among all the figures of speech under which He describes His work in the world,—the vine, the good shepherd, the door, the light of the world, the bread of life, the water of life, the corner stone, the temple,—none contains any sacrificial allusion.

The parables of Christ have a natural and ethical character. They are only esoteric in as far as the hardness or worldliness of men's hearts prevents their understanding or receiving them. There is a danger of our making them mean too much rather than too little, that is, of winning a false interest for them by applying them mystically or taking them as a thesis for dialectical or rhetorical exercise. For example, if we say that the guest who came to the marriage supper without a wedding-garment represents a person clothed in his own righteousness instead of the righteousness of Christ, that is an explanation of which there is not a trace in the words of the parable itself. That is an illustration of the manner in which we are not to gather doctrines from Scripture. For there is nothing which we may not in this way superinduce on the plainest lessons of our Saviour.

Reading the parables, then, simply and naturally, we find in them no indication of the doctrine of atonement or satisfaction. They form a very large portion of the sayings which have been recorded of our Saviour while He was on earth; and they teach a great number of separate lessons. But there is no hint contained in them of that view of the death of Christ which is sometimes regarded as the centre of the Gospel. There is no 'difficulty in the nature of things' which prevents the father going out to meet the prodigal son. No other condition is required of the justification of the publican except the true sense of his own unworthiness. The work of those labourers who toiled for one hour only in the vineyard is not supplemented by the merits and deserts of another. The reward for the cup of cold water is not denied to those who are unaware that He to whom it is given is the Lord. The parables of the Good Samaritan, of the Fig-tree, of the Talents, do not recognize the distinction of faith and works. Other sayings and doings of our Lord while He was on earth implied the same unconsciousness or neglect of the refinements of later ages. The power of the Son of Man to forgive sins is not dependent on the satisfaction which He is to offer for them. The Sermon on the Mount, which is the extension of the law to thought as well as action, and the two great commandments in which the law is summed up, are equally the expression of the Gospel. The mind of Christ is in its own place, far away from the oppositions of modern theology. Like that of the prophets, His relation to the law of Moses is one of neutrality; He has another lesson to teach which comes immediately from God. 'The Scribes and Pharisees sit in Moses' seat—' or, 'Moses, because of the hardness of your hearts—' or, 'Which of you hath an ox or an ass—' or, 'Ye fools, did not he that made that which is without make that which is within.' He does not say, 'Behold in me the true Sacrifice;' or, 'I that speak unto you am the victim and priest.' He has nothing to do with legal and ceremonial observances. There is a sort of natural irony with which He regards the world around Him. It was as though He would not have touched the least of the Levitical commandments; and yet 'not one stone was to be left upon another' as the indirect effect of His teaching. So that it would be equally true: 'I am not come to destroy the law but to fulfil;' and 'Destroy this temple and in three days I will raise it up again.' 'My kingdom is not of this world,' yet it shall subdue the kingdoms of this world; and, the Prince of Peace will not 'bring peace on earth, but a sword.'

There is a mystery in the life and death of Christ; that is to say, there is more than we know or are perhaps capable of knowing. The relation in which He stood both to His Father and to mankind is imperfectly revealed to us; we do not fully understand what may be termed in a figure His inner mind or consciousness. Expressions occur which are like flashes of this inner self, and seem to come from another world. There are also mixed modes which blend earth and heaven. There are circumstances in our Lord's life, too, of a similar nature, such as the transfiguration, or the agony in the garden, of which the Scripture records only the outward fact. Least of all do we pretend to fathom the import of His death. He died for us, in the language of the Gospels, in the same sense that He lived for us; He 'bore our sins' in the same sense that He 'bore our diseases' (Matt. viii. 17). He died by the hands of sinners as a malefactor, the innocent for the guilty, Jesus instead of Barabbas, because it was necessary 'that one man should die for that nation, and not for that nation only;' as a righteous man laying down his life for his friends, as a hero to save his country, as a martyr to bear witness to the truth. He died as the Son of God, free to lay down His life; confident that He would have power to take it again. More than this is meant; and more than human speech can tell. But we do not fill up the void of our knowledge by drawing out figures of speech into consequences at variance with the attributes of God. No external mode of describing or picturing the work of Christ realizes its inward nature. Neither will the reproduction of our own feelings in a doctrinal form supply any objective support or ground of the Christian faith.

IV. Two of the General Epistles and two of the Epistles of St. Paul have no bearing on our present subject. These are the Epistles of St. James and St. Jude, and the two Epistles to the Thessalonians. Their silence, like that of the Gospels, is at least a negative proof that the doctrine of Sacrifice or Satisfaction is not a central truth of Christianity. The remainder of the New Testament will be sufficiently considered under two heads: first, the remaining Epistles of St. Paul; and, secondly, the Epistle to the Hebrews. The difficulties which arise respecting these are the same as the difficulties which apply in a less degree to one or two passages in the Epistles of St. Peter and St. John, and in the book of Revelation.

It is not to be denied that the language of Sacrifice and Substitution occurs in the Epistles of St. Paul. Instances of the former are furnished by Rom. iii. 23, 25 ; 1 Cor. v. 7: of the latter by Gal. ii. 20 ; iii. 13.

Rom. iii. 23–25 : 'For all have sinned, and come short of the glory of God ; being justified freely by his grace, through the redemption that is in Christ Jesus: whom God hath set forth to be a propitiation through faith by his blood, to declare his righteousness.'

1 Cor. v. 7 : 'Christ our passover is sacrificed [for us] ; therefore let us keep the feast, not with old leaven, neither with the leaven of malice and wickedness ; but with the unleavened bread of sincerity and truth.'

These two passages are a fair example of a few others. About the translation and explanation of the first of them interpreters differ. But the differences are not such as to affect our present question. For that question is a general one, viz. whether these, and similar sacrificial expressions, are passing figures of speech, or appointed signs or symbols of the death of Christ. On which it may be observed :—

First : That these expressions are not the peculiar or characteristic modes in which the Apostle describes the relation of the believer to his Lord. For one instance of the use of sacrificial language, five or six might be cited of the language of identity or communion, in which the believer is described as one with his Lord in all the stages of His life and death. But this language is really inconsistent with the other. For if Christ is one with the believer, He cannot be regarded strictly as a victim who takes his place. And the stage of Christ's being which coincides, and is specially connected by the Apostle, with the justification of man, is not His death, but His resurrection (Rom. iv. 25).

Secondly : These sacrificial expressions, as also the vicarious ones of which we shall hereafter speak, belong to the religious language of the age. They are found in Philo; and the Old Testament itself had already given them a spiritual or figurative application. There is no more reason to suppose that the word 'sacrifice' suggested the actual rite in the Apostolic age than in our own. It was a solemn religious idea, not a fact. The Apostles at Jerusalem saw the smoke of the daily sacrifice; the Apostle St. Paul beheld victims blazing on many altars in heathen cities (he regarded them as the tables of devils). But there is no reason to suppose that they led him to think of Christ, or that the bleeding form on the altar suggested the sufferings of his Lord.

Therefore, thirdly, We shall only be led into error by attempting to explain the application of the word to Christ from the original meaning of the thing. That is a question of Jewish or classical archaeology, which would receive a different answer in different ages and countries. Many motives or instincts may be traced in the worship of the first children of men. The need of giving or getting rid of something; the desire to fulfil an obligation or expiate a crime; the consecration of a part that the rest may be holy; the Homeric feast of gods and men, of the living with the dead; the mystery of animal nature, of which the blood was the symbol; the substitution, in a few instances, of the less for the greater; in later ages, custom adhering to the old rituals when the meaning of them has passed away;—these seem to be true explanations of the ancient sacrifices. (Human sacrifices, such as those of the old Mexican peoples, or the traditional ones in pre-historic Greece, may be left out of consideration, as they appear to spring from such monstrous and cruel perversion of human nature.) But these explanations have nothing to do with our present subject. We may throw an imaginary light back upon them (for it is always easier to represent former ages like our own than to realize them as they truly were); they will not assist us in comprehending the import of the death of Christ, or the nature of the Christian religion. They are in the highest degree opposed to it, at the other end of the scale of human development, as 'the weak and beggarly elements' of sense and fear to the spirit whereby we cry, Abba, Father; almost, may we not say, as the instinct of animals to the reasoning faculties of man. For sacrifice is not, like prayer, one of the highest, but one of the lowest acts of religious worship. It is the antiquity, not the religious import of the rite, which first gave it a sacredness. In modern times, the associations which are conveyed by the word are as far from the original idea as those of the cross itself. The death of Christ is not a sacrifice in the ancient sense (any more than the cross is to Christians the symbol of infamy); but what we mean by the word 'sacrifice' is the death of Christ.

Fourthly: This sacrificial language is not used with any definiteness or precision. The figure varies in different passages; Christ is the Paschal Lamb, or the Lamb without spot, as well as the sin-offering; the priest as well as the sacrifice. It is applied not only to Christ, but to the believer who is to present his body a living sacrifice; and the offering of which St. Paul speaks in one passage is 'the offering up of the Gentiles.' Again, this language is everywhere broken by moral and spiritual applications into which it dissolves and melts away. When we read of 'sacrifice,' or 'purification,' or 'redemption,' these words isolated may for an instant carry our thoughts back to the Levitical ritual. But when we restore them to their context, a sacrifice which is a 'spiritual sacrifice,' or a 'spiritual and mental service,' a purification which is a 'purging from dead works to serve the living God,' a redemption 'by the blood of Christ from your vain conversation received by tradition from your fathers'—we see that the association offers no real help; it is no paradox to say that we should rather forget than remember it. All this tends to show that these figures of speech are not the eternal symbols of the Christian faith, but shadows only which lightly come and go, and ought not to be fixed by definitions, or made the foundation of doctrinal systems.

Fifthly: Nor is any such use of them made by any of the writers of the New Testament. It is true that St. Paul occasionally, and the author of the Epistle to the Hebrews much more frequently, use sacrificial language. But they do not pursue the figure into details or consequences; they do not draw it out in logical form. Still less do they inquire, as modern theologians have done, into the objective or transcendental relation in which the sacrifice of Christ stood to the will of the Father. St. Paul says, 'We thus judge that if one died, then all died, and he died for all, that they which live shall not henceforth live to themselves, but unto him which died for them and rose again.' But words like these are far indeed from expressing a doctrine of atonement or satisfaction.

Lastly: The extent to which the Apostle employs figurative language in general, may be taken as a measure of the force of the figure in particular, expressions. Now there is no mode of speaking of spiritual things more natural to him than the image of death. Of the meaning of this word, in all languages, it may be said that there can be no doubt. Yet no one supposes that the sense which the Apostle gives to it is other than a spiritual one. The reason is, that the word has never been made the foundation of any doctrine. But the circumstance that the term 'sacrifice' has passed into the language of theology, does not really circumscribe or define it. It is a figure of speech still, which is no more to be interpreted by the Mosaic sacrifices than spiritual death by physical. Let us consider again other expressions of St. Paul: 'I bear in my body the marks of the Lord Jesus.' 'Who hath taken the handwriting of ordinances that was against us, and nailed it to his cross.' 'Filling up that which is behind of the afflictions of Christ in my flesh, for his body's sake, which is the church.' The occurrence of these and many similar expressions is a sufficient indication that the writer in whom they occur is not to be interpreted in a dry or literal manner.

Another class of expressions, which may be termed the language of substitution or vicarious suffering, are also occasionally found in St. Paul. Two examples of them, both of which occur in the Epistle to the Galatians, will indicate their general character.

Gal. ii. 20: 'I am crucified with Christ: nevertheless I live; yet not I, but Christ liveth in me: and the life which I now live in the flesh, I live by the faith of the Son of God, who loved me, and gave himself for me.' iii. 13: 'Christ hath redeemed us from the curse of the law, being made a curse for us.'

This use of language seems to originate in what was termed before the language of identity. First, 'I am crucified with Christ,' and secondly, 'Not I, but Christ liveth in me.' The believer, according to St. Paul, follows Christ until he becomes like Him. And this likeness is so complete and entire, that all that he was or might have been is attributed to Christ, and all that Christ is, is attributed to him. With such life and fervour does St. Paul paint the intimacy of the union between the believer and Christ: They two are 'One Spirit.' To build on such expressions a doctrinal system is the error of 'rhetoric turned logic.' The truth of feeling which is experienced by a few is not to be handed over to the head as a form of doctrine for the many.

The same remark applies to another class of passages, in which Christ is described as dying 'for us,' or 'for our sins.' Upon which it may be further observed, first, that in these passages the preposition used is not $\dot{a}\nu\tau\acute{\iota}$ but $\dot{\upsilon}\pi\acute{\epsilon}\rho$; and, secondly, that Christ is spoken of as living and rising again, as well as dying, for us; whence we infer that He died for us in the same sense that He lived for us. Of what is meant, perhaps the nearest conception we can form is furnished by the example of a good man taking upon himself, or, as we say, identifying himself with, the troubles and sorrows of others. Christ himself has sanctioned the comparison of a love which lays down life for a friend. Let us think of one as sensitive to moral evil as the gentlest of mankind to physical suffering; of one whose love identified Him with the whole human race as strongly as the souls of men are ever knit together by individual affections.

Many of the preceding observations apply equally to the Epistle to the Hebrews and to the Epistles of St. Paul. But the Epistle to the Hebrews has features peculiar to itself. It is a more complete transfiguration of the law, which St. Paul, on the other hand, applies by way of illustration, and in fragments only. It has the interest of an allegory, and, in some respects, admits of a comparison with the book of Revelation. It is full of sacrificial allusions, derived, however, not from the actual rite, but from the description of it in the books of Moses. Probably at Jerusalem, or the vicinity of the actual temple, it would not have been written.

From this source chiefly, and not from the Epistles of St. Paul, the language of sacrifice has passed into the theology and sermons of modern times. The Epistle to the Hebrews affords a greater apparent foundation for the popular or Calvinistical doctrines of atonement and satisfaction, but not perhaps a greater real one. For it is not the mere use of the terms 'sacrifice' or 'blood,' but the sense in which they were used, that must be considered. It is a fallacy, though a natural one, to confuse the image with the thing signified, like mistaking the colour of a substance for its true nature.

Long passages might be quoted from the Epistle to the Hebrews, which describe the work of Christ in sacrificial language. Some of the most striking verses are the following:—ix. 11-14: 'Christ being come an high priest of good things to come, by a greater and more perfect tabernacle, not made with hands, that is to say, not of this building; neither by the blood of goats and calves, but by his own blood, he entered in once into the holy place, having obtained eternal redemption for us. For if the blood of bulls and of goats, and the ashes of an heifer sprinkling the unclean, sanctifieth to the purifying of the flesh: how much more shall the blood of Christ, who through the eternal Spirit offered himself without spot to God, purge your conscience from dead works to serve the living God.' x. 12: 'This man, after he had offered one sacrifice for sins for ever, sat down on the right hand of God.'

That these and similar passages have only a deceitful resemblance to the language of those theologians who regard the propitiatory sacrifice of Christ as the central truth of the Gospel, is manifest from the following considerations:—

1. The great number and variety of the figures. Christ is Joshua, who gives the people rest (iv. 8); Melchisedec, to whom Abraham paid tithes (v. 6, vii. 6): the high priest going into the most holy place after he had offered sacrifice, which sacrifice He himself is, passing through the veil, which is His flesh.

2. The inconsistency of the figures: an inconsistency partly arising from their ceasing to be figures and passing into moral notions, as in chap. ix. 14: 'the blood of Christ, who offered himself without spot to God, shall purge your conscience from dead works;' partly from the confusion of two or more figures, as in the verse following: 'And for this cause he is the mediator of the new testament,' where the idea of sacrifice forms a transition to that of death and a testament, and the idea of a testament blends with that of a covenant.

3. The author of the Epistle to the Hebrews dwells on the outward circumstance of the shedding of the blood of Christ. St. Paul in the Epistle to the Galatians makes another application of the Old Testament, describing our

Lord as enduring the curse which befell 'One who hanged on a tree.' Imagine for an instant that this latter had been literally the mode of our Lord's death. The figure of the Epistle to the Hebrews would cease to have any meaning; yet no one supposes that there would have been any essential difference in the work of Christ.

4. The atoning sacrifice of which modern theology speaks, is said to be the great object of faith. The author of the Epistle to the Hebrews also speaks of faith, but no such expression as faith in the blood, or sacrifice, or death of Christ is made use of by him, or is found anywhere else in Scripture. The faith of the patriarchs is not faith in the peculiar sense of the term, but the faith of those who confess that they are 'strangers and pilgrims,' and 'endure seeing him that is invisible.'

Lastly: The Jewish Alexandrian character of the Epistle must be admitted as an element of the inquiry. It interprets the Old Testament after a manner then current in the world, which we must either continue to apply or admit that it was relative to that age and country. It makes statements which we can only accept in a figure, as, for example, in chap. xi, 'that Moses esteemed the reproach of Christ greater riches than the treasures of Egypt.' It uses language in double senses, as, for instance, the two meanings of $\delta\iota\alpha\theta\acute{\eta}\kappa\eta$ and of $\acute{\eta}$ $\pi\rho\acute{\omega}\tau\eta$ in chap. viii. 13; ix. 1; and the connexion which it establishes between the Old Testament and the New, is a verbal or mystical one, not a connexion between the temple and offerings at Jerusalem and the offering up of Christ, but between the ancient ritual and the tabernacle described in the book of the law.

Such were the instruments which the author of this great Epistle (whoever he may have been) employed, after the manner of his age and country, to impart the truths of the Gospel in a figure to those who esteemed this sort of figurative knowledge as a kind of perfection (Heb. vi. 1). 'Ideas must be given through something;' nor could mankind in those days, any more than our own, receive the truth except in modes of thought that were natural to them. The author of the Epistle to the Hebrews is writing to those who lived and moved in the atmosphere, as it may be termed, of Alexandrian Judaism. Therefore he uses the figures of the law, but he also guards against their literal acceptation. Christ is a priest, but a priest for ever after the order of Melchisedec; He is a sacrifice, but He is also the end of sacrifices, and the sacrifice which He offers is the negation of sacrifices, 'to do thy will, O God.' Everywhere he has a 'how much more,' 'how much greater,' for the new dispensation in comparison with the old. He raises the Old Testament to the New, first by drawing forth the spirit of the New Testament from the Old, and secondly by applying the words of the Old Testament in a higher sense than they at first had. The former of these two methods of interpretation is moral and universal, the latter local and temporary. But if we who are not Jews like the persons to whom the Epistle to the Hebrews is addressed, and who are taught by education to receive words in their natural and prima facie meaning, linger around the figure instead of looking forward to the thing signified, we do indeed make 'Christ the minister' of the Mosaic religion. For there is a Judaism not only of outward ceremonies or ecclesiastical hierarchies, or temporal rewards and punishments, but of ideas also, which impedes the worship of spirit and truth.

The sum of what has been said is as follows:—

Firstly: That our Lord never describes His own work in the language of atonement or sacrifice.

Secondly: That this language is a figure of speech borrowed from the Old Testament, yet not to be explained by the analogy of the Levitical sacrifices; occasionally found in the writings of St. Paul; more frequently in the Epistle to the Hebrews; applied to the believer at least equally with his Lord, and indicating by the variety and uncertainty with which it is used that it is not the expression of any objective relation in which the work of Christ stands to His Father, but only a mode of speaking common at a time when the rites and ceremonies of the Jewish law were passing away and beginning to receive a spiritual meaning.

Thirdly: That nothing is signified by this language, or at least nothing essential, beyond what is implied in the teaching of our Lord himself. For it cannot be supposed that there is any truer account of Christianity than is to be found in the words of Christ.

§ 2.

Theology sprang up in the first ages independently of Scripture. This independence continued afterwards; it has never been wholly lost. There is a tradition of the nineteenth century, as well as of the fourth or fourteenth, which comes between them. The mystical interpretation of Scripture has further parted them; to which may be added the power of system: doctrines when framed into a whole cease to draw their inspiration from the text. Logic has expressed 'the thoughts of many hearts' with a seeming necessity of form; this form of reasoning has led to new inferences. Many words and formulas have also acquired a sacredness from their occurrence in liturgies and articles, or the frequent use of them in religious discourse. The true interest of the theologian is to restore these formulas to their connexion in Scripture, and to their place in ecclesiastical history. The standard of Christian truth is not a logical clearness or sequence, but the simplicity of the mind of Christ.

The history of theology is the history of the intellectual life of the Christian Church. All bodies of Christians, Protestant as well as Catholic, have tended to imagine that they are in the same stage of religious development as the first believers. But the Church has not stood still any more than the world; we may trace the progress of doctrine as well as the growth of philosophical opinion. The thoughts of men do not pass away without leaving an impress, in religion, any more than in politics or literature. The form of more than one article of faith in our own day is assignable to the effort of mind of some great thinker of the Nicene or mediaeval times. The received interpretation of texts of Scripture may not unfrequently be referred to the application of them first made in periods of controversy. Neither is it possible in any reformation of the Church to return exactly to the point whence the divergence began. The pattern of Apostolical order may be restored in externals; but the threads of the dialectical process are in the mind itself, and cannot be disposed of at once. It seems to be the nature of theology that while it is easy to add one definition of doctrine to another, it is hard to withdraw from any which have been once received. To believe too much is held to be safer than to believe too little, and the human intellect finds a more natural exercise in raising the superstructure than in examining the foundations. On the other hand, it is instructive to observe that there has always been an under-current in theology, the course of which has turned towards morality, and not away from it. There is a higher sense of truth and right now than in the Nicene Church—after than before the Reformation. The laity in all Churches have moderated the extremes of the clergy. There may also be remarked a silent correction in men's minds of statements which have not ceased to appear in theological writings.

The study of the doctrinal development of the Christian Church has many uses. First, it helps us to separate the history of a doctrine from its truth, and indirectly also the meaning of Scripture from the new reading of it, which has been given in many instances by theological controversy. It takes us away from the passing movement, and out of our own particular corner into a world in which we see religion on a larger scale and in truer proportions. It enables us to interpret one age to another, to understand our present theological position by its antecedents in the past; and perhaps to bind all together in the spirit of charity. Half the intolerance of opinion among Christians arises from ignorance; in history as in life, when we know others we get to like them. Logic too ceases to take us by force and make us believe. There is a pathetic interest and a kind of mystery in the long continuance and intensity of erroneous ideas on behalf of which men have been ready to die, which nevertheless were no better than the dreams or fancies of children. When we make allowance for differences in modes of thought, for the state of knowledge, and the conditions of the ecclesiastical society, we see that individuals have not been altogether responsible for their opinions; that the world has been bound together under the influence of the past; moreover, good men of all persuasions have been probably nearer to one another than they supposed, in doctrine as well as in life. It is the attempt to preserve or revive erroneous opinions in the present age, not their existence in former ages, that is to be reprobated. Lastly, the study of the history of doctrine is the end of controversy. For it is above controversy, of which it traces the growth, clearing away that part which is verbal only, and teaching us to understand that other part which is fixed in the deeper differences of human nature.

The history of the doctrine of the atonement may be conveniently divided into four periods of unequal length, each of which is marked by some peculiar features. First, the Patristic period, extending to the time of Anselm, in which the doctrine had not attained to a perfect or complete form, but each one applied for himself the language of Scripture. Secondly, the Scholastic period, beginning with Anselm, who may be said to have defined anew the conceptions of the Christian world respecting the work of Christ, and including the great schoolmen who were his successors. Thirdly, the century of the Reformation, embracing what may be termed the after-thoughts of

Protestantism, when men began to reason in that new sphere of religious thought which had been called into existence in the great struggle. 'Fragments of the great banquet' of the schoolmen survive throughout the period, and have floated down the stream of time to our own age. Fourthly, the last hundred years, during which the doctrine of the atonement has received a new development from the influences of German philosophy[1], as well as from the speculations of English and American writers.

1. The characteristics of the first period may be summed up as follows. All the Fathers agreed that man was reconciled to God through Christ, and received in the Gospel a new and divine life. Most of them also spoke of the death of Christ as a ransom or sacrifice. When we remember that in the first age of the Church the New Testament was exclusively taught through the Old, and that many of the first teachers, who were unacquainted with our present Gospels, had passed their lives in the study of the Old Testament Scriptures, we shall not wonder at the early diffusion of this sort of language. Almost every application of the types of the law which has been made since, is already found in the writings of Justin Martyr. Nor indeed, on general grounds, is there any reason why we should feel surprise at such a tendency in the first ages. For in all Churches, and at all times of the world's history, the Old Testament has tended to take the place of the New; the law of the Gospel; the handmaid has become the mistress; and the development of the Christian priesthood has developed also the idea of a Christian sacrifice.

The peculiarity of the primitive doctrine did not lie here, but in the relation in which the work of Christ was supposed to stand to the powers of evil. In the first ages we are beset with shadows of an under world, which hover on the confines of Christianity. From Origen downwards, with

[1] In the following pages I have derived great assistance from the excellent work of Baur über die Versöhnungslehre.

some traces of an earlier opinion of the same kind, perhaps of Gnostic origin, it was a prevailing though not quite universal belief among the Fathers, that the death of Christ was a satisfaction, not to God, but to the devil. Man, by having sinned, passed into the power of the evil one, who acquired a real right over him which could not be taken away without compensation. Christ offered himself as this compensation, which the devil eagerly accepted, as worth more than all mankind. But the deceiver was in turn deceived; thinking to triumph over the humanity, he was himself triumphed over by the Divinity of Christ. This theory was characteristically expressed under some such image as the following: 'that the devil snatching at the bait of human flesh, was hooked by the Divine nature, and forced to disgorge what he had already swallowed.' It is common in some form to Origen, Augustine, Ambrose, Gregory of Nyssa, Gregory the Great, Isidore of Seville, and much later writers; and there are indications of it in Irenaeus (*Adv. Haer.* v. i. 1). The meaning of this transaction with the devil it is hardly possible to explain consistently. For a real possession of the soul of Christ was not thought of: an imaginary one is only an illusion. In either case the absolute right which is assigned to the devil over man, and which requires this satisfaction, is as repugnant to our moral and religious ideas, as the notion that the right could be satisfied by a deception. This strange fancy seems to be a reflection or anticipation of Manicheism within the Church. The world, which had been hitherto a kingdom of evil, of which the devil was the lord, was to be exorcised and taken out of his power by the death of Christ.

But the mythical fancy of the transaction with the devil was not the whole, nor even the leading conception, which the Fathers had of the import of the death of Christ. It was the negative, not the positive, side of the doctrine of redemption which they thus expressed; nobler thoughts also filled their minds. Origen regards the death of Christ as a payment to the devil, yet also as an offering to God; this offering took place not on earth only, but also in heaven; God is the high priest who offered. Another aspect of the doctrine of the atonement is presented by the same Father, under the Neo-Platonist form of the λόγος (word), who reunites with God, not only man, but all intelligences. Irenaeus speaks, in language more human and more like St. Paul, of Christ 'coming to save all, and therefore passing through all the ages of man; becoming an infant among infants, a little one among little ones, a young man among young men, an elder with the aged (?), that each in turn might be sanctified, until He reached death, that He should be the first-born from the dead' (ii. 22, 147). The great Latin Father, though he believed equally with Origen in the right and power of the devil over man, delights also to bring forward the moral aspect of the work of Christ. 'The entire life of Christ,' he says, 'was an instruction in morals' (*De Ver. Rel.* c. 16). 'He died in order that no man might be afraid of death' (*De Fide et Symbolo*, c. 5). 'The love which He displayed in his death constrains us to love Him and each other in return' (*De Cat. Rud.* c. 4). Like St. Paul, Augustine contrasts the second Adam with the first, the man of righteousness with the man of sin (*De Ver. Relig.* c. 26). Lastly, he places the real nature of redemption in the manifestation of the God-man.

Another connexion between ancient and modern theology is supplied by the writings of Athanasius. The view taken by Athanasius of the atoning work of Christ has two characteristic features: First, it is based upon the doctrine of the Trinity;—God only can reconcile man with God. Secondly, it rests on the idea of a debt which is paid, not to the devil, but to God. This debt is also due to death, who has a sort of right over Christ, like the right of the devil in the former scheme. If it be asked in what this view differs from that of Anselm, the answer seems to be, chiefly in the circumstance that it is stated with less distinctness: it is *a* form, not *the* form, which Athanasius gave to the doctrine. In the conception of the death of Christ as a debt, he is followed, however, by several of the Greek Fathers. Rhetoric delighted to represent the debt as more than paid; the payment was 'even as the ocean to a drop in comparison with the sins of men' (Chrys. on *Rom. Hom.* x. 17). It is pleasing further to remark that a kind of latitudinarianism was allowed by the Fathers themselves. Gregory of Nazianzen (*Orat.* xxxiii. p. 536) numbers speculations about the sufferings of Christ among those things on which it is useful to have correct ideas, but not dangerous to be mistaken. On the whole the doctrine of the Fathers of the first four centuries may be said to oscillate between two points of view, which are brought out with different degrees of clearness. 1. The atonement was effected by the death of Christ; which was a satisfaction to the devil, and an offering to God: 2. The atonement was effected by the union in Christ of the Divine and human nature in the 'logos,' or word of God. That neither view is embodied in any creed is a proof that the doctrine of atonement was not, in the first centuries, what modern writers often make it, the corner-stone of the Christian faith.

An interval of more than 700 years separates Athanasius from Anselm. One eminent name occurs during this interval, that of Scotus Erigena, whose conception of the atonement is the co-eternal unity of all things with God; the participation in this unity had been lost by man, not in time, but in eternity, and was restored in the person of Christ likewise from eternity. The views of Erigena present some remarkable coincidences with very recent speculations; in the middle ages he stands alone, at the end, not at the beginning, of a great period;—he is the last of the Platonists, not the first of the schoolmen. He had consequently little influence on the centuries which followed. Those centuries gradually assumed a peculiar character; and received in after times another name, scholastic, as opposed to patristic. The intellect was beginning to display a new power; men were asking, not exactly for a reason of the faith that was in them, but for a clearer conception and definition of it. The Aristotelian philosophy furnished distinctions which were applied with a more than Aristotelian precision to statements of doctrine. Logic took the place of rhetoric; the school of the Church; figures of speech became abstract ideas. Theology was exhibited under a new aspect, as a distinct object or reality of thought. Questions on which Scripture was silent, on which councils and Popes would themselves pronounce no decision, were raised and answered within a narrow sphere by the activity of the human mind itself. The words 'sacrifice,' 'satisfaction,' 'ransom,' could no longer be used indefinitely; it was necessary to determine further to whom and for what the satisfaction was made, and to solve the new difficulties which thereupon arose in the effort to gain clearer and more connected ideas.

2. It was a true feeling of Anselm that the old doctrine of satisfaction contained an unchristian element in attributing to the devil a right independent of God. That man should be delivered over to Satan may be just; it is a misrepresentation to say that Satan had any right over man. Therefore no right of the devil is satisfied by the death of Christ. He who had the real right is God, who has been robbed of His honour; to whom is, indeed, owing on the part of man an infinite debt. For sin is in its nature infinite; the world has no compensation for that which a good man would not do in exchange for the world (*Cur Deus Homo*, i. 21). God only can satisfy himself. The human nature of Christ enables Him to incur, the infinity of his Divine nature to pay, this debt (ii. 6, 7). This payment of the debt, however, is not the salvation of mankind, but only the condition of salvation; a link is

still wanting in the work of grace. The two parties are equalized; the honour of which God was robbed is returned, but man has no claim for any further favour. This further favour, however, is indirectly a result of the death of Christ. For the payment of the debt by the Son partakes of the nature of a gift which must needs have a recompense (ii. 20) from the Father, which recompense cannot be conferred on himself, and is therefore made at His request to man. The doctrine ultimately rests on two reasons or grounds; the first a noble one, that it must be far from God to suffer any rational creature to perish entirely (*Cur Deus Homo*, i. 4, ii. 4); the second a trifling one, viz. that God, having created the angels in a perfect number, it was necessary that man, saved through Christ, should fill up that original number, which was impaired by their fall. And as Anselm, in the spirit of St. Paul, though not quite consistently with his own argument, declares, the mercy of God was shown in the number of the saved exceeding the number of the lost (*Cur Deus Homo*, i. 16, 18).

This theory, which is contained in the remarkable treatise *Cur Deus Homo*, is consecutively reasoned throughout; yet the least reasons seem often sufficient to satisfy the author. While it escapes one difficulty it involves several others; though conceived in a nobler and more Christian spirit than any previous view of the work of Christ, it involves more distinctly the hideous consequence of punishing the innocent for the guilty. It is based upon analogies, symmetries, numerical fitnesses; yet under these logical fancies is contained a true and pure feeling of the relation of man to God. The notion of satisfaction or payment of a debt, on the other hand, is absolutely groundless, and seems only to result from a certain logical position which the human mind has arbitrarily assumed. The scheme implies further two apparently contradictory notions; one, a necessity in the nature of things for this and no other means of redemption; the other, the free will of God in choosing the salvation of man. Anselm endeavours to escape from this difficulty by substituting the conception of a moral for that of a metaphysical necessity (ii. 5). God chose the necessity and Christ chose the fulfilment of His Father's commands. But the necessity by which the death of Christ is justified is thus reduced to a figure of speech. Lastly, the subjective side of the doctrine, which afterwards became the great question of the Reformation, the question, that is, in what way the death of Christ is to be apprehended by the believer, is hardly if at all touched upon by Anselm.

No progress was made during the four centuries which intervened between Anselm and the Reformation, towards the attainment of clearer ideas respecting the relations of God and man. The view of Anselm did not, however, at once or universally prevail; it has probably exercised a greater influence since the Reformation (being the basis of what may be termed the evangelical doctrine of the atonement) than in earlier ages. The spirit of the older theology was too congenial to those ages quickly to pass away. Bernard and others continued to maintain the right of the devil: a view not wholly obsolete in our own day. The two great masters of the schools agreed in denying the necessity on which the theory of Anselm was founded. They differed from Anselm also respecting the conception of an infinite satisfaction; Thomas Aquinas distinguishing the 'infinite' Divine merit, and 'abundant' human satisfaction; while Duns Scotus rejected the notion of infinity altogether, declaring that the scheme of redemption might have been equally accomplished by the death of an angel or a righteous man. Abelard, at an earlier period, attached special importance to the moral aspect of the work of Christ; he denied the right of the devil, and declared the love of Christ to be the redeeming principle, because it calls forth the love of man. Peter Lombard also, who retained, like Bernard, the old view of the right of the devil, agreed with Abelard in giving a moral character to the work of redemption.

3. The doctrines of the Reformed as well as of the Catholic Church were expressed in the language of the scholastic theology. But the logic which the Catholic party had employed in defining and distinguishing the body of truth already received, the teachers of the Reformation used to express the subjective feelings of the human soul. Theology made a transition, such as we may observe at one or two epochs in the history of philosophy, from the object to the subject. Hence, the doctrine of atonement or satisfaction became subordinate to the doctrine of justification. The reformers begin, not with ideas, but with the consciousness of sin; with immediate human interests, not with speculative difficulties; not with mere abstractions, but with a great struggle; 'without were fightings, within were fears.' As of Socrates and philosophy, so it may be also said truly of Luther in a certain sense, that he brought down the work of redemption 'from heaven to earth.' The great question with him was, 'how we might be freed from the punishment and guilt of sin,' and the answer was, through the appropriation of the merits of Christ. All that man was or might have been, Christ became, and was; all that Christ did or was, attached or was imputed to man: as God, he paid the infinite penalty; as man, he fulfilled the law. The first made redemption possible, the second perfected it. The first was termed in the language of that age, the 'obedientia passiva,' the second, the 'obedientia activa.'

In this scheme the doctrine of satisfaction is far from being prominent or necessary; it is a remnant of an older theology which was retained by the Reformers and prevented their giving a purely moral character to the work of Christ. There were differences among them respecting the two kinds of obedience; some regarding the 'obedientia passiva' as the cause or condition of the 'obedientia activa,' while others laid no stress on the distinction. But all the great chiefs of the Reformation agreed in the fiction of imputed righteousness. Little had been said in earlier times of a doctrine of imputation. But now the Bible was reopened and read over again in one light only, 'justification by faith and not by works.' The human mind seemed to seize with a kind of avidity on any distinction which took it out of itself, and at the same time freed it from the burden of ecclesiastical tyranny. Figures of speech in which Christ was said to die for man or for the sins of man were understood in as crude and literal a sense as the Catholic Church had attempted to gain from the words of the institution of the Eucharist. Imputation and substitution among Protestant divines began to be formulas as strictly imposed as transubstantiation with their opponents. To Luther, Christ was not only the Holy One who died for the sins of men, but the sinner himself on whom the vials of Divine wrath were poured out. And seeing in the Epistles to the Galatians and Romans the power which the law exercised in that age of the world over Jewish or half-Jewish Christians, he transferred the state which the Apostle there describes to his own age, and imagined that the burden under which he himself had groaned was the same law of which St. Paul spoke, which Christ first fulfilled in His own person and then abolished for ever.

It was not unnatural that in the middle ages, when morality had no free or independent development, the doctrine of the atonement should have been drawn out on the analogy of law. Nor is there any reason why we should feel surprised that, with the revival of the study of Scripture at the Reformation, the Mosaic law should have exercised a great influence over the ideas of Protestants. More singular, yet an analogous phenomenon, is the attempt of Grotius to conceive the work of Christ by the help of the principles of political justice. All men are under the influence of their own education or profession, and they are apt to conceive truths which are really of a different or higher kind under some form derived from it; they require such a degree or kind of evidence as their minds are accustomed to, and political or legal principles have often been held a sufficient foundation for moral truth.

The theory of the celebrated jurist proceeds from the conception of God as governor of the universe. As such, He may forgive sins just as any other ruler may remit the punishment of offences against positive law. But although the ruler possesses the power to remit sins, and there is nothing in the nature of justice which would prevent his doing so, yet he has also a duty, which is to uphold his own authority and that of the laws. To do so, he must enforce punishment for the breach of them. This punishment, however, may attach not to the offender, but to the offence. Such a distinction is not unknown to the law itself. We may apply this to the work of Christ. There was no difficulty in the nature of things which prevented God from freely pardoning the sins of men; the power of doing so was vested in His hands as governor of the world. But it was inexpedient that He should exercise this power without first making an example. This was effected by the death of Christ. It pleased God to act according to the pedantic rules of earthly jurisprudence. It is useless to criticize such a theory further; almost all theologians have agreed in reprobating it; it adopts the analogy of law, and violates its first principles by considering a moral or legal act without reference to the agent. The reason which Grotius assigns for the death of Christ is altogether trivial.

4. Later theories on the doctrine of the atonement may be divided into two classes, English and German, logical and metaphysical; those which proceed chiefly by logical inference, and those which connect the conception of the atonement with speculative philosophy.

Earlier English writers were chiefly employed in defining the work of Christ; later ones have been most occupied with the attempt to soften or moderate the more repulsive features of the older statements; the former have a dogmatical, the latter an apologetical character. The nature of the sufferings of Christ, whether they were penal or only quasi penal, whether they were physical or mental, greater in degree than human sufferings, or different in kind; in what more precisely the compensation offered by Christ truly consisted; the nature of the obedience of Christ, whether to God or the law, and the connexion of the whole question with that of the Divine decrees:—these were among the principal subjects discussed by the great Presbyterian divines of the seventeenth and eighteenth centuries. Continuing in the same line of thought as their predecessors, they seem to have been unconscious of the difficulties to which the eyes of a later generation have opened.

But at last the question has arisen within, as well as without, the Church of England: 'How the ideas of expiation, or satisfaction, or sacrifice, or imputation, are reconcilable with the moral and spiritual nature either of God or man?' Some there are who answer from analogy, and cite instances of vicarious suffering which appear in the disorder of the world around us. But analogy is a broken reed; of use, indeed, in pointing out the way where its intimations can be verified, but useless when applied to the unseen world in which the eye of observation no longer follows. Others affirm revelation or inspiration to be above criticism, and, in disregard alike of Church history and of Scripture, assume their own view of the doctrine of the atonement to be a revealed or inspired truth. They do not see that they are cutting off the branch of the tree on which they are themselves sitting. For, if the doctrine of the atonement cannot be criticized, neither can it be determined what is the doctrine of the atonement; nor, on the same principles, can any true religion be distinguished from any false one, or any truth of religion from any error. It is suicidal in theology to refuse the appeal to a moral criterion. Others add a distinction of things above reason and things contrary to reason ; a favourite theological weapon, which has, however, no edge or force, so long as it remains a generality. Others, in like manner, support their view of the doctrine of the atonement by a theory of accommodation, which also loses itself in ambiguity. For it is not determined whether, by accommodation to the human faculties, is meant the natural subjectiveness of knowledge, or some other limitation which applies to theology only. Others regard the death of Christ, not as an atonement or satisfaction to God, but as a manifestation of His righteousness, a theory which agrees with that of Grotius in its general character, when the latter is stripped of its technicalities. This theory is the shadow or surface of that of satisfaction ; the human analogy equally fails ; the punishment of the innocent for the guilty is not more unjust than the punishment of the innocent as an example to the guilty. Lastly, there are some who would read the doctrine of the atonement 'in the light of Divine love only ;' the object of the sufferings and death of Christ being to draw men's hearts to God by the vision of redeeming love (compare Abelard), and the sufferings themselves being the natural result of the passage of the Saviour through a world of sin and shame. Of these explanations the last seems to do the least violence to our moral feelings. Yet it would surely be better to renounce any attempt at inquiry into the objective relations of God and man, than to rest the greatest fact in the history of mankind on so slender a ground as the necessity for arousing the love of God in the human heart, in this and no other way.

German theology during the last hundred years has proceeded by a different path ; it has delighted to recognize the doctrine of the atonement as the centre of religion, and also of philosophy. This tendency is first observable in the writings of Kant, and may be traced through the schools of his successors, Fichte, Schelling, Hegel, as well as in the works of the two philosophical theologians Daub and Schleiermacher. These great thinkers all use the language of orthodoxy; it cannot be said, however, that the views of any of them agree with the teaching of the patristic or mediaeval Church, or of the Reformers, or of the simpler expressions of Scripture. Yet they often bring into new meaning and prominence texts on this subject which have been pushed aside by the regular current of theology. The difficulties which they all alike experience are two: first, how to give a moral meaning to the idea of atonement; secondly, how to connect the idea with the historical fact.

According to Kant, the atonement consists in the sacrifice of the individual; a sacrifice in which the sin of the old man is ever being compensated by the sorrows and virtues of the new. This atonement, or reconcilement of man with God, consists in an endless progress towards a reconcilement which is never absolutely completed in this life, and yet, by the continual increase of good and diminution of evil, is a sufficient groundwork of hope and peace. Perfect reconcilement would consist in the perfect obedience of a free agent to the law of duty or righteousness. For this Kant substitutes the ideal of the Son of God. The participation in this ideal of humanity is an aspect of the reconcilement. In a certain sense, in the sight of God, that is, and in the wish and resolution of the individual, the change from the old to the new is not gradual, but sudden: the end is imputed or anticipated in the beginning. So Kant 'rationalizes' the ordinary Lutheran doctrine of justification; unconscious, as in other parts of his philosophy, of the influence which existing systems are exercising over him. Man goes out of himself to grasp at a reflection which is still—himself. The mystical is banished only to return again in an arbitrary and imaginative form—a phenomenon which we may often observe in speculation as well as in the characters of individuals.

Schleiermacher's view of the doctrine of the atonement is almost equally different from that of Kant who preceded him, and of Hegel and others who were his contemporaries or successors: it is hardly more like the popular theories. Reconciliation with God he conceives as a participation in the Divine nature. Of this participation the Church, through the Spirit, is the medium; the individual is redeemed and consoled by communion with his fellow-men. If in the terminology of philosophy we ask which is the objective, which the subjective part of the work of redemption, the answer of Schleiermacher seems to be that the subjective redemption of the individual is the consciousness of union with God; and the objective part, which corresponds to this consciousness, is the existence of the Church, which derives its life from the Spirit of God, and is also the depository of the truth of Christ. The same criticism, however, applies to this as to the preceding conception of the atonement, viz. that it has no real historical basis. The objective truth is nothing more than the subjective feeling or opinion which prevails in a particular Church. Schleiermacher deduces the historical from the ideal, and regards the ideal as existing only in the communion of Christians. But the truth of a fact is not proved by the truth of an idea. And the personal relation of the believer to Christ, instead of being immediate, is limited (as in the Catholic system) by the existence of the Church.

Later philosophers have conceived of the reconciliation of man with God as a reconciliation of God with himself. The infinite must evolve the finite from itself; yet the true infinite consists in the return of the finite to the infinite. By slow degrees, and in many stages of morality, of religion, and of knowledge, does the individual, according to Fichte, lay aside isolation and selfishness, gaining in strength and freedom by the negation of freedom, until he rises into the region of the divine and absolute. This is reconcilement with God; a half Christian, half Platonic notion, which it is not easy to identify either with the subjective feeling of the individual, or with the historical fact. Daub has also translated the language of Scripture and of the Church into metaphysical speculation. According to this thinker, atonement is the realization of the unity of man with God, which is also the unity of God with himself. 'Deus Deum cum mundo conjunctum Deo manifestat.' Perhaps this is as near an approach as philosophy can make to a true expression of the words, 'That they all may be one, as thou Father art in me and I in thee, that they also may be one in us.' Yet the metaphysical truth is a distant and indistinct representation of the mind of Christ which is expressed in these words. Its defect is exhibited in the image under which Fichte described it—the absolute unity of light; in other words, God, like the being of the Eleatics, is a pure abstraction, and returning into himself is an abstraction still.

It is characteristic of Schelling's system that he conceives the nature of God, not as abstraction, but as energy or action. The finite and manifold are not annihilated in the infinite; they are the revelation of the infinite. Man is the son of God; of this truth Christ is the highest expression and the eternal idea. But in the world this revelation or incarnation of God is ever going on; the light is struggling with darkness, the spirit with nature, the universal with the particular. That victory which was achieved in the person of Christ is not yet final in individuals or in history. Each person, each age, carries on the same conflict between good and evil, the triumphant end of which is anticipated in the life and death of Christ.

Hegel, beginning with the doctrine of a Trinity, regards the atonement as the eternal reconciliation of the finite and the infinite in the bosom of God himself. The Son goes forth from the Father, as the world or finite being, to exist in a difference which is done away and lost in the absoluteness of God. Here the question arises, how individuals become partakers of this reconciliation? The answer is, by the finite receiving the revelation of God. The consciousness of God in man is developed, first, in the worship of nature; secondly, in the manifestation of Christ; thirdly, in the faith of the Church that God and man are one, of which faith the Holy Spirit is the source. The death of Christ is the separation of this truth from the elements of nature and sense. Hegelian divines have given this doctrine a more Pantheistic or more Christian aspect; they have, in some instances, studiously adopted orthodox language; they have laid more or less stress on the historical facts. But they have done little as yet to make it intelligible to the world at large; they have acquired for it no fixed place in history, and no hold upon life.

Englishmen, especially, feel a national dislike at the 'things which accompany salvation' being perplexed with philosophical theories. They find it easier to caricature than to understand Hegel; they prefer the most unintelligible expressions with which they are familiar to great thoughts which are strange to them. No man of sense really supposes that Hegel or Schelling is so absurd as they may be made to look in an uncouth English translation, or as they unavoidably appear to many in a brief summary of their tenets. Yet it may be doubted whether this philosophy can ever have much connexion with the Christian life. It seems to reflect at too great a distance what ought to be very near to us. It is metaphysical, not practical; it creates an atmosphere in which it is difficult to breathe; it is useful as supplying a light or law by which to arrange the world, rather than as a principle of action or warmth. Man is a microcosm, and we do not feel quite certain whether the whole system is not the mind itself turned inside out, and magnified in enormous proportions. Whatever interest it may arouse in speculative natures (and it is certainly of great value to a few), it will hardly find a home or welcome in England.

§ 3.

The silence of our Lord in the Gospels respecting any doctrine of atonement and sacrifice, the variety of expressions which occur in other parts of the New Testament, the fluctuation and uncertainty both of the Church and individuals on this subject in after ages, incline us to agree with Gregory Nazianzen, that the death of Christ is one of those points of faith 'about which it is not dangerous to be mistaken.' And the sense of the imperfection of language and the illusions to which we are subject from the influence of past ideas, the consciousness that doctrinal perplexities arise chiefly from our transgression of the limits of actual knowledge, will lead us to desire a very simple statement of the work of Christ; a statement, however, in accordance with our moral ideas, and one which will not shift and alter with the metaphysical schools of the age; one, moreover, which runs no risk of being overthrown by an increasing study of the Old Testament or of ecclesiastical history. Endless theories there have been (of which the preceding sketch contains only a small portion), and many more there will be as time goes on, like mystery plays, or sacred dramas (to adapt Lord Bacon's image), which have passed before the Church and the world. To add another would increase the confusion: it is ridiculous to think of settling a disputed point of theology unless by some new method. That other method can only be a method of agreement; little progress has been made hitherto by the method of difference. It is not reasonable, but extremely unreasonable, that the most sacred of all books should be the only one respecting the interpretation of which there is no certainty; that religion alone should be able to perpetuate the enmities of past ages; that the influence of words and names, which secular knowledge has long shaken off, should still intercept the natural love of Christians towards one another and their

Lord. On our present subject there is no difficulty in finding a basis of reconciliation; the way opens when logical projections are removed, and we look at the truth in what may be rightly termed a more primitive and Apostolical manner. For all, or almost all, Christians would agree that in some sense or other we are reconciled to God through Christ; whether by the atonement and satisfaction which He made to God for us, or by His manifestation of the justice of God or love of God in the world, by the passive obedience of His death or the active obedience of His life, by the imputation of His righteousness to us or by our identity and communion with Him, or likeness to Him, or love of Him; in some one of these senses, which easily pass into each other, all would join in saying that 'He is the way, the truth, and the life.' And had the human mind the same power of holding fast points of agreement as of discerning differences, there would be an end of the controversy.

The statements of Scripture respecting the work of Christ are very simple, and may be used without involving us in the determination of these differences. We can live and die in the language of St. Paul and St. John; there is nothing there repugnant to our moral sense. We have a yet higher authority in the words of Christ himself. Only in repeating and elucidating these statements, we must remember that Scripture phraseology is of two kinds, simple and figurative, and that the first is the interpretation of the second. We must not bring the New Testament into bondage to the Old, but ennoble and transfigure the Old by the New.

First; the death of Christ may be described as a sacrifice. But what sacrifice? Not 'the blood of bulls and of goats, nor the ashes of an heifer sprinking the unclean,' but the living sacrifice 'to do thy will, O God.' It is a sacrifice which is the negation of sacrifice; 'Christ the end of the law to them that believe.' Peradventure, in a heathen country, to put an end to the rite of sacrifice 'some one would even dare to die;' that expresses the relation in which the offering on Mount Calvary stands to the Levitical offerings. It is the death of what is outward and local, the life of what is inward and spiritual: 'I, if I be lifted up from the earth, shall draw all men after me;' and 'Neither in this mountain nor at Jerusalem shall ye worship the Father.' It is the offering up of the old world on the cross; the law with its handwriting of ordinances, the former man with his affections and lusts, the body of sin with its remembrances of past sin. It is the New Testament revealed in the blood of Christ, the Gospel of freedom, which draws men together in the communion of one spirit, as in St. Paul's time without respect of persons and nations, so in our own day without regard to the divisions of Christendom. In the place of Churches, priesthoods, ceremonials, systems, it puts a moral and spiritual principle which works with them, not necessarily in opposition to them, but beside or within them, to renew life in the individual soul.

Again, the death of Christ may be described as a ransom. It is not that God needs some payment which He must receive before He will set the captives free. The ransom is not a human ransom, any more than the sacrifice is a Levitical sacrifice. Rightly to comprehend the nature of this Divine ransom, we must begin with that question of the Apostle: 'Know ye not that whose servants ye yield yourselves to obey, his servants ye are to whom ye obey, whether of sin unto death, or of obedience unto righteousness?' There are those who will reply: 'We were never in bondage at any time.' To whom Christ answers: 'Whosoever committeth sin is the servant of sin;' and, 'If the Son shall make you free, ye shall be free indeed.' Ransom is 'deliverance to the captive.' There are mixed modes here also, as in the use of the term sacrifice—the word has a temporary allusive reference to a Mosaical figure of speech. That secondary allusive reference we are constrained to drop, because it is unessential; and also because it immediately involves further questions—a ransom to whom? for what?—about which Scripture is silent, to which reason refuses to answer.

Thirdly, the death of Christ is spoken of as a death for us, or for our sins. The ambiguous use of the preposition 'for,' combined with the figure of sacrifice, has tended to introduce the idea of substitution; when the real meaning is not 'in our stead,' but only 'in behalf of,' or 'because of us.' It is a great assumption, or an unfair deduction, from such expressions, to say that Christ takes our place, or that the Father in looking at the sinner sees only Christ. Christ died for us in no other sense than He lived or rose again for us. Scripture affords no hint of His taking our place in His death in any other way than He did also in His life. He himself speaks of His 'decease which He should accomplish at Jerusalem,' quite simply: 'greater love hath no man than this, that a man lay down his life for his friends.' The words of Caiaphas, 'It is expedient that one man should die for this nation,' and the comment of the Evangelist, 'and not for that nation only, but that he should gather together in one the children of God that are scattered abroad,' afford a measure of the meaning of such expressions. Here, too, there are mixed modes which seem to be inextricably blended in the language of Scripture, and which theology has not always distinguished. For the thing signified is, partly, that Christ died for our sakes, partly that He died by the hands of sinners, partly that He died with a perfect and Divine sympathy for human evil and suffering. But this ambiguity (which we may silently correct or explain) need not prevent our joining in words which, more perhaps than any others, have been consecrated by religious use to express the love and affection of Christians towards their Lord.

Now suppose some one who is aware of the plastic and

accommodating nature of language to observe, that in what has been written of late years on the doctrine of the atonement he has noticed an effort made to win for words new senses, and that some of the preceding remarks are liable to this charge; he may be answered, first, that those new senses are really a recovery of old ones (for the writers of the New Testament, though they use the language of the time, everywhere give it a moral meaning); and, secondly, that in addition to the modes of conception already mentioned, the Scripture has others which are not open to his objection. And those who, admitting the innocence and Scriptural character of the expressions already referred to, may yet fear their abuse, and therefore desire to have them excluded from articles of faith (just as many Protestants, though aware that the religious use of images is not idolatry, may not wish to see them in churches)—such persons may find a sufficient expression of the work of Christ in other modes of speech which the Apostle also uses. (1) Instead of the language of sacrifice, or ransom, or substitution, they may prefer that of communion or identity. (2) Or they may interpret the death of Christ by His life, and connect the bleeding form on Mount Calvary with the image of Him who went about doing good. Or (3) they may look inward at their own souls, and read there, inseparable from the sense of their own unworthiness, the assurance that God will not desert the work of His hands, of which assurance the death of Christ is the outward witness to them. There are other ways, also, of conceiving the redemption of man which avoid controversy, any of which is a sufficient stay of the Christian life. For the kingdom of God is not this or that statement, or definition of opinion, but righteousness, and peace, and joy in the Holy Ghost. And the cross of Christ is to be taken up and borne; not to be turned into words, or made a theme of philosophical speculation.

1. Everywhere St. Paul speaks of the Christian as one with Christ. He is united with Him, not in His death

only, but in all the stages of His existence; living with Him, suffering with Him, crucified with Him, buried with Him, rising again with Him, renewed in His image, glorified together with Him; these are the expressions by which this union is denoted. There is something meant by this language which goes beyond the experience of ordinary Christians, something, perhaps, more mystical than in these latter days of the world most persons seem to be capable of feeling, yet the main thing signified is the same for all ages, the knowledge and love of Christ, by which men pass out of themselves to make their will His and His theirs, the consciousness of Him in their thoughts and actions, communion with Him, and trust in Him. Of every act of kindness or good which they do to others His life is the type; of every act of devotion or self-denial His death is the type; of every act of faith His resurrection is the type. And often they walk with Him on earth, not in a figure only, and find Him near them, not in a figure only, in the valley of death. They experience from Him the same kind of support as from the sympathy and communion of an earthly friend. That friend is also a Divine power. In proportion as they become like Him, they are reconciled to God through Him; they pass with Him into the relationship of sons of God. There is enough here for faith to think of, without sullying the mirror of God's justice, or overclouding His truth. We need not suppose that God ever sees us other than we really are, or attributes to us what we never did. Doctrinal statements, in which the nature of the work of Christ is most exactly defined, cannot really afford the same support as the simple conviction of His love.

Again (2), the import of the death of Christ may be interpreted by His life. No theological speculation can throw an equal light on it. From the other side we cannot see it, but only from this. Now the life of Christ is the life of One who knew no sin, on whom the shadow of evil never passed; who went about doing good; who had not where to lay His head; whose condition was in all respects the reverse of earthly and human greatness; who also had a sort of infinite sympathy or communion with all men everywhere; whom, nevertheless, His own nation betrayed to a shameful death. It is the life of One who came to bear witness of the truth, who knew what was in man, and never spared to rebuke him, yet condemned him not; himself without sin, yet One to whom all men would soonest have gone to confess and receive forgiveness of sin. It is the life of One who was in constant communion with God as well as man; who was the inhabitant of another world while outwardly in this. It is the life of One in whom we see balanced and united the separate gifts and graces of which we catch glimpses only in the lives of His followers. It is a life which is mysterious to us, which we forbear to praise, in the earthly sense, because it is above praise, being the most perfect image and embodiment that we can conceive of Divine goodness.

And the death of Christ is the fulfilment and consummation of His life, the greatest moral act ever done in this world, the highest manifestation of perfect love, the centre in which the rays of love converge and meet, the extremest abnegation or annihilation of self. It is the death of One who seals with His blood the witness of the truth which He came into the world to teach, which therefore confirms our faith in Him as well as animates our love. It is the death of One, who says at the last hour, 'Of them that thou gavest me, I have not lost one' - of One who, having come forth from God, and having finished the work which He came into the world to do, returns to God. It is a death in which all the separate gifts of heroes and martyrs are united in a Divine excellence—of One who most perfectly foresaw all things that were coming upon Him—who felt all, and shrank not—of One who, in the hour of death, set the example to His followers of praying for His enemies.

It is a death which, more even than His life, is singular and mysterious, in which nevertheless we all are partakers— in which there was the thought and consciousness of mankind to the end of time, which has also the power of drawing to itself the thoughts of men to the end of time.

Lastly, there is a true Christian feeling in many other ways of regarding the salvation of man, of which the heart is its own witness, which yet admit, still less than the preceding, of logical rule and precision. He who is conscious of his own infirmity and sinfulness, is ready to confess that he needs reconciliation with God. He has no proud thoughts: he knows that he is saved 'not of himself, it is the gift of God;' the better he is, the more he feels, in the language of Scripture, 'that he is an unprofitable servant.' Sometimes he imagines the Father ' coming out to meet him, when he is yet a long way off,' as in the parable of the Prodigal Son; at other times the burden of sin lies heavy on him; he seems to need more support— he can approach God only through Christ. All men are not the same; one has more of the strength of reason in his religion; another more of the tenderness of feeling. With some, faith partakes of the nature of a pure and spiritual morality; there are others who have gone through the struggle of St. Paul or Luther, and attain rest only in casting all on Christ. One will live after the pattern of the Sermon on the Mount, or the Epistle of St. James. Another finds a deep consolation and meaning in a closer union with Christ; he will 'put on Christ,' he will hide himself in Christ; he will experience in his own person the truth of those words of the Apostle, 'I am crucified with Christ, nevertheless I live; yet not I, but Christ liveth in me.' But if he have the spirit of moderation that there was in St. Paul, he will not stereotype these true, though often passing feelings, in any formula of substitution or satisfaction; still less will he draw out formulas of this sort into remote consequences. Such logical idealism is of another age; it is neither faith nor philosophy in this. Least of all will he judge others by the circumstance of their admitting or refusing to admit the expression of his individual feelings as an eternal truth. He shrinks from asserting his own righteousness; he is equally unwilling to affirm that the righteousness of Christ is imputed to him. He is looking for forgiveness of sins, not because Christ has satisfied the wrath of God, but because God can show mercy without satisfaction : he may have no right to acquittal, he dare not say, God has no right to acquit. Yet again, he is very far from imagining that the most merciful God will indiscriminately forgive; or that the weakness of human emotions, groaning out at the last hour a few accustomed phrases, is a sufficient ground of confidence and hope. He knows that the only external evidence of forgiveness is the fact, that he has ceased to do evil; no other is possible. Having Christ near as a friend and a brother, and making the Christian life his great aim, he is no longer under the dominion of a conventional theology. He will not be distracted by its phrases from communion with his fellowmen. He can never fall into that confusion of head and heart, which elevates matters of opinion into practical principles. Difficulties and doubts diminish with him, as he himself grows more like Christ, not because he forcibly suppresses them, but because they become unimportant in comparison with purity, and holiness, and love. Enough of truth for him seems to radiate from the person of the Saviour. He thinks more and more of the human nature of Christ as the expression of the Divine. He has found the way of life—that way is not an easy way—but neither is it beset by the imaginary perplexities with which a false use of the intellect in religion has often surrounded it.

It seems to be an opinion which is gaining ground among thoughtful and religious men, that in theology, the less we define the better. Definite statements respecting the relation of Christ either to God or man are only figures of speech;

they do not really pierce the clouds which 'round our little life.' When we multiply words we do not multiply ideas; we are still within the circle of our own minds. No greater calamity has ever befallen the Christian Church than the determination of some uncertain things which are beyond the sphere of human knowledge. A true instinct prevents our entangling the faith of Christ with the philosophy of the day; the philosophy of past ages is a still more imperfect exponent of it. Neither is it of any avail to assume revelation or inspiration as a sort of shield, or Catholicon, under which the weak points of theology may receive protection. For what is revealed or what inspired cannot be answered *a priori*; the meaning of the word Revelation must be determined by the fact, not the fact by the word.

If our Saviour were to come again to earth, which of all the theories of atonement and sacrifice would he sanction with His authority? Perhaps none of them, yet perhaps all may be consistent with a true service of Him. The question has no answer. But it suggests the thought that we shrink from bringing controversy into His presence. The same kind of lesson may be gathered from the consideration of theological differences in the face of death. Who, as he draws near to Christ, will not feel himself drawn towards his theological opponents? At the end of life, when a man looks back calmly, he is most likely to find that he exaggerated in some things; that he mistook party spirit for a love of truth. Perhaps, he had not sufficient consideration for others, or stated the truth itself in a manner which was calculated to give offence. In the heat of the struggle, let us at least pause to imagine polemical disputes as they will appear a year, two years, three years hence; it may be, dead and gone—certainly more truly seen than in the hour of controversy. For the truths about which we are disputing cannot partake of the passing stir; they do not change even with the greater revolutions of human things. They are in eternity; and the image of them on earth is not the movement on the surface of the waters, but the depths of the silent sea. Lastly, as a measure of the value of such disputes, which above all other interests seem to have for a time the power of absorbing men's minds and rousing their passions, we may carry our thoughts onwards to the invisible world, and there behold, as in a glass, the great theological teachers of past ages, who have anathematized each other in their lives, resting together in the communion of the same Lord.

ESSAY

ON

PREDESTINATION AND FREE WILL

THE difficulty of necessity and free will is not peculiar to Christianity. It enters into all religions at a certain stage of their progress; it reappears in philosophy and is a question not only of speculation but of life. Wherever man touches nature, wherever the stream of thought which flows within, meets and comes into conflict with scientific laws, reflecting on the actions of an individual in relation to his antecedents, considering the balance of human actions in many individuals; when we pass into the wider field of history, and trace the influence of circumstances on the course of events, the sequence of nations and states of society, the physical causes that lie behind all; in the region of philosophy, as we follow the order of human thoughts, and observe the seeming freedom and real limitation of ideas and systems; lastly in that higher world of which religion speaks to us, when we conceive man as a finite being, who has the witness in himself of his own dependence on God, whom theology too has made the subject of many theories of grace, new forms appear of that famous controversy which the last century discussed under the name of necessity and free will.

I shall at present pursue no further the train of reflections which are thus suggested. My first object is to clear the way for the consideration of the subject within the limits of Scripture. Some preliminary obstacles offer themselves, arising out of the opposition which the human mind everywhere admits in the statement of this question. These will be first examined. We may afterwards return to the modern aspects of the contradiction and of the reconcilement.

§ 1.

In the relations of God and man, good and evil, finite and infinite, there is much that must ever be mysterious. Nor can any one exaggerate the weakness and feebleness of the human mind in the attempt to seek for such knowledge. But although we acknowledge the feebleness of man's brain and the vastness of the subject, we should also draw a distinction between the original difficulty of our own ignorance, and the puzzles and embarrassments which false philosophy or false theology have introduced. The impotence of our faculties is not a reason for acquiescing in a metaphysical fiction. Philosophy has no right to veil herself in mystery at the point where she is lost in a confusion of words. That we know little is the real mystery; not that we are caught in dilemmas or surrounded by contradictions. These contradictions are involved in the slightest as well as in the most serious of our actions, which is a proof of their really trifling nature. They confuse the mind but not things. To trace the steps by which mere abstractions have acquired this perplexing and constraining power, though it cannot meet the original defect, yet may perhaps assist us to understand the misunderstanding, and to regard the question of predestination and free will in a simpler and more natural light.

A subject which claims to be raised above the rules and requirements of logic, must give a reason for the exemption, and must itself furnish some other test of truth to which it is ready to conform. The reason is that logic is inapplicable to the discussion of a question which begins with a contradiction in terms : it can only work out the opposite aspects or principles of such a question on one side or the other, but is inadequate to that more comprehensive conception of the subject which embraces both. We often speak of language as an imperfect instrument for the expression of thought. Logic is even more imperfect ; it is wanting in the plastic and multiform character of language, yet deceives us by the appearance of a straight rule and necessary principle. Questions respecting the relation of God and man, necessity and free will, the finite and the infinite—perhaps every question which has two opposite poles of fact and idea—are beyond the sphere of its art. But if not logic, some other test must be found of our theories or reasonings, on these and the like metaphysical subjects. This can only be their agreement with facts, which we shall the more readily admit if the new form of expression or statement of them be a real assistance to our powers of thought and action.

The difficulties raised respecting necessity and free will partake, for the most part, of the same nature as the old fallacies respecting motion and space of Zeno and the Eleatics, and have their 'solvitur ambulando' as well. This is the answer of Bishop Butler, who aims only at a practical solution. But as it is no use to say to the lame man, ' rise up and walk,' without a crutch or helping hand, so it is no use to offer these practical solutions to a mind already entangled in speculative perplexities. It retorts upon you—'I cannot walk : if my outward actions seem like other men's ; if I do not throw myself from a precipice, or take away the life of another under the fatal influence of the doctrine of necessity, yet the course of thought within me is different. I look upon the world with other eyes, and slowly and gradually, differences in thought must beget differences also in action.' But if the mind, which is bound by this chain, could be shown that it was a slave only to its own abstract ideas—that it was below where it ought to be above them—that, considering all the many minds of men as one mind, it could trace the fiction—this world of abstractions would gradually disappear, and not merely in a Christian, but in a philosophical sense, it would receive the kingdom of Heaven as a little child, seeking rather for some new figure under which conflicting notions might be represented, than remaining in suspense between them. It may be as surprising to a future generation that the nineteenth century should have been under the influence of the illusion of necessity and free will, or that it should have proposed the law of contradiction as an ultimate test of truth, as it is to ourselves that former ages have been subjected to the fictions of essence, substance, and the like.

The notion that no idea can be composed of two contradictory conceptions, seems to arise out of the analogy of the sensible world. It would be an absurdity to suppose that an object should be white and black at the same time; that a captive should be in chains and not in chains at the same time, and so on. But there is no absurdity in supposing that the mental analysis even of a matter of fact or an outward object should involve us in contradictions. Objects, considered in their most abstract point of view, may be said to contain a positive and a negative element: everything is and is not; is in itself, and is not, in relation to other things. Our conceptions of motion, of becoming, or of beginning, in like manner involve a contradiction. The old puzzles of the Eleatics are merely an exemplification of the same difficulty. There are objections, it has been said, against a vacuum, objections against a plenum, though we need not add, with the writer who makes the remark, 'Yet one of these must be true.' How a new substance can be formed by chemical combination out of two other substances may seem also to involve a contradiction, e. g. water is and is not oxygen and hydrogen. Life, in like manner, has been defined as a state in which every end is a means, and every means an end. And if we turn to any moral or political subject, we are perpetually coming across different and opposing lines of argument, and constantly in danger of passing from one sphere to another; of applying, for example, moral or theological principles to politics, and political principles to theology. Men form to themselves first one system, then many, as they term them different, but in reality opposite to each other. Just as that nebulous mass, out of which the heavens have been imagined to be formed, at last, with its circling motion, subsides into rings, and embodies the 'stars moving in their courses,' so also in the world of mind there are so many different orbits which never cross or touch each other, and yet which must be conceived of as the colours of the rainbow, the result of a single natural phenomenon.

It is at first sight strange that some of these contradictions should seem so trivial to us, while others assume the appearance of a high mystery. In physics or mathematics we scarcely think of them, though speculative minds may sometimes be led by them to seek for higher expressions, or to embrace both sides of the contradiction in some conception of flux or transition, reciprocal action, process by antagonism, the Hegelian vibration of moments, or the like. In common life we acquiesce in the contradiction almost unconsciously, merely remarking on the difference of men's views, or the possibility of saying something on either side of a question. But in religion the difficulty appears of greater importance, partly from our being much more under the influence of language in theology than in subjects which we can at once bring to the test of fact and experiment, and partly also from our being more subject to our own natural constitution, which leads us to one or the other horn of the dilemma, instead of placing us between or above both. As in heathen times it was natural to think of extraordinary phenomena, such as thunder and lightning, as the work of gods rather than as arising from physical causes, so it is still to the religious mind to consider the bewilderments and entanglements which it has itself made as a proof of the unsearchableness of the Divine nature.

The immoveableness of these abstractions from within will further incline us to consider the metaphysical contradiction of necessity and free will in the only rational way; that is, 'historically.' To say that we have ideas of fate or freedom which are innate, is to assume what is at once disproved by a reference to history. In the East and West, in India and in Greece, in Christian as well as heathen times, whenever men have been sufficiently enlightened to form a distinct conception of a single Divine power or overruling law, the question arises, How is the individual related to this law? The first answer to this question is Pantheism; in which the individual, dropping his proper qualities, abstracts himself into an invisible being, indistinguishable from the Divine. God overpowers man; the inner life absorbs the outer; the ideal world is too much for this. The second answer, which the East has also given to this question, is Fatalism; in which, without abstraction, the individual identifies himself, soul and body, in deed as well as thought, with the Divine will. The first is the religion of contemplation; the second, of action. Only in the last, as the world itself alters, the sense of the overruling power weakens; and faith in the Divine will, as in Mahometan countries at the present day, shows itself, not in a fanatical energy, but in passive compliance and resignation.

The gradual emergence of the opposition is more clearly traceable in the Old Testament Scriptures or in Greek poetry or philosophy. The Israelites are distinguished from all other Eastern nations—certainly from all contemporary with their early history—by their distinct recognition of the unity and personality of God. God, who is the Creator and Lord of the whole earth, is also in a peculiar sense the God of the Jewish people whom He deals with according to His own good pleasure, which is also a law of truth and right. He is not so much the Author of good as the Author of all things, without whom nothing either good or evil can happen; not only the permitter of evil, but in a few instances, in the excess of His power, the cause of it also. With this universal attribute He combines another, 'the Lord our God, who brought us out of the land of bondage.' The people have one heart and one soul with which they worship God and have dealings with Him. Only a few individuals among them, as Moses or Joshua, draw near separately to Him. In the earliest ages they do not pray each one for himself. There is a great difference in this respect between the relation of man to God which is expressed in the Psalms and in the Pentateuch. In the later Psalms, certainly, and even in some of those ascribed to David, there is an immediate personal intercourse between God and His servants. At length in the books of Job and Ecclesiastes, the human spirit begins to strive with God, and to ask not only, how can man be just before God? but also, how can God be justified to man? There was a time when the thought of this could never have entered into their minds; in which they were only, as children with a father, doing evil, and punished, and returning once more to the arms of His wisdom and goodness. The childhood of their nation passed away, and the remembrance of what God had done for their fathers was forgotten ; religion became the religion of individuals, of Simeon and Anna, of Joseph and Mary. On the one hand, there was the proud claim of those who said, 'We have Abraham to our Father;' on the other hand, the regretful feeling 'that God was casting off Israel,' which St. Paul in the manner of the Old Testament rebukes with the words, 'Who art thou, O man?' and 'We are the clay, and He the potter.'

We may briefly trace the progress of a parallel struggle in Grecian mythology. It presents itself, however, in another form, beginning with the Fates weaving the web of life, or the Furies pursuing the guilty, and ending in the pure abstraction of necessity or nature. Many changes of feeling may be observed between the earlier and later of these two extremes. The Fate of poetry is not like that of philosophy, the chain by which the world is held together; but an over-living power or curse—sometimes just, sometimes arbitrary—specially punishing impiety towards the Gods or violations of nature. In Homer, it represents also a determination already fixed, or an ill irremediable by man; in one aspect it is the folly which 'leaves no place for repentance.' In Pindar it receives a nobler form, 'Law the king of all.' In the tragedians, it has a peculiar interest, giving a kind of measured and regular movement to the whole action of the play. The consciousness that man is not his own master, had deepened in the course of ages; there had grown up in the mind a sentiment of overruling law. It was this half-religious, half-philosophical feeling, which Greek tragedy embodied; whence it derived not only dramatic irony or contrast of the real and seeming, but also its characteristic feature—repose. The same reflective tone is observable in the 'Epic' historian of the Persian war; who delights to tell, not (like a modern narrator) of the necessary connexion of causes and effects, but of effects without causes, due only to the will of Heaven. A sadder note is heard at intervals of the feebleness and nothingness of man ; πᾶν ἐστιν ἄνθρωπος συμφορή. In Thucydides, (who was separated from Herodotus by an interval of about twenty years) the sadness remains, but the religious element has vanished. Man is no longer in the toils of destiny, but he is still feeble and helpless. Fortune and human enterprise divide the empire of life.

Such conceptions of fate belong to Paganism, and have little in common with that higher idea of Divine predestinatoin of which the New Testament speaks. The Fate of Greek philosophy is different from either. The earlier schools expressed their sense of an all-pervading law in rude, mythological figures. In time this passed away, and the conceptions of chance, of nature, and necessity became matters of philosophical inquiry. By the Sophists first the question was discussed, whether man is the cause of his own actions; the mode in which they treated of the subject being to identify the good with the voluntary, and the evil with the involuntary. It is this phase of the question which is alone considered by Aristotle. In the chain of the Stoics the doctrine has arrived at a further stage, in which human action has become a part of the course of the world. How the free will of man was to be reconciled either with Divine power, or Divine foreknowledge, was a difficulty pressed upon the Stoical philosopher equally as upon the metaphysicians of the last century; and was met by various devices, such as that of the confatalism of Chrysippus, which may be described as a sort of identity of fate and freedom, or of an action and its conditions.

Our inquiry has been thus far confined to an attempt to show, first, that the question of predestination cannot be considered according to the common rules of logic; secondly, that the contradictions which are involved in this question, are of the same kind as many other contrasts of ideas; and, thirdly, that the modern conception of necessity was the growth of ages, whether its true origin is to be sought in the Scriptures, or in the Greek philosophy, or both. If only we could throw ourselves back to a prior state of the world, and know no other modes of thought than those which existed in the infancy of the human mind, the opposition would cease to have any meaning for us; and thus the further reflection is suggested, that if ever we become fully conscious that the words which we use respecting it are words only, it will again become unmeaning. Historically we know when it arose, and whence it came. Already we are able to consider the subject in a simpler way, whether presented to us (1) in connexion with the statements of Scripture, or (2) as a subject of theology and philosophy.

§ 2.

Two kinds of predestination may be distinguished in the writings of St. Paul, as well as in some parts of the Old Testament. First, the predestination of nations; secondly, of individuals. The former of these may be said to flow out of the latter, God choosing at once the patriarchs and their descendants. As the author of the Epistle to the Hebrews expresses it, 'By faith Abraham offered up Isaac; and therefore sprang there of one, and him as good as dead, so many as the stars of heaven in multitude.' The life of the patriarchs was the type or shadow of the history of their posterity, for evil as well as good. 'Simeon and Levi are brethren; instruments of cruelty are in their habitations; Joseph is a goodly bough;' Moab and Ammon are children of whoredom; Ishmael is a wild man, and so on. There is also the feeling that whatever extraordinary thing happens in Jewish history is God's doing, not of works nor even of faith, but of grace and choice: 'He took David from the sheep-folds, and set him over His people Israel.' So that a double principle is discernible: first, absolute election; and, secondly, the fulfilment of the promises made to the fathers, or the visitation of their sins upon the children.

The notion of freedom is essentially connected with that of individuality. No one is truly free who has not that inner circle of thoughts and actions in which he is wholly himself and independent of the will of others. A slave, for example, may be in this sense free, even while in the service of his lord; constraint can apply only to his outward acts, not to his inward nature. But if, in the language of Aristotle, he were a natural slave, whose life seemed to himself defective and imperfect, who had no thoughts or feelings of his own, but only instincts and impulses, we could no more call him free than a domestic animal which attaches itself to a master. So, in that stage of society in which the state is all in all, the idea of the individual has a feeble existence. In the language of philosophy the whole is free, and the parts are determined by the whole. So the theocracy of the Old Testament seems to swallow up its members. The Jewish commonwealth is governed by God himself; this of itself interferes with the personal relation in which He stands to the individuals who compose it. Through the law only, in the congregation, at the great feasts, through their common ancestors, the people draw near to God; they do not venture to think severally of their separate and independent connexion with Him. They stand or fall together; they go astray or return to Him as one man. It is this which makes so much of their history directly applicable to the struggle of Christian life. Religion, which to the believer in Christ is an individual principle, is with them a national one.

The idea of a chosen people passes from the Old Testament into the New. As the Jews had been predestined in the one, so it appeared to the Apostle St. Paul that the Gentiles were predestined in the other. In the Old Testament he observed two sorts of predestination; first, that more general one, in which all who were circumcised were partakers of the privilege—which was applicable to all Israelites as the children of Abraham; secondly, the more particular one, in reference to which he says, 'All are not Israel who are of Israel.' To the eye of faith 'all Israel were saved;' and yet within Israel, there was another Israel chosen in a more special sense. The analogy of this double predestination the Apostle transfers to the Christian society. All alike were holy, even those of whom he speaks in the strongest terms of reprobation. The Church, like Israel of old, presents to the Apostle's mind the conception of a definite body, consisting of those who are sealed by baptism and have received 'the first fruits of the Spirit.' They are elect according to the foreknowledge or predisposition of God; sealed by God unto the day of redemption;

a peculiar people, a royal priesthood, taken alike from Jews and Gentiles. The Apostle speaks of their election as of some external fact. The elect of God have an offence among them not even named among the Gentiles, they abuse the gifts of the Spirit, they partake in the idol's temple, they profane the body and blood of Christ. And yet, as the Israelites of old, they bear on their foreheads the mark that they are God's people, and are described as 'chosen saints,' 'sanctified in Christ Jesus.'

Again, the Apostle argues respecting Israel itself, 'Hath God cast off his people whom he foreknew?' or rather, whom He before appointed. They are in the position of their fathers when they sinned against Him. If we read their history we shall see, that what happened to them in old times is happening to them now; and yet in the Old Testament as well as the New the overruling design was not their condemnation but their salvation—'God concluded all under sin that he might have mercy upon all.' They stumbled and rose again then; they will stumble and rise again now. Their predestination from the beginning is a proof that they cannot be finally cast off; beloved as they have been for their father's sakes, and the children of so many promises. There is a providence which, in spite of all contrary appearance, in spite of the acceptance of the Gentiles, or rather so much the more in consequence of it, makes all things work together for good to the chosen people.

In this alternation of hopes and fears, in which hope finally prevails over fear, the Apostle speaks in the strongest language of the right of God to do what He will with His own; if any doctrine could be established by particular passages of Scripture, Calvinism would rest immoveable on the ninth chapter of the Romans. It seemed to him no more unjust that God should reject than that He should accept the Israelites; if, at that present time He cut them short in righteousness, and narrowed the circle of election,

He had done the same with the patriarchs. He had said of old, 'Jacob have I loved, and Esau have I hated:' and this preference, as the Apostle observes, was shown before either could have committed actual sin. In the same spirit He says to Moses, 'I will have mercy on whom I will have mercy, and I will have compassion on whom I will have compassion.' And to Pharaoh, 'For this cause have I raised thee up.' Human nature, it is true, rebels at this, and says, 'Why does he yet find fault?' To which the Apostle only replies, 'Shall the thing formed say unto him that formed it, Why hast thou made me thus? Hath not the potter power over the clay?' Some of the expressions which have become the most objectionable watchwords of predestinarian theology, such as 'vessels of wrath and vessels of mercy,' are in fact taken from the same passage in the Epistle to the Romans.

It is answered by the opponents of Calvinism, that the Apostle is here speaking not of individual but of national predestination. From the teaching of the Old Testament respecting the election of the Jewish people we can infer nothing respecting the Divine economy about persons. To which in turn it may be replied, that if we admit the principle that the free choice of nations is not inconsistent with Divine justice, we cannot refuse to admit the free choice of persons also. A little more or a little less of the doctrine cannot make it more or less reconcilable with the perfect justice of God. Nor can we argue that the election of nations is a part of the Old Testament dispensation, which has no place in the New; because the Apostle speaks of election according to the purpose of God as a principle which was at that time being manifested in the acceptance of the Gentiles.

Yet the distinction is a sound one if stated a little differently, that is to say, if we consider that the predestination of Christians is only the continuance of the Old Testament in the New. It is the feeling of a religious Israelite respecting his race; this the Apostle enlarges to comprehend the Gentiles. As the temporal Israel becomes the spiritual Israel, the chosen people are transfigured into the elect. Why this is so is only a part of the more general question, 'why the New Testament was given through the Old?' It was natural it should be so given; humanly speaking, it could not have been otherwise. The Gospel would have been unmeaning, if it had been 'tossed into the world' separated from all human antecedents; if the heaven of its clearness had been beyond the breath of every human feeling. Neither is there any more untruthfulness in St. Paul's requiring us to recognize the goodness of God in the election of some and the rejection of others, than in humility or any act of devotion. The untruth lies not in the devout feeling, but in the logical statement. When we humble ourselves before God, we may know, as a matter of common sense, that we are not worse than others; but this, however true ('Father, I thank thee I am not as other men'), is not the temper in which we kneel before Him. So in these passages, St. Paul is speaking, not from a general consideration of the Divine nature, but with the heart and feelings of an Israelite. Could the question have been brought before him in another form—could we have been asked whether God, according to His own pleasure, chose out individual souls, so that some could not fail of being saved while others were necessarily lost—could he have been asked whether Christ died for all or for the chosen few—whether, in short, God was sincere in his offer of salvation—can we doubt that to such suggestions he would have replied in his own words, 'God forbid! for how shall God judge the world?'

It has been said that the great error in the treatment of this subject consists in taking chap. ix. separated from chaps. x. xi. We may say more generally, in taking parts of Scripture without the whole, or in interpreting either apart from history and experience. In considering the question of predestination, we must not forget that at least one-half of Scripture tells not of what God does, but of what man ought to do; not of grace and pardon only, but of holiness. If, in speaking of election, St. Paul seems at times to use language which implies the irrespective election of the Jews as a nation; yet, on the other hand, what immediately follows shows us that conditions were understood throughout, and that, although we may not challenge the right of God to do what He would with His own, yet that in all His dealings with them the dispensation was but the effect of their conduct. And although the Apostle is speaking chiefly of national predestination, with respect to which the election of God is asserted by him in the most unconditional terms; yet, as if he were already anticipating the application of his doctrine to the individual, he speaks of human causes for the rejection of Israel; 'because they sought not righteousness by the way of faith;' 'because they stumble at the rock of offence.' God accepted and rejected Israel of His own good pleasure; and yet it was by their own fault. How are we to reconcile these conflicting statements? They do not need reconciliation; they are but the two opposite expressions of a religious mind, which says at one moment, 'Let me try to do right,' and at another, 'God alone can make me do right.' The two feelings may involve a logical contradiction, and yet exist together in fact and in the religious experience of mankind.

In the Old Testament the only election of individuals is that of the great leaders or chiefs, who are identified with the nation. But in the New Testament, where religion has become a personal and individual matter, it follows that election must also be of persons. The Jewish nation knew, or seemed to know, one fact, that they were the chosen people. They saw, also, eminent men raised up by the hand of God to be the deliverers of His servants. It is not in this 'historical' way that the Christian becomes conscious of his individual election. From within, not from without, he is made aware of the purpose of God respecting himself.

Living in close and intimate union with God, having the mind of the Spirit and knowing the things of the Spirit, he begins to consider with St. Paul, 'When it pleased God, who separated me from my mother's womb, to reveal his Son in me.' His whole life seems a sort of miracle to him; supernatural, and beyond other men's in the gifts of grace which he has received. If he asks himself, 'Whence was this to me?' he finds no other answer but that God gave them 'because he had a favour unto him.' He recalls the hour of his conversion, when, in a moment, he was changed from darkness to light, and from the power of Satan unto God. Or, perhaps, the dealings of God with him have been insensible, yet not the less real; like a child, he cannot remember the time when he first began to trust the love of his parent. How can he separate himself from that love or refuse to believe that He who began the good work will also accomplish it unto the end? At which step in the ladder of God's mercy will he stop? 'Whom he did foreknow, them he did predestinate; whom he did predestinate, them he also called; whom he called, them he justified; whom he justified, them he also glorified.'

A religious mind feels the difference between saying, 'God chose me; I cannot tell why; not for any good that I have done; and I am persuaded that he will keep me unto the end;' and saying, 'God chooses men quite irrespective of their actions, and predestines them to eternal salvation;' and yet more, if we add the other half of the doctrine, 'God refuses men quite irrespective of their actions, and they become reprobates, predestined to everlasting damnation.' Could we be willing to return to that stage of the doctrine which St. Paul taught, without comparing contradictory statements or drawing out logical conclusions—could we be content to rest our belief, as some of the greatest, even of Calvinistic divines have done, on fact and experience, theology would be no longer at variance with morality.

'Work out your own salvation with fear and trembling; for it is God that worketh in you both to do and to will of his good pleasure,' is the language of Scripture, adjusting the opposite aspects of this question. The Arminian would say, 'Work out your own salvation;' the Calvinist, 'God worketh in you both to do and to will of his good pleasure.' However contradictory it may sound, the Scripture unites both; work out your own salvation with fear and trembling; for it is God that worketh in you both to will and to do of His good pleasure.

§ 3.

I. We have been considering the question thus far within the limits of Scripture. But it has also a wider range. The primary relations of the will of man to the will of God are independent of the Christian revelation. Natural religion, that is to say, the Greek seeking after wisdom, the Indian wandering in the expanse of his own dreamlike consciousness, the Jew repeating to himself that he is Abraham's seed; each in their several ways at different stages of the world's history have asked the question, 'How is the freedom of the human will consistent with the infinity and omnipotence of God?' These attributes admit of a further analysis into the power of God and the knowledge of God. And hence arises a second form of the inquiry, 'How is the freedom of the human will reconcilable with Divine omniscience or foreknowledge?' To which the Christian system adds a third question, 'How is the freedom of the human will reconcilable with that more immediate presence of God in the soul which is termed by theologians Divine grace?'

(1) God is everywhere; man is nowhere. Infinity exists continuously in every point of time; it fills every particle of space. Or rather, these very ideas of time and space are figures of speech, for they have a 'here' and a 'there,' a future and a past—which no effort of human imagination

can transcend. But in God there is no future and no past, neither 'here nor there;' He is all and in all. Where, then, is room for man? in what open place is he permitted to live and move and have his being?

God is the cause of all things; without Him nothing is made that is made. He is in history, in nature, in the heart of man. The world itself is the work of His power; the least particulars of human life are ordained by Him. 'Are not two sparrows sold for one farthing, and yet your heavenly Father feedeth them;' and 'the hairs of your head are all numbered.' Is there any point at which this Divine causalty can stop? at which the empire of law ceases? at which the human will is set free?

The answer is the fact; not the fact of consciousness as it is sometimes termed, that we are free agents, which it is impossible to see or verify; but the visible tangible fact that we have a place in the order of nature, and walk about on the earth, and are ourselves causes drawing effects after them. Does any advocate of freedom mean more than this? Or any believer in necessity less? No one can deny of himself the restrictions which he observes to be true of others; nor can any one doubt that there exists in others the same consciousness of freedom and responsibility which he has himself. But if so, all these things are as they were before; we need not differ about the unseen foundation whether of necessity or free will, spirit or body, mind or matter, upon which the edifice of human life is to be reared. Just as the theory of the ideality of matter leaves the world where it was—they do not build houses in the air who imagine Bishop Berkeley to have dissolved the solid elements into sensations of the mind—so the doctrine of necessity or predestination leaves morality and religion unassailed, unless it intrude itself as a motive on the sphere of human action.

It is remarkable that the belief in predestination, both in modern and in ancient times, among Mahometans as well as Christians, has been the animating principle of nations and bodies of men, equally, perhaps more than of individuals. It is characteristic of certain countries, and has often arisen from sympathy in a common cause. Yet it cannot be said to have been without a personal influence also. It has led to a view of religion in which man has been too much depressed to form a true conception of God himself. For it is not to be supposed that the lower we sink human nature in the scale of being, the higher we raise the Author of being; worthy notions of God imply worthy notions of man also.

'God is infinite.' But in what sense? Am I to conceive a space without limit, such as I behold in the immeasurable ether, and apply this viewless form to the thought of the Almighty? Any one will admit that here would be a figure of speech. Yet few of us free our notions of infinity from the imagery of place. It is this association which gives them their positive, exclusive character. But conceive of infinity as mere negation, denying of God the limits which are imposed upon finite beings, meaning only that God is not a man or comprehensible by man, without any suggestion of universal space, and the exclusiveness disappears; there is room for the creature side by side with the Creator. Or again, press the idea of the infinite to its utmost extent, till it is alone in the universe, or rather is the universe itself, in this heaven of abstraction, nevertheless, a cloud begins to appear; a limitation casts its shadow over the formless void. Infinite is finite because it is infinite. That is to say, because infinity includes all things, it is incapable of creating what is external to itself. Deny infinity in this sense, and the being to whom it is attributed receives a new power; God is greater by being finite than by being infinite. Proceeding in the same train of thought, we may observe that the word finite is the symbol, to our own minds as to the Greek, of strength and reality and truth. It cannot be these which we intend to deny of the Divine Being. Lastly, when we have freed our minds from associations of place and from those other solemn associations which naturally occur to us from its application to the Almighty, are we sure that we intend anything more by the 'Infinite' than mere vacancy, the 'indefinite,' the word 'not?'

It is useful to point out the ambiguities and perplexities of such terms. Logic is not to puzzle us with inferences about words which she clothes in mystery; at any rate, before moving a step she should explain their meaning. She must admit that the infinite overreaches itself in denying the existence of the finite, and that there are some 'limitations,' such as the impossibility of evil or falsehood, which are of the essence of the Divine nature. She must inquire whether it be conceivable to reach a further infinite, in which the opposition to the finite is denied, which may be a worthier image of the Divine Being. She must acknowledge that negative ideas, while they have often a kind of solemnity and mystery, are the shallowest and most trifling of all our ideas.

So far the will may be free unless we persist in an idea of the Divine which logic and not reason erroneously requires, and which is the negative not only of freedom but of all other existence but its own. More serious consequences may seem to flow from the attribute of omnipotence. For if God is the Author of all things, must it not be as a mode of Divine operation that man acts? We can get no further than a doctrine of emanation or derivation. Again, we are caught unwittingly in the toils of an 'illogical' logic. For why should we assume that because God is omnipotent He cannot make beings independent of himself? A figure of speech is not generally a good argument; but in this instance it is a sufficient one, what is needed being not an answer but only an image or mode of conception. (For in theology and philosophy it constantly happens that while logic is working out antinomies, language fails to supply an expression of the intermediate truth.) The carpenter makes a chair, which exists detached from its maker; the mechanician constructs a watch, which is wound up and goes by the action of a spring or lever; he can frame yet more complex instruments, in which power is treasured up for other men to use. The greater the skill of the artificer the more perfect and independent the work. Shall we say of God only that He is unable to separate His creations from himself? That man can produce works of imagination which live for ages after he is committed to the dust; nay, that in the way of nature he can bring into existence another being endowed with life and consciousness to perpetuate His name? But that God cannot remove a little space to contemplate His works? He must needs be present in all their movements, according to the antiquated error of natural philosophers, 'that no body can act where it is not.'

(2) Yet although the freedom of the will may be consistent with the infinity and omnipotence of God, when rightly understood and separated from logical consequences, it may be thought to be really interfered with by the Divine omniscience. 'God knows all things; our thoughts are His before they are our own; what I am doing at this moment was certainly foreseen by Him; what He certainly foresaw yesterday, or a thousand years ago, or from everlasting, how can I avoid doing at this time? To-day He sees the future course of my life. Can I make or unmake what is already within the circle of His knowledge? The imperfect judgement of my fellow-creatures gives me no disquietude—they may condemn me, and I may reverse their opinion. But the fact that the unerring judgement of God has foreseen my doom renders me alike indifferent to good and evil.'

What shall we say to this? First, that the distinction between Divine and human judgements is only partially true. For as God sees with absolute unerringness, so a wise man who is acquainted with the character and circumstances of others may foretell and assure their future life with a great degree of certainty. He may perceive intuitively their strength and weakness, and prophesy their success or failure. Now, here it is observable, that the fact of our knowing the probable course of action which another will pursue has nothing to do with the action itself. It does not exercise the smallest constraint on him; it does not produce the slightest feeling of constraint. Imagine ourselves acquainted with the habits of some animal; as we open the door of the enclosure in which it is kept, we know that it will run up to or away from us; it will show signs of pleasure or irritation. No one supposes that its actions, whatever they are, depend on our knowledge of them. Let us take another example, which is at the other end of the scale of freedom and intelligence. Conceive a veteran statesman casting his eye over the map of Europe, and foretelling the parts which nations or individuals would take in some coming struggle, who thinks the events when they come to pass are the consequences of the prediction? Every one is able to distinguish the causes of the events from the knowledge which foretells them.

There are degrees in human knowledge or foreknowledge proceeding from the lowest probability, through increasing certainty, up to absolute demonstration. But as faint presumptions do not affect the future, nor great probability, so neither does scientific demonstration. Many natural laws cannot be known more certainly than they are; but we do not therefore confuse the fact with our knowledge of the fact. The time of the rising of the sun, or of the ebb and flow of the tide, are foretold and acted upon without the least hesitation. Yet no one has imagined that these or any other natural phenomena are affected by our previous calculations about them.

Why, then, should we impose on ourselves the illusion that the unerring certainty of Divine knowledge is a limit or shackle on human actions? The foreknowledge which we possess ourselves in no way produces the facts which we foresee; the circumstance that we foresee them in distant time has no more to do with them than if we saw them in distant space. So, once more, we return from the dominion of ideas and trains of speculative consequences to rest in experience. God sits upon the circle of the heavens, present, past, and future in a figure open before Him, and sees the inhabitants of the earth like grasshoppers, coming and going, to and fro, doing or not doing their appointed work: His knowledge of them is not the cause of their actions. So might we ourselves look down upon some wide prospect without disturbing the peaceful toils of the villagers who are beneath. They do not slacken or hasten their business because we are looking at them. In like manner God may look upon mankind without thereby interfering with the human will or influencing in any degree the actions of men.

(3) But the difficulty with which Christianity surrounds, or rather seems to surround us, winds yet closer; it rests also on the Christian consciousness. The doctrine of grace may be expressed in the language of St. Paul: 'I can do nothing as of myself, but my sufficiency is of God:' that which is truly self, which is peculiarly self, is yet in another point of view not self but God. He who has sought most earnestly to fulfil the will of God refers his efforts to something beyond himself; he is humble and simple, seeming to fear that he will lose the good that he has, when he makes it his own.

This is the mind of Christ which is formally expressed in theology by theories of grace. Theories of grace have commonly started from the transgression of Adam and the corruption of human nature in his posterity. Into the origin of sin it is not necessary for us to inquire; we may limit ourselves to the fact. All men are very far gone from original righteousness, they can only return to God by His grace preventing them; that is to say, anticipating and co-operating with the motions of their will. (1) God wills that some should be saved, whom He elects without reference to their deserts ; (2) God wills that some should be saved, and implants in them the mind of salvation ; (3) God calls all men, but chooses some out of those whom He calls ; (4) God chooses all alike, and shows no preference to any ; (5) God calls all men, even in the heathen world, and some hear His voice, not knowing whom they obey. Such are the possible gradations of the question of election. In the first of them grace is a specific quality distinct from holiness or moral virtue ; in the second it is identical with holiness and moral virtue, according to a narrow conception of them which denies their existence in those who have not received a Divine call ; in the third an attempt is made to reconcile justice to all men with favour to some ; in the fourth the justice of God extends equally to all Christian men ; in the fifth we pass the boundaries of the Christian world and expression is given to the thought of the Apostle, 'Of a truth I perceive that God is no respecter of persons. but that in every nation he that feareth God is accepted of him.'

All these theories of grace affect at various points the freedom of the will, the first seeming wholly to deny it, while all the others attempt some real or apparent reconcilement of morality and religion. The fourth and fifth meet the difficulties arising out of our ideas of the justice of God, but fall into others derived from experience and fact. Can we say that all Christians, nominal and real, nay, that the most degraded persons among the heathen, are equally the subjects of Divine grace? Then grace is something unintelligible ; it is a word only, to which there is no corresponding idea. Again, how upon any of these theories is grace distinguishable from the better consciousness of the individual himself? Can any one pretend to say where grace ends and the movement of the will begins ? Did any one ever recognize in himself those lines of demarcation of which theology sometimes speaks ?

These are difficulties in which we are involved by 'oppositions of knowledge falsely so called.' The answer to them is simple—a return to fact and nature. When, instead of reading our own hearts, we seek, in accordance with a preconceived theory, to determine the proportions of the divine and human—to distinguish grace and virtue, the word of God and man—we know not where we are, the difficulty becomes insuperable, we have involved ourselves in artificial meshes, and are bound hand and foot. But when we look by the light of conscience and Scripture on the facts of human nature, the difficulty of itself disappears. No one doubts that he is capable of choosing between good and evil, and that in making this choice he may be supported, if he will, by a power more than earthly. The movement of that Divine power is not independent of the movement of his own will, but coincident and identical with it. Grace and virtue, conscience and the Spirit of God, are not different from each other, but in harmony. If no man can do what is right without the aid of the Spirit, then every one who does what is right has the aid of the Spirit.

Part of the difficulty originates in the fact that the Scripture regards Christian truth from a Divine aspect, 'God working in you,' while ordinary language, even among religious men in modern times, deals rather with human states or feelings. Philosophy has a third way of speaking which is different from either. Two or more sets of words and ideas are used which gradually acquire a seemingly distinct meaning; at last comes the question—in what relation they stand to one another? The Epistles speak of grace and faith at the same time that heathen moralists told of virtue and wisdom, and the two streams of language have flowed on without uniting even at our own day. The question arises, first, whether grace is anything more than the objective name of faith and love; and again, whether these two latter are capable of being distinguished from virtue and truth? Is that which St. Paul called faith absolutely different from that which Seneca termed virtue or morality? Is not virtue, πρὸς θεόν, faith? Is faith anything without virtue? But if so, they are not opposed at all, or opposed only as part and whole. Christianity is not the negative of the religions of nature or the heathen; it includes and purifies them.

Instead, then, of arranging in a sort of theological diagram the relations of the human will to Divine grace, we deny the possibility of separating them. In various degrees, in many ways, more or less consciously in different cases, the Spirit of God is working in the soul of man. It is an erroneous mode of speaking, according to which the free agency of man is represented as in conflict with the Divine will. For the freedom of man in the higher sense is the grace of God; and in the lower sense (of mere choice) is not inconsistent with it. The real opposition is not between freedom and predestination, which are imperfect and in some degree misleading expressions of the same truth, but between good and evil.

II. Passing out of the sphere of religion, we have now to examine the question of free agency within the narrower limits of the mind itself. It will confirm the line of argument hitherto taken, if it be found that here too we are subject to the illusions of language and the oppositions of logic.

(1) Every effect has a cause; every cause an effect. The drop of rain, the ray of light does not descend at random on the earth. In the natural world though we are far from understanding all the causes of phenomena, we are certain from that part which we know, of their existence in that part which we do not know. In the human mind we perceive the action of many physical causes; we are therefore led to infer, that only our ignorance of physiology prevents our perceiving the absolute interdependence of body and soul. So indissolubly are cause and effect bound together, that there is a mental impossibility in conceiving

them apart. Where, then in the endless chain of causes and effect can the human will be inserted, or how is the insertion of the will, as one cause out of many, consistent with the absolute freedom which we ascribe to it?

The author of the *Critic of pure Reason* is willing to accept such a statement as has been just made, and yet believes himself to have found out of time and space, independent of the laws of cause and effect, a transcendental freedom. Our separate acts are determined by previous causes; our whole life is a continuous 'effect,' yet in spite of this mechanical sequence, freedom is the overruling law which gives the form to human action. It is not necessary to analyze the steps by which Kant arrived at this paradoxical conclusion. Only by adjusting the glass so as to exclude from the sight everything but the perplexities of previous philosophers, can we conceive how a great intellect could have been led to imagine the idea of a freedom from which the notion of time is abstracted, of which nevertheless we are conscious in time. For what is that freedom which does not apply to our individual acts, hardly even to our lives as a whole, like a point which has neither length nor breadth, wanting both continuity and succession?

Scepticism proceeds by a different path in reference to our ideas of cause and effect; it challenges their validity, it denies the necessity of the connexion, or even doubts the ideas themselves. There was a time when the world was startled out of its propriety at this verbal puzzle, and half believed itself a sceptic. Now we know that no innovation in the use of words or in forms of thought can make any impression on solid facts. Nature and religion, and human life remain the same, even to one who entirely renounces the common conceptions of cause and effect.

The sceptic of the last century, instead of attempting to invalidate the connexion of fact which we express by the terms cause and effect, should rather have attacked language as 'unequal to the subtlety of nature.' Facts must be described in some way, and therefore words must be used, but always in philosophy with a latent consciousness of their inadequacy and imperfection. The very phrase, 'cause and effect,' has a dire influence in disguising from us the complexity of causes and effects. It is too abstract to answer to anything in the concrete. It tends to isolate in idea some one antecedent or condition from all the rest. And the relation which we deem invariable is really a most various one. Its apparent necessity is only the necessity of relative terms. Every cause has an effect, in the same sense that every father has a son. But while in the latter case the relation is always the same, the manifold application of the terms, cause and effect, to the most different phenomena has led to an ambiguity in their use. Our first impression is, that a cause is one thing and an effect another, but soon we find them doubling up, or melting into one. The circulation of the blood is not the cause of life, in the same sense that a blow with the hammer may be the cause of death; nor is virtue the cause of happiness, in precisely the same sense that the circulation of the blood is the cause of life. Everywhere, as we ascend in the scale of creation, from mechanics to chemistry, from chemistry to physiology and human action, the relative notion is more difficult and subtle, the cause becoming inextricably involved with the effect, and the effect with the cause, 'every means being an end, and every end a means.'

Hence, no one who examines our ideas of cause and effect will believe that they impose any limit on the will; they are an imperfect mode in which the mind imagines the sequence of nature or moral actions; being no generalization from experience, but a play of words only. The chain which we are wearing is loose, and when shaken will drop off. External circumstances are not the cause of which the will is the effect; neither is the will the cause of which circumstances are the effect. But the phenomenon intended to be described by the words 'cause and effect' is itself the will, whose motions are analyzed in language borrowed from physical nature.

The same explanation applies to another formula: 'the strongest motive.' The will of every man is said to be only determined by the strongest motive: what is this but another imaginary analysis of the will itself? For the motive is a part of the will, and the strongest motive is nothing more than the motive which I choose. Nor is it true as a fact that we are always thus determined. For the greater proportion of human actions have no distinct motives; the mind does not stand like the schoolmen's ass, pondering between opposite alternatives. Mind and will, and the sequence of cause and effect, and the force of motives, are different ways of speaking of the same mental phenomena.

So readily are we deceived by language, so easily do we fall under the power of imaginary reasonings. The author of the *Novum Organum* has put men upon their guard against the illusions of words in the study of the natural sciences. It is true that many distinctions may be drawn between the knowledge of nature, the facts of which are for the most part visible and tangible, and morality and religion, which run up into the unseen. But is it therefore to be supposed that language, which is the source of half the exploded fallacies of chemistry and physiology, is an adequate or exact expression of moral and spiritual truths? It is probable that its analysis of human nature is really as erring and inaccurate as its description of physical phenomena, though the error may be more difficult of detection. Those 'inexact natures' or substances of which Bacon speaks exist in moral philosophy as in physics; their names are not heat, moisture, form, matter and the like, but necessity, free will, predestination, grace, motive, cause, which rest upon nothing and yet become the foundation-stones of many systems. Logic, too, has its parallels, and conjugates, and differences of kind, which in life and reality are only differences of degree, and remote inferences lending an apparent weight to the principle on which they really drag, which spread themselves over every field of thought and are hardly corrected by their inconsistency with the commonest facts.

III. Difficulties of this class belong to the last generation rather than to the present; they are seldom discussed now by philosophical writers. Philosophy in our own age is occupied in another way. Her foundation is experience, which alone she interrogates respecting the limits of human action. How far is man a free agent? is the question still before us. But it is to be considered from without rather than from within, as it appears to others or ourselves in the case of others, and not with reference to our internal consciousness of our own actions.

The conclusions of philosophers would have met with more favour at the hands of preachers and moralists, had they confined themselves to the fact. Indeed, they would have been irresistible, like the conclusions of natural science, for who can resist evidence that any one may verify for himself? But the taint of language has clung to them; the imperfect expression of manifest truths has greatly hindered the general acceptance of them even among the most educated. It was not understood that those who spoke of necessity meant nothing which was really inconsistent with free will; when they assumed a power of calculating human actions, it was not perceived that all of us are every day guilty of this imaginary impiety. The words, character, habit, force of circumstances, temperament and constitution imply all that is really involved in the idea that human action is subject to uniform laws. Neither is it to be denied that expressions have been used equally repugnant to fact and morality; instead of regularity, and order, and law, which convey a beneficent idea, necessity has been set up as a constraining power tending to destroy, if not really destroying, the accountability of man. History, too, has received an impress of fatalism, which has doubtless affected our estimate of the good and evil of the agents who have been regarded as not really responsible for actions which the march of events forced upon them.

According to a common way of considering this subject, the domain of necessity is extending every day, and liberty is already confined to a small territory not yet reclaimed by scientific inquiry. Mind and body are in closer contact; there is increasing evidence of the interdependence of the mental and nervous powers. It is probable, or rather certain, that every act of the mind has a cause and effect in the body, that every act of the body has a cause and effect in the mind. Given the circumstances, parentage, education, temperament of each individual; we may calculate, with an approximation to accuracy, his probable course of life. Persons are engaged every day in making such observations; and whatever uncertainty there may be in the determination of the future of any single individual, this uncertainty is eliminated when the inquiry is extended to many individuals or to a whole class. We have as good data for supposing that a fixed proportion of a million persons in a country will commit murder or theft as that a fixed proportion will die without reaching a particular age and of this or that disease under given circumstances. And it so happens that we have the power of testing this order or uniformity in the most trifling of human actions. Nor can we doubt that were it worth while to make an abstract of human life, arranging under heads the least minutiae of action, all that we say and do would be found to conform to numerical laws.

So, again, history is passing into the domain of philosophy. Nations, like individuals, are moulded by circumstances; in their first rise, and ever after in their course, they are dependent on country and climate, like plants or animals, embodying the qualities which have dropped upon them from surrounding influences in national temperament; in their later stages seeming to react upon these causes, and coming under a new kind of law, as the earth discloses its hidden treasures, or the genius of man calls forth into life and action the powers which are dormant in matter. Nature, which is, in other words, the aggregate of all these causes, stamps nations and societies, and creates in them a mind, that is to say, ideas of order, of religion, of conquest, which they maintain, often unimpaired by the changes in their physical condition. She infuses among the mass a few great intellects, according to some law unknown to us, to 'instrument this lower world.' Here is a new power which is partially separated from the former, and yet combines with it in national existence, like body and soul in the existence of man. Partly isolated from their age and nation, partly also identified with them, it is a curious observation respecting great men that while they seem to have more play and freedom than others, in themselves they are often more enthralled, being haunted with the sense of a destiny which controls them. The 'heirs of all the ages' who have subjected nature to the dominion of science are also nature's subjects; the conquerors who have poured over the earth have only continued some wave or tendency in the history of the times which preceded them. From the thin vapour which first floated, as some believe, in the azure vault, up to that miracle of complexity which we call man, and again from man the individual to the whole human race, with its languages and religions, and other national characteristics, and backwards to the beginning of human history, in the works of mind too as well as in the material universe, there is not always development, but order, and uniformity, and law.

It is a matter of some importance in what way this connexion or order of nature is to be expressed. For although words cannot alter facts, the right use of them greatly affects the readiness with which facts are admitted or received. Now the world may be variously imagined as a vast machine, as an animal or living being, as a body endowed with a rational or divine soul. All these figures of speech, and the associations to which they give rise, have an insensible influence on our ideas. The representation of the world as a machine is a more favourite one, in modern times, than the representation of it as a living being; and with mechanism is associated the notion of necessity. Yet the machine is, after all, a mere barren unity, which gives no conception of the endless fertility of natural or of moral life. So, again, when we speak of a 'soul of the world,' there is no real resemblance to a human soul; there is no centre in which this mundane life or soul has its seat, no individuality such as characterizes the soul of man. But the use of the word invariably recalls thoughts of Pantheism:

'deum namque ire per omnes terrasque tractusque maris,
    coelumque profundum.'

So the term 'law' carries with it an association, partly of compulsion, partly of that narrower and more circumscribed notion of law, in which it is applied to chemistry or mechanics. So again the word 'necessity' itself always has a suggestion of external force.

All such language has a degree of error, because it introduces some analogy which belongs to another sphere of thought. But when, laying aside language, we consider facts only, no appearance of external compulsion arises, whether in nature, or in history, or in life. The lowest, and therefore the simplest idea, that we are capable of forming of physical necessity, is of the stone falling to the ground. No one imagines human action to be necessary in any such sense as this. If this be our idea of necessity, the meaning of the term must be enlarged when it is applied to man. If any one speaks of human action as the result of necessary laws, to avoid misunderstanding, we may ask at the outset of the controversy, 'In what degree necessary?' And this brings us to an idea which is perhaps the readiest solution of the apparent perplexity—that of degrees of necessity. For, although it is true, that to the eye of a superior or divine being the actions of men would seem to be the subject of laws quite as much as the falling stone, yet these laws are of a far higher or more delicate sort; we may figure them to ourselves truly, as allowing human nature play and room within certain limits, as regulating only and not constraining the freedom of its movements.

How degrees of necessity are possible may be illustrated as follows: The strongest or narrowest necessity which we ever see in experience is that of some very simple mechanical fact, such as is furnished by the law of attraction. A greater necessity than this is only an abstraction; as, for example, the necessity by which two and two make four, or the three angles of a triangle equal two right angles. But any relation between objects which are seen is of a much feebler and less absolute kind; the strongest which we have ever observed is that of a smaller body to a larger. The physiology even of plants opens to our minds freer and nobler ideas of law. The tree with its fibres and sap, drawing its nourishment from many sources, light, air, moisture, earth, is a complex structure: rooted to one particular spot, no one would think of ascribing to it free agency, yet as little should we think of binding it fast in the chains of a merely mechanical necessity. Animal life partaking with man of locomotion is often termed free; its sphere is narrowed only by instinct; indeed the highest grade of irrational being can hardly be said, in point of freedom, to differ from the lowest type of the human species. And in man himself are many degrees of necessity or freedom, from the child who is subject to its instincts, or the drunkard who is the slave of his passions, up to the philosopher comprehending at a glance the wonders of heaven and earth, the freeman 'whom the truth makes free,' or the Christian devoting himself to God, whose freedom is 'obedience to a law;' that law being 'the law of the Spirit of life,' as the Apostle expresses it; respecting which, nevertheless, according to another mode of speaking (so various is language on this subject), 'necessity is laid upon him.' And between these two extremes are many half freedoms, or imperfect necessities: one man is under the influence of habit, another of prejudice, a third is the creature of some superior will; of a fourth it is said, that it was 'impossible for him to act otherwise;' a fifth does by effort what to another is spontaneous; while in the case of all, allowance is made for education, temperament, and the like.

The idea of necessity has already begun to expand; it is no longer the negative of freedom, they almost touch. For freedom, too, is subject to limitation; the freedom of the human will is not the freedom of the infinite, but of the finite. It does not pretend to escape from the conditions of human life. No man in his senses imagines that he can fly into the air, or walk through the earth; he does not fancy that his limbs will move with the expedition of thought. He is aware that he has a less, or it may be a greater, power than others. He learns from experience to take his own measure. But this limited or measured freedom is another form of enlarged necessity. Beginning with an imaginary freedom, we may reduce it within the bounds of experience; beginning with an abstract necessity, we may accommodate it to the facts of human life.

Attention has been lately called to the phenomena (already noticed) of the uniformity of human actions. The observation of this uniformity has caused a sort of momentary disturbance in the moral ideas of some persons, who seem unable to get rid of the illusion, that nature compels a certain number of individuals to act in a particular way, for the sake of keeping up the average. Their error is, that they confuse the law, which is only the expression of the fact, with the cause; it is as though they affirmed the universal to necessitate the particular. The same uniformity appears equally in matters of chance. Ten thousand throws of the dice, *ceteris paribus*, will give about the same number of twos, threes, sixes : what compulsion was there here? So ten thousand human lives will give a nearly equal number of forgeries, thefts, or other extraordinary actions. Neither is there compulsion here; it is the simple fact. It may be said, Why is the number uniform? In the first place, it is *not* uniform, that is to say, it is in our power to alter the proportions of crime by altering its circumstances. And this change of circumstances is not separable from the act of the legislator or private individual by which it may be accomplished, which is in turn suggested by other circumstances. The will or the intellect of man still holds its place as the centre of a moving world. But, secondly, the imaginary power of this uniform number affects no one in particular; it is not required that A, B, C, should commit a crime, or transmit an undirected letter, to enable us to fill up a tabular statement. The fact exhibited in the tabular statement is the result of all the movements of all the wills of the ten thousand persons who are made the subject of analysis.

It is possible to conceive great variations in such tables; it is possible, that is, to imagine, without any change of circumstances, a thousand persons executed in France during one year for political offences, and none the next. But the world in which this phenomenon was observed would be a very different sort of world from that in which we live. It would be a world in which 'nations, like individuals, went mad;' in which there was no habit, no custom; almost, we may say, no social or political life. Men must be no longer different, and so compensating one another by their excellencies and deficiencies, but all in the same extreme; as if the waves of the sea in a storm instead of returning to their level were to remain on high. The mere statement of such a speculation is enough to prove its absurdity. And, perhaps, no better way could be found of disabusing the mind of the objections which appear to be entertained to the fact of the uniformity of human actions, than a distinct effort to imagine the disorder of the world which would arise out of the opposite principle.

But the advocate of free will may again return to the charge, with an appeal to consciousness. 'Your freedom,' he will say, 'is but half freedom, but I have that within which assures me of an absolute freedom, without which I should be deprived of what I call responsibility.' No man has seen facts of consciousness, and therefore it is at any rate fair that before they are received they shall be subjected to analysis. We may look at an outward object which is called a table; no one would in this case demand an examination into the human faculties before he admitted the existence of the table. But inward facts are of another sort; that they really exist, may admit of doubt; that they exist in the particular form attributed to them, or in any particular form, is a matter very difficult to prove. Nothing is easier than to insinuate a mere opinion, under the disguise of a fact of consciousness.

Consciousness tells, or seems to tell, of an absolute freedom; and this is supposed to be a sufficient witness of the existence of such a freedom. But does consciousness tell also of the conditions under which this freedom can be exercised? Does it remind us that we are finite beings? Does it present to one his bodily, to another his mental constitution? Is it identical with self-knowledge? No one imagines this. To what then is it the witness? To a dim and unreal notion of freedom, which is as different from the actual fact as dreaming is from acting. No doubt the human mind has or seems to have a boundless power, as of thinking so also of willing. But this imaginary power, going as it does far beyond experience, varying too in youth and age, greatest often in idea when it is really least, cannot be adduced as a witness for what is inconsistent with experience.

The question, How is it possible for us to be finite beings, and yet to possess this consciousness of freedom which has no limit? may be partly answered by another question:

How is it possible for us to acquire any ideas which transcend experience? The answer is, only, that the mind has the power of forming such ideas; it can conceive a beauty, goodness, truth, which has no existence on earth. The conception, however, is subject to this law, that the greater the idealization the less the individuality. In like manner that imperfect freedom which we enjoy as finite beings is magnified by us into an absolute idea of freedom, which seems to be infinite because it drops out of sight the limits with which nature in fact everywhere surrounds us; and also because it is the abstraction of self, of which we can never be deprived, and which we conceive to be acting still when all the conditions of action are removed.

Freedom is absolute in another sense, as the correlative of obligation. Men entertain some one, some another, idea of right, but all are bound to act according to that idea. The standard may be relative to their own circumstances, but the duty is absolute; and the power is also absolute of refusing the evil and choosing the good, under any possible contingency. It is a matter (not only of consciousness but) of fact, that we have such a power, quite as much as the facts of statistics, to which it is sometimes opposed, or rather, to speak more correctly, is one of them. And when we make abstraction of this power, that is, when we think of it by itself, there arises also the conception of an absolute freedom.

So singularly is human nature constituted, looking from without on the actions of men as they are, witnessing inwardly to a higher law. 'You ought to do so; you have the power to do so,' is consistent with the fact, that in practice you fail to do so. It may be possible for us to unite both these aspects of human nature, yet experience seems to show that we commonly look first at one and then at the other. The inward vision tells us the law of duty and the will of God; the outward contemplation of ourselves and others shows the trials to which we are most subject.

Any transposition of these two points of view is fatal to morality. For the proud man to say, 'I inherited pride from my ancestors;' or for the licentious man to say, 'It is in the blood;' for the weak man to say, 'I am weak, and will not strive;' for any to find the excuses of their vices in their physical temperament or external circumstances, is the corruption of their nature.

Yet this external aspect of human affairs has a moral use. It is a duty to look at the consequences of actions, as well as at actions themselves; the knowledge of our own temperament, or strength, or health, is a part also of the knowledge of self. We have need of the wise man's warning, about 'age which will not be defied' in our moral any more than in our physical constitution. In youth, also, there are many things outward and indifferent, which cannot but exercise a moral influence on after life. Often opportunities of virtue have to be made, as well as virtuous efforts; there are forms of evil, too, against which we struggle in vain by mere exertions of the will. He who trusts only to a moral or religious impulse, is apt to have aspirations, which never realize themselves in action. His moral nature may be compared to a spirit without a body, fluttering about in the world, but unable to comprehend or grasp any good.

Yet more, in dealing with classes of men, we seem to find that we have greater power to shape their circumstances than immediately to affect their wills. The voice of the preacher passes into the air; the members of his congregation are like persons 'beholding their natural face in a glass;' they go their way, forgetting their own likeness. And often the result of a long life of ministerial work has been the conversion of two or three individuals. The power which is exerted in such a case may be compared to the unaided use of the hand, while mechanical appliances are neglected. Or to turn to another field of labour, in which the direct influence of Christianity has been hitherto small, may not the reason why the result of missions is often disappointing be found in the circumstance, that we have done little to improve the political or industrial state of those among whom our missionaries are sent? We have thought of the souls of men, and of the Spirit of God influencing them, in too naked a way; instead of attending to the complexity of human nature, and the manner in which God has ever revealed himself in the history of mankind.

The great lesson, which Christians have to learn in the present day, is to know the world as it is; that is to say, to know themselves as they are; human life as it is; nature as it is; history as it is. Such knowledge is also a power, to fulfil the will of God and to contribute to the happiness of man. It is a resting-place in speculation, and a new beginning in practice. Such knowledge is the true reconcilement of the opposition of necessity and free will. Not that spurious reconcilement which places necessity in one sphere of thought, freedom in another; nor that pride of freedom which is ready to take up arms against plain facts; nor yet that demonstration of necessity in which logic, equally careless of facts, has bound fast the intellect of man. The whole question, when freed from the illusions of language, is resolvable into experience. Imagination cannot conquer for us more than that degree of freedom which we truly have; the tyranny of science cannot impose upon us any law or limit to which we are not really subject; theology cannot alter the real relations of God and man. The facts of human nature and of Christianity remain the same, whether we describe them by the word 'necessity' or 'freedom,' in the phraseology of Lord Bacon and Locke, or in that of Calvin and Augustine.

THE END.

www.ingramcontent.com/pod-product-compliance
Lightning Source LLC
Chambersburg PA
CBHW030552300426
44111CB00009B/956